MONEY
and
BANKING

THE IRWIN SERIES IN ECONOMICS

Consulting Editor
LLOYD G. REYNOLDS
Yale University

GAMBS & KOMISAR *Economics and Man* 3d ed.

GORDON *The Investment Financing and Valuation of the Corporation*

GRAMPP & WEILER (eds.) *Economic Policy: Readings in Political Economy* 3d ed.

GROSSMAN, HANSEN, HENDRIKSEN, MCALLISTER, OKUDA, & WOLMAN (eds.) *Readings in Current Economics* rev. ed.

GUTHRIE *Statistical Methods in Economics*

GUTHRIE & WALLACE *Economics* 4th ed.

HAGEN *The Economics of Development*

HARRISS *The American Economy: Principles, Practices, and Policies* 6th ed.

HERBER *Modern Public Finance*

HIGGINS *United Nations and U.S. Foreign Economic Policy*

JOME *Principles of Money and Banking*

KINDLEBERGER *International Economics* 4th ed.

KUHLMAN & SKINNER *The Economic System* rev. ed.

LEE *Macroeconomics: Fluctuations, Growth, and Stability* 5th ed.

LOCKLIN *Economics of Transportation* 6th ed.

LLOYD *Microeconomic Analysis*

LOW *Modern Economic Organization*

MEYERS *Economics of Labor Relations*

PEGRUM *Public Regulation of Business* rev. ed.

PEGRUM *Transportation: Economics and Public Policy* rev. ed.

PETERSON & GRAY *Economic Development of the United States*

PHILLIPS *The Economics of Regulation: Theory and Practice in the Transportation and Public Utility Industries* rev. ed.

REYNOLDS *Economics: A General Introduction* 3d ed.

RIMA *Development of Economic Analysis*

SCITOVSKY *Welfare and Competition: The Economics of a Fully Employed Economy* rev. ed.

SIEGEL *Aggregate Economics and Public Policy* 3d ed.

SIRKIN *Introduction to Macroeconomic Theory* 3d ed.

SMITH *Macroeconomics*

SMITH & TEIGEN (eds.) *Readings in Money, National Income, and Stabilization Policy* rev. ed.

SNIDER *Introduction to International Economics* 5th ed.

SPENCER *Managerial Economics: Text, Problems, and Short Cases* 3d ed.

VANEK *International Trade: Theory and Economic Policy*

WILCOX *Public Policies toward Business* 4th ed.

MONEY and BANKING

DOUGLAS FISHER
Chairman of the Department of Economics
University of Essex, England

1971 **RICHARD D. IRWIN, INC.** HOMEWOOD, ILLINOIS
Irwin-Dorsey Limited GEORGETOWN, ONTARIO

First Printing, January, 1971

Library of Congress Catalog Card No. 78–138416
Printed in the United States of America

To my wife

PREFACE

The principal aim of this text is to bring modern monetary economics—and monetary controversy—to the undergraduate. It is my belief that this is the way in which the student will become more interested in—and more embroiled in—the general problems with which monetary economists are grappling. Specifically, what I have done is to hang as much of the journal material of the last 15 years onto an elementary microeconomic framework as I thought it could bear. The general objectives in using these materials are, at the least, to provide a statement of their relevance and, at the best, to stimulate further work on monetary problems by trying to show exactly where the problems lie.

The general approach of the book has been to bring the powerful tools of microeconomic analysis to bear on a wide range of monetary problems. Indeed, macroeconomics has been studiously avoided (with a few exceptions) for three reasons:

1. Macroeconomic theory in itself takes up an inordinate amount of space if done properly, and some microeconomic theory is still necessary.
2. Microeconomics makes it easier to motivate students in terms of their own experiences; and, obviously,
3. More solutions to monetary problems exist in the microeconomic than in the macroeconomic idiom.

One might enlarge on the third point by adding that many problems one might be interested in—portfolio behavior, for example—are at present *only* approachable by means of micro analysis.

This text presents an integration of some of the best recent work on monetary problems. While the most exciting areas are those of direct application to monetary problems—such as the treatment of money as an item of wealth—there are excursions into other areas which have some interest in their own right, in addition to the light they may shed onto the more traditional monetary problems. In this connection the text discusses stock market prices, portfolio management, the cost of capital, the role of money in economic development, and the term structure of interest rates; these are all topics normally slighted in a course of this sort.

Traditional monetary problems still dominate the text, and traditional methods are employed even when there is some danger of arousing ancient hostilities. In particular, the Equation of Exchange is employed in a number of places, both to clarify the language and to illuminate the data. But I do not take any doctrinal stand; and when the going gets heavy and the Equation of Exchange is no longer of any special use, it is gently put aside. On the other hand, doctrine has some place in a subject whose origins lie in heated discussion; and in Chapter 9 a summary of the positions of the principal antagonists is presented in a way which ought to help the uninitiated attain some familiarity with the issues.

Actually, I have made some effort to pigeonhole the less general material in the text. I would hope the student would attempt every chapter, and certainly the book has been written with this objective in mind; but it is conceivable that some chapters—for example Chapter 11, on the term structure of interest rates—could be skipped entirely. Partly in this connection, the chapters on international monetary economics have been gathered up at the end of the book. This is somewhat of a contradiction, as you will see when you read these chapters, for the whole theme of this section is that one cannot ignore the influence of the international in his thinking about domestic monetary problems.

There is no escaping the fact that the material in this text is hard going at points, and I have tried to cope with this problem in three main ways. In the first place, I have constructed a large number of simple examples to illustrate the trickier passages. Many of these examples are constructed from data given in the *Federal Reserve Bulletin;* furthermore, these data generally refer to the 1960's, so that one necessarily acquires a knowledge of the magnitudes in the monetary sector in the course of following through the argument. In the second place I have avoided all higher level mathematics, ruthlessly restricting myself to algebra whenever words seemed inadequate. Finally, I have attempted complete coverage of the most important ideas in each chapter in a series of Discussion Questions in the text itself; and a series of Definitions, True-False Discussion Questions, and Essay Questions in the *Teacher's Manual* which accompanies this text.

I have greatly benefitted from the close reading of a substantial part of the manuscript by David E. W. Laidler and J. Michael Parkin. In addition, Michael G. Porter and Lloyd Reynolds (as Irwin's Consulting Editor) have made a number of substantive comments which were of considerable help. Others who were kind enough to make general comments or to read over one or two chapters were Alastair McAuley, Peter Lindert, Larry Moss, Pramod Junankar, B. Borkakoti, and A. L. Robb. In addition, I benefitted greatly from seeing material in manuscript written by G. C. Archibald and J. Richmond, Philip Cagan, Robert S. Clower, Alec Chrystal, Peter Lindert, and Michael G. Porter. Two drafts of the manuscript were typed by my wife who also edited out as many of the stylistic flaws as the requirements of domestic harmony could permit. All of the remaining errors will have to be charged to my account.

December, 1970   Douglas Fisher

CONTENTS

xiii

PART II: CAPITAL MARKETS

13. The Economics of Stock Prices 280

14. Some Implications of Uncertainty Analysis in Money and Banking 302

PART III: INTERNATIONAL MONETARY ECONOMICS

PART I

Domestic Monetary Economics

Chapter 1

AN INTRODUCTION TO THE ANALYSIS OF MONEY AND BANKING

1.1 INTRODUCTION

A very good reason for studying the role of money in our economic system is that its presence is felt everywhere; indeed, a world without money is quite difficult to imagine. Practically all of our daily transactions are exchanges between money and commodities, and all of our quoted commodity prices are money prices—that is, so many dollars per unit of each commodity. Much of our wealth is denoted in money terms—for example, stocks and bonds—and we receive our income in the form of money—at a rate expressed in dollars per hour of work. Not only are things this way now, but they probably always were so; some form of money undoubtedly was invented about the time the first exchanges between commodities occurred. Whether or not this is true of all economic history, it is true that since we have had economic data, we have had money, for having money around and therefore having the prices of everything quoted in terms of money makes data collection both easier and more inevitable.

In spite of the lack of actual historical examples, we will begin our study with a simple nonmonetary economy and gradually build up a full economic system comparable to our own. We do this because it seems to reveal, *as a matter of logical necessity*, what I will evasively call the monetary mechanism. Beginning at the other end, with a full description of our monetary economy in its present form, almost certainly would cause us to miss the fundamental points, and we would suffer a kind of mental indigestion from trying to appreciate too many things simultaneously. In the end, much the same ground will be covered by our ap-

3

proach; the principal danger is that you might think I am making statements about the historical development of financial institutions when I am not.

There are several things about the approach of this book which you ought to appreciate initially. The most important, by far, is that we are going to employ *microeconomics* rather than *macroeconomics* as the basic analytical technique; microeconomics emphasizes individual decisions, while macroeconomics builds its theory around broad statistical aggregates in which individual decisions cannot be identified. The main reason for approaching the financial markets in this way is that I think we can get a better picture of things thereby; but this will have to be proved to you in practice. However, there are two immediately obvious gains which we can reap. One of these is that we will be able to cut through the complications that the institutional structure of each separate financial market seems to present, and the other is that we will come into a closer contact with developments in the professional literature than has been the fashion in the money and banking books of recent years.

Another factor of some importance in my approach to money and banking is that the institutional details of the financial markets will be introduced in an *implicit* fashion in the course of the discussion of the theory of each situation. This means that you will have to make extensive use of the index—which I have gone to great pains to make comprehensive—if you wish to track down the structure of any particular market. Things have been done in this way because these details are, on the one hand, somewhat distracting and, on the other, somewhat irrelevant if you are interested in a broad statement of monetary problems. Along these lines, you should pay somewhat closer attention to the footnotes than you are used to doing, both because some important qualifications appear there and because a fair amount of cross-referencing is effected in this way.

The last point, perhaps of little interest in itself, is to note that no attempt has been made either to prune the controversy out of things or to hide my own views. Our task is a positive one, of course; but a good deal about the financial world is unknown, and a good deal which is known is appreciated in different ways by different people, so controversy is inevitable—indeed, it sometimes helps expose the structure of the problem. I will not always attempt to identify the proponents of certain views, but I will provide a sufficient list of readings for you to find them easily. In fact, it seems that certain views actually never were held in the explicit ways they will appear here; and certain people who seem to be saying one thing at one period of their work end up saying something quite different at a later stage. There is nothing surprising about either statement, for we must necessarily comprehend reality—and monetary reality in particular—from our own time and from our own perspective.

1.2 THE SCOPE OF THE STUDY

1.2.1 The Study of the Monetary Mechanism: Chapters 1 through 9

The rest of this chapter will be devoted to preliminary matters; but you should not, on this account, skip over it lightly. This section will describe the plan of the book and section 1.3 describes what is meant by money and capital—our subject. Section 1.4 begins a summary discussion of some useful elements of traditional microeconomic theory. We will find that careful attention to the formal structure of economic theory will pay us rich dividends in our study of financial marketplaces; accordingly, section 1.4 will consider the foundations of the theory, and section 1.5 will go on to present some of the apparatus of the theory of choice (that is, demand). You will be alerted to the fact that each separate situation in this book is to be attacked by breaking the forces in the market into those influencing supply and those influencing demand.

The first task will be to define our terms, and Chapter 2 will be devoted entirely to problems of definition. We will begin with a simple nonmonetary economy and introduce money in such a way that its definition will be obvious. Understanding at this point is so critical to what follows that we will dwell at great length on the distinctions made; what this amounts to is a general description of the alternative definitions which we could use and then a practical selection among them. We will conclude that there are good reasons for referring to the total of demand deposits in commercial banks and currency in the hands of the public as *money*.

We will adopt, as mentioned previously, a microeconomic framework, so we will tend to discuss each particular financial market in terms of the demand for and the supply of the product. We will begin, in Chapter 3, with the demand for money; then, in Chapters 4, 5, and 6, we will consider the supply of money. Supply takes more chapters than demand primarily because there are two suppliers of money: commercial banks (Chapter 4) and the Federal Reserve System (Chapters 5 and 6). Furthermore, the Federal Reserve attempts to exert control over the rest of the economy—in particular, control over the effects of the business cycle—so that many more complications arise. Indeed, things become so complicated that we will not really be finished with supply even after Chapter 6, for in Chapter 8—a survey of some special events in our *monetary* history—you will see that changes in the supply of money have often had a sharp impact on the American economy; and the topic will be taken up again in Part II of the book, as well.

There are two other chapters in Part I. Chapter 7 discusses the role of money in underdeveloped countries and is of interest for two reasons: (*a*) the institutional structure is so different that we might find out more clearly what is basic in monetary economics, and (*b*) we will learn something about the peculiar problems of those countries. Chapter 9, on the other hand, is almost completely backward-looking: here I will present my version of the history of monetary thought, and some of the important figures in its development will be identified in order to help to pull together the discussion of Chapters 2 through 8.

1.2.2 The Study of Capital Markets: Chapters 10 through 14

In Part II of this book you will find something which does not usually appear in money and banking books—a reasonably up-to-date summary of *capital markets* theory. We are, in fact, going to discuss the relation between money and a reasonable selection of all other financial assets; this discussion breaks down into relations affecting supply and relations affecting demand. We will begin, in Chapter 10, with comments on both the institutional structure and the potential influence of other financial institutions. Chapter 10, in other words, will attempt to set the problems up explicitly.

At first glance, Chapter 11 stands a little apart from the rest of this section; it is a generalization of the single interest rate into a *world* of interest rates, particularly on government bonds. The idea is to see what use we can make of the fact that bonds have different dates of maturity, some stretching very far into the future, and that, therefore, bond *prices* (and therefore interest rates) are quoted on bond contracts some distance into the future. It is explained in Chapter 11 that both the supply and demand for money are involved in the world of interest rates. Furthermore, we will discover that economic forecasts can be dug out of interest rate data, and this finding is of interest by itself.

In Chapters 12 and 13 we will consider material developed almost entirely outside formal monetary economics. We will argue that a fruitful way to analyze the role of money is to treat money as one of a number of assets which wealth holders can choose to hold. Then, with the theory of choice of Chapter 1 and the principles of portfolio analysis of Chapter 12, we will be able to apply some of our findings (in Chapter 14) to monetary problems. We will, by this point, have some interest in common stocks; and, it turns out, an analysis of the determination of stock prices in Chapter 13—along with some explicit institutional material— also contributes to our understanding of monetary problems. In this case we will also dwell a little on the findings about stock prices themselves.

Chapter 14, then, simply pulls together the material of Chapters 10 through 13 in the context of monetary problems. The gains, it seems, are quite substantial.

1.2.3   The Open Economy: Chapters 15 through 18

In Part III of the book we will return to a more traditional area of monetary economics—that of international finance—but our approach will not be traditional in some respects. The general idea is to ask ourselves what differences it might make to our earlier conclusions if we broaden our framework to that of the *open economy*—that is, bring in the financial aspects of foreign trade. In Chapter 15 we will discuss the determination of the balance of payments and raise the question of the effect of capital flows on the autonomy of nations. In Chapter 16 we will discuss the determination of exchange rates, and in Chapter 17 we will discuss the various proposals which have been advanced to reform the system described in Chapters 15 and 16. Chapter 18, finally, will undertake to unite the results of Part III with the earlier parts of the book; we will see that it makes a great deal of difference that countries are open and not closed to international trade and that the openness introduced by capital flows between countries is especially important.

1.3 MONEY AND CAPITAL

We must begin, from now on, to be perfectly clear about what it is that we intend to study and how our study fits into the economic world. There are two traditional paths which we might take here—either that of "money and banking" or that of "money and capital"—but we will choose a different route which combines many aspects of both. If we were to discuss money and banking, as it is often described, our discussion would center primarily around both the media of exchange—paper money, coins, and checking deposits in commercial banks—and the problems and policy of the banking sector of the economy. If we were to discuss money and capital, our discussion would concern the markets for certain financial instruments such as United States Treasury bills—often referred to as "money"—and corporate bonds and equity. But, generally, those who take one or the other path do not attempt to bring them together.

In fact, there are several obvious senses in which these subjects fit together neatly, and these will be the subject of the integration which is the purpose of this text. In the first place, the technical properties of bank and government money, on the one hand, and stocks and bonds, on the other, are remarkably similar. One form of bank money, the time deposit, is intrinsically a bond with a very short (30 days maximum) maturity date. Even demand deposits can be thought of as a kind of bond, payable on demand, even though they pay no interest. In the second place, all of these items provide returns to their users. Money, whether produced by commercial banks or by the government, is free from the risk of default and facilitates the exchange of commodities and financial instruments; while stocks and bonds provide income in lieu of services, you might say, and, like money, help to improve the allocation of resources by perfecting the capital market.

There is one other much more important reason why money and the various forms of capital should be included in the same presentation—both represent wealth to their owners, and the owners can switch among them, depending on the circumstances. That is to say, a typical economic entity (and it makes little difference at this point whether we are discussing a final unit, such as the consuming unit, or an intermediate unit, such as a life insurance company) will have a portfolio which represents that portion of its wealth which is in financial form. These forms, generically, will be money, equities, and bonds. If the price of any of these items alters, wealth holders will consider the possibility of altering their portfolios in relation to the cost of effecting the desired changes. Further than this, if the holder's wealth changes, whether the change comes about as a result of financial or nonfinancial factors, he will want to make some adjustments, again neglecting the complications of transactions costs. Each of these adjustments to some extent will involve all of the items in the wealth holder's portfolio, so that it is impossible to ignore any financial forms if we wish to be completely general about any one of them.

There is another important reason why money and capital cannot be separated, and this is that economic mechanisms are called into play and need to be studied on account of monetary policy. That is to say, when the government decides—and for the moment we will not pay any attention as to how they might carry out this plan—to increase the amount of money in the system, the repercussions generally spread throughout the entire economic system. If the government succeeds in increasing the quantity of money and if interest rates fall as banks seek to lend out the additional funds, all issuers of financial instruments will be affected; and all holders of monetary wealth, the other side of the picture, will have to readjust their portfolios. This change is no different from that mentioned in the last paragraph; but it has several additional important aspects which are of special interest if we wish to understand the financial community. For one thing, we will find that the government will be interested in all of these effects because both the direction and net effect of its policy are thereby affected; certain offsets or exaggerations of its policy could occur which it would want to anticipate. For another thing—and this is of special interest to students of the financial marketplaces—under certain conditions, the injections of money into the economy will be measurable, so that one might then be able to study the workings of the economic system, at least until the initial impulse has died down or become so confused in offsetting reactions as to be no longer identifiable. These advantages come about, in this case, *because we are in possession of the causes*, a circumstance which gives us an opportunity to perform an actual experiment.

What we will do, then, in the chapters which follow, is to consider the supply and demand for these various instruments, beginning with the fundamental one, money, and completely describe their interweavings throughout financial spheres. Before undertaking this task, however, we must discuss how an economic decision unit will operate in a world similar to the one we will be discussing in this book, so that when we recognize a problem which fits this form, we can immediately move toward the solution. This task will be undertaken in two stages so that we do not have to carry the apparatus for a long time before we use it. That is, in the next section we will discuss the "theory of choice," and this apparatus will establish the techniques to be used on the demand side of financial markets. Then, in Chapter 4, we will introduce a new set of techniques, those known as the "theory of the firm," in the context of describing the behavior of the commercial bank.

1.4 SOME REFLECTIONS ON ECONOMIC THEORY

Although the basic aim throughout the text is at decidedly practical matters, you should be alerted that we will be following a firm and consistent theoretical outline in each distinct unit and that underlying the entire text is a microeconomic model in which individuals are assumed to act consistently. We must not expect too much of our theory, in terms of practical suggestions; for unique answers, even to very simple questions, are not easy to achieve in social science. The main reason this is so is that we will have to judge our results on the basis of data generated outside of the laboratory. The chief cost will be that all results must be stated provisionally.

1.4.1 Definitions, Axioms, and Assumptions

If we approach our theory formally, we will set up a series of definitions by which we can classify our phenomena, behavioral axioms by which we can circumscribe the behavior of our subjects into a manageable set, and assumptions by which we are enabled to use certain standard techniques, such as mathematical notation.[1]

The *definitions* will be arbitrary and will be convenient or inconvenient according to their acceptability as language, their lack of ambiguity, and the like. If definitions are strictly arbitrary, it is reasonable to ask why there is so much dispute over definitions. What has just been said is that definitions cannot be "right" or "wrong"; they may be simply useful or nonuseful. Usefulness is an arguable property, of course, and so is clarity; but it is probable that most of the definitional disputes in economics concern the use of implicit definitions: the bad habit of defining concepts in the context of using the words. One frequent result, as we shall see in our discussion of the demand for money, is that disputes over the theory itself become mixed up with the definitional system in ways which make it difficult not only to pull things apart but also to understand them.

The *axioms* will be statements about human behavior which ought to be realistic, although we are aware that the statements are not always true. An example will help to clarify this use of the word "axiom." We often assert in microeconomics that people are consistent. In fact, in our theory, we are not saying that all people are consistent but that our analysis is strictly applicable only to consistent people, in whatever sense we define consistency. This means, when it comes to judging our results, that we will never be able to test our theory directly, for we know that some people are inconsistent in general and that all people are incon-

---

[1] This terminology closely follows that of H. Wold and L. Jureen in *Demand Analysis* (New York: John Wiley & Sons, Inc., 1953), who refer to "axioms of economic behavior" and "regularity assumptions."

sistent at some times. If our theory predicts well, we still do not know whether people are generally consistent or not; and if our theory predicts poorly, we do not know whether the assumption about consistency was the key error or not. What we can say is that if we know most people will react inconsistently in a certain situation, it is not wise to attempt to predict their behavior using our microeconomic model. It is in this sense that we say that the behavioral axioms ought to be realistic.

It is not always easy to tell the axioms from the assumptions in microeconomics, but the behavioral nature of the former is the key. The *assumptions* are generally adopted for convenience, are quite often expositional, and are quite properly to be viewed as restrictions. We often assume certain things about commodities, things which are strictly untrue, so that we can apply calculus. In so doing, we lose some fairly trivial generality,[2] but we gain a powerful set of techniques, those of the mathematician; further, we are entitled thereby to use any theorems the mathematician might have proved.

1.4.2 Theorems in Economics

We will have a complete example of this methodology in the last section of this chapter; in the rest of this section we can turn to the complete articulation of the model of theory itself, as it is usually understood to apply to economics. After the axioms, assumptions, and definitions have been assembled, all of the fundamental inputs of the theory are complete. The next step is the construction of logical relationships which we might refer to as *theorems*. For example, having adopted the appropriate restrictions, we might deduce that demand curves for products, in our theoretical framework, slope downward. Again, care must be taken to avoid misunderstanding. Demand curves do not necessarily slope

---

[2] When I say we "lose generality," I mean that our assumption has reduced the range of reality which can be reached by the theory. By this usage of the word "general," a model which has everything in it is the most general (an example is the "general equilibrium" model), while one with almost nothing in it (e.g., macroeconomics) is the least general. On the other hand, the latter model is the more powerful (for many problems); indeed, the assumptions and axioms serve the function of increasing the power of the theory at the cost of generality.

downward; but, under the postulated conditions of our theory, after certain theoretically suggested adjustments have been made, we will predict that they slope downward, in practical applications. Suppose, in apparent contradiction, we discover that the demand for potatoes slopes upward—that decreases in the price of potatoes seem to bring reductions, rather than increases, in the quantity demanded. Are we in trouble, since we predicted that this demand curve would slope downward? Perhaps, but there are several routes to take to extricate ourselves from this situation, routes which are suggested by the theory itself.

In the first place, if we are to regard the happening as being related to the theory, we might try to prove that there is a direct link of some kind between the data and the theory. This exercise is rarely performed in economics; and, in fact, the nature that such a proof might have is not well understood. One thing we could do is to see if our fundamental conditions, particularly the axioms, are met by the experimental data—we might simply ask if the people in the potato market are consistent. In reality, this exercise amounts to testing the axioms and promises to be a difficult process because of the psychological nature of the axioms in economics.

Another, actually complementary, approach arises because we state our theoretical results with provisional warnings, such as ceteris paribus. The ceteris paribus clause has almost a legal sense in economics, and it warns the user, formally, that certain other things are held constant. In the case of the theoretical demand curve, for example, tastes are assumed not to change from situation to situation because the theory would be vitiated if they did. Provisionally, income, too, is held constant. "Being held constant" is not a statement of fact but a device of the theory which enables us to state limited results; the downsloping demand curve is one such result. As applied to the case of the demand for potatoes, inspection of the ceteris paribus list might suggest that we look at consumer income; if we find that income had fallen during the period studied, so that the higher priced observations were taken when people were richer, we might have a possible explanation of our results. In this way, ceteris paribus is seen to be a help and not a limitation to our analysis because it spells out a list of potential troublemakers. That, in fact, is the purpose of ceteris paribus; and if the ceteris paribus list contains any items which could not affect the situation, their inclusion is simply a waste of effort.

We will also find that our theory directly throws off implications which are worth looking into in situations of the kind being considered here. One of these, which we shall work with in the last section of this chapter, is the price-induced income effect—the idea that a fall in the price of a commodity makes the consumers of that product wealthier in that they can purchase their original amount and still have money left over. This might explain the result for the demand for potatoes, as we shall see, and is of special importance in financial markets, particularly when the price involved is the general price level.

1.5 THE THEORY OF CHOICE

What we have to say in this section can be applied to any situation in which one wishes to analyze the factors behind the economic choices made by individuals. We will keep returning to this apparatus from time to time; but because prices are determined by supply and demand in the marketplace, we will turn, in section 1.6, to the choices made by the aggregate of individuals. In most cases we will find that the transition from the individual to the sum of individuals can be effected with a sweep of the pen—but not always, so we will want to know what is involved in the process.[3]

But what we have to say also applies to other than individuals. Banks, in particular, and financial intermediaries such as savings and loan associations, all have alternative portfolios before them and necessarily have to make choices. Even industrial corporations must choose among various potential financial instruments in their asset accounts and even, on occasion, with regard to their liabilities.

---

[3] Supply could also be taken up in the same way at this point—that is, first a description of the "supply decision" of an individual firm and then an aggregate description—but, it turns out, a great deal of formal supply analysis is not that useful for our problems; and we will be able to adopt a somewhat looser approach. This will be apparent in Chapter 4, when the little bit of "supply theory" we do present is introduced implicitly.

In the latter case, for example, a corporation can raise funds by issuing bonds (debt) or stocks (equity). The government, too, makes portfolio decisions, and its methods are not so dissimilar from those of the business world.

The common denominator in all of these cases is that a "constrained" choice must be made. The individual, for example, chooses assets subject to—that is, constrained by—his wealth. Banks and many financial intermediaries are constrained by the size of their deposits; the corporation management is constrained by its stockholders and by their views on the risks it should undertake, particularly with respect to issuing debt or equity. The Federal Reserve System is limited in its policies by legal restrictions and pressure from Congress. All of these units are, in addition, limited by market forces, for all operate in open marketplaces to some extent.

The theory to be elaborated in the following paragraphs is that of *choice under constraint*. At this point in our study, two objectives underlie our pursuit of this topic: the limitations of our analysis must be made obvious by listing the critical assumptions; and the separation of the choice problem into two subproblems— choice when price changes and choice when wealth changes—must be achieved. In the final analysis these methods will be applied to the particular problems just suggested and to a fairly wide range of other financial problems. To work such applications, we must state the constraints; and that statement involves, among other things, describing the most important of the institutional features of each situation. We must also in many cases find and define the price and then describe the characteristics of the product. These matters disposed of, we are then in a position to employ microeconomic analysis.

1.5.1   The Fundamental Conditions: Axioms and Assumptions

We begin by imposing some axioms on the behavior of our individual decision unit. We assume that the unit is consistent (Axiom 1): that is, when it is faced with sets of three choices, if the unit prefers choice A over choice B and choice B over choice C, then, to be called consistent, it must prefer A over C.

We might denote all this as in Equation 1–1, with $>$ suggesting "prefers" and $\Rightarrow$ suggesting "implies."

$$A > B \quad \text{and} \quad B > C \Rightarrow A > C \qquad (1\text{–}1)$$

Briefly, we will also state that our decision unit prefers more of whatever good we are studying to less (Axiom 2), that it is able to make choices among the alternatives (Axiom 3). We will also assert that it does make choices (Axiom 4), when we come to consider actual situations.

As noted above, none of these statements is expected to be true in all cases or for all decision units, particularly for individuals. On the other hand, one nice thing about financial marketplaces is that the participants believe themselves to be especially consistent, and they certainly are especially greedy; this suggests that the first two axioms are reasonable. As to whether or not individuals can always make choices of the type we wish them to make, we might ask ourselves how easily a black can buy a home in an upper middle class suburb, if it is inhabited by whites, or how easily he can acquire a mortgage from a local financial intermediary. At any rate, if the behavior suggested by these axioms dominates in the market in question, we would expect our theories to predict real-world phenomena successfully.

Eventually we want to work with simple equations and to draw smooth graphs representing demand and supply conditions, and it will be inconvenient if commodities come in large units (such as a house); accordingly, we will assume that our products, so far undefined, are continuous or offer services which can be interpreted as continuous. By continuous we will mean, nonrigorously, that the product can be divided and then divided again an infinite number of times. The damage such an assumption might make depends on the circumstances at hand but will probably not be all that serious for financial markets. One way of evading the whole issue would be to deal with the market as a whole rather than with the individual, while still employing microeconomic analysis, but this raises some other problems—those of aggregation—which we will defer to section 1.6.

As described above, the next thing we must do is define our terms. In this case, we will say no more at present than to note that definitions will be part of the institutional structure of each problem and will consequently vary with the circumstances. So far as the rest of this chapter goes, we will not have any particular market situation in mind, so definition is not important; we can turn, instead, to the formal analysis.

1.5.2 The Budget Constraint

Our typical decision unit will be faced with certain data and will be presumed to act in the manner suggested by our axioms and assumptions. Further, we have said enough about the character of our unit to assert now that it will choose, for example a portfolio; and our task, for the remainder of this chapter, is to see what the principles of this choice are.[4] Let us suppose that our unit is an individual who wishes to consider two types of consumer goods, X and Y, to be perfectly vague. Our consumer will be faced with prices for these commodities, let us say P_x and P_y, over which he has no control.[5] The consumer, we will assume, has a fixed amount of income to dispose of—let us call this income I—and let us note that he has two variables to choose between: he can purchase Y at P_y, or he can purchase X at P_x. If we were to put up the algebraic representation of these comments, we would get the following statement of the individual's choice limitation:

$$I = P_y(Y) + P_x(X) \qquad\qquad (1-2)$$

where I is known ahead of time and the prices are set in the marketplace; thus, only Y and X—the quantities of the two goods—have to be decided upon by the individual.

---

[4] It is tempting, here, to try to work with a financial problem, but there are certain matters which must be dealt with before we attempt this. For example, suppose that goods X and Y, the two consumer goods in the analysis of this section, are a bond and a stock, respectively. If the consumer is faced with a fall in the price of the stock, he might decide that this indicates a trend and move into bonds; for this reason the "demand curve" for the stock might slope upward. Then, too, if the consumer already held some of the stock, the price fall, while raising his purchasing power on the one hand, would reduce his wealth on the other. This is too complicated a set of considerations for our first use of the techniques of this text.

[5] Here the assertion is that the individual is faced with perfect competition. If the individual is in a monopolistic position, we need to consider his influence on the price as he adjusts his expenditures.

Equation 1–2 graphs to a straight line in two-dimensional space; it is usually referred to as a "budget constraint," and it expresses the limits to which the consumer can go in his acquisition of the two goods. The slope of this straight line is given by the negative of the ratio of the two prices, inverted; and its distance from the origin indicates the magnitude of the consumer's income. Figure 1–1 illustrates these points.[6]

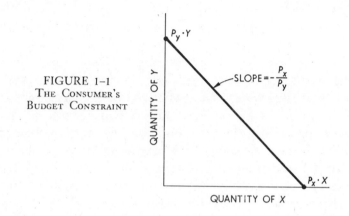

FIGURE 1–1
THE CONSUMER'S
BUDGET CONSTRAINT

1.5.3 The Consumer's Choice

Enough has been assumed about the behavior of the consumer to assert that under our conditions he will pick that point on the budget line which provides him with more satisfaction than any other point on the line. He will not pick a point to the left of the line, for such a point can be seen to be inferior to some point on the line itself; it is inferior in the sense that for any point within the line there is some point on the line which offers more of both goods—and our consumer prefers more to less. The point which the consumer actually picks depends on his tastes; but, since we have assumed that he will choose, it is unnecessary to draw any such thing as a "utility" curve to suggest how his taste patterns might look—the choice he actually makes will be

---

[6] The best way for the student to verify the statements just made is to solve for the values of the X and Y intercepts and then to compute their ratio (the Y intercept over the X intercept).

at his personal optimum, under our assumptions, and that is all we are interested in.

We cannot, in what follows, restrict ourselves to two dimensions; indeed, it should be obvious that in order to generalize in the sense of giving our consumer unit more items to choose among, all we have to do is add commodities into Equation 1-2, along with their prices. Of course the two-dimensional picture will no longer be available to us; but, on the other hand, it will often not be necessary in what follows, except as an aid to the intuition.

There are three experiments we can confront our consumer with in order to test his reactions: in economic terminology these are known as "partial experiments" because only one variable is changed at a time; they exhaust the possibilities, so far as we have specified the choice problem.[7] In the first place, the consumer's tastes can undergo a change so that he will be forced, by his own psychology, to take up a new position on his budget line. This is not a change which we will discuss very often in this book simply because taste factors, aside from the dislike of risk, do not seem very important in financial markets. We will also observe that under normal conditions it is not likely that the taste for financial instruments will change.[8]

In the second place, the consumer's income may change. This can occur for several reasons, the most usual of which is simply that he has had, or expects to have, an increase in pay. The effect of this is a rightward—and parallel—shift of the budget line in Figure 1-1. The shift is parallel because the prices, and hence the ratio of the two prices, remain unchanged; it is rightward because the consumer can purchase more of both goods after the increase in income.

In the last place, the price of one of the commodities may change—let us say that P_x falls. To understand the results of this change most clearly, we need to refer to actual situations. Let

---

[7] It is worth emphasizing here that the point of view of these experiments is that of the economist. We do not change the tastes of the individual, but we do ask what his responses would be if a change occurred.

[8] An example of an abnormal condition is the case in which there is a run on a bank. These shifts of taste occurred in waves, in the United States, until the mid-1930's.

us initially assume our consumer to be in an optimum position at the following set of prices and quantities:

Price of Y..................... $1.00 per unit
Price of X..................... $1.25 per unit
Quantity of Y consumed........ 20 units
Quantity of X consumed........ 10 units

If we rewrite Equation 1–2 for the new conditions, we have

$$\$32.50 = \$1(20) + \$1.25(10) \qquad (1\text{–}3)$$

Now, let us suppose the price of X falls to $1. In Figure 1–1 this would be represented by a new budget line which would lie to the right of the old budget line, except at the point where it intersects the Y axis. Both Equation 1–3 and the new budget line, which will be exhibited below as Equation 1–4, are shown in Figure 1–2.

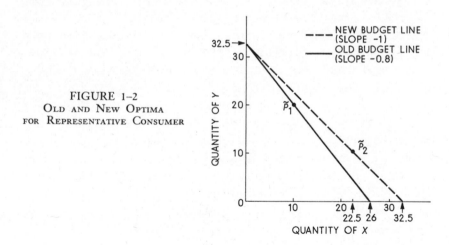

FIGURE 1–2
OLD AND NEW OPTIMA
FOR REPRESENTATIVE CONSUMER

Let us suppose that the consumer was at point $\tilde{P}_1$ when the old budget line was relevant and, after the price change, chose, because it was his new optimum, point $\tilde{P}_2$ on the new budget line.[9] Our concern is not with the criteria he uses in arriving at his choice, so long as he adheres to our assumed conditions—for all we care, he may use an astrological forecast. We should observe one point here, however; all of his choices under the new condi-

---

[9] We will use the tilde ($\sim$) to designate points in our "commodity space" in order to avoid the confusion of points with prices in the text.

tions (except at the Y intercept) can be shown to be better than some of his choices under the old; he is better off under the new conditions in a way which makes us observe that the effectiveness of his given *income* has increased. First of all, let us see what Equation 1–3 looks like under the new conditions, at the new optimum.

$$\$32.50 = \$1(10) + \$1(22.5) \tag{1-4}$$

1.5.4   Income and Substitution Effects

As Equation 1–4 makes clear, the consumer is seen to have purchased more of X and less of Y at $\bar{P}_2$; this result was not unexpected. But, and this is the important point, because of his increased income, we have mixed two influences: the effect of the change in price by itself (the *substitution effect*) and the effect of the residual change in income (the price-induced *income effect*), even though we desired only to study the change in price. There is a simple technique, both for practical and, as we shall see, for theoretical expositions, which can be used to remove accretion in income so as to leave the pure substitution effect of the change in price. The reasons why we might be interested in this separation will vary from problem to problem, but the most important is our expectation that the consumer will react one way to the price change and quite another to the income change. This will have both practical and theoretical significance. In particular, we might sometimes expect increases in income to result in cuts in the consumption of some commodities, potatoes for example, while substitution effects will only be negative, even for potatoes, when the price of the product changes.

We can perform this adjustment by "compensating" the consumer for his windfall gain in income. In the example being discussed here, the consumer was given a bonus, equal to 25 cents per unit of X, as a result of the fall in the price of X. Algebraically, we might say that:

Change in effectiveness of income
= Change in price times the original quantity of X
which, more exactly, is:

$$\Delta I = \Delta P(X) \tag{1-5}$$

In our example, this amount is $2.50. When we *remove* income from our consumer, we shift his budget line leftward—it is easy to verify that when we remove the amount suggested in Equation 1–5, the new budget line will go through the old point ($\tilde{P}_1$) and will be parallel to the new budget line representing the new price ratio.[10] Figure 1–3 illustrates the new, compensated situation along with the old.

FIGURE 1–3
OLD, NEW, AND COMPENSATED CHOICES FOR
REPRESENTATIVE CONSUMER

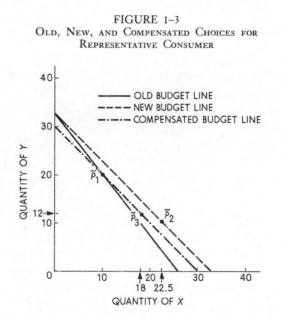

The compensation, which in this case was negative, has left the consumer with $30 of income at the new price ratio. He can, if he wishes, consume the old amount of the commodities, for $30 = $1(20) + $1(10); but, invariably, he will wish to purchase more of X and less of Y.[11] We do not know exactly where the consumer will go after suffering the theoretical compensation;

---

[10] To show this, all you have to note is that $\tilde{P}_1$ (which is 20 units of Y and 10 of X) is a point on the new budget line.

[11] It can be proved, but it is certainly not one of the tasks of this book to do so, that this substitution effect is always negative under our circumstances. The reader who wishes to verify this property ought to consult a text in intermediate microeconomic theory for both intuitive and (sometimes) rigorous proofs of this contention.

but, for example, let us assert that it is point $\tilde{P}_3$ in Figure 1–3.[12] At this point, along the compensated budget line, the consumer is seen to have purchased 12 units of Y and 18 units of X; his new budget solution is the following:

$$\$30 = \$1(12) + \$1(18) \qquad (1-6)$$

1.5.5 The Demand Curve for an Individual

Now, there are several uses for this information. In the first place, we might derive a compensated demand curve for either of the products, particularly for X; in this book we will find it important to separate income effects from substitution effects in our analysis of the demand for money. In the second place, we might be interested in "income consumption" curves, although for the moment we will not discuss their properties. Let us, then, compare a compensated demand curve with an uncompensated one; in other words, let us see what effect the residual change in income has on the individual's demand for good X. Table 1–1 gathers all of the information of this example into one place, and

TABLE 1–1

INCOME AND SUBSTITUTION EFFECTS OF A CHANGE IN THE PRICE OF X ON QUANTITY DEMANDED OF X*

	$P_x = \$1.25$	$P_x = \$1.00$
Quantity purchased, uncompensated	10	22.5
Quantity purchased, compensated		18.0
Income effect		4.5
Substitution effect (negative)		8.0
Total Effect		12.5

* All entries in the table are quantities of X.

---

[12] The information which one needs to compute the actual point is not provided in the above example. In fact, we will need some estimate of the consumer's marginal propensity to consume good X. Clearly, this propensity times the change in income will then give us the income effect, for the propensity gives the (marginal) consumption of X out of changes in income. Since the total effect, which is known, is equal to the income effect plus the substitution (pure price) effect, we also have an estimate of the substitution effect. In the example in the text, this propensity is 1.8; this means that for each additional dollar of income, the consumer will purchase 1.8 units of X. In practice, we would find this propensity by collecting data on the income of the consumers studied.

Figure 1–4 represents the two demand curves where, the reader should be careful to note, the vertical axis is now the price of X and the horizontal axis is the quantity demanded of X by our representative consumer.

FIGURE 1–4
COMPENSATED AND UNCOMPENSATED DEMAND CURVES

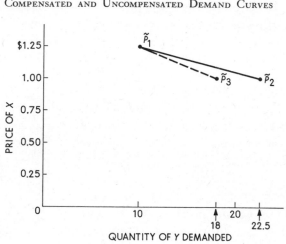

1.5.6 Conclusions

What does all of this amount to for the further understanding of financial markets, particularly the money market? For one thing, we have a general set of techniques, capable of being expanded as needed, which we can apply to a large variety of situations. We have used the examples of goods X and Y, but equally well we could have used stocks and bonds, money and commodities, or, because the apparatus generalizes easily, combinations of all of these factors. Wherever there are situations of constrained choice among economic alternatives, we will find that such an apparatus helps us to analyze the various economic problems which emerge. Indeed, we will never understand the role of money in our economic system without some such kind of microeconomic analysis.

We need to be clear on another point. While we chose to present our model in two-dimensional form, there is no problem (except visually) to the presentation of the model in as many dimensions as we desire.[13] One obvious extension, for the example just described, would be to allow our consumer to choose to hold some of his income in the form of money rather than to consume it. When we do this, however, we immediately become aware that money is not like the other two commodities because it does not seem to provide any direct satisfaction, except to misers; and a purely formal solution does not really explain this matter to us. The difficulty is that money serves as a generalized *medium of exchange*, on the one hand, and appears to be a safe *store of value*, on the other. The problems that this dual character raises are so complicated that it would be reckless to make any further statements here. In the next chapter we will go to work on these matters.

1.6 AGGREGATION AND TOTAL DEMAND

1.6.1 The Aggregation Problem

When we move from the analysis of the individual to the analysis of the market as a whole, we usually aggregate. We can take each individual separately (that is, employ general equilibrium analysis), but we usually find it convenient to sum (aggregate) individual demand curves to obtain the market demand curve. We can then use the market demand curve as if it were an individual curve; but there is a drawback, which arises because we must incur the cost of additional assumptions. Thus it is essential that we have some idea of the "cost of aggregation" before we proceed to work with aggregates. In fact, we must assume that all individuals have the same tastes and the same incomes before we sum their demand curves if we want to treat the aggregate of individuals as a single individual. This is a high cost to pay, because we know that neither income nor taste is invariant as prices change in the real world; but we are generally willing to proceed with these assumptions, since the aggregated apparatus is so useful.[14]

---

[13] This will be done explicitly in the next chapter.

[14] We should also point out that our aggregate consumer will be expected to have all the characteristics of the individual: consistency, greed, and limited means.

In addition to the aggregation of individuals just described, we sometimes wish to aggregate commodities. In order to do this—in order to be able to treat the sum of a group of commodities as a single commodity with a single price—we must assume that all of the price changes of all the commodities are in the same proportion. At some times this aggregation seems less costly than at others. For example, currency aggregates quite well with demand deposits and with time deposits to form the composite products, *narrow money* (currency plus demand deposits) or *broad money* (narrow money plus time deposits). In the latter case we have suppressed, in the aggregation, the influence of the price of time deposits on the quantity of demand deposits, and in some circumstances that might be a costly assumption.[15]

Another aggregation which will appear in this book is the aggregation of all spending into consumption, investment, and government spending in order to be able to use such devices as the macroeconomic "consumption function" in the same way that we use the demand curve. What this means, in practice, is that if we wish to treat gross consumer spending, for example, as a single product and retain the apparatus of the theory of demand, we must assume that all consumer price changes are in the same proportion.[16] This is an extremely strong condition, and it seems to deny the relevance of microeconomics for macroeconomic problems, for much of microeconomics is suppressed in the bargain. That is, when we use gross national product (GNP) as if it were a single product with a single price (the overall price level), we cannot analyze the determination of the relative prices between commodities. If we disaggregate gross national product into con-

---

[15] When money is "tight," it is said, individuals are tempted (by banks) to put their cash into time deposits by the raising of time deposit interest rates. We will see in Chapter 4 that this has monetary repercussions.

[16] Some economists felt that with the price of money (the price level), you could work under these conditions without losing too much generality. This has turned out not to be the case, for, as we shall see below, we will need nonproportionality to explain some interesting characteristics of money. There is another problem which we will have to deal with at certain points—that is, that retaining the fixture of prices becomes implausible when we sum individuals to consider market situations. In fact, we will not be able to explain how prices are determined unless we allow them to be flexible in the aggregate. This is no problem for microeconomic analysis, but if we had approached this problem by way of macroeconomics, assuming that all price changes are proportional, we should not have been able to say very much about individual prices. This is a considerable advantage of the microeconomic approach.

sumption, investment, and government spending, then we can analyze the determination of the price levels of each of these categories, taken separately, but not within the categories.[17]

1.6.2 Total Demand

Actually, after we have decided on our aggregation, the rest of the analysis is fairly straightforward. Indeed, when we sum our individuals' demands to get market demand, after we have done the same for supply, we have enough information to solve for the price which clears the market.[18] That is, the end product of the supply and demand analysis is an explanation of price; if we have done our theory carefully, we will have a list of factors which contribute to the formation of price, and, in particular cases, we will be able to estimate the force of these factors.

In monetary economics we are interested in the determination of two prices: the interest rate and the price level. There are severe aggregation problems in connection with both of these entities, particularly the latter, so we must be extremely careful to set out our analysis completely. This task we will begin in Chapter 2.

1.7 DISCUSSION QUESTIONS

1. One observes the most heated debates among economists concerning definitions. Indeed, the claim is often made that a certain

---

[17] For example, one question we might like answered concerns how certain specific reallocations of our resources might improve the rate of growth of GNP. We will have to split GNP into much finer divisions than spending on government, investment, and consumer goods to work on this problem with any hope of a useful answer, because much of both consumer and government spending is essentially investment. The best example of the overlapping is spending on education which may be an important direction—more important than business investment, even—to divert resources from other types of consumption in order to improve the rate of growth. That is, it may be more beneficial to the growth rate to push funds toward the consumer sector—if spending on education rises—than toward business investment. The aggregation suggested (into *C*, *I*, and *G*) would conceal this possibility.

[18] The intersection of the supply and demand curves or, more generally, the solution of a system of supply and demand equation, might give us a solution, but it need not be a stable one. In fact, it is possible that in certain financial markets *speculation* destabilizes the market; there are many examples of such cases, one of which is the stock market (at least for short periods), and another, the market for foreign exchange. We will discuss these and other examples in the book.

definition is incorrect. Can you reconcile the use of the word *incorrect* in such debates with the claim in the text that definitions are the property of the definer?

2. Frequently, one hears the term *the rational consumer.* Is the assumption of consistency enough to cause us to regard a consuming unit as rational, or need we assume some other characteristics as well?

3. Why do we refer to our theory as the theory of choice rather than as the theory of demand? Does it have something to do with the fact that we intend to examine data which are generated in the market place *after* choices have been made?

4. Suppose an individual chooses a large apple over a pear and a pear over a small apple, but chooses a small apple over a large apple so as not to appear greedy. Is this a violation of consistency as we have defined it? Is this a violation of rationality as you described it in question 2?

5. In addition to causing our theory to work poorly, the influence of racial prejudice in markets creates a misallocation of resources. In what ways are these problems two sides of the same coin?

6. If a consumer chooses a point inside the budget line of this chapter, he will necessarily be saving. Why is this behavior a problem to our analysis? What other information would we need before we could explain this behavior?

7. If the price of good Z, which you currently do not purchase, should fall, you would not be better off in the sense of Figure 1–2. Yet if you decided to purchase some of good Z you would be better off. Why is it necessary for you to be a purchaser for you to make a gain?

8. The total effect of a change in the price of a good is divided between the income and the substitution effect. Is it possible to have an income effect of zero? Illustrate your answer. Would a demand curve under these conditions necessarily slope downward?

9. Actually, the aggregation conditions suggested for individuals in Section 1.6.1 are stronger than they need to be. That is, I have stated *sufficient* conditions which are not completely *necessary.* What would be the nature of the gains from using a more economical set of assumptions?

10. Aggregation is inevitable in economics, but costly. What do you see as the principal advantages gained by stopping with the aggregation of individuals and not aggregating commodities? How do these aggregations actually arise in micro- and macroeconomics?

1.8 FURTHER READING

Methodology

BRONFENBRENNER, MARTIN S. "A Middlebrow Introduction to Economic Methodology," *The Structure of Economic Science* (ed. Sherman R. Krupp). Englewood Cliffs, N.J.: Prentice-Hall, Inc., 1966.

FRIEDMAN, MILTON S. "On the Methodology of Positive Economics," *Essays in Positive Economics* (ed. Milton Friedman). Chicago: University of Chicago Press, 1953.

MARGENAU, HENRY. "What Is a Theory?" *The Structure of Economic Science* (ed. Sherman R. Krupp). Englewood Cliffs, N.J.: Prentice-Hall, Inc., 1966.

Price Theory

DUE, JOHN, and CLOWER, ROBERT S. *Microeconomic Theory*. Homewood, Ill.: Richard D. Irwin, Inc., 1966.

LLOYD, CLIFF. *Microeconomic Analysis*. Homewood, Ill.: Richard D. Irwin, Inc., 1967.

Aggregation

LEIJONHUFVUD, AXEL. *On Keynesian Economics and the Economics of Keynes*. New York: Oxford University Press, 1968.

Chapter 2

DEFINITIONS: MONEY AND THE PRICE OF MONEY

2.1 INTRODUCTION

In the chapters which follow, we are going to show that what I will define as money plays an extremely important role in the economic system. We must begin our study with definition; indeed, the argument of Chapter 1 almost forces us to do so; but this procedure will be more interesting and more useful than one might have anticipated. Part of the interest flows from the fact that there is a lively controversy over the problem of the definition of money; there are (at least) two ways of "defining money" commonly employed in both theoretical and empirical work in monetary economics. Needless to say, the results one gets are not going to be invariant with respect to the definition chosen, so we have another sufficient reason for working on the problem of definition. Since we must opt for a definition ourselves, some of my comments will be intended to clarify the reasoning behind my choice.

When one "defines" something, basically he has two choices: attaching labels to real-world objects, in which case he is a *nominalist,* or attaching labels to bundles of concepts and then searching for the real-world entity which best satisfies these criteria; let us call the practitioner of such a method an *empiricist.* In the case of the nominalist, one has the best setup for empirical work possible: he begins with a real-world entity (currency plus demand deposits), gives it a name (money), and then gets on with his work (money and banking). In the case of the empiricist, for example in the case of financial markets, one introduces a set of economic characteristics and then searches among all of the possible aggregates of financial instruments to find the best aggregate. A good deal of the empirical effort is directed toward finding the correct (from some point of view) definition.

There is a third approach which seems to fit somewhere between the two just described, and that is, after listing the characteristics, to use in the working definition only those items which have all the characteristics at once. On the one hand, what this does, analytically, is to avoid the problem of trying to decide which characteristics are more important, a task which must involve, among other things, a good deal of judgment. On the other hand, it leaves room for the selection of important economic characteristics which one might, in turn, be able to define in a way satisfactory to most students of monetary economics.

The problem of the definition of money is a version of the problem of aggregation, especially if the empiricist's approach to definition is taken. That is, aggregation necessarily suppresses some factors in the data, factors which one must judge to be of less importance, explicitly or implicitly, than those retained. No matter which approach we take, so long as we have any aggregate at all, we must have this suppression. Even so, by emphasizing a certain set of characteristics which money must have—medium of exchange, store of value, and unit of account—I make the designation of what is money arbitrary and not a matter of judgment. Thus the burden of judgment falls on the explanation of and the justification of the characteristics themselves, and that is what sections 2.2 through 2.6 of this chapter are about.

2.2 AN ECONOMY WITHOUT MONEY

Let us call an economy without money a *barter economy*. For this economy, let us assume both that individuals are in possession of fixed amounts of physical commodities and that they wish to exchange these commodities because they are not satisfied, individually, with the arrangement they have inherited.[1] There certainly can be production of goods, and there may be all manner of modern techniques; but expositional convenience suggests it

---

[1] Actually, we need some fiction here to get things going. The best thing is to assert that the commodities are simply dumped on the doorstep the night before the economist arrived to study the system.

is better if we think in terms of a simple society, perhaps an island economy, which is sufficiently small so that people come into frequent contact with one another in the course of the market period, however we might wish to define that.[2] We are assuming that each individual, in some unspecified fashion, has come to possess certain amounts of consumer goods; then we can argue that the demand analysis of the last chapter can be applied perfectly to this economy and that each individual will be presumed to want to get the most satisfaction he can from his limited—and arbitrary—initial supplies of commodities.

As individuals go through the process of exchanging their products, they must keep in mind the exchange ratios between their products and all other products in the market.[3] As time progresses toward the end of the market period, there will be a number of these ratios which, we will assume, are tentative prices, really, and will differ for each individual depending on his energy and experience. However, when the market is finally cleared at the end of the week, there will be one final set of exchange ratios, agreed upon by all, which we will define as *market relative prices*, at which all deals are consumated. There are, in fact, a large number of these relative prices which must be kept in mind by anyone who wishes to have all the information available about trading conditions. If there are 10 commodities, there will be

$$9 + 8 + 7 + 6 + 5 + 4 + 3 + 2 + 1 = 45$$

price ratios to know,[4] even for a society so simple that it has only 10 commodities.

---

[2] Even the definition of the market period is not immune to controversy in economics. We will define it, rather conventionally, as the time it takes to clear the market. We can talk about clearing the market because we have no production but just "manna from heaven" in our simple exchange economy.

[3] An example of an exchange ratio, or relative price, would be one grass skirt for 10 coconuts.

[4] For example, the 10th good will have 9 exchange ratios with the 9 remaining goods, the 9th will have 8 with the 8 remaining goods (the exchange ratio with the 10th already having being counted once), and so forth, as noted in the text. Of course, if any of the natives specializes in production, that is, if any one produces only one good, he will need to know only 9 price ratios. There is another case, as well, that of the *numeraire*. A commodity, not itself money, would be termed a numeraire if it were customary to quote prices in terms of it. Actual primitive societies did have numeraires.

There is clearly a relatively considerable burden of search involved in participating in this simple market economy.[5] We will define the costs of this search and bargaining activity as *transactions costs*, and these are relatively important in our simple society because of the large number of relations a trader must consider; they would be larger, of course, in a more complicated barter economy.

A native of average intelligence would soon observe that there are ways to reduce these transactions costs.[6] One way this might be done is by accumulating transactions into bigger lots. In this case the transactions are still direct (barter), but clearly such a technique will reduce transactions costs over the week. The problem is that another kind of cost, *waiting costs*, will be increased, for while one is accumulating stores of consumer goods, he is obviously unable to consume them; and, in addition, he has to incur the costs of storage. This is important and worth emphasizing. There are, as things are laid out in our simple world, two kinds of costs which are connected with the exchange of commodities—transactions costs and waiting costs. Let us define the sum of these two costs as *exchange costs;* an economic problem then arises because waiting costs *rise* from the effort to lower transactions costs so that there must be some trade-off between the two costs. That is to say, up to a point, the lumping of transactions into bigger lots can be expected to lower exchange costs by reducing transactions costs more than it increases waiting costs. The consumers in our system can be expected, insofar as we permit them to vary the size of their consumption lots, to juggle the size of their transactions lots until the optimum-sized lot is obtained.

---

[5] You will have noticed, I hope, that the natives must live off their fat while the bargaining is going on. If some deals are actually consummated before the end of the week, it will not make sense to talk of a single set of market prices because, in general, those intermediate dealings will tend to be at other prices, either higher or lower. We will ignore this problem in our discussion in the text.

[6] We are not really talking about primitive societies as such, but we do know that in such economies one often finds conventionally determined prices. This is one way to reduce transactions costs at, presumably, the costs of having a misallocation of resources. That is, if the price is determined by law rather than by market forces, it will ordinarily be a disequilibrium price.

2.3 THE APPEARANCE OF A MEDIUM OF EXCHANGE

The system just described had no medium of exchange, as such. We can now complicate our system a little more by assuming that individuals begin to accumulate balances of certain commodities which they have no intention of consuming themselves. In the previous section, we did permit individuals to accumulate balances of their own commodities in order to reduce transactions costs; but it is only a short step to trading their own commodities for more universally acceptable commodities, such as gold and silver, holding the latter, and then trading these for the items they wish to consume. The use of commodities in this intermediate sense represents the introduction of *commodity money* into the economic system.[7]

Commodity money, which has appeared in response to the need for it, as we have set up our simple economic system, will certainly end up reducing transactions costs, hence improving the efficiency of the market system, and will probably—but not necessarily—reduce waiting costs. It will probably reduce waiting costs because it is likely, but not certain, that the average consumer will hold smaller balances of the more useful, more flexible, commodity money than he would of his own accumulated commodities. Let us be clear on another point, in case you think we have strayed into the topic of the demand for the product: if the medium of exchange (commodity money) is introduced into the system, it will have been because individuals have gained on net. If individuals gain, in turn, it is simply that exchange costs, as we have defined them, have fallen; but, and here is the main point, we are illustrating a characteristic, *medium of exchange*, which money is to have in our definition.[8]

---

[7] We had better note that we are really describing a specialized store of value. That is, an individual accumulates gold because it is immutable, acceptable, etc.; these are relatively unique properties. We will need to keep this in mind in the discussion which follows.

[8] Commodity money will have other characteristics as well. We are only considering its function in one dimension, that of facilitating exchange, and that is because we are defining medium of exchange at this point. There is practically no limit to the number of items which could serve as media of exchange; and, probably, all commodities and services do to some extent; money, we will see, serves as well as it does because it is more generally useful in this role.

We pointed out that if a medium of exchange is adopted, it must have been useful. We are saying that in some sense a society with a medium of exchange is better off than the same society without it. The question concerns what form this gain takes. In fact, as things are laid out in this section, there is a simple saving of time: perhaps it is clearest to argue that the use of a medium of exchange shortens the time necessary to get the market cleared. The consequence is that our natives are better off in having more free time on their hands. If we were to consider a more general situation—one in which production could occur—we would note that one of the choices open to each native would be the production of more commodities with his increased leisure, but we will defer further discussion of this point for the time being.

One other important characteristic of a pure barter economy can be discussed, now that we have defined the medium of exchange: the barter economy does not have any organized markets. If it did, so far as we have specified things, these markets would serve as media of exchange in the same sense, although without the same technical properties, as commodity money. This says, in effect, that the New York Stock Exchange is a form of money, or, more properly, that both money and organized exchanges have functions in common—they facilitate exchange—and provide services of value equivalent to the production of leisure in the economy. This, you can easily see, is an interesting reason why one might want to link money and capital markets, indeed any organized markets, into the monetary mechanism.

We are certainly not going to study these exchanges as money, for they lack some of the other characteristics of money, especially *universality*, but they do mediate in exchanges. We will, instead, argue that the next step is the organization of our primitive world into a series of submarkets, such as those for grass skirts, coconuts, and the like, in which commodities with similar characteristics are traded. This economy, even without the commodity *money*, has media of exchange; for exchange is facilitated by organization, in fact a utility creating organization. The next step is now obvious: we can designate, institutionally or legally, one and only one commodity which is to be traded on all of these exchanges. We then have a monetary economy which is virtually indistinguishable from ours—and it has a universal medium of exchange.

We could have taken another approach here and argued that the monetary system gradually grew, filling the need for money, until some enterprising businessman had managed to get his product accepted in exchange in every market. We have taken another approach, indeed one which evades a lot of the supply and demand problems, and said that the money which in introduced into every market is *fiat money*. By fiat money we mean money which is given an arbitrary legal existence; the way this is usually enforced is for the money, like ours, to be declared both "legal tender" and "acceptable as payment of taxes." This establishes its legal existence but not, as we shall see in the next chapter, its value. If the money is commodity fiat money, it is not hard to see that it serves a real function; but if it is paper fiat money, this is not so obvious, at least not the first time around. In fact, I am not going to elaborate further on the difference simply because commodity money is not very important anymore.

2.4 STOCKS AND FLOWS

2.4.1 Stocks

One thing that must be clear about money in setting up its definition is its dimension and, consequently, its measurement. In fact, money, expressed as so many dollars, is dimensionally a *stock* and, one might naturally suspect, ought to be so measured. A stock, formally,

> is a quantity of some good which is
> measured at an instant of time.

Thus, the stock of currency in the hands of the public can be measured as of 5:01 P.M. on December 30, 1969; it is so many dollars at a point in time. In this book we are going to link all the *stock* markets together, national as well as international, so we are going to treat money as a stock.[9] By way of emphasis, Table 2–1 contains a list of the stock items we will emphasize in our study, taking the view of individual wealth holders in the American economy.

---

[9] There is an alternative as we shall see in the section on the price of money.

TABLE 2–1

THE MAIN CHOICES OF FINANCIAL INSTRUMENTS AVAILABLE TO
INDIVIDUAL WEALTH HOLDERS IN THE UNITED STATES*

Money:	*Government Debt:*
Currency and coin	U.S. Treasury bills
Demand deposits	Government bonds
	Government pensions

Intermediary Debt:	
Commercial bank time deposits	*Corporate Debt and Equity:*
Savings and loan deposits	Corporate equity (stocks)
Mutual savings bank deposits	Direct
Life insurance savings	Indirect (mutual fund shares)
Private pensions	Corporate bonds

* The classification is arbitrary. The table represents the choices available
to individuals rather than totals, so most overlapping problems (for example the
fact that intermediaries hold corporate debt) are ignored.

Currency can be measured over a period of time, to be sure, in which case it must be given a different dimension—and, presumably, a different interpretation. That is, we can measure the stock of currency at two points in time and subtract the earlier total from the later in order to get the change per unit of time in the stock of currency. For example, the total currency in the hands of the public on April 30, 1969 was $43.5 billion, while on April 2, 1969 it was $43.7 billion. We would record −$0.2 billion as the change in the stock. The point to appreciate about this number is that it is still tied to the stock dimension in that one cannot fill in the gaps with any other number. Further, the number −$0.2 billion does not give us any idea of the size of the stock itself. Witness Figure 2–1.

In Figure 2–1 we can see the problem reasonably clearly. We connected up April 2 and April 30 and calculated a number, −$0.2 billion, which completely missed an interesting fluctuation. Furthermore, especially given the cost of producing such data, there is no way around this problem. The best we can do—for example, to get a figure for April 16 when it is too expensive to measure it directly—is to interpolate between the two end dates. If we had done this for any of the dates selected, all the interpolations would have been too low. And there is no way around this problem as things stand: the change in currency has the dimension "per unit of time," but currency is still tied to its original stock dimension, no matter how often data are collected.

FIGURE 2–1
CURRENCY IN THE HANDS OF THE PUBLIC IN THE UNITED
STATES, APRIL 1969

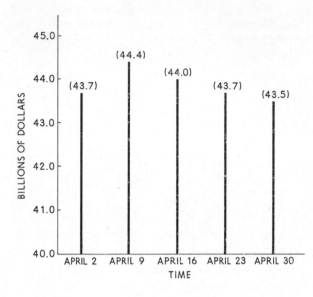

2.4.2 Flows

In economics we find another type of measurement made per
unit of time: the flow. A flow can be defined as

the *rate* of economic activity, *measured over
a period of time;*

that is to say, since activity takes time, a flow must be measured
per unit of time and cannot be measured at a moment of time,
although it can be measured over as small a period of time as
one might desire. There are many examples of flows you are already familiar with; one such is gross national product (GNP),
the market value of final goods and services sold in the country;
consider the breakdown Table 2–2. Here we see that as the
period in question gets shorter the actual amount of activity gets
proportionately smaller, approaching zero (Column 1), while the
annual rate of activity need not change (Column 2). A critical
element in the definition of the flow, clearly, is the period over
which it is measured.

TABLE 2–2
GROSS NATIONAL PRODUCT IN 1969
($ billion)

Period	Actual Rate	Annual Rate
1969 (entire year)............................	932.3	932.3
1st quarter................................	227.2	908.7
2nd quarter...............................	231.2	924.8
3rd quarter................................	235.7	942.8
4th quarter................................	238.3	953.1
February 15, 1969*..........................	2.5	908.7
Between 3 and 4 P.M. on February 15, 1969**...	0.3	908.7

* Assuming 90 days in the quarter.
** Assuming eight hours in the day.

Let us draw this discussion together a little. An economic stock is measured at a moment of time, and an economic flow is measured over a period of time. The only ways to bridge the gap are ones which are imperfect: we can get an interpretation of a stock—the change—which has the same dimension as a flow, but we will never bring the two together. In fact, we will see, we can work the other way as well—that is, convert a flow into a stock—but only on an average basis. Currency, and presumably money, is a stock; but the services in exchange provided by currency are dimensionally flows. Money, it turns out, provides other services in its role as a stock, and it is to these which we now turn.

2.5 MONEY AS A STORE OF VALUE

The items listed in Table 2–1 are financial stores of value for private wealth holders. Currency and demand deposits, the only "media of exchange" in the list, are only two among a long list of potential stores. Each of these items has different characteristics; indeed, the list of characteristics is quite long for money itself. For example, a dime, indisputably a medium of exchange by our definition, also serves as an excellent screwdriver in an emergency. The financial properties of money are another matter and need to be considered if we are to define money rather than simply a medium of exchange.

In fact, most of the items in the list in Table 2–1 pay either interest or dividends to wealth holders; and all of them change in value, as, for example, the stock market fluctuates. Money, alone, in that scheme, does not itself fluctuate in value with changes in interest rates or stock prices; that is, a dollar always fetches a dollar and generally pays an interest rate of zero (if you will agree to stick to currency plus demand deposits as money until I have completed my argument). Money provides the services of a medium of exchange, of course, and that is one reason why people have it in their collected wealth; but it also provides the service of being a relatively safe depository of value compared to the other stores of value.[10] Furthermore, it is an extremely non-specialized store of value in that little special skill is needed to become an expert in storing one's wealth in the form of money. This is in contrast to the problems of storing one's wealth in, say, common stocks or, especially, in real property such as housing.

Now, you will notice that the interest payments which money holders have to forego in order to hold money are a good measure of the net services of money. That is to say, the interest rate on Treasury bills might reflect the yield of money in an alternative sense, since money holders, judged after the fact, seem to have rejected the choice of holding Treasury bills. The interest rate is not a perfect measure of these services, not only because it is difficult to see which other store of value one ought to choose as his alternative but also because banks offer other "nonmoney" services, such as loan privileges, free checks, and the like, which confuse the issue.

The interest rate, then, in the sense of the alternatives which wealth holders have apparently foregone in order to hold "barren" money, is a useful price of money services.[11] Let us finish our enumeration of the services of money in order to complete our definition.

---

[10] Roughly speaking, I am describing the property of liquidity which, we will see later, is the subject of much of the dispute over definition in monetary economics. See sections 3.4.1, 10.2, and 14.2.1 for further discussions of the concept of liquidity.

[11] We will pursue the discussion of the influence of interest rates under the heading of the demand for money in Chapter 3; what we have done here is define the price of money services.

2.6 THE OTHER FUNCTIONS OF MONEY

The Federal Reserve, whose view we will want to know anyway, in its booklet *Purposes and Functions*, which bears the imprint of the Board of Governors of the Federal Reserve System, says

Money is most meaningfully defined in terms of how it is used. Money serves as: (1) a means of payment; (2) a standard of value; and (3) a store of purchasing power.

As a means of payment, money allows individuals to concentrate their productive efforts on those activities for which they are best equipped and in which they are trained to engage. Money is what people receive in return for their services and what they use to buy goods and other things they need for themselves and their families.

As a standard of value, money provides the means by which a day's work can be equated with, for example, a family's food, housing, and other bills, including what is set aside for old age or for children's education. It is thus the measuring rod in terms of which producer and consumer choices can be assessed and decided.

As a store of purchasing power, money enables us to set aside some of our present income for future spending or investing. It is a way in which remuneration for labor and work in the present can be stored for meeting the many contingencies, needs, or opportunities that individuals and families are likely to face in the future.[12]

The Federal Reserve makes this definition operational by arguing, in effect, that all three functions must be served at once if any item is to be identified as money in our economy; only currency and demand deposits serve all three functions, so the Federal Reserve, although it has strictly "defined" currency plus demand deposits, has a usable definition of money. Let us illustrate.

We—and the Federal Reserve—are defining money as that product or combination of products which is simultaneously a medium of exchange, a store of value, and a standard of value. Symbolically, we can represent this approach with a Venn diagram, in which sets of economic entities (to be purposefully vague) are collected according to their characteristics. Money is defined

---

[12] Board of Governors of the Federal Reserve System, *The Federal Reserve, Purposes and Functions* (Washington, D.C., 1963), pp. 5–6.

FIGURE 2–2
THE DEFINITION OF MONEY: A DIAGRAMMATIC APPROACH

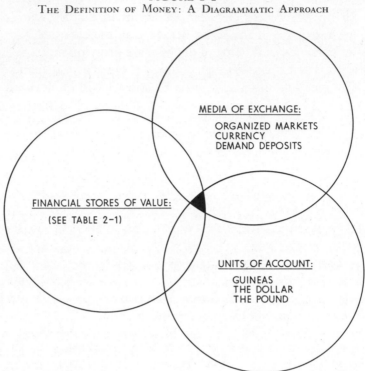

as the intersection (the shaded area) of these sets of entities; and, to the best of my knowledge, this intersection for the United States contains

currency
demand deposits

which I thereby designate *money*.

Let us notice that while these characteristics might or might not be of interest to economic decision units, the characteristics do exist in their own right. If they are of interest, there will be some point in studying the demand for money, since money is one of the ways one can obtain them; but for now, at least provisionally, we have separated the problem of definition from the problem of demand. Things are never as simple as one might wish them, and one thing we have not done is to deal explicitly with all the quality differences between the items in each of the sets. In fact, because none of the other items fits all the characteristics, and because currency and demand deposits are growing more and more alike, this is not a problem of definition; but it is a demand problem, and much of our attention in Chapter 3 will be devoted to it.

2.6.1 Money as a Unit of Account

Let us become a little bit parochial and elaborate on two other characteristics: first, that money is a unit of account, and, second, that money is a standard of value. In the first case we noted earlier, rather casually, that having money around lowered computational costs; in fact, we should now emphasize, having money around provides a ready basis for keeping one's books in terms of money values. But, as is often claimed to the contrary, money itself is not a unit of account. In point of fact, the United States is on the dollar system, and the unit of account is the dollar; the British, at present, are on the pound system, and the unit of account is the pound. Most accounts in the two countries are kept in dollars and pounds, respectively, not in currency and demand deposits. Money—that is to say, currency plus demand deposits—cannot be the unit of account because, in fact, these accounts are *kept* in the unit of account—the dollar or the pound. One can have a unit of account and not have money in his economic system; the unit of account is strictly arbitrary and has no economic existence in the sense of necessarily being the price of anything. In fact, custom sometimes designates units for which there is no legal money equivalent—the British guinea (see Figure 2–2) which is equivalent to 21 shillings "exists" as a unit of account with British shopkeepers and doctors who are aiming to create snob value for their products and services.

Because the unit of account is arbitrary, there is no conceptual problem in changing it, although there certainly would be rounding errors. In addition, being arbitrary, accounts could be kept in rubber bands, I suppose, and be in a perfectly workable and flexible system. Only the auditors would complain, and then only until they got used to the system.

2.6.2   Money as a Standard of Value

The other characteristic emphasized by the Federal Reserve is that money is a standard of value. That is to say, to go back to the simple money economy, if everyone were to quote his prices in dollar units, then one would have a handy means of comparing the values of the commodities. These prices we will define here to be money prices; and, in the economy with 10 commodities, there would be 10 money prices instead of the 45 prices which we found to exist without a medium of exchange. But we must be careful here, for it is the money price, and not the money itself, which is the standard of value—and the price of any commodity, whether it functions as money or not, could be used in this manner. In fact, there is a serious problem here, for the money price of money will always be unity (which is to say, undefined)—a dollar will always fetch a dollar in the open market. This is no problem so long as average values are the same from situation to situation—so long as the value of money is the same from situation to situation—for all we need to know about prices is the money price of each commodity. We can make direct comparisons between items, whether separated geographically or temporally, and know that our standard is reliable. But if this is not true, if the value of the dollar changes from time to time or has a different value in New York City from its value in Rome, Georgia, we must know the average value of money in each situation to have an effective "standard of value." Thus, to the Federal Reserve's definition, the qualification "given time and space" must be added in order to restore order to the definition.

It is in this way that the standard of value function of the dollar raises new questions for consideration. These are new questions because until now we have not been worried about the price of money; we turn to the definitional aspects of this problem in the next section.

2.7   THE PRICE OF NOMINAL MONEY

Money, as we have defined it, is essentially a durable good which provides a flow of services over time. The value of these services is certainly measured by the interest rate which is foregone, but one aspect of money—indeed a critical one—is not covered in this way: where does the *exchange value* of money figure in? Here, following the discussion of the last section, we are taking as our basic unit the amount of nominal money in circulation and trying to find out what it is worth in exchange—this route should lead us to its price. By nominal money what I mean is the amount, in dollar terms, of currency and demand deposits in the hands of the public. To use a popular expression: when we seek the price of money we wish to know "what the dollar is worth" at a moment in time.

Now the aggregate price we are going to define here is determined, like most prices, by the forces of supply and demand, so we are obviously jumping well ahead of our story in some respects. However, to keep things straight, we are not going to attempt any explanation of the determination of this price; we are just going to define it. Accordingly, all equations in the following pages are expressed as definitions, denoted by the mathematical identity sign ($\equiv$). This is tedious, but it does separate effectively the topic of definition from the topics of supply and demand.

For the manufacturing product, of course, it is an easy matter to find a price—easy because people buy and sell the product at a (money) price that everyone who is interested can easily become aware of. For nominal money, on the other hand, the price is not stated explicitly by either the suppliers or the demanders, so one is forced to define the price in terms of the alternatives to holding and using money, rather than the price quoted, conveniently, on some organized market.[13] The only problem is that since money is exchanged in every market, the alternatives are everything, that is, everything which is of economic consequence (which has a price). Everything, categorically, consists of goods and services on the one hand and financial instruments (stocks and bonds) on the other.

---

[13] An example where such an approach is necessary is the valuation of the services of garbage collectors employed by a municipality, where no private collectors exist. One can find the proper wage to pay by an empirical method, the union permitting, which might work as follows. If at the going wage one cannot find the man to fill the job, either in quantity or in quality, the wage is too low; it is too high, probably, if college graduates are turning up for jobs. This method "works" because the workers consider garbage collecting in terms of their alternatives, which one need not know to get a satisfactory estimate of the market price.

2.7.1 The Price Level

Let us begin with an individual, possessing a certain amount of money income (designated Y), and suppose, as in Chapter 1, that he purchases two goods, Q_1 and Q_2, with it; the situation, assuming he must spend everything, is described by Equation 2–1.[14]

$$Y \equiv P_1 Q_1 + P_2 Q_2 \qquad (2\text{--}1)$$

Now if one's income is in the form of money, as it usually is, this equation represents the exchange of a *stock* on the left for a *stock* on the right *more by assumption* (from our island economy) than by relation to reality. If we took a more realistic case, we would want to emphasize that the items on the right are usually conceived of as flows over a period of time rather than as stocks. An individual, in the course of a year, receives a certain amount of income (he receives it in the *form* of money) and spends it on a number of items over the period.

That is, if we are to interpret Equation 2–1 as a budget constraint, we are all right taking it as a stock; but if we wish to

---

[14] We are going to find it very convenient to use a more compact notation than we have used so far. In fact, Equation 2–1 can be written as

$$Y \equiv \sum_{i=1}^{2} P_i Q_i$$

in which the comparison is obvious. Then, if we wished to generalize, we need merely change the index limit from two to, say, n (any number), and we can conceive of "everything"; this is a great convenience. Σ, of course, is essentially an algebraic concept; let us establish a few things about its algebra which we will use later in this and other chapters; we can refer to these statements as properties, and you can verify them by putting in actual numbers.

$$\sum_{i=1}^{n} a_i = a_1 + a_2 + a_3 + \cdots + a_n \qquad \text{(i)}$$

$$\sum_{i=1}^{n} b = nb \qquad (b, \text{ a constant}) \qquad \text{(ii)}$$

$$\sum_{i=1}^{n} a b_i = a \sum_{i=1}^{n} b_i \qquad (a, \text{ a constant}) \qquad \text{(iii)}$$

$$\sum_{i=1}^{n} (a_i + b_i) = \sum_{i=1}^{n} a_i + \sum_{i=1}^{n} b_i \qquad \text{(iv)}$$

interpret it as a definition of exchange, we must interpret it in a flow sense, for exchange takes time. Let us recognize this formally (and rewrite Equation 2–1 in the more general way suggested in the footnote), by introducing an arbitrary averaging number, V, which converts the stock—of money—into the (averaged) "per unit" time dimension.

$$MV \equiv \sum_{i=1}^{n} P_i Q_i \qquad\qquad (2\text{–}2)$$

We see that in Equation 2–1, if we wish to think of it as an exchange, V, which we define to be velocity, was assumed to be unity.

Now Equation 2–2 is famous (or infamous, if you are a Keynesian) as the "equation of exchange," which was born, at a specific date not yet settled, sometime in the early 19th century. As it stands here, in its definitional underwear, so to speak, it is completely untouched by any doctrinal influence. We have defined exchange in Equation 2–2; and to generalize from the individual to the economy as a whole, all you have to do is sum both sides.

If this were a macroeconomic presentation of monetary economics, you would probably not object to the statement that expenditures must equal receipts; well, that, strictly speaking, is the essence of Equation 2–2, with expenditures on the right-hand side.

Let us be clear on the interpretation of this equation for an economy. We are saying that the stock of money times the number of times it circulates per unit of time equals total spending. The key to interpreting this expression lies in appreciating the use of V, which we now emphasize is velocity. In fact, velocity is the number which converts the stock M into the flow $\sum_{i=1}^{n} P_i Q_i$; it represents the average number of times money was spent. Dimensionally, it is "times" per unit of time. I grant you that this is a little abstract at the moment, but we will have something concrete to feast on in a minute.

It is all very well to have something which you know to be true, like Equation 2–2, but it is quite another thing to be able to use it. That is to say, although this equation is clearly definitionally true, it is not very useful as we have written it down. For the United States, for example, we would have no idea what number to put in for V unless we had all the information on the right-hand side of the equation; and that information is, in principle, the prices and quantities exchanged of everything. Let's take a simple example so that we can see how this equation might be worked out, if we had the information. We will assume the data exhibited in Table 2–3, with one important warning—the actual income each person receives, in the form of money, is paid out over the period, rather than all at once, so that the amount of money used need not be equal to the combined incomes of the two individuals. This economizing is reasonable even in the theoretical world we are describing because money certainly ought not to be treated as a free good.

TABLE 2–3
An Economy with Two Individuals

	Quantities Purchased		
	Individual 1	Individual 2	Prices
Good X_1.............	10	15	$5.00
Good X_2.............	20	50	$2.50
Incomes............	$100	$200	

Let us assume that the initial quantity of money is $150; then, as is readily apparent, if we put the values from Table 2–3 into Equation 2–2, we get the following results:

$$\$150 \ V = 25(\$5) + 70(\$2.50) \qquad (2\text{–}3)$$

Then we can "solve" for velocity, which is the only variable we have not stated explicitly, and we get Equation 2–4; the $150 is spent, on average, twice during the period.

$$V \equiv \frac{\sum_i P_i Q_i}{M} = \frac{\$300}{\$150} = 2 \qquad (2\text{–}4)$$

Equation 2–4, consequently, constitutes the formal definition of the concept of velocity.[15]

Let us look again at Equation 2–2 to see what further can be learned from the results of the exchange of economic commodities. We commented that the terms on the right are observable in principle, but numerous, in fact almost infinitely so, if our framework is ecomomywide. On the other hand, we do not really need all that information for our analysis of money, because we can proceed if we can estimate the average value of money in its other forms. In other words, we can substitute the average price in Equation 2–2 for the individual prices, assuming we have found some reasonably consistent way to calculate the average. If we had such an average, we would rewrite Equation 2–2 as Equation 2–5:

$$MV \equiv \sum_{i=1}^{n} PQ_i \equiv P \sum_{i=1}^{n} Q_i \qquad (2\text{--}5)$$

and we can do the factoring out shown in the right-hand side of the equation because P is a constant (repeated n times) in each of the summed expressions on the right.

If we rearrange Equation 2–5, it is obvious that we have obtained a definition of the price level. But Equation 2–5 is awkward to deal with and, more seriously, requires us to add together, in $\sum_{i=1}^{n} Q_i$, items which are measured in different units. A way around the problem is to define the price level as in Equation 2–6:

$$\bar{P} \equiv \sum_{i=1}^{n} W_i P_i \quad \text{where} \quad \sum_{i=1}^{n} W_i \equiv 1 \qquad (2\text{--}6)$$

By this definition the W_i are a set of relative weights, which would be taken to represent the percentage of total funds allocated to each commodity. Clearly, the ideas behind P and $\bar{P}$ are the same. But, in either case, there are serious problems, not the least

---

[15] Actually, this is the formal definition of transactions velocity. We are going to substitute income for transactions a little later in the chapter and obtain income velocity. The two will differ considerably in size, but their changes often will be so closely synchronized that for most of the analytical problems we will take up, it won't matter much.

of which is that quality changes tend to get mixed up with price changes.[16] Accurate definition is one thing and usefulness is another, so we will reformulate Equation 2–5 in still another way, one which is designed to use the data which are available. If we recall that on the right-hand side of Equation 2–5 we are measuring total expenditures, and if we restrict ourselves to total expenditures on final goods and services—gross national product—which we will designate as Y, then we can rewrite Equation 2–5 as Equation 2–7:

$$MV \equiv Y \qquad (2\text{--}7)$$

Now Y is actually in money terms, necessarily, as indeed were all our other concepts; which is to say, we can break out the price level (P) from Y, leaving "real" income (y). That is, we can rewrite Equation 2–7 as:

$$MV \equiv Py \qquad (2\text{--}8)$$

2.7.2 A Price Index

The price level we have just described is a fairly unambiguous concept—but is not what you will find reported in the newspapers as the price level. At the risk of causing confusion, I am going to call the latter conept a *price index* for it is, in fact, an index number of prices, expressed in abstract units (index numbers) rather than in dollars. This is usually not an important issue, but we must make the distinction here since we are going to use the level (Equation 2–6) rather than the index (Equation 2–9, which follows) as the exchange value of money in our theoretical work.

The standard formula used to calculate the price index $(\bar{P}_I)$ in the United States is the following, in its simplest form, where the subscript 1 designates something measured at the base period, and 2 at the current period.

$$\bar{P}_I = \frac{\Sigma P_2 Q_1}{\Sigma P_1 Q_1} \qquad (2\text{--}9)$$

This index, for our numerical example, would be calculated as follows, using the values given in Table 2–4; and it shows that

---

[16] For a discussion see M. L. Burstein, "The Index-Number Problem," in R. W. Clower (ed.), *Monetary Theory* (Baltimore: Penguin Books, Ltd., 1969). The general idea is that if something improves in quality, it ought to fetch a higher price; such a rise would not be considered inflation.

TABLE 2–4
PRICES AND QUANTITIES EXCHANGED IN A TWO-
PERSON ECONOMY AT TWO POINTS IN TIME

	Period 1	*Period 2**
Price of X_1.......................	$4.00	$5.00
Price of X_2.......................	$2.00	$2.50
Quantity of X_1 exchanged..........	25	25
Quantity of X_2 exchanged..........	70	70

* Formerly Table 2–3.

a 20 percent rise in prices (and in each price) has occurred between the two periods.

$$\bar{P}_I \equiv \frac{\$5(25) + \$2.50(70)}{\$4(25) + \$2(70)} = \frac{\$300}{\$240} = 1.20 \qquad (2\text{--}10)$$

Let us return to the problem of the price of money before all of this becomes too tedious. P, however measured, is not the price of money because it is an estimate of the average price of everything else;[17] but in the alternative sense in which we are trying to measure the value of money, the reciprocal of P, that is $1/P$,

$$\left[\frac{1}{P} \equiv \text{The price of money} \right]$$

is the true price of nominal money, and that is how we will define it. That is to say, the fraction $1/P$ tells us how much a dollar will get, on average, in terms of goods and services; and that, surely, is what we mean by the price (meaning exchange value) of money.

If this were any commodity other than money, we could leave matters there; but we wish to ask what happens to the quantity of money when its price falls; and, most uniquely, the fall in the price of money actually decreases the quantity of money, as we ordinarily define quantity. In order to discover the real value of something denoted in money terms in this world of paper values, we deflate the item by the average price of things. We observe that in the situation of Table 2–4 people are no better off in

---

[17] Recall that "everything else" should mean stocks and bonds, since they are exchanged; but often, in practice, it is more narrowly defined, for example as consumer goods.

Period 2 than in Period 1. In fact, a 20 percent rise in income has been absorbed by a 20 percent rise in prices. To find real income, that is to say, we would deflate the second income by the price level. This, we can readily verify, has the stated consequences; real income has not changed. What has happened to the real quantity of money, defined in the same way? As we see from the following set of calculations, the real quantity of money, in arbitrary units, has fallen.

$$\left(\frac{M}{P}\right)_1 = \frac{\$150}{1} = \$150$$

$$\left(\frac{M}{P}\right)_2 = \frac{\$150}{1.20} = \$135$$

Now, this is a curious fact: P has risen, so that the price of money $(1/P)$ has fallen and so has the real quantity of money, automatically. This does not happen to a commodity in the real world; indeed, it did not happen to the commodities in our example, although their prices changed. The converse of this case about the price of money is also interesting: a rise in the price of money (that is, a fall in the price level) is equivalent to the production of new money (a change of M) and has all sorts of interesting consequences so long as money is not a free good. But we are now ready to discuss the demand for the product, for we have, at last, defined its price.

2.8 DISCUSSION QUESTIONS

1. When we define money to be the sum of demand deposits and currency we do not mean to preclude other definitions. What are the probable consequences, then, of defining money as only currency or as currency, demand deposits, time deposits, and savings and loan deposits?

2. In a certain sense the critical element in the transactions demand for cash is the time it takes to clear a market. Indeed we "save" time in speeding up the flow of goods. How does this way of putting things help to make clear the relations between money and interest?

3. Suppose an individual were forced to complete a trade before the end of the trading period. Would the solution be any different? How is this situation similar to the experience in 1929, during

the stock market panic? Could markets actually become unstable if people are forced to trade before they planned to?

4. Historians tell us that such things as cows and even large rocks have served as money in times past. Is it conceivable that these items could fit our definition of money? Which critical functions of money, as defined in Chapter 2, are not well served by these forms?

5. The organization of markets is likened to money creation because it has the same end product: it saves time. What, however, happens to the store of value function? Seats on the New York Stock Exchange sell at fabulous prices; where do they get their value? Is this the store of value function in disguise?

6. Do we have any other choice than to treat money as a stock? Is not every consumer good a stock in some sense? How, then, can we call Gross National Product, which is final spending on goods and services, a flow dimensionally?

7. One frequently hears the statement that the dollar is losing value. What people seem to mean is that the purchasing power of money is declining. If prices are rising does this necessarily mean that the dollar is worth less? Do you have to make some assumption about the behavior of the interest rate (which represents the yield of the dollar) before you answer this question?

8. What would you say if someone suggested that all we would need, to be able to refer to the British Guinea as money, is to coin the Guinea? Would the stock of money necessarily be increased by such an act?

9. The concept of velocity is designed to deal with the problem that money, whether "credit" or "hard," can be respent. Why do we have to define velocity *per unit of time?* Does this make velocity a *flow* concept? Is there an alternative *stock* definition for velocity?

10. When the price of money (the price level) changes, we have pointed out that the quantity of money changes in the same direction. Is this fact of *economic* significance? For example, is the economic system any the worse off for the loss of quantity caused by a price decline? Does your answer depend on what causes the price fall?

2.9 FURTHER READING

Bushaw, D., and Clower, Robert W. *Introduction to Mathematical Economics*, pp. 1–22. Homewood, Ill.: Richard D. Irwin, Inc., 1957.

BOARD OF GOVERNORS OF THE FEDERAL RESERVE SYSTEM. *The Federal Reserve System: Purposes and Functions.* Washington, D.C., 1963.

LAIDLER, DAVID E. W. "The Definition of Money, Theoretical and Empirical Problems," *Journal of Money, Credit, and Banking,* 1969.

YEAGER, LELAND B. "Essential Properties of the Medium of Exchange," *Kyklos,* Vol. 7, No. 1 (1968).

THE DEMAND FOR MONEY

3.1 INTRODUCTION

Our description of the characteristics of money described not all its characteristics but, for the most part, characteristics which are of interest to cconomists. For example, one characteristic of money which is generally an important one to its owner is that of providing the feeling of economic power; others are even more psychological. In general, we say that demanders will desire (*demand*) these characteristics and that suppliers will *supply* the product, hence satisfying the desires for the characteristics. The problem of the economist, rather than to probe into the characteristics, is to find out the nature of the two functions—the demand and the supply—and to comment on their interaction in the marketplace.

We will begin with the demand function in this chapter, and this means beginning with the demand function of an individual. We will introduce the key variables which influence the decision of an individual to hold money and, in an imaginary laboratory, subject him to changes in these variables. The actual data available for study in the real world are largely aggregate, of course; so in order to secure testable results, we must add the individual demands to get a total demand relationship. We will then manipulate the total demand for two reasons: to become familiar with it, and to illustrate some fundamental points in money and banking. Then, beginning in Chapter 4, we can turn to supply.

3.2 MONEY AND LEISURE

Fundamental to the demand for any economic good, and we certainly are asserting that money is such a good, is that it provide economic services. Some goods are pure services—such as shoe-shines—and are used up upon their creation; but many goods can be reused, and most consumer goods have some durability. Those goods which do possess durability offer the chance of a rearrangement of one's using-up pattern; that is, one can *stock* durable goods against future needs. In this sense, money is a durable good and, like all durable goods, provides continuing services to its users—services which are, no doubt, also available from other durable goods, although in the end the purchase of a unit of money is a tacit confession that it was expected to be the best good in providing those services, at that time. Money, because of its low physical perishability, is especially useful in permitting the rearrangement of one's expenditure pattern; and if one has money, his options into other goods are generally open.

Most products provide both direct and indirect services, to make a distinction which is not going to be all that clear in practice. For some products the direct services dominate, as for example, an apple, which provides an obvious gustatory satisfaction. There is a range of products which provide substantial amounts of both direct and indirect services, such as a refrigerator, which chills our wine, a direct service, and enables us to stockpile consumer goods, an indirect service since we save time rather than directly satisfy one of the senses. Money, you can see, is no less a consumer product for providing mostly indirect services; and, like the storage capacity of the refrigerator, the service provided is primarily that of saving time by allowing the consumer to arrange his expenditures more efficiently. Money also permits exchange to occur at well-known prices, in an acceptable and portable medium.

The saving of time in the sense just described we will refer to as the production of leisure, and it is more noticeable in the aggregate than in the individual case. To what degree one chooses either to take his time-saving in the form of leisure or to work so as to have other consumer goods is more a sociological than an economic question, but, properly, both the leisure and the consumer goods ought to be included in the standard of living. One reason the leisure-producing capabilities of money have been ignored is that the study of leisure itself (in most Western countries) has been ignored.

3.3 THE INDIVIDUAL DEMAND CURVE

What we have said, then, is that money is one of the forms in which a consumer can hold his wealth; and, of more direct analytic importance, money provides services which can be thought of as additions to income. This means that to proceed further, we must define the concept of wealth, for durable items which produce income are part of one's wealth.

3.3.1 Wealth and Interest

Any object which offers future returns (such as a government bond) or future services (such as money) will be worth something in the open market if it can be traded;[1] these items will be *wealth*. One such item is a government bond; we can formally relate the market price of the bond (P_b) to the stream of future interest payments ($C_1, \ldots C_n$) by the relation depicted as Equation 3–1.[2]

$$P_b = \frac{C_1}{1+i} + \frac{C_2}{(1+i)^2} + \cdots + \frac{C_n}{(1+i)^n} + \frac{\text{Face value}}{(1+i)^n} \quad (3\text{--}1)$$

This is a complicated formula, although you might have seen it in a mathematics course; it is the formula from which a yield, such as those appearing in standardized bond tables, is calculated. In fact, the C's (defined as coupons) are the stream of interest payments (one for each year); the face value is the issue price of the bond, which is paid back in n years; and i is the *yield*,

---

[1] Some things cannot be traded, although their services can be directly traded. Humans have individual capital values (studied as "human capital" in economics), but, for humanitarian and other reasons, usually only working hours are exchanged. This, of course, is not true in a slave state.

[2] The formal analysis of such expressions will be left until Chapter 11, the first part of which you could read now, if you really want to pin down all the nuances of the intuitive discussion of this section. In effect, I am avoiding this formality here because it is distracting and am leaving the matter of further reading to you.

calculated as a residual after all the other information has been obtained.[3]

The yield in Equation 3–1 moves in the opposite direction from the price of the bond—as bond prices rise, their yields fall; this is more obvious in Equation 3–2, which represents the yield for a perpetual bond—one which is never redeemed.

$$P_b = \frac{C_1}{1+i} + \frac{C_2}{(1+i)^2} + \cdots + \text{to infinity} \qquad (3\text{–}2)$$

In fact, by using a simple mathematical trick, Equation 3–2 is exactly equivalent to Equation 3–3; and it is in this form that we will think of it throughout the rest of this chapter.[4]

$$P_b = \frac{C}{i} \qquad (3\text{–}3)$$

3.3.2 Nominal Money Balances

We pointed out in Chapter 2 that $1/P$ represents the exchange value (or price) of a unit of nominal money. We also pointed out that when the price level rises—and the price of money falls—the quantity of money, as we ordinarily define quantity, has fallen. Mastery of this rather paradoxical point will pay high dividends, because this result flows from the special role of money in the economic system. The key to the puzzle is noting that for the individual, *money is wealth*, so that a fall in the purchasing power of money—if one has unchanged nominal balances of money—reduces one's wealth.

The real value of physical wealth does not vary with the price level, for its market value changes along with the price level. For example, suppose that you owned a car and had a money balance of $20 and that the money price of all commodities suddenly

---

[3] The easiest way to fix all these ideas in your mind is to note that a bond is a loan from the buyer to the issuer (or seller). The loan, which offers repayment conditions and rental payments, sells in the open market, which is where we get the quotation for P_b. The reason the yield, which is also a rate of discount, is squared in the second term is that since one must wait two years for this coupon payment, the payment must be "discounted" twice, once for each year.

[4] There are perpetual bonds in Britain, but the main justification for introducing Equation 3–3 in this chapter is that money is an infinitely durable good, especially, of course, book money. The mathematics is discussed in Chapter 11.

doubled—including the money price of your car. If you were thinking of your car in the same way as you were thinking of money—as a durable good which you wished to trade—you would record no change in the value of the car; the increased price of the car would be exactly matched by the increase of all other prices, so you would be no better off. If you were not thinking of trading the car, then you would ignore both the price level and the price of the car; in either case your real wealth would remain unchanged.

3.3.3 Real Money Balances

The real wealth in the form of money balances, however, is reduced by the rise in the price level, and people generally are thinking of trading their money. Thus, if we take a wealth approach to the analysis of money—that is, if we ask what induces individuals to hold money among their items of real wealth—then we would enter nominal money divided by the price level on the list of our wealth holdings. Indeed, our argument to this point amounts to this assertion. But there is still a problem; for by dividing nominal money balances by the price level, we have, in effect, divided out the transactions function of money.

The problem can be described more easily than it can be defined. When you had $20 and the original price level of, say, $1 per item, then $20 was an adequate money balance to make 20 purchases during the period, on average. If the price level doubles, then, obviously, you will need $40 to do the same work in the same period of time. The point is that when we think of transactions, we think of the money prices of commodities versus the amount of nominal money balances in our pocket.

Now there are several traps set in the last paragraph which we will have to deal with at various points in this book. For one thing, we did not say how it came about that the price level doubled, and this is a critical question to answer, for it is inconceivable that your loss was not matched, at least in part, by someone else's gain. In fact, this is a problem which we will discuss in the aggregate—in, that is, the case of total demand. Another problem is that we have ignored the possibility that money might circulate a little faster if there were an increase in the demand for services; for example, if everyone spent money twice as fast in the above situation, you would need only $20 to do the same work as $40 did in the second case; what all of this amounts to is simply changing the length of the market period. This would seem to leave the system with money performing the same essential work as it did originally, except for one fact—wealth appears to be lower, since the real value of money balances (M/P) is lower.

3.4 MONEY AND INTEREST

In order to deal with the problems which arise at this point, we must appreciate that to a wealth holder an important alternative to holding money is holding a bond, perhaps the one described in Equation 3–3. Let us begin with real money balances (M/P) and consider just the asset selection problem, unencumbered by references to specific motives for holding money.

Suppose, for example, that the interest rate falls; then an individual who previously was happy with the distribution of his wealth between money and nonmoney will switch some of his wealth into money. That is, if the flow of *services* from holding money does not change while the flow of *yields* from a representative bond falls, the individual can be expected to hold more of the relatively higher yielding asset and less of the lower. Figure 3–1 represents this argument.

3.4.1 The Keynesian Demand for Money

Now there are actually two elements mixed into this relationship, and there is good reason to expect both to figure into the problem. In the Keynesian theory of the demand for money, three motives for holding money—which means three motives for holding some of one's wealth in the form of money—are the

transactions motive,
precautionary motive, and
speculative motive.

We understand the transactions motive already, for this arises directly from the usefulness and acceptability of money in ex-

change. Similarly, we will find it easy to understand the precautionary motive; it is closely related to the transactions motive.

In the first place, an important aspect of what we might call
the *transactions demand* for money concerns the timing of receipts
and expenditures over the foreseeable future for the individual.
We might know for certain what this pattern will be; yet, in
general, we will need to hold some average balance because the
expenditures will not coincide with the receipts. Further than this,

FIGURE 3–1

THE DEMAND FOR MONEY AS A FUNCTION OF
INTEREST RATES: THE INDIVIDUAL

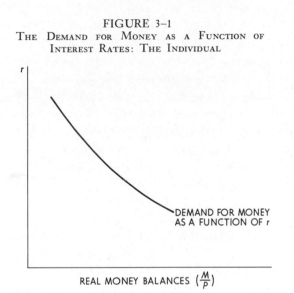

REAL MONEY BALANCES ($\frac{M}{P}$)

there is the possibility, all too familiar to all of us, that we will
need additional funds during the planning period ahead of us. In
the first case, all I mean is that payments dates are not known
with certainty; the electric bill is coming sometime this month,
but maybe not until next month. The expenditure is planned, and
all that is missing is the date of the expenditure. This, strictly
speaking, is still a part of the transactions demand for money;
the funds were allocated for that purpose; but at any moment
of time these funds are part of an individual's wealth and, when
we aggregate, part of the consumer sector's wealth.

A shade removed from this last sort of transactions demand
are the cases when the size of the future expenditure is unknown.
After all, who knows precisely how much his electric bill is going

to be, particularly in the heating season or, in the United States, in the cooling season? In these cases it is really not important whether the date of the future purchase is known, for one must still, at least until that date, hold balances which we will define as *precautionary balances*. These balances, also, are part of an individual's wealth, at a moment of time, and, perforce, part of the consumer sector's wealth, at the same moment of time.

But there is one further aspect to the individual demand for money, an especially important one because money holding is alternative to bond holding. In fact, bond yields fluctuate—or, if you prefer, bond prices fluctuate—so that part of the holding of money will be tied to the risk of bond price fluctuation. For most bonds there are two sorts of risk available: a risk that the company will default and the risk that the individual will require his funds before the bond is cashed in. If bond prices do not change over the time period—that is, if there were some law prohibiting bond price changes—this latter rise would not be a problem; but we don't live in that kind of world. As noted, bond prices are often subject to fairly wide swings; and even if they weren't, the individual still could make a small swing a wide swing for himself by buying bonds with borrowed money.[5] Wide swings, which are also unpredictable, imply risk, of course; and risk brings out the speculators. In fact, we know that there are speculators in the bond market—that is, people who believe they know better than the market what is going to happen in the market—and sizable gains are known to have been made dealing in corporate and government bonds; sizable losses, too.

Take a specific example. If bond prices have risen for a while, so that the market begins to expect bond prices to fall, it is only sensible that individuals will take action. As we have specified their choices, individuals can escape the expected fall in bond prices in only three ways: one escape route is into money, where the exchange price $(1/P)$ is fixed; the second is into common stocks, where prices might also fall; and the third is into real property, which is, among other disadvantages, often relatively perish-

---

[5] This is how one obtains *leverage*. In the United States the usual down payment on government bonds is 10 percent, although some dealers quote 5 percent. The general idea is to borrow 90 or 95 percent of the purchase price, paying the 10 or 5 percent margin as "down payment," depositing the bonds as collateral.

able. It is easy to see that money will be particularly suitable for this purpose; that at any time individuals as a whole can be expected to be holding such balances, which are defined as *speculative balances;* and that the amount of these balances held will depend on the current level of interest rates relative to the level expected to rule.[6] This dependence is such that when interest rates rise, people can be expected to move out of money into bonds, not only because the holding of money balances has become more expensive but also because they expect bond prices to rise; these things happen simultaneously, of course. Thus we have two factors leading to the negative relation between interest rates and the demand for money which we illustrated in Figure 3–1.

3.4.2   The Total Demand Curve

We have opened up a gold mine in broadening our framework to include the problems of asset selection and the speculative manipulation of assets, but for now we must restrict ourselves to answering some preliminary questions in the context of the total demand for money. We will assume that all individuals have the same tastes and incomes; then we will sum (conceptually) all individual demands and treat the aggregate, for the rest of this section, as if it were an individual. The issue which we still have to discuss here concerns the actual shape of the total demand for money as a function of interest.[7]

Figure 3–2 illustrates three versions of the demand for money as a function of interest alone. We are, that is to say, ignoring the influence of the price level, a procedure which is not advisable if we were dealing with real-world phenomena; but, of course, we have to start somewhere.[8]

I would be fair neither to Keynesians nor to classical economists if I put the extreme cases down as representative of their views; but one can see that it is a matter of degree or, if you wish,

---

[6] This dependence will be explained fully in section 14.2.

[7] We will return to the question of how one generates an aggregate demand curve from an individual demand curve in Chapter 9 (when we describe the Keynesian theory more completely) and in Chapter 14 (after we have studied the treatment of uncertainty in monetary economics).

[8] If we were to include income, we might show it shifting the curve we have here, much as a change in income shifted the demand curve in our analysis of Chapter 1.

an empirical question as to which case dominates. If the demand for money is such that large changes in interest rates cause individuals to change the pattern of their holdings only slightly, then the interest rate can be ignored in the theory of the demand for money; if this is the case, the interest rate becomes an important factor in monetary policy—important because small changes in the supply of money produce large changes in the interest rate. This is shown in the curve labeled "extreme classical." If the converse holds—if the influence of the interest rate is strong, as shown

FIGURE 3–2
THREE PROPOSITIONS ABOUT THE DEMAND FOR MONEY

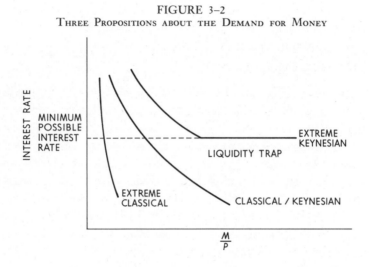

in the curve labeled "Keynesian"—small changes in the interest rate will induce large changes in the quantity of money demanded. We can neglect monetary policy (in this dimension), but we cannot neglect the effect of interest rates on the demand for money. There is one special case: that in which the interest rate is so low that no one expects it to fall any further—the section of the extreme Keynesian curve marked "liquidity trap" to imply that money is soaked up into idle balances. This is of interest in the Keynesian formulation because it was adduced, as we shall see in Chapter 8, in order to explain the events of the 1930's.[9]

---

[9] The rationale is as follows. As interest rates fall (bond prices rise), it becomes more and more unlikely that interest rates can fall any further (bond prices rise any further). The point will come when the interest rate cannot be driven any lower (or will not fall any lower) because all further additions

3.5 MONEY AND PRICES

What we have just described is essentially the Keynesian theory of the demand for money; in fact, the theory we stated also includes some classical elements, such as the references to the transactions motive. Nevertheless, as we will see in this section, some other parts of the classical framework must be added in to the Keynesian in order to achieve an overall view of the demand for money; these elements are all too often neglected in the Keynesian literature.

3.5.1 The Real Balance Effect

Let us return to our microeconomic analysis of Chapter 1 and suppose that an individual is confronted with a change in the price of his nominal money balances (M): how will he react? In the discussion of the last chapter, you will recall, we saw that the price of nominal money balances was unity over the price level ($1/P$); thus we are asking, under the conditions of Chapter 1 and with interest rates held constant, how this new situation works itself out.

Let us begin with some arbitrary data, as in Chapter 1, and employ our definitions; the data are contained in Table 3–1. Now, in the table we are arbitrarily assuming initial holdings of money wealth of $20; in Chapter 1 our consumer had no money wealth. To find the real value of money income and the real value of money balances, we would have to deflate by the price level; Equation 3–4 repeats this idea, in its general form, from Equation 2–6.

$$\bar{P} = \sum_{i=1}^{n} W_i P_i \qquad \Sigma W_i = 1.000 \qquad (3\text{--}4)$$

to the stock of money (by changing the supply of money through open market operations) will simply be held in "idle" balances; no one will expect the interest rate to fall any further, so it won't.

The empirical record is not complete for us, to be sure; but provisionally, at least, it seems that the demand for money as a function of interest is more like the hybrid classical-Keynesian curve than either of the extremes, at least for post–World War II years. There are two good studies of these and other aspects of the demand for money: they are listed in section 3.7, "Further Reading."

Let us choose as weights the percentage of income our consumer spends on each product—0.615 for X_1 and 0.385 for X_2. This was an arbitrary choice and any other set of weights, which are determined in the system as a whole, would have done. Thus, for case 1, the price level is $1.096 ($P_1$), and we could calculate real income and real (money) wealth by deflating the nominal items in the table.

Now suppose that the price of X_2 falls to $1. We will get, between X_1 and X_2, the income effect and the substitution effect; and we will get the same effects between X_2 and M (and, for

TABLE 3–1
An Illustration of the Effect of Changes in the
Price Level on Individual Demand

		Evaluated at	
	Case 1	$\bar{P}_1$	$\bar{P}_2$
Money income..............	$32.50	...	$32.50
PX_1......................	1.00	...	...
PX_2......................	1.25	...	...
Q of X_1 purchased...........	10 units	...	...
Q of X_2 purchased...........	22 units	...	...
Nominal money balances.....	$20.00	...	$20.00
Price levels................		1.096	1.000

that matter, between X_1 and M). But there is a further effect to the individual, defined as the *real balance effect*, which occurs because the price level has fallen. That is to say, if we retain the same weights as before,[10] the individual will find that the real value of his money wealth has increased. The figures appear in columns 2 and 3 of Table 3–1. This is a third effect, brought about, as it were, by including money in the analysis; the three effects work as follows. Firstly, the consumer faces a lower price of X_2, which causes him to buy more X_2 and to buy less X_1 and M on the *substitution* effect as in Chapter 1. Secondly, the con-

---

[10] We retain the same weights because we assume our consumer's decision to change his expenditure pattern does not change the economywide weights. We are not really entitled to have a change in price without there being a change in the relative amounts people spend on the product, but we consider this valid since we are only looking at one consumer. When we aggregate, this will be the chief complication we will have to deal with.

sumer's income now goes further, so he might buy more of all three goods—X_1, X_2, and M—on the *income* effect as in Chapter 1. Thirdly, and this is the new element, the consumer will receive an addition to the value of his money holdings, which are evaluated at the price level; and, in order to take advantage of this effect, he must spend more on X_1 and X_2 and hold less M, because of the *real balance* effect.

3.5.2   On Aggregation

Needless to say, the measurement of these effects in real-life situations is going to be a complicated matter; even the geometry is a bit complex since it requires that we operate in three dimensions (X_1, X_2, and M). We could, from this experiment, derive an individual's demand curve for each of the products, especially money; but because we are denied the use of geometry, we will not. Instead, we will set up a new problem in which the prices of all commodities change in the same proportion and derive a total demand curve from that situation, using geometry. The general idea behind assuming all prices change in the same proportion is to abstract from the complications introduced by having a substitution effect between commodities;[11] further, with price changes proportional, we can treat the sum of all commodities as a single commodity, as we pointed out in section 1.6.

In our earlier work we performed the aggregation of individual demand by making the assumptions sufficient to enable us to treat the aggregate of individuals as if it were an individual. The conditions under which aggregation applies are that each individual in the system has both the same tastes and the same income, conditions which are sufficient to prevent distribution effects from vitiating the analysis. The analysis is stripped of its power if we permit the distribution of income to affect our results, because then the change in prices will produce "income effects" and sub-

---

[11] There are a number of consequences of this assumption. The first of these is that when the price changes of X_1 and X_2, for example, are in the same proportion, we can treat the sum $X_1 + X_2$ as a single, composite commodity; this deals with the geometry and is an advantage. The second consequence is that since the relative price of X_1 and X_2 cannot change, we cannot evaluate substitution effects between X_1 and X_2, and between M and X_1 and M and X_2; while this is inconvenient, it is simple. Our defense is that there is a great deal of interest in the problem treated in the text, even so.

stitution effects throughout the economic system. The reason we lose power is that with some set of weights we could then get any type of demand curve—such as an upsloping one—anyone could dream up.[12] This profusion is of little use in economic analysis, as things stand, for it does not lead directly to prediction.

We are going to take a slightly different approach to the problem of the aggregate demand for money as a function of $1/P$. We are going to assume that the supply of nominal money is fixed arbitrarily, and then we are going to change that amount and catalogue the reactions of the aggregate of identical individuals. In both cases, the supply curve for money will be a vertical straight line, reflecting the assumption—if you need an institutional comment to hang on to—that the monetary authorities arbitrarily fix the amount of money for policy reasons. Whatever the method of introduction of more money into the system, it is best to argue, as in Chapter 2, that is simply dumped on the doorstep, to avoid introducing problems of supply before we get to a discussion of the actual supply mechanism.

3.5.3 The Equation of Exchange in the United States

Let us go back to the income version of the equation of exchange, introduced as Equation 2–8, which we will now consider as Equation 3–5.[13]

$$M = \frac{1}{V} Py \qquad y = \frac{Y}{P} = \text{Real income} \qquad (3\text{--}5)$$

We have added nothing new if we interpret this as another arrangement of the definition of exchange, but we now wish to interpret the equation as the result of the interaction of supply and demand—a statement about what the market does, rather than what is identically true, as it was in Chapter 2. In Equation 3–5, the stock of money (M) is assumed to be equal to $(1/V)Py$ at equilibrium only; Equation 3–5 is an equilibrium condition resulting from the interaction of supply and demand, a condition which

---

[12] If, as prices (including that on the good in question) fell, income shifted away from people who consume the product, the quantity demanded of the good in question might actually fall.

[13] Actually, the literature refers to $MV = PT$ as the equation of exchange, where T refers to transactions; Equation 3–5 is referred to as the Cambridge equation.

is not necessarily true when we are not at equilibrium. Since we generally observe economic values at equilibrium—that is, since only determined prices and quantities are available to us—Equation 3–5 is what we will have to use anyway. There is another thing about Equation 3–5 which is important to notice, and that concerns the dimensions of the variables. M is a stock, as we defined this term earlier; Y is obviously a flow, since the amount of income spent is clearly something defined over a period of time. $1/V$, then, is a number which converts the flow into a stock (V, you will recall, does the opposite).

TABLE 3–2
VARIABLES IN THE EQUATION OF EXCHANGE, UNITED STATES, 1965–69

Variables	1965	1966	1967	1968	1969
Gross national product in current dollars (Y)	684.7	749.9	793.5	865.7	932.1
Gross national product in 1958 dollars (y)	617.8	658.1	674.6	707.6	727.5
Money stock (M)	166.8	170.4	181.7	144.8	199.6
Consumer price index (P)	109.9	113.1	116.3	121.2	127.7
Velocity ($V = Y/M$)	4.106	4.401	4.376	4.444	4.669

NOTE: (1) The money stock consists of demand deposits and currency and is measured at the end of the year. (2) The consumer price level is the average of the monthly figures.
SOURCE: *Federal Reserve Bulletin.*

At this point, in order to develop some feeling for the magnitudes involved in our equations and to reinforce some of the considerations already emphasized, we ought to introduce some actual data. Table 3–2, using the American data for the years 1965 through 1969, presents the relevant figures for Equation 3–5; it also presents the calculation of velocity rather than $1/V$. The results show a fairly wide variation in velocity, which we will try to explain a little later in this chapter.

3.5.4   A Classical Proposition

One of the predictions of the quantity theory of money—in fact, its least debatable proposition—is that, other things being equal, a change in the quantity of money causes income (Y) to change in the same proportion; a 10 percent increase in M will induce a 10 percent increase in Y, assuming V is constant as a matter of assumption rather than as a matter of fact.[14] Clearly, this is practically indisputable, so far as we have specified things, for Equation 3–5 describes how things must come out in equilibrium—and if we replace M by two times M, we must replace Y by two times Y, if V is assumed to be unchanged. Furthermore, if real income (y) is assumed to be constant,[15] the change will be solely in P. A real-world interpretation of this result would be to say that if the quantity of money doubled while the economy was at full employment, a case in which one could reasonably assume y (real income) constant, then, given spending habits $(1/V$ constant), people would continue to spend the new money

TABLE 3–3
THE EFFECTS OF A DOUBLED MONEY SUPPLY:
THE CLASSICAL CASE

	Period 1	Period 2	Period 3
Price of X_1	$ 5.00	$ 5.00	$ 10.00
Price of X_2	$ 2.50	$ 2.50	$ 5.00
Quantity of X_1 exchanged	25	25	25
Quantity of X_2 exchanged	70	70	70
Money stock	$150.00	$300.00	$300.00

until prices had doubled, in which case they would be right back where they were before, in real terms. "Before," we should be careful to remember, was an equilibrium position.

Let us work an example. In Table 3–3, we present before and after situations (Period 1 and Period 3). These are both equilibrium positions; and I have made this explicit by putting in Period 2, in which $M > (1/V)Py$. In Period 2, that is, individuals have more money than they are willing to hold, at the existing price level, assuming that $150 was exactly right in the first place.

How do individuals go about getting rid of surplus money balances? By spending, of course, for they are individually un-

---

[14] For some time it was thought that classical economists were claiming the constancy of V as a matter of fact; Alvin Hansen seemed to think so, for one example (Alvin Hansen, *Monetary and Fiscal Policy* [New York: McGraw-Hill Book Co., 1949]). The main stream of classical writers probably did not, as any kind of unbiased inspection of their writings would reveal. On the other hand, certain kinds of inconsistencies and certain errors of omission, and certainly certain kinds of unhelpful emphasis, can be attributed to them. See Chapter 9 for a more complete discussion of one such classical system.

[15] That is, at full employment.

aware that the system cannot produce more goods; thus, in trying to buy products which are in fixed supply, they must continue until prices are doubled, for only in this case will they be back where they were before.[16]

Let us see what has happened to the price level between Periods 1 and 3, as we have worked it out. If we apply our index number formula to the data of the table, we find that

$$\bar{P}_I = \frac{\Sigma P_2 Q_1}{\Sigma P_1 Q_1} = \frac{\$10(25) + \$5(70)}{\$5(25) + \$2.50(70)} = \frac{\$600}{\$300} = \$2$$

That is, prices have doubled. We have learned that the price of money is unity over the price level $(1/P)$; consequently, in the case before us, the price of nominal money has fallen; Figure 3–3 represents the information so far provided.

FIGURE 3–3
THE "DEMAND FOR MONEY" AS A FUNCTION OF THE PRICE LEVEL

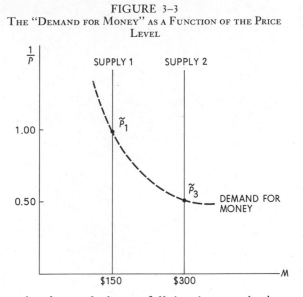

We have also learned that a fall in the purchasing power of money is equivalent to the destruction of money, just as an increase in the price of money is equivalent to the production of money. In fact, in the case before us, since the quantity of money doubled and its price halved, the real quantity of money (M/P) has re-

---

[16] Here we see that it is essential to this prediction to remove distribution effects; for if we do not, prices might be either more or less than doubled, depending on who gained in the redistribution.

mained the same, like the quantity of everything else. This result should not surprise us, for we assumed that there was full employment before we began.[17]

In our discussion leading to Table 3–3, we have not explained how things worked themselves out for individuals; such an explanation will not be presented, finally, until we get through Chapter 9; but for the moment we can simply say that the doubling of individual money balances, however the doubling comes about, induces the individuals to try to get rid of their unwanted balances. Since individuals are all alike, our assumptions make it possible that a doubling would occur. It is not essential—if we are willing to give up our theorem about doubled prices—in this respect, for velocity to remain constant; but if we do so, we are left with some qualification such as "prices will rise" or prices will "tend to rise." All this seems straightforward enough, but we have avoided some questions. For one thing, we must know how the new money enters the system, for if it enters simply because individuals decided they wanted to use more, all of our analysis is essentially irrelevant. Further, of more serious import because it is a demand problem, we must find some explanation of what governs velocity.

3.6 VELOCITY AND INTEREST RATES

We have, so far, emphasized two variables, in addition to wealth, as explaining the aggregate demand for nominal money: the interest rate and the price level.[18] Let us push a little bit harder on the empirical side of things. The classical view on the demand for money emphasizes the role of money income. That is, since money services income, the higher the level of money income, the greater the quantity demanded of money (M) will be.

Of course, to be a proper old-fashioned economist, you might be tempted to go a little further: income is the only determinant of the demand for money, or, in other words, velocity (V in

---

[17] There is one thing about Figure 3–3 which we should notice. The points shown, $\tilde{P}_1$ and $\tilde{P}_3$, and the locus of other points in between them are all equilibrium points, in other words, points at which supply and demand are equal, by Equation 3–5. The locus is a demand curve for money because of our tacit assumption of a vertical supply curve. That is, each of the points measured is on the demand curve for money.

[18] We will return to wealth in Chapter 9.

Equation 3–5) is constant. We have seen, and any fool can plainly see in Table 3–2, that V is nothing like a constant; this leaves us with a problem of rationalization. The fact is that many classical economists have argued several alternatives to the version of the theory of this paragraph. One of them is that velocity is not constant, but follows its own laws, independent of the supply and demand for money—and, to add a little bit free of charge, only changes slowly. This disposes of the matter as far as the demand for money is concerned although not, you can be sure, as far as Figure 3–5 is concerned; but if the laws of change of velocity can be determined, you can predict $\tilde{P}_3$, after all. The second modern version of the theory, and one which we shall pursue more energetically through the rest of this book, is that while there is some relation between velocity and the supply of money, this relation is a stable one and therefore a predictable one and offers, on that account, no important contradiction to the theory. By stable relation, let us hasten to point out, we do not mean that velocity is constant, but we do mean that the effect of whatever it is that changes velocity is consistent and (we hope) predictable. This view is clearly different from the case in which velocity itself was interpreted simply as a constant.

Now if we wish to explain what determines velocity, the interest rate must be introduced simultaneously into the analysis. In fact, if the analysis of the last section is to apply perfectly with an interest rate in the problem, then that interest rate must be the same at both end points $\tilde{P}_1$ and $\tilde{P}_3$. That is to say, by and large, we expect that a rise in the interest rate, given the amount of money in the system, will by itself induce individuals to economize on their cash balances (M). In the market approach we have now adopted $(MV = Py)$, this means that velocity will rise (people will get rid of money more rapidly), which, in turn, means that the price level will rise. When interest rates are introduced into the picture, we run into a lot of problems, so it might be just as well to see if there is any overall observable connection between velocity and interest rates. Figure 3–4 has a summary; and it is clear that there is indeed a firm relation and that the relation, taken at five-year intervals, is reasonably, but not perfectly, "stable" in appearance. Stability, here, is judged by the comparative shapes of the two profiles in the figure.

There are a lot of other issues about the demand for money, and we are going to get to them as we progress through the financial markets. But for now, let us summarize. We seem to have found both theory and data to suggest that two variables have to be included in the analysis of the demand for money: the price

FIGURE 3–4
VELOCITY AND THE INTEREST RATE, THE UNITED STATES, 1915–54*

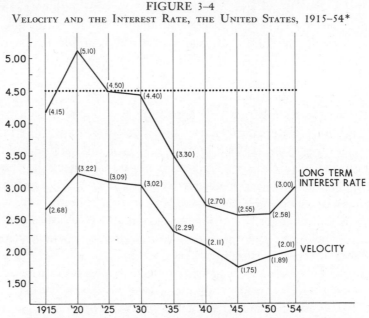

* The interest rate is the 30-year yield reported by David Meiselman, *The Term Structure of Interest Rates* (Englewood Cliffs, N.J.: Prentice-Hall, Inc., 1962). (The data were originally compiled by David Durand.)

Velocity is that for currency and demand deposits appearing in Milton Friedman and Anna J. Schwartz, *A Monetary History of the United States* (New York: National Bureau of Economic Research, 1963).

level and the interest rate. We have actually covered a lot of ground in this way; but before we get back to the demand, especially in Chapter 9, we must discuss the other side of the coin.

3.7 DISCUSSION QUESTIONS

1. Can you think of an economic good or service that has no durability whatsoever? What about some of the proposed computerized

banking systems in which no checks change hands? Does the notion of durability imply that the good must have a physical existence?

2. Why can we unashamedly assert that an individual is poorer when
the price level rises? Does this simple truth extend to the aggregate
of individuals? Do we have to know how the gains and losses are
distributed before we conclude that a change in the price level is
undesirable?

3. We have made a distinction between transactions motives, precautionary motives, and speculative motives for holding money.
Why do we use a bond yield as our basis of comparison for the
speculative demand? Will an individual speculator ever hold money
and bonds at the same time? Is the consistency of the speculator
involved? What would the individual demand curve, as a function
of the interest rate, look like?

4. Would individuals hold transactions balances if all future cash
needs were known with certainty? Do we have to know something
about the mechanics and costs of conversion between money and
bonds before we answer this question?

5. The notion that individuals hold idle money (or time deposits)
while waiting for bond prices to fall runs counter to one's intuition,
while the converse does not. Explain this statement. Why is the
latter sufficient to give us a downsloping (negative sloping)
speculative demand for money (as a function of interest rates)?

6. When one wishes to illustrate the real balance effect, it is an easy
matter with an individual, but a difficult matter with the aggregate
of individuals. Why is this so? Would it help to know what caused
the change in the price level? Why did we introduce the "composite commodity" to deal with the aggregate case?

7. Why is it necessary to treat velocity as a residual in our analysis?
Does this imply that velocity is an intangible concept? Why do we
distinguish between *transactions* velocity and *income* velocity? Can
you think of any cases in which these two measures might not be
perfectly synchronized in their movements?

8. We posed a test—in connection with our discussion of the Quantity
Theory of Money—in which a change in the quantity of money
was completely absorbed by a change in the price level. What role
do our assumptions play in this result? Suppose that during the
process of adjustment the rich got richer and the poor got poorer,
but that no other changes occurred; could we then "prove" our
theorem?

9. Explain why, when the quantity of money enters the economic system in response to an increase in the demand for money, the direction of causation in Equation (3–5) is from right to left. What sorts of factors would lead to this result (explain in terms of $1/V$, P, and y)? Why is it important to know which direction of causation rules, in general, in the American economy?

10. Explain why, in our theory, we emphasize the stability of the relation between velocity and interest rates rather than the constancy of velocity as such. Is the game necessarily up if velocity and interest do not move together? What other factors might also be involved—themselves in a stable relation with velocity and/or interest rates—which could restore order to things?

3.8 FURTHER READING

FRIEDMAN, MILTON. "The Quantity Theory of Money—A Restatement," *Studies in the Quantity Theory of Money* (ed. Milton Friedman). Chicago: University of Chicago Press, 1953.

JONES, DAVID M. "The Demand for Money: A Review of the Empirical Literature," *Staff Economic Study*. Federal Reserve Board of Governors, February 1966.

LAIDLER, DAVID E. W. *The Demand for Money*. Scranton, Pa.: International Textbook Co., 1969.

THE SUPPLY OF BANK MONEY

4.1 INTRODUCTION

We are going to emphasize in this chapter that banks are business firms, engaged in the activity of *producing* money, subject to specific cost conditions. We are going to begin the discussion with a full-blown banking system rather than with a single bank; furthermore, the system which will be described will be as similiar to the American banking system as we can manage from the beginning.

There are several points in the following discussion which you should not miss. One of these is that in switching the emphasis from money creation to money production, we are sidestepping the whole debate over whether or not—or, more properly, in what sense—commercial banks actually create money.[1] When we come to consider the business of banking, we will take the view that banks produce checking accounts and bookkeeping services; we will imply that their decisions as to both production and retailing influence their desire to hold reserves and that these decisions help to determine the quantity of money in the economy. Because banks are regulated on the one hand and produce deposits which are callable on demand on the other, there are two other major decision units involved in the creation of money: the public and the Federal Reserve System. For the sake of clarity we will present in this chapter an analytical framework which includes all three sectors at once; further, we will go some way toward analyzing

---

[1] James Tobin, "Commercial Banks as Creators of Money," in Deane Carson (ed.), *Banking and Monetary Studies* (Homewood, Ill.: Richard D. Irwin, Inc., 1963). We will pursue this topic in Chapter 10, however.

the decisions in each of these sectors. But the main thrust of the chapter will be toward commercial banks.[2]

4.2 A BANKING SYSTEM WITHOUT A CENTRAL BANK

We will begin by assuming that we have two commercial banks and a stock of currency issued by the Treasury;[3] in terms of balance sheets the initial situation for commercial banks might look like Table 4–1. In this example, we see that each bank has "issued"

TABLE 4–1
A TWO-BANK ECONOMY

Bank A

ASSETS		LIABILITIES	
Currency	$10	Demand deposits	$50
Loans	40	Capital accounts	10
Investments	10		
Total Assets	$60	Total Liabilities	$60

Bank B

ASSETS		LIABILITIES	
Currency	$10	Demand deposits	$50
Loans	40	Capital accounts	5
Investments	5		
Total Assets	$55	Total Liabilities	$55

deposits of $50 which are backed by currency of $10. Bank *A* has accumulated, either by not paying out all its profits or by selling stock in the bank, $10 of capital, matched by $10 of investments.[4] Bank *B* has $5 in its "capital account." Finally, we will assume that individual consumers hold $100 of currency in addition to the $100 of deposits shown in the table.

---

[2] I am going to introduce institutional materials in this chapter mostly in an implicit way—as examples—rather than in their own right. The exception is in section 4.6, which takes up competition in the banking industry.

[3] The system corresponds, in outline at least, to that which existed in the United States from the Civil War until 1914, although there were then many different types of banks.

[4] The matching up of capital accounts and investments for both banks is strictly arbitrary. The profits arise mainly because the bank pays lower interest (and incurs lower expenses) on its deposit liabilities than it earns on its loan assets.

4.2.1   Currency versus Deposits

It has already been explained why individuals will hold money, but that analysis did not provide any direct analysis of the way in which they divide their holdings between bank money (demand deposits) and central bank money (currency). Actually, ownership of a bank account provides the following advantages over owning currency: bank deposits

a)   Are safer to hold than currency.
b)   Enable the individual to pay through the mail more safely.
c)   Provide a receipt.
d)   Provide an accurate accounting of expenditures.
e)   Provide access to loan facilities.

In contrast, currency is easier to spend and has a physical existence which is pleasing. Currency and deposits have different characteristics; and, accordingly, it is reasonable to suppose that consumers will hold both in their portfolios so long as it costs something (in time, in this case) to convert from one to the other.

We will assume that both banks and consumers are in their desired positions in this example. We can express these desires in various ways—for example, by including the entire balance sheet in our analysis—but one efficient way is to concentrate on the ratios of important components in their respective balance sheets. Let us suppose that the relevant ratio for consumers is the ratio of currency to deposits held—1 in our example—and that the relevant ratio for each bank, and thus for banks as a whole, is the ratio of its currency to its deposit liabilities—0.2 in our example. Each of these items—that is, reserves for the bank and currency for the consumer—represents ultimate liquidity to its respective sector, although the consumer's attitude will differ from the banker's, since the initiative (if we ignore loans and investments) between currency held by the public and bank deposits lies with the public rather than with the banks. At any rate, the ratio of the currency in bank vaults to bank deposit liabilities is essentially a matter of safety in this system; further, we will assume that the amount of currency in banks is held voluntarily rather than in response to a legal regulation. This assumption must be made so as not to confuse an important issue to which we will return a little later in this chapter.

4.2.2 The Determinants of the Money Stock

Let us illustrate this information with a model which will be very useful to us at several points in our discussion; the data are from Table 4–1. Let us define the money supply (M) as consisting of:

$$M = C_p + D \qquad \$200 = \$100 + \$100 \qquad (4\text{--}1)$$

where C_p is money in the hands of individuals and D refers to demand deposits; we do not count currency in the banks as part of the money supply, for it is not to be spent but is to be held as reserves against another type of money—deposits. Further, let us define the base of the system, which we will call *high-powered money* (H) as:

$$H = C_b + C_p \qquad \$120 = \$20 + \$100 \qquad (4\text{--}2)$$

C_b is currency in the hands of the banks. Now we can divide Equation 4–1 by Equation 4–2 to produce Equation 4–3.

$$\frac{M}{H} = \frac{C_p + D}{C_b + C_p} \qquad (4\text{--}3)$$

Further, we may simplify the terms on the right side to get our final equation.

$$M = H\left[\frac{C_p/D + 1}{C_b/D + C_p/D}\right] \quad \$200 = \$120\left[\frac{1 + 1}{0.2 + 1}\right] = \$120\left[\frac{2}{1.2}\right]$$
$$(4\text{--}4)$$

This equation, in which C_p/D and C_b/D have the assumed values of 0.2 and 1 respectively,[5] permits us to analyze the effect on the quantity of money of changes in bank preferences (changes in C_b/D), changes in the public's preferences (changes in C_p/D), and changes in the central government's contribution (changes in H).[6]

---

[5] We generally refer to such concepts as parameters.

[6] For this equation to be used successfully in the manner I am suggesting, it is necessary that the three variables C_p/D, C_b/D, and H be independent of each other; this is not obvious, as the text makes clear.

4.2.3 A Change of Consumers' Preferences

Now suppose that individuals—merely altering the form in which they hold wealth as far as they can see—decide to switch $50 from demand deposits to currency, perhaps in response to a doubt about the safety of commercial banks. If you want something historical to fix on, think of the financial panic in 1873, in which just such an event occurred on a broad scale. It is clear that bankers do not have the funds; and, it should also be clear, bankers will not want to run down all their cash anyway; let us assume that bankers wish to keep $1 of currency for every $5 of demand deposits, whatever the actual size of their demand deposit accounts. We will ignore the interactions between the three "sectors" here; and we see a resolution of the dilemma is possible only if we interpret the actions of individuals as suggesting a new currency-deposits ratio, for if they continue to try to get $150 of currency when only $120 exists, they will destroy the banking system and still end up with only $120. They will also lose all of their loans, and the stock of money will finally stand at $120 in nominal terms. We do not know precisely what will happen to real consumer wealth, but if we judge the loss of money as a loss of a flow of services, it is likely that real consumer wealth will have fallen; there is, at the end, only currency and no more banks; and this was neither intended by the public nor desirable in general, since the reallocation required was only the conversion of one kind of spending power into another.

If we take the point of view that individuals want three fourths rather than one half of their money wealth in the form of currency, we can find a formal solution to our problem, assuming that bankers' preference for a one to five reserves-deposits ratio is not altered.[7] In our case, we said that individuals decided to hold smaller deposits and more cash, and we can now interpret this to mean that C_p/D has risen to three. If we put this new result into Equation 4–4, we get:

$$M = \$120 \left(\frac{3 + 1}{0.2 + 3} \right) = \$120 \left(\frac{4}{3.2} \right) = \$150 \qquad (4\text{–}5)$$

---

[7] This is a fairly strong assumption, actually. It is known that as a panic proceeds, bankers' attitudes toward liquidity change. This happened in the middle 1930's, when they seem to have opted for a larger cushion of reserves, as discussed at length in Chapter 8.

which represents both a satisfactory solution for all parties and also a considerable reduction in the supply of money to the system. Let us emphasize this result, for it is fundamental to the understanding of the behavior of the American financial system until the end of the depression of the 1930's: changes in individuals' tastes, represented by shifts of their preference for cash which need not be related in any way to events in other parts of the economy, were capable of vast destructions of money, depending on how expanded the system was; that is, the contraction forced on the system in such an event depended on the size of bankers' reserves in relation to their deposit liabilities.[8]

TABLE 4–2
THE TWO-BANK SYSTEM AFTER THE CURRENCY DRAIN

Consolidated Banks

ASSETS		LIABILITIES	
Currency............	$ 7.50	Deposits.............	$37.50
Loans..............	30.00	Capital accounts......	15.00
Investments.........	15.00		
Total Assets.......	$52.50	Total Liabilities.....	$52.50

But there are other consequences, for along with the expansion of money one customarily finds an expansion of credit. Indeed, in our example, as Table 4–2 makes clear, loans by the banking system have fallen from $80 to $30. This is another of the consequences of a financial panic (which we might be describing), for so long as the stock of currency is not expanded, all banks must call in loans, since the currency preferences of the public have to be met.[9] The destruction of credit which financed business spending, consumer spending, and even stock market speculation,[10] forces on all sectors of the economy a readjustment which is serious in proportion to the extent of the currency panic.

·

[8] In principle, this situation is still possible today for the United States, although institutional changes—notably the creation of deposit insurance—have made it quite unlikely.

[9] If there were financial intermediaries also offering credit (that is nonbank lenders), things might not work out this way, as Chapter 10 illustrates.

[10] As in 1929.

4.2.4 The Banking Multiplier

Let us discuss one other aspect of Equation 4–4 before we consider a system more in keeping with the modern American one. We notice that H, which is currency in this case, can be increased directly by the central government; and we observe the fairly obvious point—at least these days—that increases in H could have offset completely the damage caused by the change in consumer asset preferences. The public could have been given its cash, without affecting the amount of lending in the system. Of course, one must have a monetary authority with the will to do this; but, at least as far as our system is specified, it is the obvious solution (next to eliminating the cause of the panic).[11]

Actually Equation 4–4 is an orthodox banking multiplier equation, but one which is fairly fully spelled out from the beginning. The value of the multiplier, k, can be calculated as in Equation 4–6; in our case it is 1.7.

$$M = kH \tag{4–6}$$

Now, to use the language of multiplier analysis, changes in H will induce changes in M, depending on the banking multiplier; if the multiplier is very large—if banks prefer small amounts of reserves to back their deposits and the public uses little currency in comparison to its use of bank deposits—the system is very vulnerable to all changes in H and is, consequently, especially vulnerable to monetary policy, represented in this case by changes in the quantity of currency. This is an interesting result and one which has a great deal of historical relevance; for, in our country, this multiplier (not, of course, interpreted as a constant) has varied considerably from period to period. We will pursue this topic below and in Chapter 8, but for now let us continue to develop our system as it exists today—with a central bank.

4.3 A MULTIPLE BANKING SYSTEM WITH A CENTRAL BANK

Actually, in the full-blown example of the past section, we implicitly assumed a central monetary institution, for we had cur-

---

[11] There is the problem, to be discussed more completely in Chapter 6, that the real world is not as simple as our model world and, consequently, that it is difficult to judge how much of a change in H might be needed.

rency, the creation of which was impossible by commercial banks; we handled currency in this way in order to explain one way in which the supply of money by banks might be considered to be limited. We did not explain how banks arrive at their decisions; but the public, which was featured in Chapter 3, has by now been adequately handled. But before we consider banks' decisions, we must introduce a central bank into the system. By central bank we mean an institution which holds—as reserves—the deposits of commercial banks—a banker's banker, if you will.[12]

4.3.1 A Rationale for Central Banking

Probably, it is safe enough to argue, a central bank would arise even if explicit policy did not create it. Banks, for example in the United States prior to 1914, were seen to hold their reserves in safer (or bigger) banks; and what could be safer than a bank which has a government guarantee? But safeness is not really the critical aspect of modern central banking, at least if safeness against currency panics is meant, as reference to the example of section 4.2 illustrates. To see that, simply assume that the ratio of 0.2 for C_b/D is required and not optional (required to be held in a central bank)—the final result would have been exactly the same so long as the ultimate quantity of currency (now only C_p) in the system remains the same. Further, as we noted in the discussion there, it need not take a central bank to deal out currency, for a treasury could do it just as well. Thus, the mere holding of reserves is not the sort of unique function which justifies the existence of central banks.

There are, however, two unique features of a central bank:

a) It (usually) is empowered to lend reserves to commercial banks.[13]

---

[12] What follows is not a complete rationale of central banking; that will be presented in Chapters 5 and 6. Note that central banks—for example, the Bank of England—can hold private deposits. The holding of commercial banks' reserves establishes the uniqueness of the central bank and is enough to get things going here. We will see that this uniqueness is not on account of holding the reserves per se but arises on account of the ability of the central bank to create or destroy reserves and the inability of the commercial banks to do the same thing, at least by any direct means.

[13] See Chapter 5 for a more complete discussion of the lender of last resort function of modern central banks.

b) It (usually) is empowered to control the absolute quantity of reserves in the economic system.

There are, in turn, two main methods which the central bank will generally have at its disposal to effect the second item: it may change the reserve requirement; or it may buy and sell securities from the public, thus indirectly changing banks' reserves. The latter are termed *open market operations*, and have the advantage over the former that they work through the market and can be conducted in any amount, no matter how small, the authorities might wish.

TABLE 4–3

A SIMPLE BANKING SYSTEM WITH A CENTRAL BANK

Commercial Banks

ASSETS		LIABILITIES	
Balances with the Federal Reserve...............	$ 20	Demand deposits..........	$100
Loans...................	80		
Investments.............	15		
		Capital accounts...........	15
Total Assets...........	$115	Total Liabilities........	$115

The Central Bank

ASSETS	LIABILITIES	
	Bank reserves.............	$ 20

For the moment, let us assume that the central bank does not have to hold any assets. Whether or not it does is not all that important anyway, as we shall see; but for now the intention of the assumption is to simplify matters. In fact, until very recently, all money in the United States was fractionally backed by gold; but it is now clear that the gold backing is not a constraint on the money supply.[14] In the final analysis we will include the gold backing in its proper place, but in Table 4–3 this factor is ignored. The consequence is that the Federal Reserve appears only in a skeletal form, with an unbalanced "balance" sheet. The only difference between Table 4–3 and Table 4–2 is that banks are

---

[14] See Table 15–4 for the relation, in the United States since 1956, between the total gold stock and the Treasury gold stock which is legally required to be held. There it is clear that the law adjusts to the supply of gold, vitiating the requirement.

now represented as holding balances with the Federal Reserve instead of holding idle currency, and a properly amended version of Equation 4–4 would read

$$M = H\left[\frac{C/D + 1}{C/D + R/D}\right] = kH \qquad H = C + R \qquad (4\text{–}7)$$

in which R, for reserves, takes the place of C_b and in which high-powered money is now defined to be C plus R.[15] Let us breathe some life into this equation, which we claim to have some present-day application, by looking at some recent figures for the United States (see Table 4–4).

TABLE 4–4

THE MONEY STOCK AND ITS DETERMINANTS, THE UNITED STATES, 1965–69
($ billion)

End of December	Money Stock	Currency	Deposits		Reserves		$\frac{C}{D}$	$\frac{R}{b}$	H
			De-mand	Time	Actual	Re-quired			
1965......	166.7	36.3	130.4	146.7	23.26	22.83	0.278	0.178	59.56
1966......	170.4	38.3	132.1	158.5	23.52	23.17	0.290	0.178	61.82
1967......	181.7	40.4	141.3	183.7	25.94	25.60	0.286	0.184	66.34
1968......	194.8	43.4	151.4	204.9	27.96	27.61	0.287	0.185	71.36
1969......	199.6	46.4	153.7	192.0	27.93	27.71	0.302	0.182	74.33

SOURCE: *Federal Reserve Bulletin;* the data are seasonally adjusted.

During the period covered, the money stock seems to have risen fairly steadily and, indeed, so did its components—currency and demand deposits. These are year-end figures, so some variation is concealed, particularly that for the credit squeezes in 1966 and 1969. Even so, the rates of growth of the various elements obviously changed from year to year; and time deposits at commercial banks, which we have ignored so far, actually declined during the squeeze in 1969; so did the actual reserves held by the member banks of the Federal Reserve System.[16]

---

[15] Banks are here assumed to hold no vault cash as reserves. This assumption is not necessary to what follows, nor is it valid for the United States of the present, but it does simplify the arithmetic.

[16] I am going to neglect time deposits until we reach the chapters on intermediaries, for as we have defined money, time deposits, which cannot be spent as such, are not money. If we were to include time deposits in our definition of money, we would have to adjust our multiplier equation to account for the lower reserve requirements on time deposits than on demand deposits. This

4.3.2   The Contribution of the Three Determinants: 1965–69

The two sets of reserve figures suggest that commercial banks held quite low—but positive—excess reserves during the period; but the main interest here is in the performance of the three "contributors" (by Equation 4–6) to the money stock. As individuals shift from currency to bank deposits—that is, if there is a fall of C/D—the money stock will tend to grow (if none of the other ratios change to offset it). This happens because the banking multiplier—of the given stock of high-powered money—rises on account of bank lending activity; banks will lend because we assume they hold no excess reserves. If banks move toward higher reserve

TABLE 4–5
QUALITATIVE PERFORMANCE OF THE DETERMINANTS
OF THE MONEY STOCK, 1965–69

Year	C/D	R/D	H
1965–66	Incorrect	Incorrect	Correct
1966–67	Correct	Incorrect	Correct
1967–68	Incorrect	Incorrect	Correct
1968–69	Incorrect	Correct	Correct

ratios—that is, if there is a rise of R/D—the money stock will decline. Both of these results can be verified directly from Equation 4–7. Finally, as H increases, so does M, if the banking multiplier remains constant.

When we compare the influence of the three variables on the data of Table 4–4, we see that neither of the two ratios performs well overall, although a fall in the ratio of C/D did seem to contribute to the growth of the money stock in 1967, and the reduction of R/D in 1969 did seem to help banks meet the credit squeeze of that year. But far and away the most important influence seems to have come from the stock of high-powered money, which predicted correctly for every year in the sample; a qualitative summary is given as Table 4–5.

---

is a somewhat arbitrary exclusion, but one obvious justification would be that time deposits "act" more like the deposits in savings and loan associations than like demand deposits. One observation of this is seen in Table 4–4 for 1969, when time deposits go in a different direction from M, C, or D.

4.3.3 A Balance Sheet for Commercial Banks

Throughout this discussion most of the institutional details have been avoided, but the avoidance has been at the cost of fixing magnitudes in our minds; now we must be careful to show things as they are in the two financial sectors we have been describing. With some simplifications, a balance sheet for large commercial banks, for June 25, 1969, is shown in Table 4–6. There are really

TABLE 4–6
CONSOLIDATED LARGE COMMERCIAL BANK BALANCE SHEET
JUNE 25, 1969
($ million)

ASSETS		LIABILITIES	
Vault cash................	3,094	Demand deposits.............	128,623
Federal Reserve balances.....	15,276	Time deposits...............	103,967
Other cash balances (mostly		Borrowing from Federal Reserve	1,049
items in collection)........	35,776	Other borrowings (mostly from	
Loans:	(171,683)	other banks)...............	15,156
Commerce and industry....	78,369	Other liabilities...............	25,620
Real estate..............	33,327	Capital accounts..............	22,602
Consumer installment......	19,627		
Other...................	40,360		
Investments:	(60,358)		
U.S. government..........	22,516		
States and localities........	33,625		
Other...................	4,217		
Other assets...............	11,830		
Total Assets..........	298,017	Total Liabilities........	298,017

SOURCE: *Federal Reserve Bulletin.*

no unexplained mysteries in Table 4–6, but to put the figures into perspective we should note that large commercial banks, usually members of the Federal Reserve System, comprise a large percentage of the banking system. In fact, on June 25, 1969, all commercial banks had demand and time deposits of $407 billion, in comparison to the $232 billion represented in Table 4–6.[17]

---

[17] One other fact of some importance, particularly when we come to our historical survey of the situation, is that member banks of the Federal Reserve stand in the following relation to the total banks (from the *Federal Reserve Bulletin,* as of June 25, 1969):

	Number of Banks	Total Deposits (Millions)
Federal Reserve banks..........	5,938	$330,191
Total banks...................	13,674	407,120

4.3.4 A Balance Sheet for the Federal Reserve Banks

Turning to the balance sheet of the Federal Reserve banks, Table 4–7 presents a summary of their consolidated financial position.[18]

The principal activity of these banks is not the banking business, although their balance sheet is quite similar to that of commercial banks. In fact, the two interesting liability items in Table 4–7— Federal Reserve notes and member banks' reserves—can be recognized as the high-powered money of our earlier analysis; and it is the manipulation of these items which is the chief activity of

TABLE 4–7
THE FEDERAL RESERVE BANKS, JUNE 25, 1969
($ million)

ASSETS		LIABILITIES	
Gold certificates..............	10,022	Federal Reserve notes..........	44,550
Cash.......................	183	Member bank reserves..........	21,170
Discounts and advances (member		Treasury account..............	1,547
bank borrowing).............	1,348	Other deposits.................	564
U.S. government securities......	54,206	Deferred available cash items....	7,176
Cash in process of collection.....	9,466	Other liabilities................	449
Other assets.................	2,749	Capital accounts...............	1,518
Total Assets............	76,974	Total Liabilities.........	76,974

the Federal Reserve banks. On the other side of the balance sheet we see what we might call their actual reserves; these reserves consist primarily of a portfolio of government securities of $54 billion and cash in the process of collection.[19]

Capital accounts, in Table 4–7, represents the interest of the member banks of the Federal Reserve System, the ultimate (legal) owners of the Federal Reserve banks. This ownership is strictly nominal, since the Federal Reserve banks do not seek profits (although they do make earnings on their portfolio). Since there is no intention of profit, there is no reason to value the securities

---

[18] We do not intend to emphasize that for primarily political reasons the central bank of the United States is really 12 regional banks with a board of governors as overseer. We will not emphasize this structure because the 12 have very little power, individually.

[19] The Federal Reserve performs the function of clearing checks for commercial banks. Since checks are credited and debited to commercial bank accounts before the final clearance is achieved, there are partly offsetting items on each side of the balance sheet reflecting this activity: "cash in the process of collection" and "deferred available cash items."

held by the Federal Reserve banks at market value; the nominal values recorded in Table 4–7 will do. Similarly, the gold certificates, which are provided by the Treasury (are "liabilities" of the Treasury) to "back" Federal Reserve notes, are essentially a nominal concept, since the debt involved is a legal fiction.[20] The legal fiction is exposed most clearly if anyone attempts to obtain gold from the Federal Reserve in exchange for a $5 bill; in fact, all that can be obtained is five $1 bills or another $5 bill. The word liability, in reference to Federal Reserve notes at least, seems shorn of any practical meaning in Table 4–7.

This is not to say that the words "assets" and "liabilities" are unambiguous in Table 4–6 either. In that table we observe that certain items have dubious economic importance; the most serious of these seems to be the valuing of investments at par rather than at market values, a practice which throws the whole arrangement into shadow. Specifically, if interest rates rise, the value of the securities held in the investment portfolio of commercial banks will fall; if banks do not hold all of their investments until maturity, they will suffer capital losses. Since they probably won't hold their assets if the high interest rates are the result of tight money,[21] the asset side of the balance sheet should reflect expected interest rates.

On the liability side of Table 4–6 the problem is that deposits, too, should reflect the behavior of interest rates.[22] We have argued that money is net wealth to the community and, as such, must be revalued in response to changes in interest rates. When a bank "borrows" funds from individuals in the form of demand deposits, it guarantees to repay the funds on demand. When individuals actually do "withdraw" cash from commercial banks, commercial banks suffer a loss of earning power and the community as a whole suffers a loss of wealth, since money is destroyed. But whether or not money is withdrawn, a rise in interest rates reduces the present value of the stock of money to the consumer,[23] for it

---

[20] Since the end of 1969, special drawing right certificates (SDR's) are included at this point. SDR's are described in section 17.5.2.

[21] This is simply because banks will want to keep their borrowers happy.

[22] We will ignore the price level here (that is, we will assume it unchanged) and ignore the distinction between time deposits and demand deposits.

[23] This statement is not invariant with respect to the cause of the rise in interest rates, a matter which we will pursue in Chapter 9.

means that the sacrifice made to hold idle money is greater; individual money holders must forego increased earnings on alternative assets. Since money holders have suffered a loss of value in some of their assets, it follows that money issuers have suffered a loss of value in their liability; on the other hand, bank profits are not affected by the loss of "value" to consumers of their money balances, so no entry is required in Table 4–6 on this account. It is in this sense that the wealth produced by commercial banks ceases to be of interest to them.[24] Of course if banks hold no excess reserves, the amount of deposits they produce is determined by the other two sectors in the analysis; even so, it is still production even though they cannot choose to produce more. We will take this point of view into the next section in order to examine the business side of money production.

4.4 THE BANKING BUSINESS

A typical firm, that is to say the management which guides a profit-making organization, can be visualized as trying to maximize profits in its chosen product market, subject to the constraints imposed by the real world in which it operates. In economics, this real world is represented by cost and productivity conditions on the one hand, and demand conditions on the other. Let us first assume that the firm of our analysis is attempting to maximize profits; this assumption takes the place of the set of consistency assumptions which individuals were presumed to possess in the demand analysis. Profits, then, can be defined as equal to total revenue (TR) less total costs (TC) as in Equation 4–8.

$$\text{Profits} = TR - TC \qquad (4\text{–}8)$$

Our analysis breaks down into the discussion of, first, TR and, then, TC, with the former flowing from a consideration of the demand side of the market. The constraints will be seen to enter into both revenues and costs, at least in commercial banking.

---

[24] In this connection banks are like the producers of ordinary consumer durables. These firms do not carry their past output as liabilities; but, then, they cannot be forced to take back their output either. This suggests that banks ought to include as their liability some reference to the likelihood that deposits will be "cashed in." This likelihood becomes greater as interest rates rise—as, that is, the cost to money holders of holding idle balance rises.

4.4.1 The Revenue from Money Creation

Let us assume that the bank we are studying is operating in a competitive environment, so that it can expand the quantity of its deposits and loans without affecting the general price level; this assumption must be relaxed if we are discussing either a monopoly bank or the system as a whole. Parallel to Equation 4–8, we note that the profits of commercial banks can be represented by Equation 4–9:

$$\text{Profits} = \text{Net revenue from money creation} - \text{total costs} \quad (4\text{--}9)$$

The commercial bank makes its money from earning assets, as we noted in Table 4–5; consequently, we can consider the bank's "leverage" to be the ratio of earning assets to deposits. This ratio gives us the amount that a deposit increases earning assets.[25] We will designate this ratio as E; and it is especially important to realize that E is equivalent to $(1 - r)$, where r is either the required reserve ratio or the desired actual reserve ratio, the latter being the case when banks decide to hold excess reserves.[26] If we multiply the amount by the average interest rate on earning assets (i_a), we derive the total revenue from deposits.

$$\text{Revenue} = E(D)i_a \quad (4\text{--}10)$$

For example, suppose the bank has to, and does, hold reserves of 20 percent of deposits; then earnings would be calculated, for deposits of $4,000 and an interest rate of 5 percent, as equal to $160:[27]

$$\$160 = (0.8)(\$4,000)(0.05) \quad (4\text{--}11)$$

The revenue described in Equation 4–10 is gross revenue to the commercial bank, however, because it omits one factor: commercial banks suffer losses on their existing stock of investments when interest rates fall and achieve gains when the rates rise. Thus,

---

[25] Actually, the use of this particular equation is hampered by the fact that banks sometimes sell off their investments at a capital loss—especially in times of tight money—in order to meet the needs of their borrowers. The amendment to the equation is obvious, however.

[26] We saw, in Table 4–4, that banks actually do hold small excess reserves.

[27] If we were analyzing a monopoly bank, then we would want to put Equation 4–10 into real terms by deflating D and E; in this case, that is to say, we could not ignore the influence of the bank expansion of deposits on the price level.

to obtain net revenue, for use in Equation 4–9, we must adjust gross revenue for the change in value of commercial bank portfolios. For example, for one set of recent years in the United States, the gross and net earnings of the commercial banks which are members of the Federal Reserve System are described in Table 4–8.

The period described in Table 4–8 is a particularly interesting one because it contains what is now known as "the credit crunch of 1966," a period when interest rates rose rapidly and the rate

TABLE 4–8
MEMBER BANK INCOME, 1964–67
($ million)

	1964	1965	1966	1967
Revenue on:				
Government securities	1,742	1,686	1,702	1,934
Other securities.	911	1,079	1,265	1,561
Loans	8,111	9,295	11,086	12,128
Service charges	607	653	705	757
Other	1,015	1,128	1,314	1,479
Adjustments for changes in value, etc	−570	−653	−1,046	−737
Net Revenue	11,816	13,189	15,026	17,122

SOURCE: *Federal Reserve Bulletin.*

of growth of the money stock was slowed. We see offsetting influences at work on bank revenues: while they suffered capital losses on their portfolios, the earnings from their other securities and loan portfolios rose rapidly. Even so, net revenue expanded rapidly during the year.

4.4.2　Costs in Commercial Banking

The next question to which we address ourselves concerns the other side of Equation 4–8, the costs of commercial banking. We can measure the output which banks produce either in nominal units of deposits or in "accounts." Whichever system we choose to employ, the critical aspect of the analysis is that the output decision is made for the banks: banks only lend out money entrusted to them by their depositors. This being the case, the profit-maximizing decision of the firm is located in the selection and combination of the *factors of production*, so far as costs are concerned.

Total costs, which entered into Equation 4–8, can be broken down into the payments made to factors of production in the productive process. Let us suppose, for example, that money is produced by three factors, F_1, F_2, and F_3, and that the firm is faced with factor prices f_1, f_2, and f_3 for these factors. The problem of maximizing profits breaks down into the problem of maximizing the total return in Equation 4–12.

$$\text{Profits} = \text{Net revenue} - f_1F_1 - f_2F_2 - f_3F_3 \qquad (4\text{–}12)$$

Now, where we go from here depends on what is variable in Equation 4–12; that is to say, the firm may have the ability to choose either the product price or the quantity it chooses, given the price; may have some influence in picking the factor prices f_1 and f_2 and f_3; and may have control over the quantities of the factors. In practice, we usually assume that the firm is subject to pure competition in product and factor markets; this implies that P, f_1, f_2, and f_3 are fixed to the firm. Here we also are assuming that the quantity of output (Q) is fixed; thus the strategy of the firm is to pick F_1, F_2, and F_3 subject to the demand curve—and subject to production conditions—in order to maximize profits.

The actual firm is restricted in its choices of the factors hired by the production process in use in its industry. That is to say, the firm manufactures a particular product subject to a particular production process; after all, you cannot manufacture demand deposits with a meat grinder. We will adopt the convention, for argument, that the checking or savings *account* is the basic unit for costing purposes for commercial banks; then, the factors of production of commercial banks will be seen to fall, roughly, into three groups as follows:

Labor:	Tellers
	Supervisors
	Technicians
Capital:	Adding machines
	Computers
	Bank property
Materials:	Stationery

all of which can be presumed to be hired in fairly competitive markets.

As with Table 4–8, we can look at the actual costs incurred by commercial banks for the years 1964 through 1967; the data are given as Table 4–9. Again, examination of the results for the credit crunch of 1966 put the data into perspective. We see that the rise in "factor costs" in 1966 was pretty much like that for 1965 and 1967; tight money did not affect operating costs in an unusual way. But commercial banks are also intermediaries in that

TABLE 4–9
Costs and Profits for Member Banks, 1964–67
($ million)

	1964	1965	1966	1967
Salaries and wages.............	2,840	3,024	3,290	3,648
Benefits to officers and employees	420	448	507	563
Net occupancy expenses........	550	598	654	709
Other costs..................	1,701	1,922	2,277	2,496
Factor costs................	5,511	5,992	6,728	7,416
Interest on time deposits........	3,384	4,214	5,213	6,091
Total costs..............	8,895	10,206	11,941	13,507
Net revenues................	11,816	13,189	15,026	17,122
Profits.................	2,921	2,983	3,084	3,616

Source: *Federal Reserve Bulletin.*

they offer time deposit accounts. This function, properly, does not belong in this chapter as we have defined things; but, even so, to pursue the credit crunch problem, we see that there was a somewhat higher payout of interest on time deposits. It seems likely, particularly lately, that time deposits are not especially profitable for commercial banks because of the high cost of attracting them.

The profits of commercial banks seem to have expanded during the credit crunch, in fact at a slightly higher rate than in 1965, but what really leads to bank profits is expansion of the money stock. As Table 4–4 showed, the growth of the money stock was $3.7 billion in 1966, but $11.3 billion in 1967; and that, more than anything else, in spite of the continuing rise of interest rates and other costs, led to a rapid takeoff in bank profits in 1967.

4.5 COMPETITION IN COMMERCIAL BANKING

I am not going to develop the topic fully, but one important policy question concerns whether or not banks are sufficiently competitive to ensure the best allocation of our monetary resources. Since bank profits depend in part on monetary policy—which has little to do with resource allocation directly—and since entry into the banking industry is highly restricted legally, this is not an easy question to answer with reference to the data. Probably, one can generalize, the commercial banking industry is too fragmented; and lower costs, without sacrificing output, could be achieved by merging banks. There have been several pilot studies leading in this direction, and the Federal Reserve is sponsoring a number of ongoing research efforts. One such study, performed on Massachusetts banks, revealed that for these banks expansion of all operations except time deposits and safe deposit boxes would lead to lower costs per unit, with the unit being defined according to the circumstances. Table 4–10 carries a summary of the results of this study.

If these results turn out to be general, we may conclude any or all of the following:

a)   Banks will tend to expand their size through merger.
b)   A monopoly problem might emerge in commercial banking.
c)   The supply of money has been restricted so much that an efficient allocation of resources in the banking industry has not been obtained.

We do know that the industry as a whole is expanding rapidly, and we also know that concentration in banking, in terms of deposits held by the largest banks, has not been growing. The results in Table 4–11 are supplied by the Federal Reserve. This pattern has varied considerably from state to state, and one important factor has been the legal possibility of branching. In more than half (12) of the 20 states which permit statewide branching (e.g., California), concentration has been increasing;[28] in the 16 states which permit limited branching (e.g., Pennsylvania), concentration has increased in only 3 states;[29] and in the 15 states

---

[28] This category includes the District of Columbia.

[29] Massachusetts (the subject of Table 4–10), which has limited branching, has shown a decrease in concentration.

TABLE 4–10

Impact on Overall Bank Cost of a 10 Percent Increase in the Scale of Operation in Each Function

Function	Measure of Output	Average Cost per Bank before Increase	% Increase in Costs with Increase in Scale	Average Cost per Bank after Increase*
Fund supplying:				
Demand deposits............	Account	$225,360	9.1	$245,868
Time deposits...............	Account	41,230	10.0	45,353
Fund using:				
Installment loans...........	Account	85,635	9.7	93,941
Business loans.............	Account	45,410	9.2	49,588
Real estate loans...........	Account	28,090	8.4	30,456
Securities.................	Portfolio**	8,936	8.0	9,651
Overhead:				
Business development.......	Total assets†	28,200	8.2	30,512
Administration.............	Total assets†	91,300	9.3	99,791
Occupancy.................	Total assets†	70,105	9.6	76,835
Other:				
Safe deposit boxes.........	Boxes rented	8,312	10.4	9,176
Trust department††	Account	35,743	9.4	39,103
Total.................		$668,327	9.3	$730,274

* In this example it is assumed that loan deposit ratios and capital deposit ratios do not change as the bank expands.

** The value of the securities portfolio is used as a proxy for output.

† Excludes cash, building, and equipment, used as a proxy for output.

†† Some data on trust department operations were obtained outside the functional cost program.

Source: Bell and Murphy, *Costs in Commercial Banking*, Federal Reserve of Boston, 1969.

TABLE 4–11
PERCENTAGE OF TOTAL DEPOSITS HELD BY LARGEST BANKS AND BANKING
ORGANIZATIONS,* JUNE 1961 AND JUNE 1968

Number	1961		1968	
	Banks	Banking Organizations	Banks	Banking Organizations
5 largest............	13.70	14.33	14.02	14.25
100 largest............	46.31	49.44	45.06	48.99
300 largest............	60.29	62.95	59.23	62.80

* Some banks are controlled by bank holding companies which have an interest in more than one bank. Thus the concept "banking organizations" defines concentration from the point of view of who controls the bank.

SOURCE: *Federal Reserve Bulletin*, March 1970, p. 198.

which permit no branching at all (e.g., Illinois), only two have shown an increase in concentration. Thus it is that legal restrictions play an important role in determining the form of the industry and, possibly, its efficiency.

4.6 DISCUSSION QUESTIONS

1. Generally, when we talk about the production of an economic entity, we think of something being fashioned from raw materials. Bank money is intangible; and, surely, the raw materials in its production are fairly trivial. What then permits us to treat bank money as a commodity produced by banks? Are things more obvious when you think of currency? of coins?

2. Think of some ways in which the three determinants (H, R/D, C/D) might interact. Are these serious possibilities? What are the consequences, for monetary management, of a variable relation between the determinants? Would things be helped if the relations were predictable?

3. Why do we refer to the stock of currency and reserves as high-powered money? Does currency have the same "power" as reserves? Would open market operations in currency be feasible? How does the Federal Reserve actually go about getting reserves into commercial banks?

4. Milton Friedman has been one of the more enthusiastic supporters of the 100 percent reserve plan for commercial banks. How would a bank acquire its earnings under such a system? Would banks tend to disappear then? Would the stock of loans be smaller under this system?

5. What difficulties might the Federal Reserve have in providing currency for a currency panic? How, exactly, would you advise the Federal Reserve to meet the currency needs of the public in a panic? Do you still run up against the need for commercial banks to meet reserve requirements or else to dispose of their assets?

6. Milton Friedman includes time deposits in his definition of money, even though time deposits cannot be spent. Friedman claims that the technical differences are small enough to ignore. What are these differences? Would it be better to classify time deposits as a bond? Is a time deposit "money at rest," "an investment," or both?

7. We have cast doubt on the usefulness of balance sheet accounts for the banking sector in testing economic hypotheses. What is the problem? What additional information would you need? Would it help to know what the items in the portfolio yielded? How would we deal with a bank's bad debts?

8. Why might a commercial bank sell off a security during periods of tight money? Does the liquidity of the asset have anything to do with its usefulness in the bank's portfolio? In what respects is the bank's problem here similar to the individual's, when the latter holds precautionary balances in one form or another?

9. We noted that time deposits, because banks must pay interest on them, would not necessarily be as profitable as demand deposits. What qualifications would you enter to this statement in connection with the costs of servicing the accounts, the earnings from the assets held, and the relative reserve requirements? Work out a rough comparison in terms of the model of this chapter.

10. How would you expect bank profits to fluctuate over the business cycle? Construct a diagram of the relevant factors, using data from the *Federal Reserve Bulletin*, which predicts at which stage profits are greatest. Do we need legislation on this account, or do these fluctuations serve an economic purpose?

4.7 FURTHER READING

BUCHANAN, JAMES M. "An Outside Economist's Defense of Pesek and Saving," *Journal of Economic Literature*, Vol. 7, No. 3 (September 1969).

SCHNEIDER, ERICH. *Money, Income, and Employment*, Part I: chaps. 1, 2. London: George Allen & Unwin, 1962.

TOBIN, JAMES. "Commercial Banks as Creators of 'Money,'" *Banking and Monetary Studies* (ed. Deane Carson). Homewood, Ill.: Richard D. Irwin, Inc., 1963.

| Chapter 5 | # THE OBJECTIVES AND INSTRUMENTS OF MONETARY POLICY |

5.1 INTRODUCTION

We have found, in Chapter 4, that commerical banks certainly do not determine the money stock and only actively participate in its determination to the extent that they keep and alter their cushion of excess reserves. The changing needs of the public have, in recent years, not appreciably affected the money stock because the Federal Reserve generally has neutralized the impact of these changes. The implication is that we will not have completed our discussion of the supply of money until we finish with the central bank and, most importantly, until we have dealt with monetary policy itself. We are now interested primarily in the determination of the stock of high-powered money (currency plus reserves) and its effect on both the quantity of money and on economic activity. In this chapter we will discuss the general climate in which policy decisions are taken; in Chapter 6, we will turn to the more technical questions involved in controlling the financial community. We will see, eventually, that there is good reason to doubt that the Federal Reserve can control H, let alone M; and we will find that the whole monetary process is much more complex than the working assumptions of Chapters 2, 3, and 4 have implied. But the first problem is to try to see what the authorities are up to, and that is the main topic of this chapter.

5.2 THE MONETARY AUTHORITIES

First of all, we should state that by the monetary authorities we mean:

the managers of the Federal Reserve System
(at present the Board of Governors),
the Secretary of the Treasury, and
the President of the United States,

although we will often talk as if the Board of Governors is the authority.[1] The Board of Governors has seven members appointed by the President of the United States and confirmed by the Senate. Most of the general decisions, concerning both the overall regulation of banks and the conduct of monetary policy, are made by the Board. The one exception is "open market operations," which are passed on by the Federal Open Market Committee (FOMC); but, even so, the FOMC itself is dominated by the Board members. While its strong air of personal independence partly determines the relationship between the two, the Federal Reserve is responsible directly to Congress.

There is a debate over the amount of freedom the Federal Reserve should have to follow its own policy lines. As things stand, the Federal Reserve is formally independent of the executive branch of the government although, as we shall see, economic realities have tumbled the two into the same bed.[2] One tack which has been taken is simply that coordination of fiscal and monetary policy is more likely to occur when the fiscal authorities (the Executive) have some control over the monetary; the converse would be illegal, if not unconstitutional. This is indisputable, but at its root would involve the sacrifice of congressional power to the Executive. The problem is that "checks and balances" which seem valid on the political level can lead to inactivity when applied to stabilization policy.[3]

---

[1] For the details of the structure you should read: Board of Governors of the Federal Reserve System, *The Federal Reserve System: Purposes and Functions* (Washington, D.C.). This is an essential supplement to this book.

[2] The Federal Reserve has the nominal task of holding most of the Treasury's funds, of lending to the Treasury, and of acting as the agent for the Treasury in both domestic security and foreign currency markets. It has the more real task of helping the Treasury float its bond issues, a task which involves the Federal Reserve heavily in security-price supporting operations. This matter is pursued in section 5.5, where it is argued that open market operations have been little more than supporting operations in our recent history.

[3] One possibility—not an empty set—is that the two separate agencies end up responding to each other's errors rather than to the signals from the private economy. This is all the more likely when the lags in the effects of fiscal and monetary policy are different. This topic is discussed further in section 6.5.

Another tack, associated with Milton Friedman, is to argue that any active monetary authority, no matter where located, is a mistake. The general idea—and it seems to follow from classical quantity theorizing—is that since the essential role of money is a passive one (servicing the needs of trade), the best we can hope for from a monetary policy is neutrality. Mopping up one's own past mistakes, or the mistakes of other agencies, is a valid enough exercise, given the mistakes in the first place; but we would be better off (it is argued) if the rate of growth of the money stock were steady, at 2 to 4 percent per year, than if we tried to conduct active monetary policy. We simply don't know enough about the links between the monetary "sector" and the rest of the economy to judge this argument; but there seem to be some clear examples of mistakes, which establish, at the least, that the argument will go on for some time.[4]

Even so, there are some formal policy links between the Executive and the Federal Reserve; in fact, both the Treasury and the President do exert an influence which varies with the time and with the problem. For example, the decision to devalue the dollar, internationally, which would have all sorts of monetary repercussions and which would involve the Federal Reserve in all sorts of supporting actions, is made by the Executive. Thus we must treat the authorities in a collective sense; and, in working on the problems of policy, we will assume that they, like individuals, have both the collective objectives and the means to satisfy those objectives. But this is an *analogy;* and we will argue that the objectives they have are, first, personal—for example, having to do with their own careers—or, second, economic and social—for example, having a stable price level—and that their "means" are the instruments—for example, open market operations—which they have to achieve their objectives.

5.3 THE OBJECTIVES OF THE MONETARY AUTHORITIES

In practice, there are at least three sets of objectives which the American monetary authorities have had to consider; and these are not entirely reconcilable. In the first place, the authorities, particularly the Federal Reserve, have been instructed by the

---

[4] We will discuss several possibilities in Chapter 8.

Congress, at various times, to pursue certain objectives, usually, in fact, some quite obscure objectives. In the second place, the Federal Reserve officials have their own ideas about what objectives they should achieve; and in the third place, economists have an entirely different view. To complicate things still further, all of these sets of objectives have been subject to constant revision over the years, with the economists' views showing the greatest variability both over time and within the profession at a given time.

5.3.1   The Legal Formula

To begin with, let us look at the legal prescriptions. The Federal Reserve Act of December 23, 1913, instructed the system managers

to accommodate commerce and business with regard to the general credit situation of the country

and, in particular,

to furnish an elastic currency, to furnish means of rediscounting commercial paper, and to establish a more effective supervision of banking in the United States.

Of these objectives of the original planners, the most vital one at that time seems to have been the provision for an "elastic" currency. In fact, the principal apparent defect of the patchwork system which preceded the Federal Reserve System was that shifts in the taste for currency, particularly at times of currency panic, tended to cause havoc in the financial system. We worked an example in Chapter 4 to show how rises in C/D would tend to reduce the quantity of money and, in particular, how the large dislocations in times of currency panic would tend to destroy, temporarily, both the monetary and the credit systems. The idea behind "elastic," then, is permitting the public to have its cash while simultaneously keeping the money supply constant.[5] This was a modest enough beginning to monetary policy; but growing out of its central position and the Federal Reserve's assumption

---

[5] The idea is that in the equation $M = H\left(\dfrac{C/D + 1}{R/D + C/D}\right)$ the effect of a change in the multiplier (any of the terms in the parentheses) can be offset by a change in H. In fact, currency panics went on until customers' deposits were insured by the Federal Deposit Insurance Corporation, which was not until 1934.

of broader duties in the 1920's and 1930's, the Employment Act of 1946, somewhat after the fact, instructed the Federal Reserve as an arm of the government to take responsibility for

maintaining, in a manner calculated to foster and promote free competitive enterprise and the general welfare, conditions under which there will be afforded useful employment opportunities, including self-employment, for those able, willing, and seeking to work, *and to promote maximum employment, production, and purchasing power.* [Italics added.]

This prescription is quite vague; and many have argued that it is little more than an umbrella shielding the Federal Reserve from criticism in that it does not provide any firm objectives quantitatively. But this is where things stand, and this is as far as the lawmakers have gone in setting up the guidelines for monetary policy.

5.3.2 The Federal Reserve's Formula

The Federal Reserve itself had taken a fairly broad view of its objectives even before 1946. It is clear from the discussions of the Board of Governors in the 1920's and 1930's that responsibility for the condition of the money market, a responsibility implicit in the instructions of the Federal Reserve Act, suggested keeping an eye on things happening in the economy in general. But there is a direct way to get at what the Federal Reserve regards as its objectives, and that is through its published statements in the *Purposes and Functions* publication, which has gone through five editions since 1939. Most of the following summary is taken from Lawrence Ritter's fascinating study of the first four of these volumes.[6]

In the first edition of their book, in 1939, the Federal Reserve took responsibility for

contributing to economic stability and
maintaining sound monetary conditions with regard to
     productive facilities,
     full employment, and
     a rate of consumption reflecting widespread well-being.

---

[6] Lawrence Ritter, "Official Central Banking Theory in the United States, 1939–1961," *Journal of Political Economy*, Vol. 70, No. 1 (February 1962).

This statement of their 1939 objectives has one enclosure which is unusual by modern standards, and that is the reference to *full* employment, a term which is not easy to define in practice and is, at the same time, uncharacteristically precise for the Federal Reserve. Also of interest, in view of later developments, is the neglect of explicit mention of the price level and the neglect of the rate of growth either of the economy or of any of the other variables in their domain.

In 1947, reflecting the Employment Act of 1946, the Federal Reserve exhibited the most marked shift of emphasis in its stated objectives; at that time it assumed responsibility for

> helping to prevent inflation and deflation;
> sharing in creating conditions favorable to
>   sustained high employment,
>   stable values, and a
>   rising level of consumption; and
> establishing a money supply which is neither too large nor too small for the maintenance of stable economic progress.

In 1947, then, the imprecision of the legal prescriptions is perfectly mirrored in the Federal Reserve's own conception, particularly with the ubiquitous presence of the qualifying words around each objective—especially "high" rather than "full" employment—and a shift to the employment side of the picture from the unemployment side. The reference to the money supply in relation to economic progress is the first explicit reference to the growth objective, a reference which becomes increasingly strong as the editions go by.

The 1954 edition is really the definitive version of the Federal Reserve's objectives and contains, in addition to a set of objectives similar to those pursued today, all of the qualifications we are used to receiving from our policy makers: here their purpose is

To help counteract inflationary and deflationary movements, and to share in creating conditions favorable to sustained high employment, stable values, growth of the country, and a rising level of consumption.[7]

We see explicitly the reference to a stable price level, steady high employment, and growth.

---

[7] Board of Governors, *op. cit.*, 1954, p. 1.

Now there are two curious things about all of this: one is that there is no recognition of the international situation,[8] and the other is that there is no feeling that the Federal Reserve perceives any conflicts between the objectives. Little is changed in the 1961 edition of *Purposes and Functions;* the only substantive change is to qualify the commitment to growth. It is not until the 1963 edition (following the 10-year-old balance of payments deficit of the United States) that the Federal Reserve explicitly expressed its interest in the international picture:

Today it is generally understood that the primary purpose of the System is to foster growth at high levels of employment, with a stable dollar in the domestic economy and with over-all balance in our international payments.[9]

The just-mentioned failure to discuss the interrelations between objectives is both curious and serious. It is easy to think up conflicting relationships; for example, we know that when the price level begins to rise, possibly as the result of an increase of overall demand relative to overall supply, an improvement of the unemployment picture will be accompanied with the worsening of the balance of payments situation. The latter occurs because, for one thing, American goods tend to become more expensive relative to foreign goods.[10] What I am doing now is asking how the monetary authorities weight their various objectives; and, unfortunately, neither in the United States nor, to begin to develop a comparison, in the United Kingdom do the authorities give us adequate direct information on this question.[11]

It is probable that the authorities' silence on this all-important issue is mostly on account of the fact that they solve problems in such an ad hoc way that they do not know what their trade-offs

---

[8] As we shall verify in our historical survey, there have been only a few times in American history that international considerations have not had an influence on domestic monetary policy.

[9] Board of Governors, *op. cit.,* 1963, p. 2.

[10] A further complication can be introduced by reflecting that it is possible that the whole situation is caused by too fast a growth rate of the economy in general.

[11] I am going to carry the British view of their policy objectives along because the comparison helps to focus the discussion. At several other points in the text the British will pop up again, so this information will also serve as an institutional prop for later analysis.

are. We shall see that this is probably the case when we begin to appraise the techniques of the Federal Reserve. But their actions reveal their implicit judgments, even as to magnitude; and it is possible to be more precise, although here I will only suggest what has been revealed in a fairly general way. In fact, the following summary suggests how the two governments might have ordered their decisions in recent years:

> United Kingdom: Balance of payments over
>   Unemployment over
>   Prices over
>   Growth
>
> United States: Unemployment over
>   Prices over
>   Growth over
>   Balance of payments

These choices reflect primarily the actual situations each authority has been faced with; and the only essential difference in the rankings is the elevation of balance of payments stability, for Britain, to the prime spot, apparently as a matter of necessity.[12]

What then are the actual goals of the authorities, when goals are defined in this general and ambiguous way? My feeling is that the above paragraphs translate to the following at the present day:

United States		*United Kingdom*[13]
Fairly rapid economic growth.	(G)	A satisfactory rate of growth.
A balance of payments equilibrium.	(B)	A satisfactory balance of payments.
Moderate rise in the price level.	(P)	Price stability.
Reasonable level of unemployment.	(U)	Full employment.

---

[12] Exactly what is meant by the "balance of payments" objective and why things are ordered in this way must await the discussion of Part III (international monetary economics) of this book.

[13] *Report* of the Committee on the Working of the Monetary System, Her Majesty's Stationery Office, Cmnd. 827, 1959.

In spite of the vagueness of the objectives at this stage, it is possible to be more precise about the goals if one is willing to exercise his own judgment. The following tabulation compares the British and the Americans in their quantitative magnitudes by stating what is a zero action level for each of the objectives. *Zero action level* means that if the measured value of the item listed as the objective is as good as or better than the tabled one, the monetary authority would probably consider that it had no

TABLE 5–1
THE OBJECTIVES OF MONETARY POLICY IN BRITAIN
AND THE UNITED STATES (CIRCA 1970)

	Britain	United States
Maximum tolerable unemployment.............	1–2%	3–4%
Maximum tolerable inflation per year.........	3%	2–3%
Minimum tolerable rate of growth of real GNP..	2½%	3%
Balance of payments*......................	Short run Balanced	Long run Balanced

* Actually, the American authorities, until the late 1960's, have not shown any special interest in this balance; the qualification "long run" is added to suggest that they are willing to continue running a deficit until a better international payments system can be achieved. See Part III of this book.

business taking any (further) positive action. These are not, of course, official figures, and we must be aware that the figures change with the circumstances.

5.3.3 Economists' Views

The only remaining area concerns the opinions of economists; they, too, have shown themselves to be fairly eclectic about the proper objectives of the monetary authorities. Roughly speaking, economists are more precise, individually, than the monetary authorities, no doubt because their jobs do not depend on hitting a target that they have enunciated, and more diverse, mostly on account of differing theoretical models. We are, for the present, evading questions concerning different theoretical models, but the gamut runs all the way from asserting that the monetary authorities have no business at all interfering with the economy to the view that no matter what objectives they choose to aim at, they have no influence over any of them because "money doesn't matter." But we shall explain these polar views in the context of describing the techniques the authorities have at their disposal.

5.4   THE INSTRUMENTS OF MONETARY POLICY

We will not be able to define an instrument in a totally unambiguous way, as you will see; but we can start by defining an instrument as a policy tool (or technique) over which the authority has absolute control. Let us start with an instrument which is not an instrument. We have been saying that the Federal Reserve can control the stock of money by means of open market operations;[14] indeed, we explained the expansion of deposits in terms of such an example. All of this seems to imply that the quantity of money is an instrument, and that if one can work out the relationship between money and the economy, including the feedback, then he can get to work. In fact, a lot of hands got involved in the creation of money; and, of more importance, we must remember that money is a product whose quantity depends on the behavior of the price level. It is best, under these circumstances, to say that the Federal Reserve can, if it wishes, control the nominal stock of money (M), with the instrument of open market operations. This is no small statement.[15]

5.4.1   Open Market Operations

In practice, most references to instruments of monetary policy are references to open market operations. When we assume that the Federal Reserve can control the quantity of money, we mean that it can always buy and sell government securities, in exchange for money, and achieve any reserve position for commercial banks

---

[14] Specifically, an open market operation is the buying or selling (by the Federal Reserve) of Treasury securities in the "open market." The open market in the United States consists of a small number of commercial banks and nonbank brokers located in New York City. See Robert V. Roosa, *Federal Reserve Operations in the Money and Government Securities Market* (Federal Reserve Bank of New York, 1956).

[15] In the case of a totally open economy, as we shall see in Chapter 18, a capital inflow, due to tighter money at home, can wipe out the effectiveness of the domestic monetary contraction by providing the capital the domestic authorities are rationing.

that it desires.[16] This is strictly true for the buying of securities, for in that case all it has to do is provide money in exchange; and, after all, it is the ultimate producer of money. In particular, when the authorities are faced by a recession and prices and employment are falling, the proper approach is to increase the money supply; in other words, the authorities monetize assets and create all sorts of pressures in the system—driving up asset prices, altering expectations, and distorting the differences between the real and the monetary sectors—which result in increased economic activity. The only limit to this process, so far as we have specified things here, is the legal ability of the Federal Reserve to buy privately issued securities. But in the other direction, in the case of fighting an inflation, there is an absolute limit to the ability of the Federal Reserve because it has to sell what it has in its portfolio; this limit has had an influence on Federal Reserve decisions up until World War II, as we will see in Chapter 8.

5.4.2 The Lender of Last Resort

Actually, the Federal Reserve has acquired a large number of techniques over the years; in fact, it seems to have many more techniques than it has objectives, as things stand. All of these have been used, at one time or another, to exert influence over the monetary system and thereby over the economy as a whole. One of these was planted in the list of original purposes, and you might have noticed it in that list: "furnish a means of rediscounting" for commercial banks. In particular, the Federal Reserve can lend reserves to commercial banks, accepting Treasury bills as collateral; and, indeed, it has made wide use of this instrument. I am not going to minimize the complications which we run into here; but if you keep in mind that in this particular operation commercial banks are merely borrowing their kind of money (reserves)

---

[16] In practice, the Federal Reserve places its buy and sell orders with the New York Federal Reserve Bank, which, in turn, deals with the New York money market. The Federal Reserve, acting also for foreign buyers and sellers as well as the Treasury, is always "in" the market, often on both sides, so it is in a good position to judge the "feel" or "tone" of the market. Most of its policy task, as it sees it, is to stabilize this market, in the sense of containing any interest rate fluctuations which are "abnormal." Whether this role is consistent with the broader objectives is a moot point and is discussed later in this chapter.

with acceptable collateral at a rate specified by the Federal Reserve, in a fashion exactly analogous to an individual's personal automobile loan, you will get the mechanics out of the way. Now the process of borrowing reserves (or rediscounting, if you prefer to emphasize the collateral side) gives the Federal Reserve an absolute instrument in three senses: it can agree or refuse to lend; it can set the rate at which loans are negotiated; and it can determine the quality of the collateral which it accepts. It is, truly,

TABLE 5–2
FEDERAL RESERVE BANK DISCOUNT RATES: NEW YORK FEDERAL RESERVE BANK,
1950–69

Effective Date	*Discount Rate*	*Effective Date*	*Discount Rate*
1950 August 21	$1\frac{3}{4}$	1959 March 6	3
1953 January 16	2	May 29	$3\frac{1}{2}$
1954 February 5	$1\frac{3}{4}$	September 11	4
April 16	$1\frac{1}{2}$	1960 June 10	$3\frac{1}{2}$
1955 April 15	$1\frac{3}{4}$	August 12	3
August 5	2	1963 July 17	$3\frac{1}{2}$
September 9	$2\frac{1}{4}$	1964 November 24	4
November 18	$2\frac{1}{2}$	1965 December 6	$4\frac{1}{2}$
1956 April 13	$2\frac{3}{4}$	1967 April 7	4
August 24	3	November 20	$4\frac{1}{2}$
1957 August 23	$3\frac{1}{2}$	1968 March 22	5
November 15	3	April 19	$5\frac{1}{2}$
1958 January 22	3	August 30	$5\frac{1}{4}$
January 24	$2\frac{3}{4}$	December 18	$5\frac{1}{4}$
March 7	$2\frac{1}{4}$	1969 April 4	6
April 18	$1\frac{3}{4}$	In effect:	
September 12	2	1969 August 31	6
November 7	$2\frac{1}{2}$		

SOURCE: *Federal Reserve Bulletin.*

the lender of last resort in our monetary system, insofar as commercial banks are concerned. We will see in our historical survey that it has varied all of these aspects; this implies that the rediscounting instrument is really a set of three instruments. From now on we will ignore the qualitative aspects of rediscounting because they are not relevant to recent history. Thus in Table 5–2 we show just the quantitative aspects of rediscount policy: the changes in the rediscount rate since 1950.[17]

---

[17] The 12 Federal Reserve banks, generally, all change their rediscount rates simultaneously. There are some minor variations, and some of the variations reflect policy differences or asserted regional differences, but rates are usually brought into line within a few days.

5.4.3   Minimum Reserve Requirements

We noted in Chapter 4 that minimum reserve requirements for commercial banks are set by the Federal Reserve. In fact, if banks are not holding excess reserves, then a rise in the minimum reserve requirement can force banks to call in reserves and a fall can provide them with funds, which were previously labeled "required reserves" and are now labeled "excess reserves," which are available for further lending. This obviously is about as direct a technique as a monetary manager could wish for, but this technique has not been employed that aggressively in recent years. The changes since 1949 are listed in Table 5–3.

It is noticeable in Table 5–3 that with the exception of the adjustment in April 1969, all of the changes since 1951 have been to relax reserve requirements. This is not surprising, in some respects, for this technique is much resented by commercial bankers, perhaps because it forces them to make rapid adjustments; and lately the Federal Reserve has used the technique mainly to allow the money supply to increase, rather than to work on stabilization problems. The exception, in April 1969, reflects the unusual panic the Federal Reserve got into then, in the face of continuing inflation (but not continuing rapid expansion of the money supply), and is not necessarily an indication of more aggressive use to come in the future. We pointed out in Chapter 4 how these changes would work themselves out; so, it is obvious, we have identified one of the important factors contributing to the growth of the money stock in recent years. Further, clearly, the multiplier is increasing in value as the reserve ratio drops, increasing the sensitivity of the system to changes in other factors, including open market operations; this is just one way in which the instruments of monetary policy are themselves interrelated.

5.4.4   Margin Requirements

The Federal Reserve also has control over margin requirements, which are specified not only for banks, under Regulation U, but for brokers and dealers in the stock markets themselves, under Regulation T, and for everybody else under Regulation G (dating from March 11, 1968). The general idea behind margin requirements is that minimum down payments on the loans to stock

TABLE 5–3
RESERVE REQUIREMENTS OF MEMBER BANKS
(percent of deposits)

December 31, 1949 through July 13, 1966

Effective Date*	Net Demand Deposits			Time Deposits (All Classes of Banks)
	Central Reserve City Banks	Reserve City Banks	Country Banks	
In effect Dec. 31, 1949......	22	18	12	5
1951 January 11............	23	19	13	6
January 25............	24	20	14	...
1953 July 9...............	22	19	13	...
1954 June 24.............	21	...	...	5
July 29..............	20	18	12	...
1958 February 27..........	19½	17½	11½	...
March 20...........	19	17	11	...
April 17..............	18½	...	...	...
April 24..............	18	16½	...	...
1960 September 1..........	17½	...	...	...
November 24.........	...	...	12	...
December 1...........	16½	...	...	...
1962 October 25............	...	...	...	4

Beginning July 14, 1966

Effective Date	Net Demand Deposits				Time Deposits**		
	Reserve City Banks		Country Banks			Other Time Deposits	
					Savings		
	Under $5 Million	Over $5 Million	Under $5 Million	Over $5 Million	De- posits	Under $5 Million	Over $5 Million
1966 July 14..........	16½		12		4	4	5
September 8.....	...		...		...	...	6
1967 March 2........	...		...		3½	3½	...
March 16.......	...		...		3	3	...
1968 January 11.......	16½	17	12	12½	...	...	...
1969 April 17.........	17	17½	12½	13	...	...	...
In effect:							
1969 August 31.......	17	17½	12½	13	3	3	6
Present legal require- ment:							
Minimum..........	10		7		3	3	3
Maximum..........	22		14		10	10	10

* The actual date recorded is that for central reserve or reserve city banks; sometimes country banks lagged behind.

** All classes of banks.

SOURCE: *Federal Reserve Bulletin.*

market speculators—defined as anyone who borrows to buy or sell (short) stocks—decrease the speculators' leverage factors; indeed, it does have this effect, since the leverage is the direct result of using someone else's money, and the margin reflects the amount of the initial loan which is to be covered by the market value of the securities. Thus, one could obtain, in 1968, a loan of $20 for a $100 purchase and has, as a result, a margin of his own money of $80 to absorb a fall in the price of the stock, an amount which seems enough, under present conditions, for most stocks listed or unlisted.

Table 5–4 contains the recent adjustments in margin requirements. These have not been changed much in recent years, and one of the reasons might be a fairly widespread feeling that this sort of control is not part of the Federal Reserve's responsibility.[18] In fact, this technique was adopted as an outgrowth of the stock market crash of 1929 and the attendant belief that the speculation of 1929 had something to do with the banking crises of the early 1930's. It is not easy to prove that this particular instrument operates on the economy through the monetary mechanism, to say the least, so it is not easy to prove that it is the Federal Reserve's responsibility.[19] One reason the Federal Reserve might have an interest in controlling stock market margins is that it has taken on much of the responsibility for stabilizing the economy, under the Employment Act of 1946; but, we should recall, many other agencies of the federal government could do so under the same act. We might note that, whatever else it has done, manipulation of the margin requirement has had a strong influence on stock market lending and, for short periods at any rate, a strong effect on stock market prices.

5.4.5 Control over Interest Rates

The Federal Reserve also controls the maximum rates of interest which commercial banks can pay on their time and savings deposits (Regulation Q). In order to appreciate all the reasoning behind

---

[18] The enabling legislation is the Securities and Exchange Act of 1934.

[19] Margin requirements do tend to dry up one source of funds to the market, and for high margins (e.g., 70 to 90 percent), the chances of there being waves of "margin calls," as there were in 1929, is not very great. Of course, this observation is not evidence for having a discretionary margin policy, but only for policing credit deals in stock markets.

TABLE 5-4

MARGIN REQUIREMENTS: PERCENT OF MARKET VALUE OF SECURITIES HELD AS COLLATERAL

Regulation	Effective Date								
	Apr. 23, 1955	Jan. 16, 1958	Aug. 5, 1958	Oct. 16, 1958	July 28, 1960	July 10, 1962	Nov. 6, 1963	Mar. 11, 1968	June 8, 1968
Regulation T:									
For credit extended by brokers and dealers on:									
Listed stocks................	70	50	70	90	70	50	70	70	80
Listed bonds convertible into stocks.....	70	..	..	..	..	..	..	50	60
For short sales..........	70	50	70	90	70	50	70	70	80
Regulation U:									
For credit extended by banks on:									
Stocks................	70	50	70	90	70	50	70	70	80
Bonds convertible into listed stocks.....	..	..	..	..	..	..	..	50	60
Regulation G:									
For credit extended by other than brokers and dealers and banks on:									
Listed stocks.........	..	..	..	..	..	..	..	70	80
Bonds convertible into listed stocks.....	..	..	..	..	..	..	..	50	60

NOTE: Regulations G, T, and U, prescribed in accordance with the Securities Exchange Act of 1934, limit the amount of credit to purchase and carry registered equity securities that may be extended on securities as collateral by prescribing a maximum loan value, which is a specified percentage of the market value of the collateral at the time the credit is extended; margin requirements are the difference between the market value (100 percent) and the maximum value.

Regulation G and special margin requirements for bonds convertible into stocks were adopted by the Board of Governors effective March 11, 1968.

SOURCE: *Federal Reserve Bulletin.*

the obvious use of this technique revealed in Table 5 5—for recent years, we have to develop more fully our understanding of the links between banks and financial intermediaries. The main factor can be explained now, however; and it involves the fear that if banks lose their savings deposits to other intermediaries on account of not being able to compete by raising their borrowing rate, the Federal Reserve will lose some of its control over the credit base of the economy. Its grip on the money supply, of course, is not especially impaired; but the worry is that its grip on the spending of the economy will be. Certainly the mechanism of transmission becomes more complicated, although it remains to be proved that it becomes unstable, as we shall see in Chapter 10.

5.4.6 Moral Suasion

But this is not all—the Federal Reserve's arsenal is still not exhausted; even if all of the weapons described to this point have been fired off, the Federal Reserve still has the ability to apply "moral suasion." Moral suasion is a qualitative instrument, and this introduces some new problems because it is hard to judge the effect of an adverb or an adjective on the money stock; that is, a Federal Reserve instruction to "tighten your lending appreciably" seems to defy precise analysis. We have not said much about the British counterpart of the Federal Reserve, the Bank of England; but they have made wide use of this technique and, in recent years, of a technique which the Federal Reserve has not employed, direct limitations on the quantity of lending.[20] The vagueness, in the former case, is probably partly deliberate, particularly with the British, who have explicitly favored more secrecy in their operations than have the Americans.

5.4.7 Conclusions

Let us take stock of our discussion in this chapter up to this point. We have said that the Federal Reserve considers certain

---

[20] The Bank of England relies more on their form of the rediscount rate (which is known as bank rate) and on controls on consumer credit than does the American Federal Reserve. In fact, consumer controls, while always a potential device, are no longer in employ by the Federal Reserve and can be dismissed for the present.

TABLE 5-5

MAXIMUM INTEREST RATES PAYABLE ON TIME AND SAVINGS DEPOSITS
(percent per year)

Rates: January 1, 1962–July 19, 1966

Type of Deposit	Effective Date			
	Jan. 1, 1962	July 17, 1963	Nov. 24, 1964	Dec. 6, 1965
Savings deposits:*				
12 months or more	4	4	4	4
Less than 12 months	$3\frac{1}{2}$	$3\frac{1}{2}$	4	4
Other time deposits:**				
12 months or more	4	4	$4\frac{1}{2}$	$5\frac{1}{2}$
6 months to 12 months	$3\frac{1}{2}$	4	$4\frac{1}{2}$	$5\frac{1}{2}$
90 days to 6 months	$2\frac{1}{2}$	4	$4\frac{1}{2}$	$5\frac{1}{2}$
Less than 90 days (30 to 80 days)	1	1	4	$5\frac{1}{2}$

Rates: Beginning July 20, 1966

Type of Deposit	Effective Date		
	July 20, 1966	Sept. 26, 1966	Apr. 19, 1968
Savings deposits:	4	4	4
Other time deposits:**			
Multiple maturity:†			
90 days or more	5	5	5
Less than 90 days (30 to 80 days)	4	4	4
Single maturity:			
Less than $100,000	$5\frac{1}{2}$	5	5
$100,000 or more:			
30 to 59 days	$5\frac{1}{2}$	$5\frac{1}{2}$	$5\frac{1}{2}$
60 to 89 days	$5\frac{1}{2}$	$5\frac{1}{2}$	$5\frac{3}{4}$
90 to 179 days	$5\frac{1}{2}$	$5\frac{1}{2}$	6
180 days and over	$5\frac{1}{2}$	$5\frac{1}{2}$	$6\frac{1}{4}$

* Closing date for the Postal Savings System was March 28, 1966. Maximum rates on postal savings accounts coincided with those on savings deposits.

** For exceptions with respect to certain foreign time deposits, see *Federal Reserve Bulletins* for October 1962, p. 1279; August 1965, p. 1084; and February 1968, p. 167.

† Multiple-maturity time deposits include deposits that are automatically renewable at maturity without action by the depositor and deposits that are payable after written notice of withdrawal.

NOTE: Maximum rates that may be paid by member banks as established by the Board of Governors under provisions of Regulation Q; however, a member bank may not pay a rate in excess of the maximum rate payable by state banks or trust companies on like deposits under the laws of the state in which the member bank is located. Beginning February 1, 1936, maximum rates that may be paid by nonmember insured commercial banks, as established by the FDIC, have been the same as those in effect for member banks.

SOURCE: *Federal Reserve Bulletin.*

objectives which are, in fact, attempts to make Americans (on net) better off, and has available certain instruments which can be presumed to influence these objectives. Figure 5–1, with some additional elements which are not unimportant in any historical perspective of the Federal Reserve's actions, illustrates the argument to this point.

As mentioned above, the Federal Open Market Committee makes the decisions on open market operations, but another ele-

FIGURE 5–1
A Partial Model of Federal Reserve Behavior

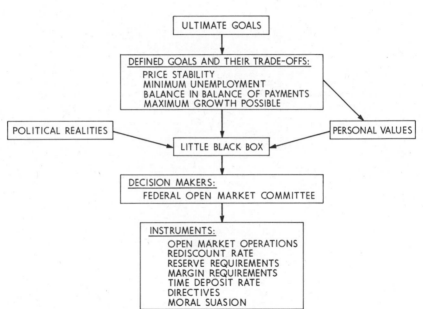

ment entering into this is a kind of collective mental process, here identified as the "Little Black Box," in which the personal characteristics of the committee members, including their views of the political realities, are given an explicit place in the model. It is not that their own satisfactions are directly involved; but we must recognize that in the context of a particular problem a conservative will approach things one way and a liberal another—and each will consider himself perfectly justified in so doing. Indeed, we will not understand some of the clearly unusual events we have witnessed in the history of American monetary policy unless we consider the influence of the Little Black Box; the rest of the diagram is simply a summary of things to this point.

5.5 MONETARY POLICY IN ACTION

The next thing we must do is pry into the Little Black Box and observe the formulation of a typical (recent) monetary policy. We might expect, after looking at the exact figures in Chapters 4 and 5 (to this point), that policies and instructions would be couched in technical language and studded with numerical goals. Nothing could be further from the truth for most of our recent history. It is ending this particular discussion on an admittedly flat note, but it is instructive to look at some recent policy directives to see what is done in practice.

When the Federal Open Market Committee meets, all of the Federal Reserve bank presidents, including those elected and therefore eligible to vote, participate in the discussion. Another representative at these meetings is the system open market account manager, a member of the staff of the New York Federal Reserve Bank, whose ultimate responsibility it is to translate the final resolutions into "action."

In fact, the committee will review the evidence and, after deliberation, draft and vote on a resolution to be passed on to the manager. A recent memo is the following, quoted in *full* from the *Federal Reserve Bulletin*.

Economic policy directive to the Federal Reserve Bank of New York adopted by FOMC on January 9, 1968:

The information reviewed at this meeting indicates that over-all economic activity has been expanding vigorously, with both industrial and consumer prices continuing to rise at a substantial rate, and that prospects are for further rapid growth and persisting inflationary pressures in the period ahead. The imbalance in U.S. international transactions worsened further in late 1967, but the new program announced by the President should result in a considerable reduction in the deficit this year. Following announcement of the program, foreign purchases of gold slackened abruptly and the dollar strengthened in foreign exchange markets. Long-term bond yields have declined in recent weeks but some short-term interest rates have risen further. Bank Credit has changed little on balance recently as banks have disposed of Government securities to accommodate strengthened loan demands. Growth in the money supply has slackened and flows into time and savings accounts at bank and nonbank financial intermediaries have continued to moderate. In this situation, it is the policy of the Federal Open Market Committee to foster financial conditions conducive to resistance of inflationary pressures and progress toward reasonable equilibrium in the country's balance of payments.

To implement this policy, System open market operations until the next meeting of the Committee shall be conducted with a view to maintaining the somewhat firmer conditions that have developed in the money market in recent weeks, partly as a result of the increase in reserve requirements announced to become effective in mid-January; provided, however, that operations shall be modified as needed to moderate any apparently significant deviations of bank credit from current expectations.

Now in this statement we see that the Federal Reserve wishes to "restrain inflation" and will do so by "maintaining somewhat firmer conditions" in the money market. How on earth, we are entitled to ask, will they judge their results at the end of the month? And, more urgently, what does "somewhat firmer conditions" mean in quantitative terms? This sort of instruction really does reduce one to metaphoric expressions, the fashion of the Federal Reserve officials.

Let us take another example, the resolution passed on April 1, 1969.

The following current economic policy directive was issued to the Federal Reserve Bank of New York.

The information reviewed at this meeting suggests that, while expansion in real economic activity has moderated somewhat further, current and prospective activity now appears stronger than earlier projections had indicated. Substantial upward pressures on prices and costs are persisting. Most long-term interest rates have risen further on balance in recent weeks, but movements in short-term rates have been mixed. In the first quarter of the year bank credit changed little on average, as investments contracted while loans expanded further. In March the outstanding volume of large-denomination CD's continued to decline sharply; inflows of other time and savings deposits were moderate; and growth in the money supply remained at a sharply reduced rate. It appears that a sizable deficit re-emerged in the U.S.

balance of payments on the liquidity basis in the first quarter but that the balance on the official settlements basis remained in surplus as a result of further large inflows of Euro-dollars. In this situation, it is the policy of the Federal Open Market Committee to foster financial conditions conducive to the reduction of inflationary pressures, with a view to encouraging a more sustainable rate of economic growth and attaining reasonable equilibrium in the country's balance of payments.

To implement this policy, System open market operations until the next meeting of the Committee shall be conducted with a view to maintaining firm conditions in money and short-term credit markets, taking account of the effects of other possible monetary policy action; provided, however, that operations shall be modified if bank credit appears to be deviating significantly from current projections.

The language and tone, for a quite different experience, was astonishingly similar to the earlier directive, but now we find the instruction to "foster conditions conducive to the reduction of inflationary pressures." Significantly, however, given this positive objective, the instruction, again, is to "maintain firm conditions" in the money market.

What the Federal Reserve means by "firm conditions" is not entirely obvious, but probably the intention is to stabilize interest rates. Since the stated objective was to stabilize prices, this seems to imply that the authorities think that a stable interest rate implies a stable price level. That fact is that this may not be the case and that the two can diverge—that, in fact, holding the interest rate constant, for example by increasing the quantity of money, can directly product inflation.[21]

Another possibility is that the choice to stabilize interest rates is generated by the institutional arrangements between the Treasury and the Federal Reserve, and not by any particular view of the economic realities. We know that up until 1951, and particularly during the war financing periods from 1940 to the end of the Korean War, the Federal Reserve was put into the position of "making" the market for Treasury debt.[22] The Treasury, that

---

[21] This is very obvious, it seems to me, but there is scant mention of such a likelihood in the Federal Reserve's pronouncements. We will return to this problem in section 6.3.

[22] Almost exactly the same situation has existed in the United Kingdom, between the Treasury and the Bank of England, since the beginning of financing for the second World War.

is to say, had massive new and refunding operations to undertake which would have been very expensive to the taxpayer. These operations, if undertaken in a thin market, would tend to. become expensive; this is so because in a relatively thin market the interest rate necessary to pay to lenders might shoot up around the issue date of a big issue. An alternative, which must have made sense during the war period, is for the Federal Reserve to support the Treasury bill rate, a support which would take the form of actually buying securities in order to hold up the price of bonds in general (and therefore to hold down interest rates). In effect, the Federal Reserve financed a good share of the war effort, ending up, at the end of the war, with a much larger portfolio of government securities than it had at the beginning.

Since the buying of Treasury securities funnels reserves into the banking system, we can argue that under these conditions the quantity of money really depends on the needs of the Treasury, or at least importantly so; and, clearly, the Federal Reserve would not have much scope for active monetary policy. In 1951, we are told, the Federal Reserve and the Treasury had it out and produced, over the conference table, the well-known Accord of that year. In the Accord, it is argued, the Federal Reserve convinced the Treasury of the need for an independent monetary policy; and it is noticeable that from that point on, interest rates began to rise. Usually, this is where things are left: the Federal Reserve now has control over the money stock but chooses, instead, to smoothe out fluctuations in the so-called money market (Treasury bill market). In fact, in recent years, one of the functions of the Federal Reserve has still been to smooth out the impact effect of the large and numerous Treasury fiscal operations, a smoothing which must have somewhat the same effect as during the period before 1951. The Federal Reserve still cannot simultaneously soften the impact of Treasury operations, whatever its view toward interest rates, and control the money stock.

5.6 DISCUSSION QUESTIONS

1. In Chapter 5 we have gone to some pains to point out that political considerations influence monetary policy. What would the consequences be of having the Federal Reserve completely independent

of Congress and the President? What role does the Treasury play in the present interdependence? Should the Federal Reserve be entirely dependent on the Executive?

2. Suppose the Treasury were to raise new funds simply by printing currency instead of selling bonds. Would the ultimate monetary repercussions be any different in the two cases? Do present legal arrangements permit this to be done? How, in fact, does an increase in the quantity of currency come about?

3. How can the Federal Reserve influence the level of unemployment and prices *at the same time*, when the two generally move in opposite directions? Give some examples. Does it necessarily confuse things if we add in the growth objective? the balance of payments objective?

4. How would you rank the four objectives stated in the text? Can you think of any more objectives, which the Federal Reserve ought to be considering (perhaps because it influences them whether it wants to or not)?

5. Why do we think the Federal Reserve ought to take an interest in the balance of payments? Does it matter, with an increase in demand, whether the source is foreign or domestic? Illustrate, in the tables of Chapter 4, how the purchase of a domestic product by a foreigner is carried on the books of commercial banks and the Federal Reserve.

6. We have distinguished between the *nominal* and the *real* stock of money both in terms of supply and demand. How do the two interact? If the interest rate were to fall would people hold more nominal balances? What did you assume to happen to the price level when you gave your answer? What "caused" the fall in the interest rate?

7. By being strict in its rediscounting, the Federal Reserve keeps such dealings to a minimum and prevents banks from taking advantage of the marginal differences in rates. What is their objection to unlimited borrowing? How might they police a system with unlimited borrowing? Does the present system imply that the instrument of rediscounting is ineffective?

8. Bankers object to the use of variable reserve requirements in the conduct of monetary policy. Why, do you suppose, do they do this? Is it a question of who has to suffer from monetary policy? Why don't banks just raise their interest rates? What is the difference implied between the change of quantity given price and the change of price given quantity?

9. Stock brokers allow their customers to keep "margin accounts" where the minimum down payment is defined by the "margin requirement." Does it matter, to monetary management, where the broker gets his funds? Explain carefully. Does a rise in the margin requirement make money tighter? What, then, is the source of the effect we observe in the stock market?

10. One reason for not having specific "policy directives" is that conditions might change rapidly so that things might go badly wrong before the next directive came out. Could the directive be worded in some way to avoid this? What sort of exact instructions might be given, in practice? Is it possible that Federal Reserve officials merely like to conceal their hand by wording things vaguely? What advantages do you see to a policy of concealment?

5.7 FURTHER READING

GUTTENTAG, JACK M. "The Strategy of Open Market Operations," *Quarterly Journal of Economics*, Vol. 80, No. 1 (February 1966).

JACOBY, NEIL. "The Structure and Use of Variable Bank Reserve Requirements," *Banking and Monetary Studies* (ed. Deane Carson). Homewood, Ill.: Richard D. Irwin, Inc., 1963.

JOHNSON, HARRY G. "The Objectives of Monetary Policy," *Maintaining and Restoring Balance in International Payments* (ed. William Fellner *et al.*). Princeton, N.J.: Princeton University Press, 1966.

JORDAN, JERRY L., and RUEBLING, CHARLOTTE E. "Federal Open Market Committee Decisions in 1968—A Year of Watchful Waiting," *Review*, Federal Reserve Bank of St. Louis, May 1969.

MAYER, THOMAS. *Monetary Policy in the United States*, chaps. 1–2. New York: Random House Press, 1968.

MEEK, PAUL. *Open Market Operations*. Federal Reserve Bank of New York, 1963.

POLAKOFF, MURRAY F. "Federal Reserve Policy and Its Critics," *Banking and Monetary Studies* (ed. Deane Carson). Homewood, Ill.: Richard D. Irwin, Inc., 1963.

SMITH, VERNON L. "The Treasury Bill Auction," *Review of Economics and Statistics*, Vol. 48, No. 2 (May 1966).

YOHE, W. P. "A Study of Federal Open Market Voting, 1955–64," *Southern Economic Journal*, Vol. 32, No. 4 (April 1966).

Chapter 6

THE LINKS BETWEEN THE QUANTITY OF MONEY AND THE ECONOMY

6.1 INTRODUCTION

In the process of linking the quantity of money to the rest of the economy, we have two main tasks. The first of these is to investigate the links between the instruments described in Chapter 5 and the financial variables—the money stock and the interest rate—and the second is to search out the principal routes through which changes in the quantity of money affect the final variables, especially real economic activity and the price level. Along the way we will again face the question of "money" control versus "interest rate" control; and, when we are done, we will have another look at our "model of economic activity." But for now we will turn to the important questions concerning links within the financial sector.

6.2 EXCESS RESERVES, FREE RESERVES, AND THE MONETARY BASE

In Chapters 4 and 5 we established that unless continually perverse changes occur in the reserve and deposit ratios, the Federal Reserve, by conducting open market operations (that is, by varying the quantity of high-powered money), can make the stock of nominal money (M) anything it likes. We qualified this statement in one direction only, and that was to note that its ability to withdraw money from the system (that is to say, its ability to sell securities) is limited, obviously, by the quantity of securities in its portfolio. In the other direction, however, there is no practical limit to open market operations if we ignore the problem of the gold "backing" to the dollar: the Federal Reserve can buy up all the existing securities in the economic system and, with adjustments in the law which are not particularly crucial, can begin to monetize real property. Clearly we can get out of a depression by means of monetary policy unless some other type of disequilibrium, possibly something having political implications or having to do with labor markets, is in force.

Be all this as it may, the Federal Reserve has chosen not to work with the money supply even though numerous economists have urged it on them; instead, they work with the more elusive concept of *free reserves*. Thus, in Federal Reserve policy free reserve targets have been aimed at; and it is the effect of changes in free reserves on the money supply or, even, directly on the rest of the economy which they seem to think critical for the management of the system. Other measures are available, and we will discuss two of these—excess reserves and the monetary base—in this section. We will introduce the discussion of each measure with its definition; and, because it is the most elementary, we will begin with excess reserves.

6.2.1 Excess Reserves

Table 6–1 contains the basic data for this section. In the table, I have divided total reserves, first of all, into vault cash, which is presumably held by banks in order to service the needs of their customers, and reserves which are held with the Federal Reserve banks. During the period from 1965 to 1969 recorded in Table 6–1, actual reserves were, at each of the points measured, in excess of the reserves that banks were required to hold; that is to say,

$$\text{Total reserves} - \text{required reserves} = \text{Excess reserves} \quad (6\text{–}1$$
$$(TR) \quad - \quad (RR) \quad = \quad (ER)$$

It is possible that excess reserves are a good indicator of Federal Reserve pressure on the system; presumably when commercial banks are under pressure, they will allow their excess reserves to run down before actually denying funds to their customers. Indeed, there is some visible indication of this effect in Table 6–1, at least for the credit squeeze in 1969. On the other hand, 1967, a year of rapid expansion of the monetary system, saw excess

TABLE 6-1

A Breakdown of the Reserves of All Member Banks of the Federal Reserve System
($ billion)

End of	Demand Deposits	Total Reserves	Vault Cash	Resv.s with F.R.	Required Resv.s	Excess Reserves	Borrowing at F.R.	Free Resv.s	Monetary Base
Dec. 1965........	111.0	22.7	4.0	18.7	22.3	0.45	0.45	−0.002	64.9
Dec. 1966........	111.7	23.8	4.3	19.6	23.4	0.39	0.56	−0.165	67.2
Dec. 1967........	118.9	25.3	4.5	20.8	24.9	0.34	0.24	0.107	71.3
Dec. 1968........	128.2	27.2	4.7	22.5	26.8	0.46	0.76	−0.310	76.0
Dec. 1969........	129.4	28.0	5.0	23.1	27.8	0.26	1.08	−0.829	78.3

rcscrves actually fall when they should have risen. But we still must conclude that the level of excess reserves tells us something about how tight the system is.

6.2.2 Free Reserves

One aspect which is not picked up by the level of excess reserves is that member banks, using the rediscount privilege, can and do borrow from the Federal Reserve; in fact, borrowing often exceeds excess reserves so that banks have net borrowed reserves. One thing they can do when pressed by monetary policy—rather than letting their excess reserves fall—is to borrow reserves; to the extent that they do this, we will find the excess reserves indicator will not give us the correct signals. On the other hand, if we calculate the difference between banks' excess reserves and their borrowings, we have some idea of the net borrowings of the banks; we define free reserves—that is to say, excess reserves which are free to be lent rather than held to back borrowings at the Federal Reserve—to be excess reserves minus borrowed reserves, as noted in Equation 6–2.

$$FR = ER - BR \qquad (6–2)$$

The Federal Reserve claims all manner of virtues for the level of free reserves or the ratio of free reserves to deposits as a measure of net tightness or ease in the money market.[1] The reason they take this position is that they firmly believe that a commercial bank's attitude toward its debt to the Federal Reserve is similar to your attitude toward your debts: you want to repay them. The Federal Reserve encourages this attitude by being unpleasant to "chronic" borrowers. There was a time, in the early days of the Federal Reserve System, when this was not the case; when, in fact, borrowed reserves exceeded required reserves.[2] This situation would tend to arise whenever the rediscount rate (the interest rate charged by the Federal Reserve) is less than the interest rate earned by the bank. In recent years banks have not taken "advantage" of this situation, though, and this is the result of the

---

[1] We would use the ratio of free reserves to deposits—or of excess reserves to deposits, for that matter—in order to remove the (largely irrelevant) effects of changes in the size of the system from the data.

[2] Prior to 1921.

sternness of the authorities; indeed, banks are reminded that their borrowing is only a privilege—and a very short-term one at that. Policing the system this way has proved easier than any attempt to keep the rediscount rate in line with market rates. Further, this essentially qualitative approach has helped to make the free reserves concept a viable one, since it discourages the sort of borrowing which could frustrate open market operations.[3]

The process works as follows. The free reserve ratio, FR/D, where D is the level of demand deposits, is judged to be a measure of the tightness of the system: it is an indicator of the pressure of monetary policy. The Federal Reserve does not operate directly on free reserves, but it does operate on total reserves by means

FIGURE 6–1
THE POSITION OF FREE RESERVES IN THE FINANCIAL SYSTEM

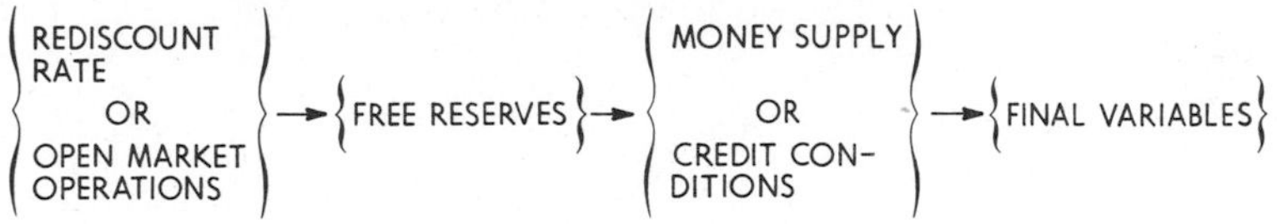

of open market operations, and it can change the value of the rediscount rate. The process they seem to visualize is something like that in Figure 6–1. We see, in this scheme, that free reserves are closer to the instruments and further from the final variables, so that a change in an instrument can be linked more readily to a change in free reserves and not be much obscured by the backwash from the final variables in the economy.

Of course, one must still work out the other links in the system; and free reserves ought to be both firmly linked to either the money supply or the interest rate and free from backwash in order to be an ideal target variable. In fact, the links are variable; and banks have had a recognizable and changeable view toward free reserves. This view has varied with interest rates and is liable to change if banks change their attitudes toward the rediscounting privilege; certainly it will change if there are changes in the degree of toughness by the authorities. The latter has actually happened, in some recent periods; and over the entire stretch of the Federal

---

[3] In the United Kingdom the authorities lend as a right of the borrowers, so they must set their discount rate above market rates.

Reserve System, the free reserve indicator has often been misleading.[4] In our data in Table 6–1, during both of the credit squeezes (1966 and, especially, 1969) we see negative free reserves, while in 1967 we see positive free reserves; but in 1968, a year of rapid expansion of the monetary system, the free reserve indicator was "incorrect." The reason, no doubt, was that the pressure of a rising demand for credit forced banks to borrow from the Federal Reserve. Again, the free reserve indicator seems to be a useful, but not perfect, indicator of the tightness of monetary policy.

6.2.3   The Monetary Base

It is partly in this context—the free reserve ratio needs to be tempered with other data—that economists at the Federal Reserve Bank of St. Louis have suggested another target variable: the monetary base. Let us define the concept mechanically and then consider its rationalization. The monetary base is the sum of the items listed in Table 6–2. The general idea of the monetary base concept is the establishment of a sharper identification of the role of the authorities than can be obtained from the stock of high-powered money: this measure looks at the financial backing of the system rather than at the total of high-powered money.

The biggest item in the table, we see, is the portfolio of securities (1-i) which the Federal Reserve acquires in the process of creating reserves; the Federal Reserve also lends reserves (1-ii) directly to the commercial banks and provides reserves (2) in exchange for gold certificates. This last figure, which arises between the Federal Reserve and the Treasury, must be netted by subtracting the idle Treasury balances at the Federal Reserve banks (4, 5, and 6). *Float* (1-iii) arises because the Federal Reserve credits commercial banks with reserves before checks have actually cleared—this item, too, must be included in the base. Finally, shifts in deposits between banks (7-i) create changes in the quantity of high-powered funds, both because member banks have different reserve requirements and because nonmember banks are subject to still another set of reserve requirements.[5] Changes in reserve requirements (7-ii)

---

[4] A. James Meigs, *Free Reserves and the Money Supply* (Chicago: University of Chicago Press, 1962).

[5] See Table 5–3 for the present status of these requirements. Milton Friedman in his *Program for Monetary Stability* (New York: Fordham University Press,

are a potential instrument of monetary policy; and their effects must also be included in the monetary base.

Table 6–1 also presents figures for the monetary base for the same periods for which we did calculations for the other target variables. We expect changes in the monetary base to be synchronized with changes in the level of deposits (column 1 in Table 6–1), and so they are, at each point recorded. But the relative severity of the squeezes in 1966 and 1969 is missed by the reserve

TABLE 6–2

The Definition of the Monetary Base
June 1968 Figures
($ million)

(1) Federal Reserve credit:
     (i) Holdings of securities.................................... +51,396
     (ii) Discounts and advances................................. +   705
     (iii) Float.. + 1,712
(2) Gold stock.. +10,369
(3) U.S. Treasury currency outstanding.......................... + 6,744
(4) Treasury deposits at Federal Reserve......................... −   960
(5) Treasury cash holdings...................................... −   973
(6) Other deposits and accounts at Reserve Banks.................. −   177
(7) Reserve adjustment factor due to: (i) Shifts in Deposits among
     classes of banks, (ii) changes in reserve requirements............ + 4,500
(8) Total.. 73,316

Source: *Review*, Federal Reserve Bank of St. Louis, August 1969, pp. 7, 14.

base in each case; indeed, the monetary base actually grew faster than the level of deposits both times, a fact which, to say the least, suggests that something is missing. But something has been gained, as well, in the sense that our descriptive powers have been sharpened.

6.3 CONTROL OF THE MONEY STOCK OR CONTROL OF THE INTEREST RATE

To this point we have linked the monetary instruments to a set of intermediate variables whose purpose is primarily to judge

---

1959) was one of the first to condemn this variability, which you can see is still not inconsiderable. There has been a trend to unify these requirements; but, one notes, there is still the instrument "changes in reserve requirements" left.

the degree of tightness or ease of monetary policy;[6] further, we have shown that the intermediate variables are themselves reasonably firmly linked to the supply of deposits, an essential linkage, of course, if the policy is to work. Now we wish to ask whether the authorities, who *can* control the monetary base—which *can* dominate the money stock—ought to be aiming at interest rates or at the stock of money. This discussion involves bringing in the final variables (the price level and the level of real income); we have not connected up the money stock to these final variables and will not until section 6.4; but, for now, we will take that linkage for granted and work on the problem of which variable ought to be influenced.

Interest rate policy can be effected either directly or indirectly. A direct change would occur if a change in the rediscount rate tended to induce direct changes in other rates. About the only way that this can occur, at least as a necessary process, is to have some legal or customary links between the rediscount rate and the structure of lending rates; and we do not have this in the United States.[7] An indirect change in interest rates would come about primarily through open market operations; and, in fact, this is the technique used by the Federal Reserve in its stabilization policy. Quantities can be controlled by open market operations or by changes in reserve requirements, but we will concentrate on the former in the following paragraphs. Let us try to develop an analytical framework.

---

[6] These also are referred to as indicators of monetary ease or tightness.

[7] In Britain there are explicit links between a large number of lenders (especially commercial banks) and the level of "bank rate." Bank rate is the rate at which the Bank of England, which is thereby the lender of last resort, lends to the discount houses. The discount houses, intermediaries between the banks and the government, serve the function of taking up the government's issue of Treasury bills on a wholesale basis and retailing it to commercial banks and other customers. The discount houses obtain their working capital from the commercial banks, and they make their profits on the margin between the rate they pay to the banks versus the Treasury bill rate, plus commissions. When banks are pressed, they do not renew their loans to the discount houses which are, in their turn, forced to borrow from the Bank of England at bank rate. Rediscounting, in the United States, is a privilege of commercial banks, while in Britain it is a right of the discount houses. This possibly accounts for the more frequent use of bank rate in Britain; that is, the authorities cannot control the quantity of lending but can control the price. Even so, the American and the British systems are essentially alike, and this similarity is especially noticeable when you note that the departments of the New York City commercial banks which deal with the bill market are, essentially, wholesale departments.

In Chapter 3, in order to illustrate one of the propositions of the modern quantity theory of money, we used the equation of exchange. But that framework has no real mention of the time element, in the sense of having only a once-for-all change in the money stock, and is consequently unsuited to considering the dynamic problems we have before us: especially the determination of the rate of growth of income and the rate of inflation, two of the variables of interest to the authorities. Let us, instead, use a dynamic form of Equation 3–5; we will not worry about its justification, but Equation 6–3 is this dynamic form:[8]

% Change in M + % change in V

$$= \text{\% Change in } P + \text{\% change in } y \quad (6\text{–}3)$$

or

$$\frac{\Delta M}{M} + \frac{\Delta V}{V} = \frac{\Delta P}{P} + \frac{\Delta y}{y} \quad (6\text{–}4)$$

The first thing to notice about Equation 6–4 is that G and P, as defined in the section on objectives, appear explicitly: P is $\Delta P/P$, and G is $\Delta y/y$; this is handy, especially if velocity is assumed to be constant. Then, if we assume the percentage change in real output is steady at 4 percent, we see that the needs of trade could be met without inflation by a steady 4 percent expansion of the money supply. Under these circumstances, V and P can then plausibly be assumed to remain constant, and so could interest rates at, let us say, 6 percent.

We will have to return to causes, from time to time; but, for the moment, let us suppose that $\Delta y/y$ suddenly slows down, say to 2 percent, perhaps as a result of the economy's approaching full employment; real income is still growing, but its rate of growth has fallen to 2 percent. Under these circumstances, with the rate of change of the money stock assumed to be unchanged, the price level will tend to rise because the increase in the quantity

---

[8] Actually, all you need to appreciate is that if you write $MV = Py$ in log form, you get

$$\text{Log } M + \text{Log } V = \text{Log } P + \text{Log } y$$

and that the derivative of this expression with respect to t (for time) is

$$\frac{1}{M} \cdot \frac{dM}{dt} + \frac{1}{V} \cdot \frac{dV}{dt} = \frac{1}{P} \cdot \frac{dP}{dt} + \frac{1}{y} \cdot \frac{dy}{dt}$$

which is equivalent to Equation 6–4 for $dt = 1$, that is for one unit of time.

of money (nominal) is greater than the increase in the demand for it. Real money balances will rise by 2 percent, in line with the expansion of real output; this is illustrated in Equation 6–5.

$$\frac{\Delta M}{M} + \frac{\Delta V}{V} = \frac{\Delta P}{P} + \frac{\Delta y}{y} \qquad (6\text{–}5)$$

$$4\% + 0\% = 2\% + 2\%$$

We have said that the Federal Reserve could adopt one of two policies here—for, after all, they cannot control P or G directly: either they can hold interest rates steady or they can hold the rate of growth of the quantity of money at 4 percent. We will refer to stabilizing M and i, then, as their alternative *targets*. First of all, let us suppose that the Federal Reserve has decided to stabilize the interest rate.[9]

When the Federal Reserve stabilizes the interest rate, the interest rate they work on is a money rate of interest—a rate which includes the effect of expected inflation as well as the underlying "real" rate of interest. Indeed, when there is an increase in the rate of inflation, bond prices tend to fall, since the interest returned in later years is worth increasingly less than if the rate of inflation were steady.[10] This being the case, bond yields will tend to rise.[11] Let us suppose that this rise in bond yields raises the rate of interest to 8 percent, 2 percent more because of the expected increase in the rate of inflation. Now, if the Federal Reserve is controlling money interest rates through open market operations, it will want to try to reestablish the money rate of interest at 6 percent. It will do this by increasing the money stock, let us say, by an additional 2 percent per year. This expansion will throw Equation 6–5 out of balance; and if we argue that real income cannot expand any further and the velocity remains constant (it might in the short run), then the rate of change of prices would tend to rise to 4 percent per year. Obviously, things can go on like this forever,

---

[9] We will allow that there are perfectly good reasons for doing this, the most important of which is simply that they think that stabilizing the interest rate means stabilizing the economy. They might also think that stability in financial markets—in the sense of unchanging prices—is more important than anything else.

[10] We will have more to say about all this in Chapter 9 when we introduce price expectations more explicitly into the picture.

[11] This relationship was discussed in Chapter 3 and will be described completely in Chapter 11.

for interest rates again would tend to go up, and so would the rate of inflation if the Federal Reserve continued to try to restrict the money interest rate to 6 percent by increasing the money supply. The economy might now be described as over-heated because the rate of inflation is increasing, and money might be described as tight because interest rates are higher; but these words do not describe the situation correctly for the money supply is plentiful in relation to the demand for it. Even gross national product would be rising—by 6 percent—mostly on account of the increasing rise in prices which the Federal Reserve, by this time, is directly causing.

In this case the opposite policy—that of controlling the rate of growth of the money stock—would not have produced this result. This is easy to appreciate because, clearly, the worst we would have managed was the original 2 percent inflation if our authorities did nothing.[12] Further, if the authorities reacted to a rise in the rate of inflation by reducing the rate of growth of the money stock to 2 percent, there would have been no increase in the rate of inflation at all.[13] Control of the money stock rather than control of interest rates is essential if we are to have stability of the price level under these conditions. The limit to this process in our example is, of course, some reversing action, based on the realization that the policy is misguided. Most likely, of course, is the possibility that the Federal Reserve will suddenly decide to let interest rates go higher and slow down the rate of growth of the money stock. But, as you can see, an important potential cause of the observable instability in our economy is that which is produced by our managers; in our historical survey in Chapter 8 we will produce some examples.

6.4 THE INFLUENCE OF MONEY ON ECONOMIC ACTIVITY

The best way to see how money influences economic activity is to assume some arbitrary increase in the quantity of money

---

[12] We are ignoring other causes of inflation and the possibility that people might come to expect an accelerating inflation and act in such a way as to make it likely to come about. We will continue the discussion of that topic in Chapter 7.

[13] When inflation is caused by other factors, as we shall see in Chapter 7, things are not so easily explained.

and follow along as it percolates through the system. We did something like this in Chapter 3 when we illustrated one of the propositions of the classical quantity theory of money, and again in the last section when we compared interest rate targets with money stock targets. But those developments were both arbitrary and incomplete and came nowhere near to laying bare some of the important complexities which emerge.

We must be very careful to keep several things apart in the following discussion. In the first place, while our theoretical discussion will demonstrate that changes in the quantity of money *can* have a significant impact on the system, it does not follow that money has. In the second place, we must be careful to distinguish between the once-for-all changes in our analytic framework and the continuous changes in the real world. We are going to comment on the latter—in fact, we did this in section 6.3—but the main objectives of this section will be to consider the dislocations produced in the economy following a sudden injection of money.

6.4.1 An Open Market Operation

Suppose, then, that the Federal Reserve increases the quantity of money by buying bonds, let us say, from the public. The action of buying bonds will, of course, drive up bond prices; but we will ignore the effect which this element has for now[14] and concentrate on the direct monetary repercussions. Individuals will, of course, deposit their funds in commercial banks and, almost immediately, will switch into some other interest-yielding asset. Someone else will acquire the funds, in turn; and, obviously, the prices of all marketable assets will have to adjust to the new price of government bonds established by the open market operation. Eventually, with the general level of interest rates lowered by the action, the new money will be held willingly in asset portfolios; and the portfolio effects of the open market operation will have ceased.[15]

---

[14] We will return to the effect of this change in private wealth in Chapter 9.

[15] At a lower interest rate, you will recall, a larger quantity of money will be demanded, for the interest rate measures the opportunity cost of holding money balances in a portfolio. This statement amounts to a reminder that the demand for real money balances slopes downward as a function of interest rates.

6.4.2 Commercial Bank Responses

Commercial banks, as a whole, will have acquired excess reserves as a result of the original open market purchase; and the subsequent switches among wealth holders, as they realign their portfolios, will merely have the effect of switching the funds from one bank to another. But let us ignore those distributive effects in order to concentrate on the more important fact that commercial banks probably will desire to lend out, or invest, their newly acquired excess reserves.[16] There is a multiplicative effect of this lending operation;[17] but be that as it may, commercial banks will offer funds to the credit market and, probably, offer them at a lower interest rate. There is no reason for the interest rate which satisfies lenders and borrowers to be the same as the portfolio rate which satisfies wealth holders, but it is clear that the interest rate will move in the same direction; downward, in this example.[18]

Even though banks are "liquid," they may experience some difficulty finding borrowers at a profitable interest rate, especially if businessmen expect general business conditions to worsen. The question here concerns the timing and the degree to which investment and consumption are sensitive to interest rate changes. The reason for our interest in this question is that such changes in spending are probably the primary avenues to the economy in general—and especially to prices and employment—along which monetary influences will travel. In particular, if open market oper-

---

[16] One of the (overrated) objections to the use of open market operations in depressions is that commercial banks might permit the excess reserves produced by the purchase of government bonds to pile up.

[17] We have already derived the banking multiplier in Chapter 4. The derivation there was direct and, probably, lacked some potential intuitive appeal. What happens is that lending occurs (or rather can be thought of as occurring) in successive rounds (as the funds circulate from bank to bank) which diminish as the initial funds disappear into the required reserve accounts of commercial banks. $100 of new money, with a one-fifth required reserve, will disappear at the rate of one-fifth per round if no bank decides to increase its excess reserves above the required level and if there are no other leakages.

[18] It is conceivable, if not likely, that initially the interest rate will shoot way down to absorb the initial impact and then bounce back. One reason this might occur, thinking of the portfolio side of the problem, is that many wealth holders will not pay any attention, since they never buy Treasury Bills and, more significantly, because they intend to hold the bonds they have until maturity, so that intermediate fluctuations do not impress them. In this case we would have a "thin" market which would overreact.

ations do lead to a lower price of credit and to a greater availability of funds, and if investment and/or consumption spending respond significantly, there could be a firm jolt to the economic system.[19]

6.4.3 Interest and Consumption

The first question concerns whether or not consumers increase their borrowing and spend more as a result of lower interest rates. It is fair to say that the majority of economists doubt this, primarily on empirical grounds. Most studies of aggregate consumption have not shown much long-run impact of the interest rate on the saving decision. But there have been some recent results which contradict these findings: we have found spending on consumer durables both directly and indirectly affected through the availability of consumer credit; and we have found corporate saving—a substitute for direct saving by consumers—affected. Further, we have found that small percentage effects, which are sometimes not picked up by statistical tests, have large actual impacts on the final variables in our system.[20]

We have also found that indirect effects on consumer spending exist, caused by altering the value of consumers' portfolios; indeed, they exist perhaps to a fairly substantial degree.[21] That is, when an open market operation (say, a purchase) occurs, capital gains are made by wealth holders; and it seems likely that some of these capital gains will find their way into consumer spending. This effect, too, could have a sizable impact on prices and employment, even though the percentage of the (billions of dollars of) open market operations involved is quite small.

6.4.4 Interest and Investment

There has been a good deal of research on this problem; and, it is best to confess, a consensus is far from established. Indeed,

---

[19] This statement ignores the timing aspect of the changes; the discussion of this topic follows, in section 6.5.

[20] We should note that even impact effects can be large; but, in addition, the final effect (known as the spending multiplier effect), after all the rounds of spending induced by the original disturbance have run their course, could be a multiple of the impact effect.

[21] The theory behind these empirical remarks is discussed in Chapter 9.

the methods employed by researchers have varied—from inter-views of businessmen to full-scale econometric models—almost as much as the findings. Roughly, the interviews tend to find no effect and the latest empirical works tend to find considerable effects, and we are left with a difficult problem of rationalization. Somehow we must integrate the findings that businessmen say the interest rate is not given much weight when they formulate their investment plans with the findings of some economists which imply that they do.

For one thing, we know the businessman is unlikely to connect the *causes* of the changed interest rate with his own situation; in fact, he is likely to limit his appraisal of the effects of a change in interest rates to the effect on his costs. From the cost point of view, it would seem that long-term investment commitments, where the interest cost will go on for a long time, will be more affected than short-term ones. In particular, with a rise in interest rates, long-term plans could be curtailed temporarily, producing a sizable effect on investment. With respect to short-term borrow-ing (perhaps financing inventories or working capital), the effect seems to be more on the firm's profitability (and, consequently, on its long-run ability to stay in business) than on its investment. This result obtains because the firm generally must keep its in-ventories and working capital financed.

Another aspect missed in the interview surveys is the effect of business expectations induced by a change in interest rates. In-deed, a fall in interest rates could be part of a fall in rates of return in general such that the businessman, in responding to the fall in his own expected profit rate, forgets to mention that it is the difference between his profit rate and the interest rate charged to him which matters to his investment rather than the level of interest rates as such. This statement, as we will see in Chapter 7, is not invariant with respect to the causes of the fall in interest rates.

Obviously, we are in the realm of empirics. We don't know whether the price of credit is more important—as it seems to be to the firm with long-range plans—or whether the availability of funds dominates—as it seems to do for the firm with an inven-tory problem. There is some evidence which was taken over the business cycle which suggests that both can matter: in particular, near the peak of business expansion, when plant capacity is fully utilized, availability dominates the interest rate, while in the early stages of the downturn, the two roles are reversed.[22] But little other firm evidence is available.

6.5 LAGS IN MONETARY POLICY

One of the reasons we would not expect successful empirical predictions from our analysis is that it takes some time for changes in financial variables to affect the economic system. In fact, if we have to wait until interest rates have affected investment, it could be a very long wait. Needless to say, any time any of the data facing an individual decision unit alter, it will take some time for the unit to react and some time for the entire reaction to pass through the economic system in general. Let us not be precise, just yet, as to the possible length of such lags in monetary policy; but let us note that if the lags are very long, there is the possibility that a particular policy might make things worse. Suppose that a rise in the price level induces the monetary authorities to reduce the quantity of money, but, for various reasons, the bulk of the effect of the reduction does not reach the economy for several years. Further, suppose the economy itself has reversed, so that the effect of the reduction on the money supply comes when prices are already falling (for other reasons). This would worsen things, when the effect hits, because it would tend to drive down the price level still further. This is an adequate justification for studying the problem.

But there is an even more serious problem, since one can learn to live with a given lag, and that is that the lags seem to vary from period to period. In fact, at least one economist[23] believes that the lag in effect in monetary policy for the United States has been as long as 18 months and as short as 6 months and has varied so much as to defy practically all serious prediction. This is a serious charge.

Actually, a whole series of lags in the policy model of Chapter 5 can enter here. In the first place there is an *information lag,*

---

[22] J. R. Meyer and R. R. Glauber, *Investment Decisions, Economic Forecasting, and Public Policy* (Cambridge, Mass.: Harvard University Press, 1964).

[23] Milton Friedman.

often longer than three months, which exists between the occurrence of an event and its measurement by the authorities. To a certain extent this lag can be reduced by finding economic variables which forecast economic events—an obvious example is to use planned business investment—but so far, such forecasts have not served us very well.[24]

The next lag in the policy system is the so-called *inside lag,* the lag between the appearance of the need for policy action and the taking of the action. The inside lag itself consists of a *recognition lag,* induced by the delay in recognizing that a change is needed, and an *action lag,* representing the time it takes to get things moving. When the data change and are fed into the Federal Reserve's meetings, patterns must emerge—that is to say, events must repeat themselves—before a decision to act will be made. The best that can be done, if data are collected monthly with an information lag of three months, is to arrive at a decision to do something four months after the event. Here, it turns out, monetary policy has a special advantage over fiscal policy, for once the decision to have an open market operation is made, the system manager can begin to operate on the next day.[25] Thus, the potential action lag for the most important instruments of monetary policy—open market operations, changes in the rediscount rate, changes in reserve requirements, and changes in margin requirements—is essentially zero.

We have seen that each of these instruments works on the system in a slightly different way; and each, too, works with a lag. Actually, the *lag-in-effect* or, if you will, the *outside lag* is a very long series of future adjustments which can only be measured arbitrarily, for example, by picking some percentage of the total effect (say, 95 percent) which must be realized and measur-

---

[24] There is another problem with respect to information, and that is that "fresh" or "preliminary" information tends to be less accurate than revised information, so that decisions taken on the basis of the former tend to have a wider range of uncertainty. Our gross national product figures, for example, are continually being revised; and in one case in early 1967, it is even conceivable that the wrong direction was given to monetary policy because of a sizable statistical error of this sort.

[25] There are some bits of fiscal policy in the hands of the Executive, but most major changes must go through Congress. This is an uncertain and time-consuming route; and, more seriously, the action lag has been very long in some instances.

ing the time it takes to be realized (say, 32 years). When an instrument is changed—when reserves, for example, are altered by an open market operation—it takes time for the money stock to alter; then, perhaps six months later, the effect of the change in the stock of money will begin to dominate the price level. If the first part of this lag, perhaps caused by the slowness of banks to run off their excess reserves, is two months—which we can refer to as the *instrument-effect lag*—and the later part is six months—which we may refer to as the *final lag*—the lag-in-effect, in our arbitrary example, would measure eight months. The total lag of the monetary policy would then measure 12 months in our (possibly understated) example, as suggested in Table 6–3.

TABLE 6–3
THE LAGS IN MONETARY POLICY:
OPEN MARKET OPERATIONS

Lag	Months
Information lag.......................	3
Inside lag { Recognition lag.............	1
{ Action lag.................	0
Lag-in-effect { Instrument-effect lag.......	2
{ Final lag................	6
Total lag.........................	12

Table 6–3 describes lags for open market operations and changes in reserve requirements when money is already tight; in this case, the instruments directly attack the availability of funds. But 12 months is about the best we can expect, and the methods which attack the price of credit (for example, the rediscount rate, which also operates fairly indirectly) probably take a very long time to work themselves out. In particular, if the main effect of an interest rate is to stimulate or retard investment spending and if we have to wait around for the effect to work itself out, we might well have gone through a cycle or two before the main impact occurs, because some private investment plans have a very long horizon indeed in our economy.[26] Thus we run the risk of having

---

[26] Phillip Cagan and Arthur Gandolfi have done a preliminary empirical study of the length of time it takes for changes in interest rates to affect income; they conclude that ". . . the main effects occur over a period beginning six months later and lasting over two years" ("The Lag in Monetary Policy as Implied by the Time Pattern of Monetary Effects on Interest Rates," *American Economic Review*, Vol. 59, No. 2 [May, 1969], p. 283).

our particular effect at a time when the situation calls for the opposite effect; monetary policy, if the lags are long enough, can be destabilizing.

6.6 SOME OTHER INTEREST RATE EFFECTS: A COLLAGE

Changes in the quantity of money affect the economic system—with varying time lags—in indirect ways, in addition to the direct ways we have emphasized. When interest rates change, all asset holders and liability owners are involved; we saw in Chapter 4 that an intermediary, such as a commercial bank (in its time deposit function), seems to break even; but this, too, depends on the extent to which funds are rationed.[27] We might summarize all of these effects by looking at the effects of tight money on the distribution of income: surprisingly, tight money seems to favor the lower income brackets.[28] This result is surprising because we presume that lower income recipients are net borrowers, but the facts show that they pay out less interest than they receive.[29]

Perhaps the widest debate over the differential effects of tight money concerns its effect on small business. It is known that small firms depend for funds more heavily on commercial banks than they do on the open stock and bond markets, but it is not clear that banks themselves "suffer" more than the markets. Further, there is no convincing evidence that banks actually engage in open discrimination; bankers, themselves, will say that small firms, which often have no alternatives and often need the funds to stay afloat, are the last rather than the first to go.

We might also wonder whether consumers are discriminated against when money is tight. It is likely that they are not, for the same reasons we mentioned in connection with small business;

---

[27] We will see in Chapter 10 that financial intermediaries and their customers have suffered in the recent bouts of tight money.

[28] Oswald Brownlee and Alfred Conrad, *The Impact of Monetary Policy* (Commission on Money and Credit) (Englewood Cliffs, N.J.: Prentice-Hall, Inc., 1962), p. 520.

[29] I should point out that this way of presenting things catches the essential effect of differing rates of inflation on the distribution of income, at least insofar as debtor-creditor relations are concerned, because the interest rates in the study cited are nominal ones (see Chapter 9). Of course, all of this discussion is neutral with respect to the actual causes of inflation, and this matters, as we will see in Chapter 7.

but there is another aspect worth mentioning here. Sales finance companies, which lend to consumers while they borrow from commercial banks, could be the subject of special pressure when banks are hit, so that consumers would be affected directly through reductions in their ability to borrow "on time." This would directly affect consumers' welfare and might force consumers, if they tried to maintain their current standard of living, to sell off some of their assets in a falling market.

6.7 THE FEDERAL RESERVE'S VIEW OF THE ECONOMY: A SUMMARY

It should be clear that it is critical that the Federal Reserve, if it is going to function effectively, has to have both effective techniques and a perception of the economy adequate to enable it to work out the influence of its actions on the economy. In this chapter we have shown how oversimplified was the apparatus of Chapters 1 through 5; and, it follows, we have shown how important it is that the managers of our monetary system have

FIGURE 6–2
THE COMPLETE MODEL OF FEDERAL RESERVE BEHAVIOR

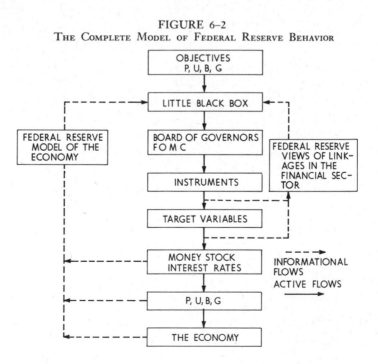

a model with *at least* the linkages spelled out here. There are good models about, the Federal Reserve Board–M.I.T. model, for example; and these models do have the features mentioned in this chapter; but one is not certain the decision makers can or do make much use of them.[30] Be that as it may, and putting the best light on things, Figure 6–2 illustrates a complete model of the economy, rearranged from Figure 5–1 to fill in the new infogmation we have introduced in this chapter, which might describe how American monetary policy is constructed.

6.8   DISCUSSION QUESTIONS

1. Would an accumulation of excess reserves be an indication of the operation of the liquidity trap? What assumptions are needed to get from the demand for money by individuals to the stock of bank excess reserves? What role do interest rates play in your answers?

2. Why is it considered dangerous to let banks borrow at will from the Federal Reserve? Would there be damaging cyclical consequences? How else could one police the system to keep down procyclical borrowing?

3. What is the relation between unemployment and prices which cause the latter to rise as full employment is approached? Give both a macroeconomic and microeconomic explanation. In what sense is the money supply involved?

4. What does the Federal Reserve hope to achieve by stabilizing the money rate of interest? Could they stabilize the real rate of interest, as this concept is defined in chapter 6? If the authorities did not interfere in bond markets, would these two rates tend to move together?

5. The association of rising interest rates with tighter money is a pronounced one, especially among government officials and businessmen. Under what assumptions, especially about the supply of money, would such an association be valid? What assumptions might you make about the expected rate of inflation?

6. It has been alleged by other economists that, following an open market operation, some time elapses before individuals get their

---

[30] One factor is that by relying on such models—which use a lot of complicated data—we increase the information lag of monetary policy.

portfolios readjusted. I have seen estimates of as much as six *years* for this time lag. Does this seem reasonable? If you sold a bond to the government would you let the cash sit in your account even for six *days?* In what ways might the interest rate be involved in the length of this lag?

7. Compare the length of the lags for fiscal and monetary policy. How does your comparison depend on your choice of fiscal or monetary instrument? Which of the monetary instruments has the longest lag?

8. How might one shorten the lags in the operation of monetary policy? To what extent is the lag's length itself an economic variable which costs resources to reduce? What sort of lags might we expect from the operations of direct controls on the quantity of credit?

9. Why ought one to emphasize the *variability* rather than the *length* of the lags in the operation of monetary policy? Do we know much about this variability? Compare the potential variability of the lags in fiscal versus monetary policy, for various policy instruments.

10. Economic variables are so intertwined that it is difficult to disentangle cause and effect. In what respects is this task likely to be easier when we are considering the effects of monetary policy on the economy? Does your answer depend on which instrument you are discussing? At what stage is it most obvious what is causing what?

6.9 FURTHER READING

ANDERSEN, LEONALL C., and JORDAN, JERRY L. "The Monetary Base—Explanation and Analytical Use," Federal Reserve Bank of St. Louis, *Review* (August 1968).

BROWNLEE, OSWALD, and CONRAD, ALFRED. *Impacts of Monetary Policy* (Commission on Money and Credit). Englewood Cliffs, N.J.: Prentice-Hall, Inc., 1962.

CAGAN, PHILLIP. "Theories of Mild Continuing Inflation," *Inflation: Its Causes, Consequences and Control* (ed. Stephen W. Rousseas). Wilton, Conn.: Calvin K. Kazanjian Economics Foundation, Inc., 1968.

GIBSON, WILLIAM E. "The Effects of Money on Interest Rates," Board of Governors, *Staff Economic Study*, No. 43 (January 1968).

JOHNSON, HARRY G., and WINDER, JOHN W. L. "Lags in the Effect of Monetary Policy in Canada" (working paper). Ottawa: Royal Commission on Banking and Finance, 1964.

KAREKEN, JOHN, and SOLOW, ROBERT M. "Lags in Fiscal and Monetary Policy," *Stabilization Policies* (Commission on Money and Credit). Englewood Cliffs, N.J.: Prentice-Hall, Inc., 1964.

MAYER, THOMAS. *Monetary Policy in the United States,* chaps. 4 and 6. New York: Random House, 1968.

MEYER, J. R., and GLAUBER, R. R. *Investment Decisions, Economic Forecasting, and Public Policy.* Cambridge, Mass.: Harvard University Press, 1964.

TUSSING, E. DALE. "Can Monetary Policy Influence the Availability of Credit?" *Journal of Finance,* Vol. 21, No. 1 (March 1966), pp. 1–14.

Chapter
7

MONEY AND DEVELOPMENT

7.1 INTRODUCTION

The text to this point has been somewhat remiss in its concentration on the monetary economics of the advanced world; we have not given equal time to the "other" two thirds of the world. To redress matters to some extent, I am going to undertake a comparison of the monetary problems in the two spheres. The main objective of this chapter is the exposure of some new areas—both in the advanced world and in the backward—where monetary analysis is relevant. One of these areas, the analysis of the causes of inflation, could have appeared in Chapter 6, but because inflation is more endemic—and less bound up with other factors—in underdeveloped countries, a greater clarity is possible by discussing it in this context. Other problems arise because underdeveloped countries also have underdeveloped monetary sectors.

7.2 ECONOMICS AND THE UNDERDEVELOPED COUNTRIES

What I wish to claim is that a "comparative advantage" in solving some problems in both advanced and underdeveloped economies can be gained by applying the techniques in one area to the problems of the other. This advantage would seem to be most obvious when the techniques from our world, such as microeconomic analysis, are carried over into development studies; but, as it turns out, even this claim is in dispute.

One line of attack is frontal: economic theory, as it exists in the advanced world, is irrelevant to the problems of the underdeveloped world. There are a lot of reasons given for taking this

view, and some of them are bound up in the war of competing
ideologies. Indeed, the most devastating arguments simply say that
the principal problems of the underdeveloped world are sociological and political—that is, the chief constraints on economic decisions are introduced through the rigidity of the society and the
rigidity and corruptness of its political institutions—so that economic policy as we understand it is simply not applicable: it is
constrained out of existence. I suppose that we are not competent
to judge the issues which arise here; but another target which is
more in our range is the claim that economics, designed as it is for
capitalistic and materialistic societies (if such a distinction is
valid), is irrelevant because the underdeveloped society is in perpetual disequilibrium and the tools of economics are useful only in
equilibrium. That is, it is claimed that while supply and demand
operate in underdeveloped countries, the typical movements in
prices and quantities either are random or, worse, tend to be away
from equilibrium, so that the techniques from advanced countries
give out the wrong answers: prices are not "determined" by supply and demand, for they are not "determined" at all.

7.2.1   The Dual Economy

Let us consider a specific proposal. It is said frequently, and
a certain empirical verification is undeniable, that underdeveloped
countries are often subdividable into "dual economies," that is,
subsistence and advanced sectors which exist side by side. Now
this is unusual and a little perturbing to our formal economics
because such dual systems, which are essentially different economies with different price and wage structures and even with
different amounts of unemployment and standards of living, should
be impossible in the long run, since most factors of production
appear to be reasonably mobile within a country.[1] In India, for
example, one notices that large cities often have advanced tech-
nologies, with the appearance, Indian-style, of Western urbanized
societies; at the same time, in the hinterland, there are separate,
village-based societies which have none of the appearances of the
Western world. The usual argument for the persistence, sometimes

---

[1] It is too easy, and probably incorrect, to shrug off the duality we observe
as merely transitory (short run) in nature.

even the spread, of such enclaves is that economic forces are not sufficient to move factors from one society to the other because in the village a kind of social insurance scheme—whereby the total output is divided evenly among the workers whether they are employed or not—makes it inconvenient and even risky for an individual unemployed worker to advance to the city where an unemployed worker is often paid nothing. In effect we have, in the village, what is known as the *extended family system*, which is also reinforced by religious, social, and educational factors.

Of course it would be absurd to argue that such barriers are impervious to social and economic erosion, and no one really does; but the known persistence of dual economic systems, one which is a highly articulated and financial economic system and one which is practically a barter economy, is remarkable enough. We might note, also, that the methods of manufacturing in such cases are equally different, with the advanced sector featuring relatively large-scale modern techniques and the retarded sector featuring small-scale and handicraft methods.

7.2.2 Is There a Monetary Dual?

The obvious question which emerges concerns whether or not monetary capital flows readily between the observed dual sectors. In fact, while we do not usually observe barter in the backward economies—that is, we do observe the existence of a medium of exchange—we do not find money serving as a financial store of value (except in the obvious accounting sense), and we find an impressive lack of other financial stores of value. The principal stores of value we do find are real—especially property—and under these circumstances there is little exchange of capital between the sectors; consequently, the rate of return on capital differs in the two sectors. Thus, a critical condition of dualism (in this case, that individuals store their wealth in a real form on other than marginal principles) is met to some extent; and monetary duality is a likely reality.

7.2.3 Trade and Economic Development

There is another aspect to the disappointment many have felt with the application of economic principles to the problems of the underdeveloped world: the interlocking of the advanced with the retarded world, through international and interregional trade, has produced a systematic milking of the poor for the rich. If anyone were to try to cure this alleged evil, he would not call on economic techniques, for what is needed is a series of transfers from the rich to the poor, transfers which are exactly the reverse of the flow suggested by the "correct" economic allocation. These transfers are effected, for example, by setting up barriers (tariffs) sufficient to improve the rate of development, barriers which, at the same time, frustrate the "best" worldwide allocation of resources.

But it must be pointed out that most of the positive development programs in underdeveloped countries today involve the attempt to build a modern economic system in which initiative, when it is productive, is rewarded with economic success and in which prices respond to the forces of supply and demand. Of central importance in most of these schemes—whether the project is inspired by the central government and can be referred to as social-ist or whether the impetus has a more decentralized origin—are the stock of venture capital and, of similar importance, the stock of entrepreneurial skills. Virtually all economic plans for under-developed countries emphasize both of these aspects; indeed, a developing country must have individual savings on the one hand and individual entrepreneurial ventures on the other, on a broad scale. Further, and this is where the financial mechanism comes in, such countries must have a mechanism for transmitting—and encouraging—the flow of savings into the most productive chan-nels of investment. But before we tackle the positive program, we must take up the terminological problems.

7.3 THE GREAT DEBATE OVER INFLATION

7.3.1 The Definition of Inflation

We must attempt a definition of inflation before considering its causes. Actually, we have worked with a rate of change of prices, which has already been defined, so inflation can be defined most readily as a rise in the price level.[2] This definitional approach

---

[2] It might be just as well to recognize that inflation could also be defined qualitatively as an *undesirable* rise of prices. *Undesirable* could then be defined

allows us to separate inflation from noninflation without ambiguity; but, we must note, as was the case for the definition of money, some people define inflation in terms of its causes[3] or, even, in terms of their own prejudices. One popular definition, for example, is that inflation is "too much money chasing (too few) goods." In fact, you should see immediately, if too much money is chasing too few goods, inflation might be caused, not defined. Further than that, such a situation may not produce inflation, and that too is a problem: in this case, if the velocity of money were falling at the same time, inflation might not occur even if the quantity of money were expanding more rapidly than the rate of growth of real income.[4]

7.3.2 The Extent of Inflation: A World View

Before we consider the causes of inflation, we should attempt to establish the extent of the problem. In Table 7–1, countries are grouped according to a five-way classification ranging from very wealthy to very poor. This list is somewhat biased numerically, and exclusion of the extremes at the top would change the picture a little; but, one notices, it is clearly difficult to generalize about inflation in the world. In fact, it seems that there are a few countries, underdeveloped as we noted above, in which rapid inflation is rather obvious; but that for the rest of the world, both advanced and backward countries seem to have about the same rates of inflation. Further, in the table, there is no apparent relationship between the growth rate and the rate of inflation.

7.4 THE CAUSES OF INFLATION: THE ADVANCED WORLD

The most obvious cause of inflation in the advanced world would be increases in the money supply. We have pointed out that increases in the quantity of money can change the price level;

---

as a rate which depends on some collective viewpoint, for example, that of the Federal Reserve as modified by political and social processes. This enables us to *shift the definition*, as it were, to deal with local conditions—for example, a 10 percent rate in Brazil would produce a celebration, while in the United Kingdom it would produce a new government.

[3] Harry G. Johnson, "A Survey of Theories of Inflation," *Essays in Monetary Economics* (London: George Allen & Unwin, Ltd., 1967), pp. 106–107.

[4] If that is what is meant by "too much money chasing too few goods."

TABLE 7–1
A Sample of Rates of Inflation in the World*
(mostly 1953–61, with some variations)

Countries	Average Inflation	Average Growth Rate of Per Capita Gross Domestic Product
Very wealthy:		
United States	1.1	1.2
Canada	1.3	1.0
Sweden	2.7	3.4
New Zealand	2.4	1.9
Wealthy:		
Belgium	1.2	2.3
Australia	2.5	1.4
France	3.6	3.7
United Kingdom	2.1	2.0
Average:		
Venezuela	1.0	2.7
Iceland	3.8	2.5
Germany, F.R	1.5	5.7
Netherlands	2.2	3.4
Finland	3.6	4.0
Austria	1.9	5.7
Israel	4.9	6.3
Poor:		
Italy	1.9	5.4
Denmark	2.3	3.4
Ireland	2.0	2.4
Jamaica	2.0	7.2
Greece	3.7	5.2
Nicaragua	1.5	0.3
Japan	1.6	8.8
Colombia	7.0	2.1
Mexico	6.0	3.0
Argentina	24.0	0.4
Chile	33.0	0.6
Brazil	18.0	2.8
Very poor:		
Malaysia	−0.2	0.8
Portugal	1.3	4.3
Honduras	1.3	0.7
Philippines	1.2	2.1
Ecuador	0.9	1.1
Guatamala	0.3	2.3
Morocco	2.7	−2.2
Peru	2.6	0.3
Syrian A.R	2.3	0.7
Ceylon	0.3	1.1
United Arab Republic	0.4	2.1
Nigeria	2.4	2.7
Thailand	2.8	1.2
India	2.0	1.4
Pakistan	1.6	0.6
Burma	1.2	2.8
China, Republic of	8.0	3.4
Turkey	10.0	1.9
Paraguay	12.0	−1.0
Korea	13.0	2.0
Indonesia	11.0	1.7

* The countries are ranked by per capita gross domestic product.

Source: Graeme S. Dorrance, "Inflation and Growth: The Statistical Evidence," International Monetary Fund *Staff Papers* (Washington, D.C., 1966), Vol. 13, pp. 96–97.

and there is little doubt that such increases, which we know to have exceeded the rate of growth of real income at times, have influenced the price level. There is little doubt because we know that the Federal Reserve has, on occasion, permitted the money supply to expand to support the Treasury bill rate; such knowledge permits us to trace and claim cause-and-effect. But such a statement is a long way from attributing all, or even a significant amount, of our actual inflation to changes in the quantity of money. In fact, we will see that most rival theories require an increase in the quantity of money in a passive sense, so that it is not going to be easy to be definite about what the causes are, especially in particular cases.

For convenience, let us refer to Keynesian and classical theories of inflation. The latter, which we just described, differs from the former both in terms of emphasis and in terms of the causal mechanism, although they overlap in that for every Keynesian disturbance there is a monetary explanation. This occurs because P, after all, is the inverse of the price of money. Both sets of theories, then, have an "aggregate demand exceeds aggregate supply" or, if you wish, "too much money demand chasing too few goods" version, with the Keynesian throwing the causal burden on shifts in investment and government spending and the classical emphasizing the impact of increases in the supply of money, whatever their origin.

In an important variant of the Keynesian model, which in recent years has become extremely popular with both laymen and academics, the cause of much of our recent inflation has been attributed to *cost-push* forces. There are two principal elements to cost-push forces:

a) The price expectations of businessmen.
b) The price expectations of (organized) wage earners.

The general idea is that workers and their bosses collectively agree, in the course of negotiating a wage-price structure, on the degree of inflation. Workers, for their part, press for higher wages, partly on the expectation of inflation; and businessmen agree, in turn, in terms of what they can give up and in terms of how fast they expect prices (and their own product prices) to rise. Other causes are involved, also, of a more mechanical sort: the main one in the worker-management nexus is the "purchasing power clause" in existing wage contracts, which establishes an automatic link between prices and wages.

Unions are often singled out as the prime element in all of this; but, in fact, a union demand for higher wages would lead, ceteris paribus, to a redistribution of income rather than to inflation; thus, other factors are required if unions are to be blamed for inflation. One of these, often adduced by the Keynesians, is that since downward shifts in wages (and hence prices) are impossible—since we can only adjust upward—a kind of ratchet is set up so that what would otherwise work out on average to a zero rate of inflation works out to a positive rate. The downward adjustment of prices which is frustrated by union action must show up somewhere, of course, and it shows up (or tends to show up) in unemployment. This raises another problem, because the monetary authority will react to the rise in unemployment.

Even the ratchet, at least in our world, is incapable of explaining the persistent rise in prices we have experienced. In fact, no inflation, we can assert, can persist without a *validation* by the monetary mechanism. Validation is an idea which accepts the essence of the Keynesian causal mechanism by reinterpreting it in monetary terms; it is, however, a reinterpretation which brings out some new points. In particular, if wage contracts are the problem, then, as unemployment rises, the Federal Reserve, in responding to its mandate from Congress, will expand the money supply to attack the problem. This will validate the inflationary pressure which would have been "self-correcting" as the labor market found some way to absorb the unemployed workers. It follows that increases in investment and in government spending—indeed, in net foreign spending[5]—will have validated effects on the price level if the Federal Reserve is "alert" enough.

7.5 THE CAUSES OF INFLATION IN THE UNDERDEVELOPED WORLD

Inflation has been somewhat more obvious in underdeveloped countries, and, accordingly, there is an extensive debate—parallel

---

[5] This is claimed to be the case with Germany in recent years. Leland B. Yeager, "The German Struggle Against Imported Inflation," *International Monetary Relations* (New York: Harper & Row, © 1966), chap. 23.

to that of section 7.3.3—concerning its causes. In point of fact, Keynesians become "structuralists" and classicals become "monetarists," and roughly the same essential points are made. But the force and specific nature of the causes is different because, on the one hand, money production is often an essential fund-raising activity of the central government and, on the other, there are few strong labor unions in underdeveloped countries.

7.5.1 Monetary Factors

We pointed out in Chapter 4 that money creation was a revenue-earning activity for the "producer" of money; in underdeveloped countries, this revenue production is often—necessarily, it is said—in the hands of the government. That is to say, in underdeveloped countries, we often find all money-creating activities either directly in the hands of the treasury or in an official central bank, which also holds all private deposits. Clearly, when other types of taxation are difficult because of the low level of literacy and the high level of evasion, avoidance, and corruption, appropriating the revenues from money creation is an important matter for a central government. We may even refer to it as "taxing idle balances," except that we realize that the tax will not succeed unless individuals are willing to hold the balances, in real terms.

People's willingness to hold money balances is embodied in the velocity term of the equation of exchange; in order to state the argument more clearly, let us repeat the dynamic form of this equation (first described in Chapter 6), along with some numbers by way of example:

$$\frac{\Delta M}{M} + \frac{\Delta V}{V} = \frac{\Delta P}{P} + \frac{\Delta y}{y} \qquad 4\% \text{ revenues} \qquad (7\text{--}1)$$
$$6\% - 1\% = 2\% + 3\%$$

In Equation 7–1 we see a 6 percent increase in the money supply, of which 1 percent is willingly absorbed (the 1 percent fall in the velocity of money); 3 percent services real income; and only 2 percent is washed away in inflation. Thus, the government's proceeds amount to 4 percent (of the money stock). If the government wished to obtain more revenue, it might step up the rate of production of new money, as in Equation 7–2.

$$\frac{\Delta M}{M} + \frac{\Delta V}{V} = \frac{\Delta P}{P} + \frac{\Delta y}{y} \qquad 4\% \text{ revenues} \qquad (7\text{–}2)$$
$$10\% - 1\% = 6\% + 3\%$$

But in this example, it actually fails to gain revenue, because the increases in the money stock are assumed to be eaten away by inflation.

Now suppose the rapid inflation causes people to expect inflation and consequently causes velocity to rise, independently, as it were. Witness Equation 7–3.

$$\frac{\Delta M}{M} + \frac{\Delta V}{V} = \frac{\Delta P}{P} + \frac{\Delta y}{y} \qquad 1\% \text{ revenues} \qquad (7\text{–}3)$$
$$10\% + 2\% = 9\% + 3\%$$

In this case the government's take, in money terms, actually has been reduced to 1 percent; individuals, by spending faster, are servicing most of the needs of the rising real national income and thus are depriving the government of its revenues. The reaction of the government to its loss of revenues is critical here. With only the money taxing power, the government, in this situation, might actually decide to step up the rate of production of nominal money; if they do, and if velocity continues to respond in a perverse fashion, they might end up as in Equation 7–4 or, for that matter, as in Equation 7–5, where the game is really up since revenues have turned negative.

$$\frac{\Delta M}{M} + \frac{\Delta V}{V} = \frac{\Delta P}{P} + \frac{\Delta y}{y} \qquad \text{no revenues} \qquad (7\text{–}4)$$
$$15\% + 3\% = 15\% + 3\%$$

$$\frac{\Delta M}{M} + \frac{\Delta V}{V} = \frac{\Delta P}{P} + \frac{\Delta y}{y} \qquad \text{negative revenues} \qquad (7\text{–}5)$$
$$80\% + 10\% = 87\% + 3\%$$

Probably, in fact, the government can count on lags in the process giving it some revenues; and if it is faster than individuals, it may even be able to keep its share constant as prices run away— it is, essentially, only a matter of adding zeros onto the medium of exchange—but what must happen eventually is a drop in the real rate of growth as financial chaos develops. Further, we have illustrated one important cause of hyperinflation: an irrational increase in the money stock.[6]

7.5.2 The Structuralist View

All of the foregoing has concentrated on the monetarist's point of view; and the monetarist's analysis is extremely helpful in cases in which an inflationary tax is known to have been used. But how does the Keynesian view translate into the framework of underdeveloped countries? In our survey of the situation in advanced countries, we noted that labor unions could produce inflation from the cost-push side and that increases in real demand could directly push up prices as resources are diverted from other uses. We do not observe powerful unions in underdeveloped countries, so what can stand in their place?

What is usually argued is that an underdeveloped country, possessed with all sorts of rigidities due to ignorance, poor transportation, shortage of skilled workers, and the like, begins to press forward. In the process, scarce workers are called from the agricultural sector to the rapidly growing sector at ever rising rates, rates which contribute directly to the rise in prices as they are passed on by businessmen. Thus, inflation is a result of growth and, more particularly, a result of pressure on fundamental bottlenecks. In dualistic underdeveloped countries, to pursue the point a little further, one might even find it necessary, in order to persuade workers to leave the farm, to pay workers by their average product rather than by their marginal product. This would come about if all workers in a farm household are paid some average amount, whether they are working or not. Usually, one supposes, the marginal product is lower than the average product, so some further push to prices can be presumed. We have, in other words, substituted several kinds of rigidities—specific to underdeveloped countries—in place of union pressures in the argument of section 7.4.

As the country's rate of inflation picks up, it begins to lose its export markets and, consequently, the foreign exchange to pay

---

[6] Hyperinflation is also referred to as "runaway" inflation; it is important to realize that hyperinflation seems to require a runaway money stock.

for imports. This forces the country, if it is to grow even at the same pace as it was, to develop the domestic import-competing industries more intensively, and further accelerates the bidding up of resource prices. Thus, we cannot have growth without inflation; and if we tried to *reduce* the money supply to attack inflation, we would merely generate unemployment and a general credit shortage. The role of money, though, would be passive.

We noted above that cost-push forces in developed countries had to be validated, or there would simply be redistribution among the factors and no particular reason for prices to rise. This is also true in underdeveloped countries. We may suppose, for example, that the government simply tries to keep its share of the revenues constant, as structuralist forces begin to press on the price level; or we may suppose an active monetary policy exists to contain unemployment. At any rate, whatever the structuralist "force" we have in mind, an increase in the money supply must occur to validate the inflationary pressures. Please be careful to note what is being said here. The structuralist causes of inflation are nonmonetary; and the quantity of money, which is associated with the price rise, is only associated passively. Note, too, that we emphasize that it is not the quantity of money which must be attacked in this situation but the rigidities themselves. The two views are genuinely different; and, we cannot doubt, both are relevant, perhaps to all countries at all times.[7]

7.6   A POSITIVE ROLE FOR MONEY IN DEVELOPMENT

All of the preceding material in this chapter, because it has concentrated on seemingly inexorable causes, has an air of the pessimistic about it. At best, we seem to be saying (*a*) that money can remain neutral, and (*b*) that aside from being a source of revenue to hard-pressed governments, its neutrality is guaranteed by both the poor articulation of financial markets and the primarily noneconomic or structural causes of economic events. This posi-

---

[7] One reason it is hard to tell them apart in practice is that playing the inflationary tax game practically requires the government to attempt to conceal its operations, for, as we noted, if people come to expect the inflation accurately, or, even to overanticipate, the game is up, except when the government is quicker. Actually, one suspects, this is where things have gotten to in some underdeveloped countries, where the balances of rather poor (and slow) people seem to bear the tax.

tion, indeed, is far too strong; and, as we shall see, there is considerable scope for an independent role for the monetary authority in assisting growth and development.

7.6.1 A Model of Development

Let us take, as our model of development, that developed by W. W. Rostow out of the classical tradition.[8] This model, which identifies five arbitrary stages in the growth process, is illustrated

FIGURE 7–1
THE STAGES OF ECONOMIC GROWTH

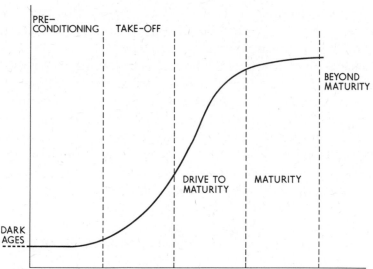

in Figure 7–1. In the first active stage, that of preconditioning, a society is altered by social and economic processes—for example, by "cultural revolutions," education, and the like—until it is perched as it were, on the brink of rapid growth. The building up of these qualitative aspects is referred to as the building up of spread mechanisms or, more particularly, market mechanisms, until the society is sensitive to cultural or other shocks. Then, some sharp shock, perhaps an invention like the Bessemer con-

---

[8] W. W. Rostow, *The Stages of Economic Growth* (Cambridge, England: Cambridge University Press, 1960).

verter, in a basic industry, sets up an imbalance in the structure; and, because the shock occurs in a basic industry—i.e., an industry which is on net resource-creating rather than resource-destroying—the effects begin to spill over into the rest of the economy. The shock takes effect if the spread mechanisms are strong—here we see that spread mechanisms are really links between sectors—and, one hopes, with various multiplier and accelerator effects operating, some kind of sustained economic growth might occur. All of this is suggested in Figure 7–1, in which the later stages are relevant primarily to the more advanced societies.

We now see that there are two features of this framework which are particularly useful to us in our search for the potential role of money in such countries. That is, money can operate as a spread mechanism—essentially qualitatively—and money can operate as a leading sector. To put matters more explicitly, we can think of a positive development strategy in which the government builds up the institutions, strengthening the economy by establishing confidence in the monetary unit, encouraging the development of financial intermediaries, and the like, which are "spread" activities; and we can envisage shocks being administered to the economy through direct increases of the money supply. The latter, I would guess, has been more used in underdeveloped countries than the former. Let us look more closely into the possibilities.

7.6.2   Money as a Spread Mechanism

Let us assume, for the reasons we have already stated, that our typical underdeveloped sector is a dualistic one and that in the undeveloped part the climate is typically found to be inhospitable to economic growth and development. Whatever keeps the undeveloped sector from merging with the developed, there are two characteristics of the undeveloped sector which deserve special attention here: agriculture is generally of the subsistence variety, and no economic surplus exists, to speak of. The discussion must begin with careful definitions of the terms to be used, particularly since we are going to make a somewhat unorthodox recommendation. The general aim of the next few paragraphs will be to remind ourselves of the properties of money which are particularly relevant to the problem of development.

A medium of exchange, you will recall, is anything which facilitates exchange, whether real or financial, without itself being a part of the exchange. Two types of media of exchange are especially important in the economic process: organized markets and money. By organizing markets, for example by bringing together the various agents into some central location, we permit exchange to occur more rapidly, and development resources (especially time) are saved in the bargain. By providing a hand-to-hand currency, which individuals can obtain for their products or services and use to obtain other products and services, we see that individuals' time is saved: time which is then available to be consumed—perhaps directly, in the form of leisure—or used productively. Both of these media cost resources to create, of course; the former requires some physical facilities and communications equipment, and the latter involves the costs of production of the means of payment to the producer and waiting costs (costs of foregone consumption) to the users.

One significant characteristic of the underdeveloped world is the comparative absence of both of these media and, additionally, the absence of financial stores of value. Money (currency and demand deposits) can serve as a store of value. But in developing nations, particularly those enduring rapid falls in the value of money because of inflation, it is safe to say that the uses of money in the backward sectors make the existing stock of cash purely "money on the wing," which is not particularly useful even as a measure of value, primarily because changes in money values are either unperceived or considered irrelevant. In fact, the growth of a firmly held money stock and its substitutes, a stock which is also a reliable standard of value, is probably a necessary condition to development of that sector. The principal reason that we should consider money as vital in this sector is that the task of creating an effective entrepreneurial system must involve driving a wedge between saving and investment by the creation of marketable stores of value. The gains from such an effort are clear: savings will be increased and, because of the marketability feature, savings will tend to find their way into the most productive uses rather than into the safest or most convenient uses. Such a view of things leads directly to more detailed prescriptions.

The development problem on the specific level is that of providing a monetary form in which savings (often small in size) can be held with confidence. A clearly related problem is that of having the form available as a medium of exchange, for we are discussing the creation of a credit—that is, confidence—arrangement, where no such tradition exists. The broad lines of the ultimate institutional arrangements are simple enough. In fact, for the prototype "savings and loan" institutions which might be suggested, there probably ought to be purchasing power arrangements to protect small balances. In practice, small, dispersable units like the mutual savings banks in the United States could be created, and the proviso added that balances be readjusted whenever there are price level changes. Naturally enough, real development resources will be involved here in two ways: directly, in the form of building up the banking and financial sector, and indirectly, in seeing that the real resources released by the saving decision find their way into projects which are desirable from the point of view of the retarded sector. This, clearly, is true development strategy.

What has been said so far is positively directed: media of exchange are resources and can be created by the government in anticipation of the need for them as part of the preconditioning task. But the question of the role of inflation in development remains. To begin with, we must be careful to recall that the exchange price of money is unity over the price level $(1/P)$ and that money, on account of its unique position in the markets (it is the only item exchanged in all markets) has a unique property— an increase in its price (decrease in the price level) is the same thing as an increase in its quantity, given economic activity. Here is the point at which the most serious shortcoming of the causes-of-inflation debate is seen: another avenue for increasing the money stock has been ignored, that of deflation. The advantage seems clear; if money is created in this fashion (or any other), we not only have the money but, in addition, have increased the likelihood that money substitutes, in which advanced countries are so rich, will become acceptable as stores of value. The difference in strategy is that between the carrot and the stick; the carrot, in this case, is an extra reward to holders of financial instruments provided by the fall in the price level.[9] We will see that a similar point can be made about the use of money as a leading sector.

7.6.3 Money as a Leading Sector

Actually, in the preceding section we have put emphasis on the quality of money; it was especially important, for the pre-conditioning we found important in the development process, that people's confidence in the medium of exchange be maintained. In this section I want to consider the problems of an already pre-conditioned society which is poised on the brink of a take-off. The question, then, concerns the potential role of money in this take-off.

The basic point follows from the definition of a leading sector; such a sector, we noted, was both fundamental to other sectors and capable of generating spill-over into other sectors, involving them all in its success. Clearly, it seems to me, the monetary sector is especially well placed for this role; in particular, if one is able to increase the real stock of money, he is creating wealth (capital) of the most general sort. Indeed, it is clear, given the low cost of this operation, that the authorities in underdeveloped countries should always see that the rate of growth of monetary resources is at its maximum, whether this maximum is achieved by inflation or deflation of the general price level.

Let us revert to the example of a growing economy and, again, use an example to fix ideas; the equation of exchange in its dynamic form will again serve as our model:

$$\frac{\Delta M}{M} + \frac{\Delta V}{V} = \frac{\Delta P}{P} + \frac{\Delta y}{y} \qquad (7-6)$$

In Table 7–2 three different strategies are collected; each of these has the same growth rate of income (in nominal terms), but not all of these strategies are equally feasible. Further, all of these strategies have different ultimate consequences for real economic growth. The balance will probably depend on the particular in-stitutional context of the situation; even so, there are certain general points we can make.

---

[9] This fall can be effected by keeping the rate of growth of the money stock below, rather than above, the general rate of growth of the economy.

If all were equally likely, we would prefer the third state because of the beneficial effect a falling price level would have on the balance of payments; you should note that balance of payments problems are a persistent nuisance to underdeveloped countries. There is another case in which the third choice might be likely, and that is the case when it is impossible to generate savings through inflation. Suppose that real money balances could be increased by 2 percent through *increases* in the quantity of money, but that for some reason any increases faster than 2 percent would be accompanied by a rise in velocity, as in our examples earlier in the chapter. It might even be true that the *only* way

TABLE 7–2
THREE GROWTH STRATEGIES

	$\frac{\Delta P}{P}$	$\frac{\Delta V}{V}$	$\frac{\Delta y}{y}$	$\frac{\Delta M}{M}$
Steady prices..................	0	0	3%	3%
Gently rising prices............	1%	0	3%	4%
Gently falling prices...........	−1%	0	3%	2%

to get the rate of growth up to 3 percent would be to increase the quantity of money by means of a lowering of the price level; this proposition, again, flows out of the psychology of the carrot versus the stick.

There are problems, of course. One is the problem of price rigidity which figures so importantly in the Keynesian literature. The idea is that a price decline is simply not a symmetrical case to a price increase—as is the argument here—but a special case. In fact, in advanced countries, the Keynesians argue, there is a bias toward upward prices, and unions advance wages but will not accept wage decreases (we noted other contractual arrangements which also work in this direction). Of course, unions are not strong in underdeveloped countries; but in their place we find institutionally and culturally rigid prices, so to some extent this is a potential factor.

But we need not belabor the point. The generalization that there is *some* appropriate rate of growth of the money stock, depending on the institutional structure and its rate of change, is clearly a sensible one. This range is all the way from a fairly rapid rate to a negative one, and individual development strategy will take it into consideration in the context of a leading sector.

7.7 MONETARY POLICY IN UNDERDEVELOPED COUNTRIES

Most of the techniques of monetary policy we have discussed throughout this book are not relevant, at least in the exact form we gave them, in underdeveloped countries. We will not, in this section, discuss any actual efforts which have been made to implement a monetary policy in this world, but we will make some general observations. The first of these is to emphasize that we have been discussing monetary policies for both growth and development which have involved direct manipulation by the authorities of their monetary liabilities. In this section we turn to a consideration of anticyclical policy in underdeveloped countries, a topic which has been relatively slighted in the literature.

Let us assume that there is a private banking sector in what follows, for without it, control over the nominal money supply is simply an automatic operation. We can then assert that the principal difference between developed and underdeveloped countries is the lack of an effective capital market and, accordingly, a lack of capital market instruments. In particular, especially in those cases in which the rate of inflation has been rapid and/or variable, no one will be willing to hold "paper" debt (debt denominated in the local currency unit), although there will be no shortage of potential issuers. Neither the government nor individuals will have this ability; so, presumably, those monetary operations which require that there be financial instruments will be impossible. The chief casualty in the list of instruments of monetary policy is the rediscounting function, which could be replaced by direct lending—although finding collateral, presumably nonfinancial, would be difficult.

Open market operations, if they are legally defined as the buying and selling of bonds denominated in the domestic currency, will be impossible, of course. Although there is no purely economic reason why open market operations cannot be given a wider scope (even, if necessary, to the point of dealing in stocks of commodities), the authorities will find it inconvenient to stockpile real resources in order to be able to reduce the money supply at a later date; so we may assume that there is little scope here. We may note in passing that active open market operations are conducted only in a few of the advanced countries anyway, primarily, if the official literature is to be trusted, on account of the thinness of capital markets. Even in the United States we hear about the "thinness" of the long-term market. Thinness is considered to be a disadvantage because it means that there will be sizable interest rate effects, which, in turn, may induce substantial allocative effects of an arbitrary nature.

The main monetary techniques available in underdeveloped countries appear to be connected either with changes in government accounts at the central bank or with changes in minimum reserve requirements. The latter work best if commercial banks stay fully loaned up, an assumption which is unlikely if there are frequent changes in reserve requirements. The latter is also a powerful technique, especially if the multiplier is relatively high. The former—the manipulation of the treasury's account—in comparison with the latter, involves the treasury explicitly; and because it has its own fiscal operations to consider, the treasury is unlikely to participate willingly in anticyclical policy.

We may conclude, then, that there is some scope for monetary policy, particularly in changing reserve requirements, but that the techniques available are not the most sensitive ones. In particular, the loss of open market operations is a serious matter. Of course, we should add, there has to be a central bank and some data collection, as well as a legal responsibility for business cycles, a set of presumptions which actually rules out a large number of underdeveloped countries which have not even begun to worry seriously about cycles. We might note that the central bank will also have to be free of the treasury, a highly unlikely circumstance in the case in which "inflationary finance" is an important tax.

7.8 DISCUSSION QUESTIONS

1. Why do we link the general problem of development with the problem of financial development? Is there any sense in which financial sophistication is a necessary—or even an important—element in the development process?

2. We said in Chapter 1 that one disadvantage to our using market data is that such data tend to be generated in equilibrium. In this chapter we seem to have noted that the converse can be a problem. Can you reconcile these two views?

3. The "extended family system" is a kind of home-made social insurance scheme, but it is one which can frustrate the efficient working of the economic system. Explain. How might one keep the desirable features of the system yet permit human and physical capital to flow readily between sectors of the economy? Is there a monetary aspect to this problem?

4. Give an economic explanation of why a steady rate of inflation of 6 percent per year might be better than a rate which is variable, but fluctuates between 1 and 3 percent. Should we take this into account when criticizing the "excessive" rates of inflation in underdeveloped countries?

5. Describe the difficulties which exist in going from the microeconomic statement that a union demand leads to a rise in a particular product price to the (essentially) macroeconomic statement that unions can and do cause inflation. Are price expectations involved in your answer?

6. Actually, the example of hyperinflation in the text is close to an explanation of most of the hyperinflations we have observed, although the motives have varied from situation to situation. What other objectives—in addition to taxing idle money balances—might a monetary authority have in perpetrating a hyperinflation? Does the effect of the hyperinflation vary with the financial sophistication of the community?

7. Part of the dichotomization of this chapter is a *defined* rather than an actual dichotomization; for example, we made a distinction between growth and development strategy. Explain in what respects there are simply *degrees* of difference between the two strategies. That is, what would constitute "growth" strategy for an unpreconditioned society and a "spread" strategy for a growing (advanced) society?

8. Explain why, when we argue that money is not an effective store of value in an undeveloped sector, we do not mean to imply that it is not a store of value. What do we mean then? In answering, describe how such money balances arise in this sector.

9. I have emphasized the role of deflation in underdeveloped countries in order to focus clearly on the problem of developing a strategy which helps the backward sectors of such countries. Discuss the difficulties inherent in actually following such a policy.

Do businessmen's expectations get involved? Why do some argue that a gently rising price level might be a desirable strategy, if feasible?

10. Explain why countries with relatively underdeveloped capital markets are not necessarily underdeveloped. Give some examples. In what respects does your answer depend on what sort of anti-cyclical monetary policy has been followed?

7.9 FURTHER READING

DORRANCE, GRAEME S. "The Instruments of Monetary Policy in Countries without Highly Developed Capital Markets," International Monetary Fund *Staff Papers*, Vol. 12, 1965.

GUDIN, EUGENIO. "Inflation in Latin America," *Inflation* (ed. D. C. Hague). London: Macmillan & Co., Ltd., for the International Economic Association, 1962.

MEIER, GERALD. *Leading Issues in Development Economics*, chap. 4. New York: Oxford University Press, 1964.

PORTER, RICHARD C. "The Promotion of the 'Banking Habit' and Economic Development," *The Journal of Development Studies*, Vol. 2, No. 3 (July 1966).

WECKSTEIN, R. S. "Money and Inflation in a Dual Economy," *Social Research*, Vol. 33, No. 1 (Spring 1966).

| Chapter 8 | # A SURVEY OF AMERICAN MONETARY POLICY FROM 1914 |

8.1 INTRODUCTION

While we have had some forms of monetary policy prior to the inception of the Federal Reserve in 1914, the main events in the history of our monetary policy begin at that point. The most exciting period, of course, runs from 1928 to 1938, and the discussion of the events of that period will be the main topic of this chapter. Even so, there have been other incidents from which we can draw conclusions in the more peaceful periods before and after that disaster, and we will not neglect the successes even though we will emphasize the more dramatic failures.

I am going to spend a little time, before beginning the survey of recent events, describing the situation prior to 1914; the main reason for this is that such a discussion makes clear the objectives the Federal Reserve System was designed to achieve; after all, the Federal Reserve System had the specific purpose of correcting some of the alleged shortcomings of its predecessor. Indeed, it seems to me that only under these conditions—that we know its aims—can we come to understand its actions completely. You will see that the Federal Reserve's actions were often peculiar when judged by the framework laid down in Chapters 1 through 6.

8.2 THE AMERICAN MONETARY SYSTEM FROM THE CIVIL WAR UNTIL 1914

In 1863, in the National Currency Act, the National Banking System was created. Prior to that, commercial banks were only chartered by states. This system had two main flaws: first, banks were often poorly run; and, second, even with the best of intentions, the right of individual banks to print currency was an invitation both to chaos and to the slow development of the financial system. The National Banking System, accordingly, had two purposes:

a)   To increase the amount of currency in circulation, on a once-for-all basis.
b)   To create a system of national—as opposed to state—banks, which could enjoy the privileges of currency issue and which could be closely regulated.

Banks did not exactly rush into the fold, because the tight regulations were considered repressive; so in 1866, to make the system operative, Congress taxed state bank notes out of existence. From then until 1914, the two types of banks—state and national—existed side by side, with the national banks showing a much better record.

With both uniform currency and a more closely regulated banking system, one would have thought that the problem of financial crises—which had been especially severe in 1837 and 1857—would have been materially alleviated; but there were severe pinches in 1873, 1884, 1893, and 1907, with the monetary system most heavily involved in 1873 and 1907. It probably was not the fault of individual banks that they often had to suspend; the financial panics of the period can mainly be traced to the failure of the system to provide an elastic currency, defined in the modern sense. It is true that there was a notion of elasticity in the National Currency Act; approximately, an elastic currency was judged to be

> one which expanded and contracted with the needs of trade, thus insuring the neutrality of money.

Indeed, this definition persisted well into the 1920's and is, no doubt, the proper definition to attach to the term "elastic currency" in the Federal Reserve Act. The problem is that this definition does not recognize the distinction between money and high-powered money; the consequence is that the supposed neutrality would not come about and that changes in the stock of currency so supplied would tend to accentuate the business cycle. Multiplier effects would be the source of the accentuation.

An elastic currency, as we would now define it, is

> one which can expand or contract to meet changes in the public's taste for currency versus demand deposits.

Indeed, it was the failure to provide elasticity in this sense—that is, the failure to provide currency when there were general runs on commercial banks—which was one of the principal defects of the pre-1914 banking system. It is important to realize that the actions of the public were not really irrational; they were instructed that they had a right to substitute currency for deposits at any time. In fact, Congress had made it impossible for the promise to be honored for everyone at once, since the quantity of currency could not readily expand without congressional action; further, such action was rarely adequate. Of course the "power" of high-powered money is what is really critical; that is, the size of the banking multiplier measures the potential impact of a $1 switch. Thus, in February 1873 the banking multiplier stood at a modest 2.07, but in June 1907 it was 4.12; in the latter case, a dollar of high-powered money "produced" four dollars of money.[1]

One other feature of the National Banking System is important in considering the Federal Reserve Act: while the scheme had a system of minimum reserve requirements, it was not an effective scheme. The system was differentiated by type of bank, as is the Federal Reserve System; but, unlike the Federal Reserve System, there was no provision for either drawing on or increasing reserves in an emergency. Commercial banks, since they could not cash in reserves, had two main options left to them:

a) They could hold idle excess reserves in cash form.

b) They could suspend whenever there was a panic, reopening after the panic was over.

---

[1] These results both here and later are the result of using the expression $(C/D + 1)/(C/D + R/D)$ and the data given in Milton Friedman and Anna J. Schwartz, *A Monetary History of the United States, 1867–1960* (Princeton, N.J.: Princeton University Press, 1963), Table B–3.

By December 1907, this multiplier had dropped to 3.60. That is, the multiplier itself changes over the cycle. In October 1928, the multiplier stood at 6.58 and remained at this level until the banking system began to collapse in 1931.

The advantage of the second alternative to commercial banks was that interest earnings were not forgone; and, not surprisingly, a significant number of banks actually did prefer this alternative.

8.3 THE EARLY YEARS OF THE FEDERAL RESERVE SYSTEM: 1914 TO 1929

As Table 8–1 indicates, the Federal Reserve came to life in a period of fairly high unemployment;[2] this did not become a con-

TABLE 8–1
UNEMPLOYMENT AS A PERCENTAGE OF THE
LABOR FORCE, 1914–29

Date	Unemployment
1914	8.0
1915	9.7
1916	4.8
1917	4.8
1918	1.4
1919	2.3
1920	4.0
1921	11.9
1922	7.6
1923	3.2
1924	5.5
1925	4.0
1926	1.9
1927	4.1
1928	4.4
1929	3.2

SOURCE: Stanley Lebergott, "Annual Estimates of Unemployment in the United States, 1900–1954," *The Measurement and Behavior of Unemployment* (National Bureau of Economic Research) (Princeton, N.J.: Princeton University Press, 1957), pp. 215–16.

cern to them, since after 1915 war prosperity pushed unemployment to a low 1.4 percent of the labor force. In this period, then, 1921 stands out as a significant year because a short—but sharp—depression is visible, unemployment having reached almost 12 percent of the labor force. The war, which seems to have produced the main low point of the unemployment cycle, also influenced the peak in 1921, largely through the financial system; in fact

---

[2] We will use the percentage of the labor force unemployed as our measure of the general level of economic activity.

in 1919 a bottled-up inflation burst over the economy, exerting pressure on the Federal Reserve to act.

The Federal Reserve did not respond until well into 1920; and they have been widely criticized both for not moving to stem the inflationary tide sooner and, after the recession had turned to depression, for not removing the controls sooner, thus prolonging and deepening the general depression of 1921 and 1922. Both charges seem valid when one looks at the timing of the Federal Reserve's responses, for the last step of the interest rate pinch was put on in June 1920, just after the price bubble had burst, by means of a rise in the rediscount rate to 7 percent. The rediscount rate was not dropped—and then only to 6.5 percent—until May 1921; this was 16 months after the cyclical peak and only two months before the trough. In fact, the fall in prices and in the money stock during the depression was the second largest in our recorded monetary history[3] and leaves one with little doubt that monetary events can influence the rest of the economy, especially when the money stock is aimed in the wrong direction.

It is just not clear why the Federal Reserve did not move against the price boom earlier,[4] or in a more measured way, but their decisive actions to prolong the depression have been explained. The usual view of the latter is that they were constrained from increasing the money supply by the 40 percent gold backing of currency required; indeed, since the gold backing had fallen to 42.2 percent in May 1920 and did not rise appreciably for the rest of the year, this might have been a constraint.[5] If this did operate to limit the authorities' actions, it is a defect of the system rather than of its managers; but it is also possible that Federal Reserve officials felt that taking an active interest in the stabilization of the economy was outside their policy domain. Indeed, it has been suggested that they might even have regarded a little deflation as a necessary purge for the system;[6] this approach to monetary management is by no means extinct even today.

---

[3] 1929–33 is larger, but not faster, per unit of time.

[4] It has been suggested that personalities had something to do with these events; from 1928 to 1934 personalities again appeared to be influential.

[5] Some Federal Reserve banks were actually "insolvent" and had to borrow from each other.

[6] Elmus R. Wicker, "A Reconsideration of Federal Reserve Policy During the 1920–21 Depression," *Journal of Economic History*, Vol. 26, No. 2 (June 1966).

8.4 THE 1930'S

There are actually two interesting subperiods in the Great Depression period for the study of banking history. The first of these
is not the period of the crash itself but the period from 1930
through 1933 when the Federal Reserve, with a helpful assist from
the new President, seemed to be following a perverse domestic
monetary and banking policy. In this case some of the explanation
will be seen to lie in the personal makeup of the directors as well

TABLE 8–2
UNEMPLOYMENT AS A PERCENTAGE OF THE
LABOR FORCE, 1929–41

Date	Unemployment
1929	3.2
1930	8.9
1931	15.9
1932	23.6
1933	24.9
1934	21.7
1935	20.1
1936	17.0
1937	14.3
1938	19.0
1939	17.2
1940	14.6
1941	9.9

SOURCE: Stanley Lebergott, "Annual Estimates of
Unemployment in the United States, 1900–1954," *The
Measurement and Behavior of Unemployment* (National
Bureau of Economic Research) (Princeton, N.J.:
Princeton University Press, 1957), pp. 215–16.

as in explicit policy decisions. The second subperiod is that of
the short, but sharp, recession of 1937–38, which might have been
precipitated by the doubling of reserve requirements which occurred immediately prior to it. These periods are also apparent
in Table 8–2, which continues the unemployment data from Table
8–1. What is important about these two periods is that to some
extent the difficulties we experienced, including the huge increase
in unemployment, can be attributed to poorly conceived monetary
policy. It is important that we know—if we are to have a sensible
view of, and policy for, our economic well-being—whether our
economic system is subject to wild fluctuations in real magnitudes,

which must be tempered by the prudent decisions of our managers if we are to survive, or whether it is the managers themselves who have made big ones out of little ones. It may seem surprising, but the issue is still not settled.

8.4.1 The Early Years of the Depression

The first thing to notice about the period from 1929 to 1934 is that the quantity of money fell quite drastically; the figures appear in Table 8–3. In fact, the money supply fell almost 25 percent in the four years from March 1929 to March 1933, with the latter representing the low point of the series. Now one of the problems with the literal interpretation of these figures is that since trade had declined considerably, the demand for money had

TABLE 8–3
THE MONEY SUPPLY AND ITS DETERMINANTS, 1929–34

Date	Money Supply ($ Billions)	H	$\frac{D}{R}$	$\frac{D}{C}$
March 1929	26.3	7.15	13.02	10.84
June 1929	26.2	7.10	13.16	10.74
September 1929	26.4	7.08	13.07	11.12
December 1929	26.4	6.98	13.24	11.07
March 1930	26.3	6.96	13.07	11.42
June 1930	25.3	6.91	12.90	11.31
September 1930	25.0	6.83	12.97	11.41
December 1930	24.9	7.12	12.14	10.57
March 1931	24.8	7.09	12.39	10.37
June 1931	23.9	7.30	11.67	9.66
September 1931	23.4	7.50	11.42	8.54
December 1931	21.9	7.74	10.46	7.11
March 1932	21.1	7.54	11.09	6.54
June 1932	20.4	7.79	10.44	5.95
September 1932	20.2	7.90	9.82	5.87
December 1932	20.3	8.03	9.13	6.05
March 1933	19.0	8.41	8.42	4.44
June 1933	19.2	7.94	8.39	5.08
September 1933	19.2	8.09	7.80	5.27
December 1933	19.8	8.30	7.50	5.37
March 1934	20.7	9.00	6.23	6.09
June 1934	21.1	9.26	6.09	6.21

NOTE: Deposits include time deposits.

SOURCE: Money supply (currency plus demand deposits) from Milton Friedman and Anna J. Schwartz, *A Monetary History of the United States, 1867–1960* (Princeton, N.J.: Princeton University Press, 1963), pp. 712–14. *H*, *D/R*, and *D/C* from *ibid.*, pp. 803–804.

obviously fallen, as well as the supply. One consequence, is that the stock of money in existence, determined as it is by supply and demand, would naturally be smaller—that is to say, we can expect the money stock series to conform positively with the business cycle. But since data corrected for the change in demand do not exist for this period, we will have to live with the problem and see what might have caused the observed decline.

The first question concerns which of the three determinants most influenced the fall in the money stock: D/C, D/R, or H. The last three columns in Table 8–3 show the values these determinants took in the period. We see that from March 1929 to March 1931, D/C did not decline appreciably, a reflection of the fact that the public was not panicked but that banks, as shown by the fall in D/R, were requiring more reserves per dollar of deposits than before and that the Federal Reserve was not offsetting this change. The last can be concluded because H, the indicator of Federal Reserve policy, remained fairly constant (it actually declined in the middle of the period).

One might wonder why the Federal Reserve allowed the stock of high-powered money to fall in the year and a half after the crash of 1929. Several explanations have been offered. One view, as explained by Harold Barger, is that there was considerable conflict within the system, with the result that the most that could be agreed upon was a mild tendency toward "cheap money" (lower interest rates) without any explicit policy toward quantities by means of open market operations.

As the recession in business took hold, considerable disagreement developed within the system as to the usefulness of cheap money in stemming the decline. In general, the New York Bank under Harrison pressed for cheaper money, and the Board rather reluctantly went along. . . . Despite these reasons for hesitation, the System's reaction to declining business was to cheapen money, and the cheapening, as measured by rediscount rates, was considerable.[7]

Cheaper money, to the laymen who ran our finances, need not have meant more abundant. Further, we are probably not too far off when we note that the Federal Reserve seems to have fol-

---

[7] Harold Barger, *The Management of Money* (Chicago: Rand McNally & Co., 1964), pp. 97–98.

lowed market interest rates downward, so that the interest rate they set was always too high—although falling—in the sense of being above rather than below the equilibrium rate. Whether conditions are tight or not cannot be judged from the fall in the rate, but only in relation to the demand for funds; but there seems to have been little recognition of this fact at the time. As Friedman and Schwartz note,

> This is a striking illustration of the ambiguity of the terms "monetary ease" and "tightness" and of the need stressed above to interpret Federal Reserve actions in the light of all the forces affecting the stock of money and credit conditions. It seems paradoxical to describe as "monetary ease" a policy which permitted the stock of money to decline in fourteen months by a percentage exceeded only four times in the preceding fifty-four years and then only during extremely severe business-cycle contractions.[8]

Further, underscoring Barger's comments on the indecision, Friedman and Schwartz assert the following:

> The stalemate within the system continued, with only minor variations throughout the next year [1931]. Harrison was pressed on the one side by his officers and directors—though less consistently by the directors than in the preceding year—to work for greater easing and larger open market purchases. On the other side, he felt strongly his responsibilities, as Chairman of the Open Market Policy Conference, to carry out loyally the policy adopted by the Conference.[9]

In this case we ought to see fairly clearly why personal values needed to be entered into the policy model of Chapters 5 and 6.

There has been a serious attempt to explain all this apparent inaction as part of a systematic policy followed from 1922 until 1933, when it became untenable. Elmus R. Wicker argues that the Federal Reserve used the rediscount rate to push gold toward Britain (1927) or to attract it toward the United States (1931) depending on international circumstances, and that the authorities were never as naive as Friedman and Schwartz imply in the above quotations.[10] It turns out that the fall in interest rates in the early

---

[8] Friedman and Schwartz, *op. cit.,* p. 375.

[9] *Ibid.,* p. 376.

[10] Elmus R. Wicker, "Federal Reserve Policy 1922–1933: A Reinterpretation," *Journal of Political Economy*, Vol. 73, No. 4 (August 1965).

1930's is consistent with this position, because interest rates were falling in Britain too; all that had to happen in order to attract gold to the United States was for interest rates to fall more slowly in the United States; and this, indeed, happened. We see, as claimed in Chapter 5, the likelihood that international factors were important in Federal Reserve decisions long before such factors were officially mentioned as relevant.[11]

8.4.2 From Recession to Depression, 1930 to 1933

From October 1930 until early 1933 the United States went through the most protracted and severe monetary and financial crisis in its history. There were three great waves of bank failures which spread throughout the country. The first began in October 1930, and in November and December of that year 608 banks closed their doors; the figures for the entire period appear in Table 8–4. In March 1931, partly precipitated by international events, especially bank failures in Europe, a second wave of failures hit the system. This one, in contrast to the first wave, severely affected bankers and depositors; and, as Table 8–4 suggests, the sharp fall in D/R and D/C, which was to continue in the former case until the late 1930's and in the latter case until June 1933, begins at this point. As Friedman and Schwartz note,

Once bitten, twice shy, both depositors and bankers were bound to react more vigorously to any new eruption of bank failures or banking difficulties than they did in the final months of 1930.[12]

Large-scale open market purchases begin in April 1932, a year and a half after the first banking panic; but by then we were deep into the depression, the figure for unemployment standing at 23.6 percent of the labor force for the year 1932. In fact, there was another wave of bank failures beginning late in 1932 which resulted in a series of state bank holidays, beginning in October 1932, which in turn culminated in the nationwide bank holiday of 1933. In the national holiday, beginning on March 6 and lasting until March 13, 14, or 15 depending on the location of the bank, all banks were closed and were not permitted to reopen without

---

[11] We saw in Chapter 5 that official mention of the international objective did not appear in the Federal Reserve's *Purposes and Functions* book until the 1960's.

[12] Friedman and Schwartz, *op. cit.*, p. 314.

TABLE 8–4

COMMERCIAL BANK SUSPENSIONS IN THE UNITED STATES,
1926–40

Date	Number of Suspensions	Deposits Involved ($ Million)
1926	975	260
1927	669	199
1928	498	142
1929	659	231
1930	1,350	837
1931	2,293	1,690
1932	1,453	706
1933	4,000	3,597
1934	61	37
1935	31	14
1936	72	28
1937	82	34
1938	80	58
1939	71	159
1940	48	143
1960	2	30

NOTE: Failures and suspensions are not synonymous, of course, because many banks eventually reopen after a suspension.

SOURCE: Milton Friedman and Anna J. Schwartz, *A Monetary History of the United States, 1867–1960* (Princeton, N.J.: Princeton University Press, 1963), p. 438.

federal or state licenses to do so. Needless to say, this eliminated, for reasons which are far from convincing, a large amount of the money stock. Further, and of more lasting seriousness, there was a permanent fall in the number of banks as a result of the holiday:

More than 5,000 banks still in operation when the holiday was declared did not reopen their doors when it ended, and of these, over 2,000 never did thereafter. . . . The "cure" came close to being worse than the disease.[13]

Again, as in 1920–21, we find our leaders *purging* the system of its *alleged* weaknesses, rather than directly reconstructing it.

When we return to the figures of Table 8–3, we see that panic is indeed writ in the behavior of depositors (the severe fall in D/C) and in the increasing desire of commercial banks to hold excess reserves. The latter are not explicitly identified in the table;

---

[13] *Ibid.*, p. 330.

but it is obvious that with reserve requirements unchanged, a fall in the actual ratio of deposits to reserves held by commercial banks will result in excess reserves, as a matter of arithmetic. The behavior of the stock of high-powered money, while in the correct direction, is woefully inadequate to the task at hand; further, there is the year-and-a-half delay in the beginnings of large-scale open market operations which needs to be explained.

We already have one explanation: the personal disagreements of the early years. But there are other factors, as well, this time centering around the authorities' continued disregard of the rising tide of bank failures; these failures were shown in Table 8–4. Friedman and Schwartz adduce three reasons for the Federal Reserve's disregard of the failures.

a)   Federal Reserve officials felt no responsibility for nonmember banks, which failed more frequently than member banks.

b)   The failures were concentrated among smaller banks which were not influential in policy matters.

c)   The few large banks which failed were thought to have done so due to poor management.

Now the first two factors, if valid, establish some myopia, but the third raises some fundamental issues. Since banks were business firms which could fail, failure was always part of banking history; and when times were bad in general, so that other firms were failing, banks suffered their share of the load. If business in general collapses, business firms and individuals will become insolvent; and the holders of their liabilities will suffer real losses. Banks, that is to say, as lenders to business firms, will feel the same cycles business firms feel.

It seems to me that banks, like business firms, need not be accused of mismanagement if they do not anticipate business cycles correctly. We do have, and did have, agencies empowered to deal with cycles; and it is at their door that bank failure is to be laid insofar as the rate of failure of banks is not out of line with the general rate. We do not know if bank managers did make foolish loans in the overly enthusiastic 1920's, for no student of banking has yet separated the cyclical effect from the mismanagement effect. But we do know that the total of bank failures probably did not reach excessive heights (cyclically) until the bank holiday of 1933, when a lot of solid banks were purged from the system.

8.4.3 The Great Recession of 1937

There is one aspect of the previous discussion which ties in with the events of the later 1930's; and that is that banks, which started to acquire excess reserves in 1931, continued to hold substantial amounts until the 1940's. In fact, the deposit-reserve ratio

TABLE 8–5
EXCESS RESERVES AND REQUIRED RESERVES FOR
UNITED STATES COMMERCIAL BANKS, 1935–38

	Reserve Ratios	
Date	*Required*	*Usable (Excess)*
June 1935	8.9	9.4
December 1935	8.6	11.4
June 1936	8.7	9.4
December 1936	13.0	7.9
June 1937	17.5	3.5
December 1937	16.9	5.9
June 1938	15.3	9.9
December 1938	14.9	11.2

SOURCE: Philip Cagan, *Determinants and Effects of Changes in the Money Stock: 1875–1960* (New York: National Bureau of Economic Research, 1965), p. 192.

for banks, which stood at 8.39 in June 1933, was down to 3.14 in June 1940 and only then began to move gradually upwards, reaching 10.08 by 1960. But from 1931 onwards, there were substantial excess reserves, and that is the principal fact of interest in the late 1930's; some figures are given for 1935 to 1938 in Table 8–5.

If you believe that the Federal Reserve had done all it could to make money plentiful prior to 1936, then you, like the Federal Reserve, would begin to worry, as the economy began to pull out of the depression, about banks having a reservoir of lending power which could frustrate anti-inflationary policy. It seems a little early, in these early stages of recovery, to worry about the other extreme, but so it was in the 1930's. The figures which guided officials are contained in Table 8–5; the table distinguishes between the *required* reserve ratio and the *usable* reserve ratio, rather than the excess reserve ratio.[14]

As is visible in the figures, the required reserve ratio was doubled over a very short period. The changes came in three steps, beginning with August 1936 and occurring again in March and May 1937. The timing of these changes was most unfortunate, for the peak of the business cycle expansion was also reached in May 1937.[15] This coincidence is probably not an accident, and thus it is that the Federal Reserve is accused by many of killing the boom in its attempt to solve a problem which probably did not exist.

But things are even worse than that, for the short recession of 1937–38 was quite deep, with unemployment averaging 19 percent of the labor force in 1938. Further, as Table 8–5 shows, excess reserves were not eliminated by the action; and by December 1938, with the Federal Reserve still firmly maintaining its repressive reserve requirements, excess reserves were almost exactly restored to the December 1935 figures. The result was that the money stock, which actually fell from March 1937 to May 1938, only reached the level of December 1936 by October 1938.[16]

But things are never as simple as they might seem, even if it is obvious that the Federal Reserve's timing was uninspired; and we must recognize that the swing in the money stock might have been caused by the recession rather than the other way around.[17] Further, we must have some doubts about why banks held excess reserves even after the public had regained confidence in the banks themselves. That is, we see from Table 8–3 that the deposit-currency ratio began to rise almost immediately after the banking holiday, which had the virtue, at least, of helping to restore the public's confidence in the system. At this point we could argue that commercial bankers were "thrice bitten" and simply decided

---

[14] The usable reserve ratio is a somewhat broader concept, along the lines of Chapter 6, of the lending ability of commercial banks.

[15] According to the dating of the National Bureau of Economic Research.

[16] A fall in the money stock, we have observed, is an unusual event.

[17] George Horwich, "Effective Reserves, Credit, and Causality in the Banking System of the Thirties," in Deane Carson (ed.), *Banking and Monetary Studies* (Homewood. Ill.: Richard D. Irwin, Inc., 1963). The explanation is a Keynesian one; others have suggested certain "structural" reinforcement.

to set their own reserve requirements, much in excess of those officially set. This, as just noted, was not so obviously necessary, since it was the public's loss of confidence which (most often) brought down commercial banks.

And there is a further fact: the Federal Deposit Insurance Corporation began operating on January 1, 1934, and

Within six months, nearly 14,000 of the nation's 15,348 commercial banks, accounting for some 97 percent of all commercial bank deposits, were covered by insurance.[18]

If, as seems likely, commercial bankers were aware of this fact and if, in turn, they understood that the public would now not engage in runs on banks, then the excess reserves were simply unusable and could not have been held for protection by the banks. As things stand, we must conclude that this important issue is not yet resolved. But there is one aspect worthy of special note: in spite of the complicated and repressive legislation of the 1930's aimed at making commercial banking safe from failure, the single piece of legislation which stands out as having significantly altered the economic climate in favor of stability is the Banking Act of 1933 which created the Federal Deposit Insurance Corporation.[19]

8.5 HOW TO PAY FOR A WAR: 1940 TO 1953

From 1940 until the end of the Korean boom—in the summer of 1953—the American economy grew rapidly, and unemployment was as low as it had ever been in the 20th century. World War II seems to have rescued the economy from the dullness of the 1930's, and the spending on the Korean War—along with the rising tide of the Cold War—seems to have eliminated the word "depression" from our economic lexicon. The unemployment figures from 1940 until 1954 are given in Table 8–6.

In order to avoid the impression of promoting a serious fallacy, which I will not dignify by further identification, I should emphasize that the war spending—in either case—was associated with substantial budgetary deficits and that it is the latter, the deficits

---

[18] Friedman and Schwartz, *op. cit.*, pp. 436–37.

[19] Refer to Table 8–4 for the miraculous effect of the FDIC on our financial community.

TABLE 8–6
UNEMPLOYMENT AS A PERCENTAGE OF THE LABOR
FORCE, 1939–54

Date	Unemployment
1939	17.2
1940	14.6
1941	9.9
1942	4.7
1943	1.9
1944	1.2
1945	1.9
1946	3.9
1947	3.6
1948	3.4
1949	5.5
1950	5.0
1951	3.0
1952	2.7
1953	2.5
1954	5.0

SOURCE: Stanley Lebergott, "Annual Estimates of Unemployment in the United States, 1900–1954," *The Measurement and Behavior of Unemployment* (National Bureau of Economic Research) (Princeton, N.J.: Princeton University Press, 1957), pp. 215–16.

themselves, which wrought the economic miracle. Even so, the federal deficits in this period were not designed to mop up unemployment (which they did in the years 1940–42 and 1951–53), but to direct resources, whether employed or not, toward the war effort. Indeed, the deficits went on, especially in 1943–45, even after the economy was fully employed.

8.5.1   The Successful Financing of World War II

Up until the end of 1942, until the economy was fully employed as indicated in Table 8–6, one might not expect deficit financing to create much monetary distortion. After that, however, and continuing until the peak of the general cycle in 1948, prices rose substantially, the rise averaging 8.7 percent per year over the entire 1939 to 1948 period. What is remarkable in this case, at least as compared to the Civil War and World War I, is that so little inflation followed such a large dislocation of economic activity; indeed, the percentage of dislocation in World War II has been estimated as the largest of our three major wars to that point, as Table 8–7 makes clear.

We see, in Table 8–7, that increases in the money stock played a much smaller role in the two 20th-century wars; further, with regard to the two world wars, we see that even though the expansion of the money stock was the same in each case, a doubled war effort was achieved with a little more than half the inflation in World War II. The explanation, obviously (since $MV = Py$), will lie in a sharp fall in velocity in World War II, and the following comments are meant to provide an explanation for that fall.

TABLE 8–7
INFLATION, REALLOCATION, AND THE RATE OF CHANGE OF THE
MONEY STOCK IN THREE WARS

	Civil War 1861–65	World War I 1914–20	World War II 1939–48
Annual rate of inflation*..................	24.5	15.3	8.7
Dislocation (% of resources diverted to government sector)**......................	14.0	9.0	18.0
Annual rate of change of money stock†......	24.0	12.9	12.1

* Wholesale prices in Milton Friedman and Anna J. Schwartz, *A Monetary History of the United States, 1867–1960* (Princeton, N.J.: Princeton University Press, 1963), p. 546.
** Milton Friedman, "Price, Income, and Monetary Changes in Three Wartime Periods," *American Economic Review*, Vol. 42, No. 2 (May 1952), pp. 624–25.
† Broad money in Friedman and Schwartz, *op. cit*, p. 546.

Two important considerations are tied up in two "real" factors:

a) The proportion of revenues raised by taxes was much greater in World War II.

b) The expansion of real income was faster in World War II, particularly insofar as the prewar depression left a greater margin for expansion without inflation.

A consideration which probably did not matter—although it is often thought to be relevant—is that price and other direct controls repressed inflation:[20] this factor is accounted for by continuing the data (in Table 8–7) until well after the controls were relaxed.

An important consideration in World War II, absent from World War I, was the method (and effectiveness) of deficit financing. Velocity fell, you might say, because the money stock was held voluntarily; and this was effected—following the

---

[20] They were strongest in World War II.

Keynesian argument of Chapter 3—by keeping "money" cheap.[21] There were two main elements to this successful program:

a) More money was held because the rate of interest, representing the opportunity cost of holding idle balances, was low.

b) More government bonds were bought directly as a result of an aggressive campaign aimed at individual savers.

Both of these factors were relevant during the war, and both failed to be reversed *significantly* after the war because the pegging of bond prices continued until 1951. That is, the relative return on the Series E bonds was still quite good, and the opportunity cost of holding idle money balances still quite low until just before the Accord of 1951.

8.5.2 The Restoration of Monetary Policy in 1951

During the Korean boom (actually from 1936), in contrast to almost all of the period from 1860 until then, the velocity of money began to rise; indeed, it has generally risen since. Thus, the inflationary potential of the deficit financing of the Korean War was realized in a way which shocked the authorities into abandoning the support of Treasury bills in 1951 (the Accord), and an independent monetary policy was once again possible. The main instrument of this policy—in its anticyclical sense, at any rate—was the rediscount rate; this rate was brought more closely into line with market rates, starting soon after the Accord.[22]

There is no escaping the fact, as I pointed out first in section 3.6, that an essential force behind the upward drift in velocity is the upward drift of interest rates. The authorities, prior to 1951, were caught in the awkward position of trying to hold down market interest rates when there was a strong push upward.[23] It is not entirely clear, of course, why velocity itself was rising. It is possible that the principal component was the long-awaited readjustment to the method of war financing; and, indeed, this

---

[21] The word "money" is put in quotation marks to emphasize that what is really involved is keeping up the price of government bonds.

[22] The data for 1950–69 appear in Table 5–2.

[23] One reason for keeping money cheap—known to be the case in Britain, which also had an accord in 1951—was the fear of a recurrence of the Great Depression.

cannot be discounted. But probably more likely—and, at any rate, more understandable—was the marked improvement in the quality of other liquid assets (such as savings and loan deposits) and the partly related rise in the opportunity cost of holding idle money balances.[24]

This leaves us with the problem of explaining why intermediaries grew so rapidly during the period. Most of the issues will be considered in Part II of this book, but one underlying factor of critical importance should be mentioned now: the expectations of businessmen and consumers—expectations based on an already rapidly growing economy—were bullish and thus produced a more rapid rise in the demand for credit than could be met out of the expansion of credit directly based on the money stock. In other words, the growth of intermediaries was demand-inspired.

8.6 THE 1950'S: HAS THE RECESSION REPLACED THE DEPRESSION?

No doubt much of the writing on the experiences of the 1950's is overly optimistic about the exorcism of "it." The principal component of this optimism is the Keynesian belief that "it" was produced by real factors and that the real factors can and will be counteracted speedily and effectively by fiscal policy. We have cast doubt on this statement by pointing out that the lags of fiscal policy are potentially very long and that much of the disaster of the 1930's can be traced to events in the monetary sector. We might further point out that it is still unproved that fiscal policy works, for, aside from the undoubted influence of deficit spending during periods of war activity, there is little direct evidence of the efficacy of fiscal measures. This is certainly true of the 1950's.

The cycles of the 1950's are revealed in Table 8–8, in the now familiar unemployment sense; in this case I have also added the rate of inflation because unusual if not neurotic concern over this variable plays an important role in the period, particularly in the recession of 1958. We see a recession in 1954–55 and again in 1958 (or 1958–60) and the relatively unexpected event of an in-

---

[24] The opportunity cost can here be judged in terms of the advantages of holding a savings and loan deposit.

crease in prices of 2.7 percent in 1958 when unemployment was quite high, at 6.8 percent of the labor force.

It seems likely that the end of the Korean inflation which did not, in turn, result in an immediate recession, can be related to the Accord mentioned in section 8.5.2: the authorities retained their grip over the money supply and, apparently, over the price level. But from 1954 until the end of the period, and especially around 1958, the authorities appear to have favored moral suasion

TABLE 8–8
UNEMPLOYMENT AND PRICES IN THE UNITED STATES,
1950–60

Date	Unemployment, % of Labor Force*	% Change in Consumer Price Level**
1950	5.0	...
1951	3.0	8.0
1952	2.7	2.2
1953	2.5	0.8
1954	5.0	0.3
1955	4.0	−0.3
1956	3.8	1.5
1957	4.3	3.4
1958	6.8	2.7
1959	5.5	0.9
1960	5.6	1.5

* 1949–54 from Stanley Lebergott, "Annual Estimates of Unemployment in the United States, 1900–1954," *The Measurement and Behavior of Unemployment* (National Bureau of Economic Research) (Princeton, N.J.: Princeton University Press, 1957), p. 216, 1955–60 from the *Federal Reserve Bulletin.*

** *Federal Reserve Bulletin.*

more than firm quantitative controls.[25] Throughout the period, the quantity of high-powered money was almost constant, while the money supply expanded steadily, even through the 1958 recession. That recession has proved a puzzle to economists, but two facts seem to help sort it out:

a)   Intermediation had begun to be a factor, so that the authorities were losing their grip on the quantity of credit.

b)   The monetary contraction begun at the end of 1957 did not affect prices seriously until 1959 and possibly slowed the recovery (as well as eliminating inflation in that year).

---

[25] This became known as "open-mouth" policy.

8.7 THE 1960'S: AN INTRODUCTION

Much of the theory of this book is illustrated by data from the 1960's—particularly from 1964 through 1969, when signs of stress appeared—but, even so, an overview at this point will help to pull together this chapter and to stimulate some interest in the further elaborations of the theory in Parts II and III, below. Some important data are gathered in Table 8–9, and they show some curious phenomena. Unemployment drifted steadily lower during

TABLE 8–9
ACTIVITY IN THE 1960'S IN THE UNITED STATES

Date	Unemploy-ment	GNP		Consumer Price Change	Money Stock		Time Deposits	
		Billions	Change	Change	Billions	Change	Billions	Change
1960......	5.6%	$487.8	...	...	$141.1	...	$ 72.9	...
1961......	6.7	497.3	1.9%	1.1%	145.5	3.1%	82.7	13.4%
1962......	5.5	529.8	6.5	1.2	147.5	1.4	92.8	18.2
1963......	5.7	551.0	4.0	1.2	153.1	3.8	112.2	14.7
1964......	5.2	580.0	5.3	1.3	159.7	4.3	126.6	12.8
1965......	4.5	614.4	5.9	1.7	167.2	4.7	146.9	16.0
1966......	3.8	647.8	5.4	2.9	170.4	1.9	158.5	7.9
1967......	3.8	674.6	4.2	2.8	181.7	6.6	183.7	15.9
1968......	3.6	707.6	4.9	4.0	194.8	7.2	204.9	11.5
1969......	3.5	727.5	2.8	5.4	198.3	1.8	198.3	−3.2

SOURCE: *Federal Reserve Bulletin.*

the period, indicating a pressure on resources which began to result in inflation from about 1966; and the real rate of growth of the economy (column 3) was at or better than 4 percent until 1969 when, by December of that year, it had probably ceased entirely.

What is curious about 1969 is that even though the growth of the economy had ceased and even though there was a firm squeeze on commercial banks—as judged by the unprecedented contraction of time deposits and the relatively slow growth of the money stock (which was mostly growth in currency)—the pace of inflation picked up steadily, to 5.4 percent in 1969. Even the surtax on consumer and corporate income and the attempts to curtail government spending seem not to have affected prices, although they probably had much to do with the slowed economy.

It will be some time before we know what happened in this period, but three additional factors, not presented in the table, are certainly involved.

a) Commercial banks obtained funds from Europe, in dollar form, in fact in the amount of $9 billion.

b) Financial intermediaries, which had been crushed in the squeeze of 1966 (which was, accordingly, more successful in the policy sense) were able to stay afloat in 1969.

c) Price rises became anticipated, and, consequently, interest rates shot up while cost-push forces accelerated.

Thus, it would seem, we have a dramatic demonstration that new elements, having to do with the increasing articulation of the financial community and the growth and flexibility of the international sector, must be integrated into our analysis. This we will begin to undertake in Chapter 10, following our survey of conventional monetary theory in Chapter 9.

8.8 DISCUSSION QUESTIONS

1. If being a member of the National Banking System did not attract state banks, banks must have expected higher profits as a result of staying out. What, do you think, might have been the source of these profits? Did the ability to create currency seem to matter much?

2. Would a system of 100 percent reserve requirements be immune to financial panic? Would it be immune to discretionary anti-cyclical monetary policy? What would be the financial effects of such a system?

3. It has been claimed that Federal Reserve policy during the 1920s and 1930s had a deflationary bias? How might this be substantiated? Explain how it is possible that they may have been pursuing some other goal and that the deflationary bias was only an unfortunate coincidence.

4. Is the claim that the money stock only influences activity in a negative way verified by the discussion in Chapter 8? Which events might contradict this position? Are there, in turn, alternative explanations of these events?

5. Again and again we have emphasized that a fall in interest rates does not imply that money is "easier." Explain why this is so.

Why, then, does the business world seem to insist on this usage? Is the distinction between macro- and microeconomics of any use in your discussion?

6. Why would it be unwise to blame all (or even many) of the bank failures of the 1930s on unsound business practices? Are there analogies you could draw with individual bankruptcies in the stock market crash? What does constitute unsound management then?

7. Explain in detail the mechanism by which the rise in reserve requirements could have led to the recession of 1937. Why is there any dispute over the issue of what caused what during that episode? Is it more comforting to think it was a failure of the managers rather than a failure of the system?

8. It is an ill wind indeed which blows no good at all. In some respects the data presented in Chapter 8 suggest that war activity has had some positive influence on our general level of activity. How, then, does one account for our recent observations in the stock market that stock market prices move downward when the war news is unfavorable?

9. During World War II the demand for currency seems to have increased to an unusual extent. Why, do you suppose, did this happen? What influence must this result have had in the efforts of the government to finance the war effort?

10. After the Accord of 1951 the Federal Reserve was free to vary interest rates; this, it is claimed, has enabled them to conduct monetary policy. What *more*, however, must be possible before monetary policy can really become active? Is fiscal policy in any way constrained if there is an active monetary policy?

8.9 FURTHER READING

CAGAN, PHILIP. "The First Fifty Years of the National Banking System—an Historical Appraisal," *Banking and Monetary Studies* (ed. Deane Carson). Homewood, Ill.: Richard D. Irwin, Inc., 1963.

FRIEDMAN, MILTON, and SCHWARTZ, ANNA J. *A Monetary History of the United States, 1867–1960.* National Bureau of Economic Research. Princeton, N.J.: Princeton University Press, 1963.

Chapter 9 | MONETARY THEORY: AN INTRODUCTION

9.1 INTRODUCTION

This chapter is necessarily going to be a little harder going than those which have preceded it. I am going to divide my topic into two main parts: the first will be a survey, with only passing reference, of my impression of what is most relevant in the history of recent monetary thought; and the second, sections 9.3 and 9.4, will consider two topics in modern monetary theory which are especially relevant to the study of money and banking.

The survey discussion of the first part is broken down into two main segments. First we will consider a version of the classical system; then, in section 9.3, we will consider amendments to the system offered by a variety of economists, of whom John Maynard Keynes is the best known. The general idea is to present a paraphrase of these ideas (from a modern viewpoint), a paraphrase which is "reasonably consistent" with the published record. It will not be possible to document this theory, for I am not claiming anyone ever said anything exactly as I have put it down. On the other hand, I will claim that our work in this book will be given a useful perspective, and that this is a productive activity in itself.

The two topics in section 9.3 and 9.4 concern some important, but difficult to understand, mechanisms left out in our earlier analysis. We will find a certain amount of shading into empirics at this point, but it can be reported that at present the relative importance of these factors is certainly suspected by a number of economists.

9.2 A CLASSICAL MONETARY SYSTEM

9.2.1 Money Is a Veil

There is a tendency to write off the classical writers on the subject of money as somehow not being in the mainstream of scientific economics as we employ it today. One accusation is that they did not perceive the realities of the economic world in which they lived: that being unable to see depressions and inflations and the like, they consequently built a theoretical structure of very limited practical use. I think this view is neither accurate nor well-taken; it sprang, in the first place, from a misreading of their intentions—and their books—and in the second place, from a misunderstanding of the role of economic thinking; let us make the general point first.

The aim of any theory, and certainly any theory in social science, is to explain something big from something small. This is a kind of "theoretical leverage," and the ratio of explanation achieved to the strength of the assumptions used is some measure of the power of the theory. If, for example, we assume that the critical element in the cost of production is the labor cost and if we assume away the influence of demand by arguing that all consumers will simply adjust their demands to the prices dictated to them, we are on our way to a "labor theory of value." Then, if it works—if, in fact, there are no missing equations and markets can clear themselves and the like—we judge the theory, highly special as its assumptions appear to make it, a powerful theory if it successfully explains or predicts a broad range of observed phenomena.

The classical economists can be interpreted as fully understanding these principles. In the area of monetary economics, in order to get answers to problems which perplexed them, because their observations of the real world were not easily explained, they began by trying to break the general problem of value into two parts: the problem of real values and the problem of monetary values.

This brings us to what is meant by the statement that "money is a veil." There are five somewhat nonexclusive possibilities:

a) They actually thought money was a veil in fact.
b) They assumed money was a veil.

c) They wished to construct a system in which money was a veil.

d) "Money is a veil" is a theoretical deduction from their analytical system.

e) Money is, in fact, a veil.

While it is likely that there are elements of all of these usages in classical writings, it is easier to find these views as accusations in the writings of their critics than in the works of the classical writers themselves.

All of these descriptions can be explained, and all are "correct" under certain theoretical or practical conditions. We won't go into the empirical propositions (*a*) and (*e*), and we will assert that (*b*) is untrue of any important classical economist; which leaves us with the mainstream of writings contained in (*c*) and (*d*), the two cases in which some specific theoretical role is played by the monetary mechanism.

9.2.2 Walras' Law

If we imagine ourselves to be placed in an economy, such as our island economy of Chapter 2, which has $n-1$ commodities and money (making n goods in all), which have already been produced, then the only interesting problems concern the determination of the prices of the goods $(P_1, \ldots, P_{n-1}, P_n)$ and the distribution of the goods between individuals. We will evade the latter issue entirely and, instead, concentrate on the solution for the n prices in the economy. The first thing which must be appreciated is that a solution must be feasible, and this is not all that obvious—it is, in fact, a mathematical problem. If we have one equation and two unknowns, e.g., $y = 2 + 3x$, we cannot solve for x or y in terms of the parameters 2 and 3; we have a straight line as things stand. The very least we need is another independent equation (independent, here, means a nonparallel line). In fact, to get a solution for two variables, we will generally need two independent equations; and to get a solution for n variables, we will usually need n equations.[1]

---

[1] Because it has not been that much of an issue in monetary economics to date, I will not apologize any further for the incompleteness of my statements about the mathematical problems of finding solutions to systems of equations.

Now all of this is fine: we have n equations and n prices, so a solution seems feasible; but we run into a classical assumption: Walras' law. Stated most generally, Walras' law asserts that the supply and demand for all n goods at once in an exchange economy are *always* equal. In one sense, all this says is that, at any moment of time, at an arbitrary set of initial prices, the sum of all the quantities demanded, plus and minus, will equal the sum of all the quantities supplied, plus and minus, where a minus quantity demanded is a quantity supplied and a minus quantity supplied, a quantity demanded. Intuitively you are best off thinking in terms of a balance sheet: if you are given n entries (the quantities demanded, plus or minus) and the fact that all entries must sum to a certain figure (the total of supply), you really have too much information. That is, given that you have the data

$$10, 20, 30$$

and are told *independently* that they must sum to 60, you are able to eliminate any single piece of information (e.g., 30) and still have all the information. You have all the information because the statements

$$10, 20, x$$

and

$$10 + 20 + x = 60 \tag{9-1}$$

enable you to deduce x. Walras' law is similar in nature to Equation 9–1.

Now what happens in a system of n independent equations when they are tied together by another equation is that one of the original n equations becomes redundant. In this case, because of the assumption of Walras' law, you can only solve for $n - 1$ independent variables. Symbolically, we cannot solve for the $P_1, \ldots,$ P_n prices, but only for the $n - 1$ money prices (goods in terms of money) as listed in Equation 9–2.[2]

$$\frac{P_1}{P_n}, \ldots, \frac{P_{n-1}}{P_n}, 1 = P_1', \ldots, P_{n-1}' \qquad \text{money prices} \quad (9-2)$$

---

[2] In an equation system with, say three unknowns and only two equations, you can only solve for ratios of unknowns, as you can easily verify. Whether or not you have a sensible solution in economics depends on whether or not the variables have an economic interpretation. In the above example, money prices do.

The money price of money, P_n', will be unity at all points, as we saw in Chapter 3 it should be when solved in this explicit fashion. The model of Chapter 3, you now can see, had a Walras' law assumption: the statement that everything must be spent.[3]

The system just specified is complete and has a solution, including a solution for the price level; but its strength (having everything in the model) is also its weakness: it is essentially incapable of making useful theoretical prediction, so it is essentially useless in practice. It seems fairly obvious now that if in some way we can separate the monetary problem from the real problem, we can work out whole sets of predictions, particularly if the separation can be justified in some way. Say's law, when applied to this framework, does just that.

9.2.3   Say's Law

Say's law is the further statement that the supply and demand for the $n - 1$ commodities as a whole must always be equal. If you have followed the argument to this point, you see that this is equivalent to the elimination of another equation in our system, so that we now have $n - 2$ independent equations and can, at most, solve for $n - 2$ variables. If we continue to try to solve for prices, this means that we can only solve for the following set of relative prices (goods in terms of goods), taken from Equation 9–2:

$$\frac{P_1'}{P_{n-1}'}, \; \ldots \;, \frac{P_{n-2}'}{P_{n-1}'} \qquad \text{of which there are only } n - 2 \quad (9\text{--}3)$$

Now, earlier in this book we defined a price level which, we noted, was the inverse of the price of nominal money; it appears as Equation 9–4.

$$P = \sum_{i=1}^{n-1} P_i Q_i \qquad (9\text{--}4)$$

If we have a Walras' world but not a Say's law world, this price level is determinate—at equilibrium—given the amount of money

---

[3] The role of money, if it is one of the goods in the system, is decidedly ambiguous. For one thing there are only stocks here, since all quantities are given—so money cannot service a flow of income—and for another, transactions costs, which must exist if money is to be held, have not been defined. Furthermore, we could use a bond in the system to establish the opportunity cost of holding money. Nevertheless, we will plough on.

in the system, with the Q_i as the fixed quantities of commodities and the P_i the $n - 1$ money prices of Equation 9–2. But, and this is a critical point, if we have a Say's law world, so that we can only solve for the $n - 2$ relative prices of Equation 9–3, the price level of Equation 9–4 becomes indeterminate. By indeterminate we mean that the price level now does not depend in any way on anything that happens in the "real" economy. Say's law, therefore, is a sufficient assumption to give us a theoretical system in which money is a veil. This explains (c) in the above system if you argue this was intentional and, I suppose, (d) if you argue that it was accidental in some actual classical writings.

We have not made any predictions yet from this system, and that is because the system is incomplete. In fact, with Say's Law, we do not have a system capable of explaining overall equilibrium. To do this, we can add another equation which asserts that the quantity of money is supplied by the central bank (or, if you want to stick to the assumed classical work, is in fixed supply like all of the other goods) and that it is demanded according to Equation 9–5.

$$M_d = kPT \qquad (9-5)$$

This equation, which is the equation of exchange appearing not as an identity (when it was interpreted as a definition of exchange) but as a behavioral relation, completes the system.[4] Furthermore, we now have a model which predicts the real world phenomena which some classical monetary economists desired to predict: the price level. The way you use the model depends on the problem you have, but if the Q's are given from the real sector and the velocity of money is constant, tends to change rather slowly, or is itself predictable, we would expect prices and money to be closely correlated. That is to say, we isolate, by our assumptions, a phenomenon which is clearly of some general validity: changes in the quantity of money will tend to change the price level and, even, will tend to change it without significantly upsetting relative values. This is predicting something big—a good deal of the variation in the price level—with something small—the classical model with the very strong assumption of Say's law.

---

[4] We also need the equilibrium statement that the supply of money equals the demand for it.

9.2.4   The Homogeneity Postulate

There is one offshoot of this discussion which has tended to obscure this rather clear approach, and that is the use by some writers of the "homogeneity postulate." Classical economists used it, especially in their more informal writings; but it is still used in international trade theory, where those working on what they call "pure trade" will often divorce their study from that of the balance of payments mechanism by invoking the explicit assumption (postulate) that real demands do not depend on money prices but only on relative prices.[5] You cannot obtain very good results in the monetary side of trade if you ignore the real, but the converse does not seem to be the case (something big from something small). To return to monetary problems, this case is essentially that of (*b*) above: money is really assumed to be a veil. Further, in the classical system with Walras' law applied, we get the same result as with the Say's law restriction: the real is divorced from the monetary, and the nature of the money market must be spelled out more completely if we are to get predictions (and to complete the system). This must be done because there are no means left to determine the price level, since people ignore it in their everyday life (the $n - 2$ relative prices).

All of this implies, I hope, that whether we use Say's law—a statement applied to the equilibrium—or the homogeneity postulate—a statement applied to the commodity demand equations— the result is a dichotomization between the monetary and real sectors. What cannot be done, and it does seem to have occurred in some spots in later classical writings, is to use both at the same time; for if we do, we get inconsistencies in the system, since they are two quite different theoretical statements. The fact that they

---

[5] There is no escaping the problem of explaining the use of the word homogeneity, although the above discussion is actually complete. Actually, the assumption is that commodity demand functions are "homogeneous of degree zero in money prices." Formally, a function (e.g., demand) $f(X_1, \ldots, X_n)$ is homogeneous of degree zero if

$$f(\lambda X_1, \ldots, \lambda X_n) = f(X_1, \ldots, X_n)$$

What our definition means in practice is that if you double all money prices ($\lambda = 2$), the equilibrium quantities demanded of the products are not changed, as asserted in the text.

both get the same result ("money is a veil") is no protection against the fallacy of overdetermination of a result. But this is enough on this rather peripheral matter.

9.3 KEYNESIAN MONETARY THEORY

In the following discussion I am going to consider three aspects of what I will call Keynesian monetary economics. In the first section we will consider the precursors to Keynes—notably Knut Wicksell—upon whose work John Maynard Keynes built. They will be summarily treated here primarily because their work has been discussed implicitly throughout the text; I will simply show where this material can be found in this text. The next section describes some of the monetary theory of Keynes himself; and, in the final section, there is a brief discussion of some of the recent work of the so-called Keynesians.

9.3.1 Neoclassical Monetary Theory

Neoclassical monetary theory really begins when concern is expressed over the role in the system of the interest rate or, in some versions, of the velocity of money. In section 9.2, velocity was tacitly assumed to be a constant; but the neoclassical economists, including Keynes in his early writings, ventured a number of opinions concerning the variables which governed it. We have gone over much of this ground in sections 3.6 and 6.3, so several general comments will serve us here.

The main thrust of neoclassical monetary writing was toward money as a flow-servicing medium of exchange. The interest rate was governed by real factors; and while the authorities could determine a "money" interest rate which was unequal to the "natural" interest rate at which real savings and real investments were equal, they had to suffer the consequence of an unstable price level. The velocity of money was widely thought to be a stable function of principally nonmonetary variables—such as payments "habits"—and, in the long run, the stock of money was determined by the demand for money.

9.3.2   Keynes as a Monetary Theorist

In the 1930's it began to become apparent that the solution of the problem of describing the role of money in the economic system depended on the integration of the flow aspects of money with the stock. Money is defined in such a way that it is clearly measured as a stock; but for such constructs as the equation of exchange, it is also clear that the stock of money directly services economic activities (such as gross national product) which are flows. In Chapter 3, the price level was brought in to reflect the flow-servicing dimension, and the interest rate to reflect the stock; but, we have seen, things are not as simple as this dichotomy would imply.

In Keynes, generally, the stock aspect of money dominates the flow; indeed, much of the uniqueness associated with Keynes' theory flows from the way he organized it. For example, in his definitional structure, Keynes combines bonds with long-term investment, so that the notion of equity is suppressed while the representative interest rate becomes a long-term rate. Money and short-term bonds are lumped together (or, rather, short-term bills are ignored) so that the role of the interest rate as an opportunity cost factor is suppressed in favor of its role as a speculative factor. Indeed, he favors using the interest rate on perpetuities, a type of security which, since it is never redeemed, represents the ultimate in interest rate risk (for mortals, at any rate).

Keynes, on the formal monetary theory of section 9.3, is said to have denied the efficacy of Say's law; but in fact his attack is on Walras' law. While the particular device of Say's law might not be the best one for the purpose of separating the real from the monetary, Keynes accepts its function. Indeed, Keynes effects his own separation, by his ignoring of short-term debt and by his discussion of the determination of real money balances (M/P) rather than nominal balances.[6]

Walras' law comes under an attack from Keynes because a system with this mechanism is (overly) concerned with the final

---

[6] As pointed out in Chapter 3, the effect of dividing out the price level is to remove the influence of the transactions motive; this makes consistent the ignoring of short-term debt.

equilibrium of the system, rather than with the approach to that equilibrium. In the Walrasian system, in which a clearing is assumed to occur instantaneously, at a single price, two important features of the real world (that is, the Walrasian real world) are ignored:

a) It takes time to effect an equilibrium, and time has economic properties.
b) Deals are closed at prices other than the final price, especially before the final price is determined.

Keynes, indeed, emphasizes that in the process of groping for an equilibrium, the traders in a market would respond to false signals, would close deals, and might even prevent the attainment of that equilibrium. In particular, Keynes is thinking of that special type of disequilibrium known as a depression; the critical element, in his thinking, is the failure of the system to solve its n equations in the time period allotted to it by the classical economists.

The role of money in the adjustment process in Keynes' model follows both from its definition as a stock and from Keynes' emphasis on the long-term rate of interest. By concentrating on the stock property of money—in particular its liquidity—Keynes directly evades the problem of linking up money with activity in general (e.g., GNP). Liquidity is defined as the ability to obtain the full market value of an asset instantly and with no cost. These are the sorts of criteria which wealth holders take account of; and since liquidity is a scarce item, a price (the interest rate) would be attached to it. The opposite to a liquid asset, in turn, is an illiquid one (long-term bond or equity), so when a wealth holder chooses money, he is expressing his liquidity preference.

The long-term rate of interest governs the demand for money, in Keynes, for it measures the market value of liquidity preference. Furthermore, since the long-term rate is relatively immobile, there is little hope for monetary policy to do much more than simply alter people's portfolios of money versus short-term assets. The general idea is that unless people's expectations about the long-term rate were altered—and they are not likely to alter just because the relative price between two kinds of money alters—long-term rates would not change; thus neither consumption nor investment would change substantially.[7] Of course the open market operation would affect short-term interest rates, and this would bestow capital gains and losses on wealth holders; but these effects, while certainly mentioned in Keynes, do get buried in the mud of his prose style.[8]

9.3.3   Some Keynesian Innovations in Monetary Theory

Keynes can be distinguished from the later Keynesians—whose citations of chapter and verse are often specious—by the more complete analysis by the latter of

     a)   The relation between short-term bonds and money and
     b)   Uncertainty.

With regard to the former, we commonly find in the writings of the Keynesians a disaggregation of short-term bonds and money, and a lumping together of short-term bonds with long-term bonds. This system produces some oddities for, on the one hand, it is difficult to discuss liquidity preference when your representative assets (money versus Treasury bills) are almost equally liquid; and, on the other hand, the ignoring of the transactions motive, when money is sharply distinguished from Treasury bills, is patently unsound.

With regard to uncertainty—that is, with regard to the possibility that expectations concerning the future might be vague—the post-Keynesian period has seen the rapid development of the analysis of this problem. I am not going to spend any time here on this topic, for it will be introduced in Chapter 12 and applied to monetary problems in Chapter 14; but I ought to note that this is a development of Keynesian economics (i.e., post-Keynes) rather than of Keynes himself, whose speculators were never vague about the future.

9.3.4   The Real Balance Effect

There has been one recent dispute which has remained somewhat unresolved; it began almost as a debating point between

---

[7] He did say that *if* the long-term rate of interest changed sufficiently there would be a substantial effect on investment.

[8] We will return to the discussion of the wealth effect in section 9.5.

Keynes and A. C. Pigou. This is the existence of a mechanism whereby full employment might be restored through persistent monetary injections. The Keynesians have argued that whether or not there is any effect of the interest rate on investment, if the demand for money is perfectly horizontal at a low interest rate (the liquidity trap of Chapter 3) we will get neither the investment spending effect nor any changes in the value of individuals' portfolios from the increase in the money supply because interest rates will not fall; consequently, monetary policy will not work. Pigou, then, suggested that as a depression worsened prices would fall continuously, creating both an increase in the value of monetary assets and a decrease in the value of monetary liabilities. Then, since the government ignores the real value of its monetary liabilities,[9] the eventual increased spending of consumers, who are wealthier on net insofar as they hold the liabilities of the government, will not be matched by a decrease of government spending; thus, a force exists which eventually will restore the system to full employment.[10]

We now refer to this mechanism as the *real balance effect*; and some of the important aspects of it, particularly its elusiveness, were discussed in Chapter 3. We might add that we no longer feel so strongly that the government need "ignore" its liabilities, for we find it implausible to take the money stock, for example, as a liability of the government. Even so, there seems little chance that we will ever be able to verify the existence of this effect; and, in fact, work has concentrated more on the "wealth effect" of a change in the money stock. The advantage—of M over P in the expression M/P—is that changes in M can be tied to specific known policy actions, while changes in P simply occur.

9.4 THE WEALTH EFFECT: A SUMMARY

How do increases in the quantity of money affect the economic system? We said in earlier chapters that since money is useful in exchange, it follows that increases in its quantity, however effected, might speed up the exchange mechanism, providing ser-

---

[9] The government, that is, exhibits *money illusion*.

[10] Pigou agreed with Keynes that "eventually" was probably a very long time; this is why I referred to this as a discussion arising from a debating point.

vices to consumers. We also stated what is then obvious, that if an increase in the nominal stock of money (M) from one period to another does provide additional services, it will add to the stock of wealth; and the proportion it adds to wealth can be judged by comparing M/P for the two periods. Indeed, we pointed out that M/P is an item of individual wealth, and that when you aggregate, it is an item of aggregate wealth, since the services which people might expect to receive from money do not disappear in the aggregation.

One of the recently conventional views is that when you aggregate over the wealth of the private sector, paper assets and liabilities cancel out; in fact, some economists appear to want to net out the assets and "liabilities" of the government. In Chapter 4 we made an assault on this problem. There we argued that in order to decide whether an item is wealth or not, we must ask if it provides a stream of future services; further, we pointed out that the market will provide an estimate of the value of the item. In fact, the market will form a collective judgment as to the value of the stream of returns; and the broader the market, the less likely it is that unsound views or random shocks will disturb this valuation and the more likely it is that we can have faith in the market's valuation.

Money, that is M/P, is traded in every market, and if M/P rises over a period, wealth in this form has increased because someone thinks it is going to be useful. It is important to notice that the accountant would enter M as an asset in the balance sheet of the individual and not M/P. When he does the former, and if the individual counts his wealth (a real concept) in money form, they are both suffering from money illusion. The individual will actually suffer, for he will make inconsistent decisions on the basis of purely money quotations, while the accountant will not.

Now we must ask if we should record a liability to the producers of money. If you want to go on with the "money game," I would not object to the demand deposit component of M being recorded as the liability of the commercial bank—for it obviously is, in the sense that a customer can demand currency for his deposit. But, in reality, our system is protected from there being any consequences of this action because the Federal Reserve tends to sterilize the money supply from shifts in consumer preferences between currency and demand deposits. It was not always so, and the following *reductio ad absurdum* shows why the liability notion is incomplete.

Suppose there were a currency panic not counteracted by the Federal Reserve. As the money stock shrinks, both assets and liabilities would tend to disappear at the same rate; so would a good deal of the credit arrangements which have grown, parasitically, onto the money stock. Even so, for each canceled asset, there would be canceled liability and, *reductio ad absurdum*, in the end, no money, precious little credit, and no accounting change in wealth, while the economic system may have crashed to the ground. Thus, whatever else it does, the accounting procedure does not deal with this phenomenon.

In fact, a commercial bank or the Federal Reserve creates a product, M, and markets it. They are liable to convert any M they have issued into some other form of M; but they are not, as producers at any rate, liable for M/P. This is clear: no matter what happens to the price level, the commercial bank need only pay back in nominal units; once it "creates" the money, it has no further interest in its purchasing power. Of course there is some likelihood that individual banks will not get their share, so there is some liability; but for a big bank with many branches, this probabilistic liability is going to be a very small percentage of its total demand deposits.

There is one difference between the creation of money by the government from the creation by commercial banks, and that is that the government doesn't have to peddle its services; it can arbitrarily change the quantity of money. When it does so, insofar as the price level does not adjust completely, it has created wealth. For example, suppose the Federal Reserve bought Treasury bills from individuals. An accountant who kept his books in nominal and par values would not notice this transaction; but, in fact, the consumer sector will be wealthier insofar as the interest rate has fallen. In Figure 9–1 we indicate the effect this open market operation has, in the money market, as the system moves from $\tilde{P}_1$ to P_2. Indeed, the fall in the interest rate (or rise in the price of bonds) is useful in getting people to hold the new money.

Now it is possible that the price level will begin to rise, thus destroying some of the gain in M/P, so that the system moves back to, say, $\tilde{P}_3$. Even so, the change in the price level has not entirely eaten up the change in the quantity of money, so the new money has ended up performing additional services on net— and wealth has increased. It is true that the capital gains at $\tilde{P}_3$ are less than those at $\tilde{P}_2$; nevertheless, there are some. The capital

FIGURE 9–1
THE APPEARANCE OF THE WEALTH EFFECT IN THE MARKET
FOR MONEY

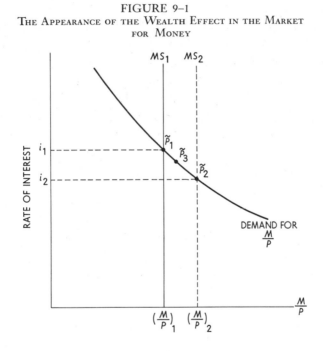

gains, the fall in the interest rate, and, above all, the increase in the real value of the money stock, all flow from the same phenomenon: the flow of money services has increased. Further, to flog the dead horse, as this occurred in the market place, no accounting entry would be made on anyone's balance sheet.

There is one factor I have glossed over in the discussion so far: what explicitly happens to the capital gains introduced into consumers' portfolios? Actually, this is an important issue because we also have not explained how it came about that the price level rose. As a matter of fact, some people will actually spend their capital gains on consumer goods, and this spending will drive up prices to the extent that the economy is in full employment. We refer to this as the wealth effect on consumer spending, and its existence has been established by economists working on the empirical side of the problem. This figures in the plot because, as we noted in Chapter 3, it seems unlikely that all of the increase in wealth going to individuals would be "spent" on bonds and money and none on consumer goods.

Commercial banks come into the picture again because it is likely that they are not in their optimal positions. That is, a profit-maximizing commercial bank will tend to acquire deposits and, *pari passu,* expand their lending activities so long as the revenue obtained from the last unit of lending exceeds the costs incurred. The cost of servicing the accounts falls as the deposit base rises;[11] thus, it is likely that changes in bank reserves, however induced, will produce wealth effects. The fact that banks pay no interest on demand deposits also enters at this point, because we are more likely to observe wealth effects if commercial banks are in permanent disequilibrium: every change in the money stock changes private wealth in this case. Other regulations on banks also have this feature. If there are wealth effects, then monetary policy will affect the economy. Further, if these are stable wealth effects, we will be able to measure them and to calculate and predict the effect of monetary policy on the economy.

9.5 INTEREST AND PRICES

One of the serious omissions in our work on interest rates so far is that we have made no mention of the connection between interest rates and prices. In fact, we have been working with nominal interest rates rather than with real interest rates—in Chapter 3, for example, the entire analysis was in nominal terms. In contrast, from the beginning of the 19th century, economists have noted a positive correspondence between interest rates and prices. It is a very strong correlation, and it is safe to say that speculation over the cause has been responsible for many of the main developments in monetary theory. The fact that prices and interest rates

---

[11] We pointed this out in Chapter 4, section 4.5.

move together does not necessarily imply that one causes the other. We will see that it is extremely difficult to set up a firm linkage; indeed, it is easier to find some other extraneous factor which causes both to change in the same direction than to find the direct link. Consider the following case.

Suppose that there is a technical innovation (the cause) which produces a change in investment plans. Clearly there will be two results, particularly if we are at full employment: one on the price level and one, raising the interest rate, in the capital markets. Thus, if the business cycles can be explained as investment cycles, in the Keynesian tradition, we are home free. But if the business cycles are monetary phenomena, or, rather, to the extent that they are monetary phenomena, the predictions of the classical view of the economy are quite different. An increase in the money supply clearly will cause prices to rise and, in the money market, interest rates to fall; to the classical writers the evidence of a correlation between money and prices posed a strong contradiction to their theoretical structure, and the phenomenon has come to be called the Gibson paradox.

The first really successful explanation belongs to what is sometimes called the neoclassical school, and it follows the lines of the Keynesian view, but with a more effective recognition of the role of the money supply on events. The first thing one must distinguish here is that the interest rates which are quoted on bonds are in fact nominal rates, but nominal rates in a special sense. We found that we could distinguish a real from a nominal value by deflating the nominal value by the average price of everything (P); what this division did was remove from the variable the effect of changes in the value of money. Now interest rates, because they are the ratios of money in the future to money in the present, are already real in the sense of being deflated automatically. Consider, however, the following example. Suppose that the interest rate for money to be paid back next year was 5 percent and that over the same period prices were expected to rise by 2 percent. Clearly, a person paying back funds at the end of the year pays back in dollars which are worth 2 percent less than they were this year; the purchasing power of the returned loan has fallen. If both lenders and borrowers have the same expectation about the price level change (the borrowers gain what the lenders lose) and both act consistently, we can say that the 5 percent interest rate consists of two parts:

$$
\begin{array}{ccccc}
\text{Nominal interest} & = & \text{Real interest} & + & \text{Expected rate of} \quad (9\text{--}6) \\
\text{rate} & & \text{rate} & & \text{change of prices} \\
5\% & = & 3\% & + & 2\%
\end{array}
$$

Now suppose the expected rate of change of prices rises to 4 percent, with the real rate of interest constant at 3 percent. In these circumstances we can say that the nominal rate of interest will rise to 7 percent if both sides of the market agree on the degree of the change to occur and both act accordingly in their financial deals. Notice what has happened: the price level has risen and so has the observed nominal interest rate. We would seem to have our explanation. But we do not, except for the circumstances we have postulated; for, as we can directly observe, suppose that the expected rate of change of prices falls back to 2 percent. We have gone through the following cycle:

	Interest Rate	Price Level	Rate of Change of P
Period 1........	5%	1.00	2%
Period 2........	7	1.04	4
Period 3........	5	1.06	2

In Period 3 the rise in the price level is in fact associated with a fall in the observed rate of interest.

Let us take stock of our results. We have, in the tradition of monetary economics, not solved the problem set before us; but we have found an important link between the price level and interest rates. If we can predict the changes expected in the price level (perhaps by predicting the changes in the money stock), we can predict an important influence on interest rates. We have found out something about interest rates which is not all that obvious. There is another gain, and that is in the form of the split of the observed (nominal) interest rate into "real" and "price determined" components. That leads us to an explanation of the Gibson paradox which is consistent with our development of the monetary theory in this chapter.

Suppose, for example, that the real rate of interest rises, as in the Keynesian case above, on account of an invention—that is to say, suppose the productivity of capital rises so that the demand for capital funds rises; Figure 9–2, with investment and saving measured on the horizontal axis and the interest rate on the vertical axis, shows the change in the form of a rightward shift of the investment line. Now, businessmen are willing to pay the higher real interest rate; but suppose the monetary system, perhaps be-

FIGURE 9–2

An Explanation of the Gibson Paradox

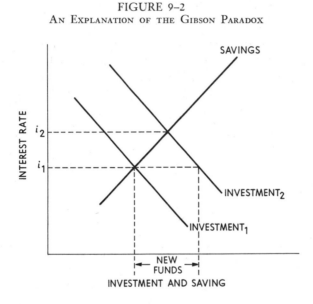

cause it is centrally directed by a group of conservative bankers (see Chapter 5 for one such system), does not adjust to the higher interest rate immediately. Suppose that the monetary authorities try to keep the interest rate at its old level (i_1). In this case, the demanders of funds (investors) wish to take up more funds than the suppliers of funds (lenders or savers) wish to provide; to make that lower nominal (or money) interest rate effective, the central bank will have to provide more funds, equal to the distance marked "New Funds" on the horizontal axis. With these funds pouring into the system, prices must rise. That is to say, the funds will remain in the system and circulate because money holders will have to be persuaded to hold the additional funds.

Thus, while the interest rate gradually rises toward i_2, which we would call the equilibrium interest rate, prices also rise. Furthermore, the analysis of this paragraph is symmetrical: if the real interest rate falls, we will observe falling nominal interest and falling prices until the adjustment is complete.

It should be fairly clear that the system I just went through is approximately the same as the Keynesian one and works most clearly insofar as the impulses come from the real side. One unhappy by-product of this result, however, is that one seems to be put into the position of arguing that the proper function of the monetary authority is just to adjust to the "needs of trade," in the sense of keeping the real and the monetary rates of interest equal. Of course this is impossible to do, for the "real rate" is not really observable and, in fact, our authorities follow an alternative: they try to stabilize the *money* rate. When they stabilize the money interest rate, they destabilize the system; for whenever the real rate is above the (rigid) money rate—that is, whenever businessmen's expectations are bullish—the authorities pump money into the system, and whenever the real rate is lower than the money rate, they pump it out. Both actions tend to make the business cycle worse.

9.6 DISCUSSION QUESTIONS

1. Keynes referred to his opus as the General Theory. Does his use of the word *general* imply that he thought his theory embraced all important economic phenomena or simply that he judged his version of monetary theory to be more complete than his predecessors' versions? Explain.

2. Clearly, the function in economic theory of Walras' Law is quite different from that of Say's Law. Explain the *purpose* of each, interpreting them as assumptions. Are their purposes in any sense comparable, then?

3. Discuss the reasons why the homogeneity postulate and Say's Law have virtually the same effect on the classical system. Does Walras' Law also have to hold in each case?

4. Explain why the fact that money and prices are closely synchronized in their movements does not help us in picking out a model on which to base this prediction. That is, explain why this observation does not help us pick between the homogeneity postulate

and Say's Law, as devices for separating the monetary from the real. What evidence would? Be fairly specific.

5. I have suggested—following Leijonhufvud—that Keynes was not a Keynesian in the sense that his theory was much richer than his successors'. One classical proposition which Keynes attacked was Walras' Law; the Keynesians in turn, attacked Say's Law. Explain these attacks. Which do you think the more fundamental, or can both attacks be justified?

6. Keynes attacked Walras' Law because the latter implied "false trading." Explain, and explain the meaning of the word *false* in this context. Could one attribute unemployment to false trading as you just defined it? Be specific and, if you can, be a little empirical.

7. Does it matter, to the ultimate effect of the wealth effect, whether increases in the quantity of money come as a result of government or of bank initiative? Suppose the initial change was demand inspired—would this case be any different?

8. Would we have stronger wealth effects if money illusion were a widespread phenomenon? Is it, then? Give some examples perhaps from your experience; you should not restrict your answer to the specific case cited in the text.

9. We pointed out that if there is no interest paid on demand deposits, all changes in the money stock might have wealth effects. Why is this so? Can we predict the direction of such changes? Are these an important or a minor part of the wealth effect? Explain carefully.

10. Why do we emphasize *expectations* about prices when we distinguish nominal from real interest rates? What assumption, then, validates the use of *actual* price changes in place of expected price changes? Does the behavior of the money supply play any role in your answer?

9.7 FURTHER READING

CLOWER, R. S. (ed.). *Monetary Theory* (Readings). Harmondsworth, England: Penguin Books, Ltd., 1969.

FRIEDMAN, MILTON S. "Interest Rates and the Demand for Money," *Journal of Law and Economics*, Vol. 9 (October 1966).

JOHNSON, HARRY G. "Monetary Theory and Policy" and "Recent Developments in Monetary Theory," *Essays in Monetary Economics* (ed. Harry G. Johnson). London: George Allen & Unwin, Ltd., 1967.

LAIDLER, DAVID E. W. "The Definition of Money, Theoretical and Empirical Problems," *Journal of Money, Credit, and Banking,* Vol. 1, No. 3, August 1969.

LEIJONHUFVUD, AXEL. *On Keynesian Economics and the Economics of Keynes,* pp. 191–98. New York: Oxford University Press, 1968.

MEISELMAN, DAVID. "Bond Prices and the Price Level: The Gibson Paradox Regained," *Banking and Monetary Studies* (ed. Deane Carson). Homewood, Ill.: Richard D. Irwin, Inc., 1963.

PESEK, BORIS P., and SAVING, THOMAS R. *Money, Wealth, and Economic Theory,* pp. 1–38. New York: Macmillan Co., 1967.

PART II

Capital Markets

Chapter 10

FINANCIAL INTERMEDIARIES

10.1 INTRODUCTION

Since World War II the growth of nonbank financial institutions, taken collectively, has been spectacular. The consequences—both real and imaginary—are equally spectacular; and they concern almost every aspect of our monetary analysis to this point. The main concern has been with the possibility that the control which the Federal Reserve is presumed to have over the money stock will somehow be undermined. The general idea can be stated now: if the authorities try to squeeze credit by reducing the money supply, they could be frustrated if lending by financial intermediaries replaces lending by commercial banks. It can happen; and, we will see in this chapter, it did happen in 1969.

This chapter, in addition to considering the monetary problem just introduced, will also undertake to describe to some extent the characteristics of financial intermediaries. Partly because the task is critical to our understanding of monetary matters, we must be careful to define our terms; the concepts we are most concerned with are *intermediation* and *credit*, and the formal questions we will consider are:

a) Are commercial banks unique in comparison to financial intermediaries?

b) What are time deposits: "money" or "intermediary claim"?

We begin with our definitions.

10.2 INTERMEDIATION AND CREDIT

A financial intermediary will have the following characteristics.[1] It will accept deposits, and it will make loans, paying interest on the former and receiving interest on the latter. It will achieve profits from the services it renders in

a) spreading the risk of its smaller depositors,
b) lending longer than it borrows, and
c) helping to improve the allocation of financial resources.

Finally, it will tend to hold its reserves neither in currency nor in the Federal Reserve, but in commercial banks. An example of a financial intermediary is the savings and loan firm, which holds the savings of individuals and lends to individuals, particularly when they purchase houses.

It is easy enough to distinguish intermediaries from banks—if we ignore the time deposit problem—by these criteria, but there are other systems of definition which do not effect this distinction. One such is the more popular view that "financial intermediaries exist to transfer financial resources from surplus units (savers) to deficit units (spenders)." By this definition, since the money balances of individuals are part of net wealth (accumulated savings), intermediation is taking place in the commercial banks as well as in the savings and loan firm. I can't help feeling that this approach conceals too much; particularly serious is the submersion of the fact that money is a medium of exchange and consequently has a direct economic function to perform, while all other financial instruments serve primarily in indirect capacities.

Paying interest, indeed, is a sign of a credit arrangement, and it is more helpful to keep money and credit apart than to confuse them by equating the interest rate aspect of a credit arrangement with the medium of exchange function of money. Credit, of course, arises in a large variety of ways, many of which do not involve financial institutions at all. A bill of exchange might be drawn up, for example, when a business firm wishes to pay for some materials later than it receives them; it will want to do this because there will be a delay until it receives its funds, with the

---

[1] I am defining an intermediary by its characteristics; see Chapter 2 for a discussion of the problems involved in such definitional schemes.

delay depending partly on how long it takes to manufacture the firm's product. The business firm which supplies the materials acquires the bill of exchange (which includes a provision for the interest cost of the operation), and it may

a)   Hold it, being satisfied that the interest earned thereby is adequate, in which case the business firm is the surplus unit.

b)   Rediscount it at the local bank in exchange for the cash it needs, in which case an individual depositor is the surplus unit.

c)   Rediscount it at an accepting house, in which case a financial intermediary's depositor is the surplus unit.

d)   Sell it directly to a surplus unit.

e)   Exchange it directly with its own suppliers, in which case we might be tempted to call it money.

Money, you can see, is a lot easier to analyze than credit.

10.3 THE SCOPE OF THE FINANCIAL MARKETS: A SURVEY

At the base of our financial system is obviously the commercial bank. Most financial dealings, except direct swaps, must be effected by means of transfers of money funds. We have not yet classified time deposits, but obviously they are going to be in a class by themselves, since they don't fit the definition of a financial intermediary (in that the reserves behind them are held in the Federal Reserve) or of money (in that they are not a medium of exchange). Even so, primarily because the reserve requirement on time deposits is lower than it is on demand deposits, and because the interest rate on time deposits is determined by the Federal Reserve, important destabilizing effects occur—on both money and credit—of exactly the same sort which we anticipate from intermediaries. We will see some of this later in this chapter, in connection with events in 1969.

Savings and loan associations (S. & L.'s) are the epitome of a financial intermediary, and their deposit rates are moderately variable; a balance sheet for S. & L.'s at the end of 1968 is given in Table 10–1. The principle business of S. & L.'s is to absorb individuals' savings, in the form of deposits which are essentially *demand* liabilities, and, while *spreading* the risk of lending among the class of individual savers, to provide funds to the private housing market. Since the assets of the S. & L.'s are both long-term and hard to dispose of, we see revealed two of the essential reasons why intermediaries (of all sorts) arise: they spread the risk of demand liabilities among a large group of individual deposit holders, *thus reducing risk*, and earn their profit on the positive margin between long-term assets (mortgages) and short-term debt (savings deposits).

TABLE 10–1
BALANCE SHEET FOR SAVINGS AND LOAN ASSOCIATIONS
(end of 1968; billions)

ASSETS		LIABILITIES	
Mortgages	$130.8	Savings capital (deposits)	$131.6
U.S. government securities	9.5	Borrowed money*	5.7
Cash	3.0	Loans in process	2.4
Other	9.5	Reserves and undivided profits	10.3
		Other	2.8
Total Assets	$152.8	Total Liabilities	$152.8

* Borrowed money is from the Federal Home Loan Bank, primarily.
SOURCE: *Federal Reserve Bulletin.*

Another big lender to the private housing market, operating in exactly the same fashion as the S. & L.'s are the state chartered mutual savings banks (MSB's); the MSB's are essentially depositor-owned—hence, the term *mutual*. As Table 10–2 indicates, they too earn their bread by performing the economic task of spreading risk, along with their usefulness in improving the allocation of capital funds. In several respects, the MSB's differ from the S. & L.'s. One is that they hold a substantial number of corporate securities, and have a wider scope in general in arranging their portfolios; a second is that they generally do not borrow from the Federal Home Loan Bank, although they now have that privilege. Both of these factors might make the MSB's more vulnerable to cyclical swings. Apparently their deposits are also more variable, and thus we find the MSB's do not lend as heavily to the mortgage market as do S. & L.'s. As we will see in section 10.6.2, the MSB's did suffer a severe cut in their deposits during the credit squeeze in 1966.

The last big lender to the private housing market is the life insurance company.[2] In their case, with mortality being an easily predictable and stable phenomenon, they must go far into the future indeed to earn a profit on their assets; they find that providing funds for large projects and purchasing long-term government and corporate bonds does give them a margin. Table 10–3 gives their position at the end of 1968. Life insurance companies, of course, provide another service—other than absorbing the

TABLE 10–2
BALANCE SHEET FOR MUTUAL SAVINGS BANKS
(end of 1968; billions)

ASSETS		LIABILITIES	
Mortgages	$53.3	Deposits	$64.5
Other loans	1.4	Other liabilities	1.4
U.S. government securities	3.8	General reserve accounts	5.3
State and local	0.2		
Corporate and other	10.2		
Cash	1.0		
Other assets	1.2		
Total Assets*	$71.2	Total Liabilities	$71.2

* First column does not add to total due to rounding.
SOURCE: *Federal Reserve Bulletin.*

TABLE 10–3
BALANCE SHEET FOR LIFE INSURANCE COMPANIES
(end of 1968; billions)

ASSETS		LIABILITIES	
Government securities	$ 10.5	Life insurance in force	$149.5
Business bonds	68.6	Other liabilities	38.2
Business stocks	10.8		
Mortgages	70.1		
Real estate	5.6		
Policy loans	11.3		
Other loans	10.9		
Total Assets*	$187.7	Total Liabilities	$187.7

* First column does not add to total due to rounding.
SOURCE: *Federal Reserve Bulletin.*

private risk of small savings—and that arises in connection with the insurance itself. That is, in taking the bets which their customers make on their lives, they are unlike the S. & L.'s and the MSB's; the life insurance company has a final product (insurance). There are a large number of intermediaries not covered by this survey. For example, stock brokers extend credit ($6.2 billion to

[2] Other than commercial banks, whose $65.1 billion lent on real estate at the end of 1968 was primarily to large customers.

margin customers), and commercial finance companies underwrite short-term consumer and business loans. The federal government sponsors credit agencies. Finally, mutual funds provide a spread of risk, investment, advice, and possibly monopoly and insider leverage to individuals interested in holding common stocks in general, rather than in particular.

10.4 INTERMEDIARIES AND COMMERCIAL BANKS: A DISTINCTION

From one point of view—that of Part I of this book—there is no problem in arriving at a distinction between the two types of institutions, because the liabilities of intermediaries do not serve as a medium of exchange.[3] But having decided to look at the stock of wealth, and recognizing that S. & L. deposits and demand deposits seem to merge together from some points of view, I must offer up more than a definition if I am to convince anyone that the distinction is worth anything. The best procedure, it seems to me, is to describe the fundamental differences between the three types of monetary institutions we have considered—the Federal Reserve, commercial banks, and financial intermediaries—and then to see what effects we might anticipate as funds circulate among them.

We pointed out that the Federal Reserve is unique in that it exercises discretionary control over the money stock, control which takes the form of open market operations, changes in reserve requirements, and changes in the discount rate at which commercial banks borrow from the Federal Reserve. Actually, what underlies the uniqueness of the Federal Reserve is the simple fact that it holds the reserves of commercial banks. That is, whether or not the Federal Reserve can use any of its instruments depends on reserves being in its hands, reserves which commercial banks cannot create at their own discretion. This is obvious enough with the discount rate and reserve requirements, but it is also true that if there were no reserve requirements—if commercial banks held their reserves at other commercial banks—the consequence of a Federal Reserve sale of a bond from its portfolio would cease with the initial exchange.[4] For example, if I buy a bond from

---

[3] This is a matter of *fact* rather than a matter of theory.

[4] Aside from interest rate and wealth effects.

the Federal Reserve and draw down my balance at a commercial bank, the Federal Reserve will own my balance at the commercial bank; but the commercial bank will not care, so long as the Federal Reserve does not seek currency for its deposit.[5]

10.4.1 Are Commercial Banks Unique?

The Federal Reserve is unique in our trilogy of financial institutions because commercial banks hold their reserves in it; are commercial banks unique because S. & L.'s hold their reserves in commercial banks? The answer is yes, the analogy holds—even though commercial banks lack the discretionary powers of the Federal Reserve. The general idea is that a pyramid of intermediary credit is built on the reserve held at the commercial bank such that

a) Changes of the public's allegiance among the intermediaries do not affect the total of credit.
b) Changes in the demand for reserves by commercial banks have a greater influence on credit than similar changes by financial intermediaries.

These aspects are formally identical to two points we made earlier about the relationship between the Federal Reserve and commercial banks, viz:

c) Changes in the public's allegiance among commercial banks do not affect the money supply.[6]
d) Changes in the demand for reserves by the Federal Reserve have a far greater impact on the money supply that do changes in the demand for reserves by the commercial banks.[7]

Let us illustrate. The point made under (a) is obvious, so long as all financial intermediaries have identical reserve requirements

---

[5] This is a different problem.

[6] Except, of course, insofar as different commercial banks have different reserve-deposit ratios, whether by legal prescriptions or by their own devices.

[7] The result obtains if we suppose that the reserves of the Federal Reserve are some sort of gold backing in a fractional sense. For example, with a gold backing of Federal Reserve liabilities of 25 percent and a reserve requirement of 2 percent for commercial banks, $1 of bank reserves supports $5 of money while $1 of gold supports $20 of money (assuming currency is issued by the Treasury).

because, on the one hand, commercial banks will take no notice of who owns their deposit liabilities and, on the other, the total stock of credit will not be affected, although its distribution will be.[8] But the establishment of (*b*) needs an illustration.

Let us begin with the commercial banks of Chapter 3. There we saw that the quantity of money could be explained in terms of Equation 10–1.

$$M = H\left[\frac{C/D + 1}{C/D + R/D}\right] \tag{10-1}$$

Let us construct a simpler system, without currency in it, so that Equation 10–1 reduces to 10–2:

$$M = R_B\left[\frac{1}{R_B/D_B}\right] = D_B \qquad \text{where } B \text{ indicates "banks"} \tag{10-2}$$
$$(M = D_B)$$

We will assume a reserve ratio of $1/5$ ($= R_B/D_B$) and initial reserves of $20. Deposits, then, are $100 (as is the money supply) and loans are $80.[9]

S. & L.'s, we will assume, arise in this system because individuals place $5 in S. & L.'s for every $4 held in their demand deposit accounts at commercial banks. In addition, we can construct an equation which is similar in purpose to Equation 10–2, but this time for S. & L.'s.

$$D_{SL} = R_{SL}\left[\frac{1}{R_{SL}/D_{SL}}\right] \tag{10-3}$$

Here, it should be clear, deposits are not created in the process of making a loan, but only accepted; whatever loans the S. & L. makes come later. If we assume that $R_{SL}/D_{SL} = 1/5$, then S. & L.'s will have deposits of $100 and make loans of $80.

This formulation contains the essence of proposition (*a*), for intermediaries are aggregated, and of proposition (*c*), for commercial banks will not react to switches between the $20 of deposits by S. & L.'s and the $80 of private deposits. The total

---

[8] That is, if you shift your funds from an S. & L. to an insurance company, small mortgagees who are customers of the S. & L. will suffer relative to large mortgagees who are the customers of the insurance companies.

[9] From the first $20, which was a primary deposit, the first bank put $4 in its reserve account and lent out $16, simultaneously creating $16 in new deposits.

stock of credit is $160, and it is the magnitude of this item which is involved in proposition (b). If S. & L.'s decided to hold $2 of reserves for every $5 of deposits, then from Equation 10–3, with $R_{SL}/D_{SL} = 2/5$ and deposits still equal to $100, R_{SL} would equal $20; and the stock of credit would fall by $10. This fall is one for one.[10]

If commercial banks decided to hold $2 of reserves for every $5, not only would the stock of money fall (something which did not happen with S. & L.'s in our example), but S. &. L.'s deposits—and hence their loans—would fall as well. This result is clear in our example, for we assumed that customers held $5 in their S. & L. account for every $4 in their demand deposit account.

10.4.2 Reserve Requirements and Intermediaries

If S. & L.'s were pressed with extra demands for loans or desired to hold more reserves, it is conceivable that commercial banks would extend credit to them. In this case commercial banks would be the "lender of last resort" to the S. & L.'s, and we would not need to assume a fixed preference for the two types of deposits in order to establish the point just made about the uniqueness of commercial banks. On the other hand, if S. & L.'s were to hold their reserves in the Federal Reserve, this rigidity would be necessary—at least for the case of the change in the demand for reserves by each of the institutions—in order to establish any real distinction between the two types of institutions, because commercial banks would have lost their "power" over S. & L.'s.

This whole approach of using fixed ratios where variable ones are more plausible is meant only to establish a test case. To see how dramatically things change when we make the ratio of the two types of deposits variable to the private wealth holder, consider the case of a deposit of new savings in an S. & L. and S. & L. reserves held either

a)   In commercial banks.
b)   In the Federal Reserve.

---

[10] Of course, in fact, if S. & L.'s cut their loans to their customers, it is likely that all the ratios which depend on customers' preferences would change as the borrowers searched around for funds.

In the first instance, no change in the money stock occurs, for both the reserves and the proceeds of the loans of S. & L.'s return to commercial banks. But in the second instance, with S. & L. reserves held in the Federal Reserve, commercial banks will tend to lose reserves, and hence the monetary base of the economy will shrink. There is a reserve loss because the Federal Reserve will receive reserves from the S. & L.'s which it will credit to the S. & L.'s while it simultaneously debits the reserve accounts of commercial banks.

Thus there is plenty of reason to ponder the questions of the influence—on the money stock and on the stock of credit—of shifts of consumer tastes for the various forms of wealth. In the following pages, more in illustration rather than in confirmation of any particular view, I will serve up two examples for you—the credit crunch of 1966 and the squeeze of 1969. We will see, using the events in 1966 as evidence, that tight money can hurt the inter-mediaries; and we will see, with reference to the events of 1969, that intermediaries can frustrate monetary policy. I mean to leave the issue unresolved in your minds because I feel that is where things stand; it is not clear whether we ought to worry about intermediation as such or simply to worry about the tendency of monetary policy to affect the financial sector unevenly.

10.5 THE CREDIT CRUNCH OF 1966

The period immediately preceding 1966 was one of an histori-cally rapid expansion for the United States; as the following figures illustrate, some sign of a "heated" economy had begun to appear in 1965, and historically low levels of unemployment were reached. This, of course, was the period of Vietnam escalation. The underlying causes of the situation were connected with the Vietnam War expansion, particularly in connection with the monetary consequences of the attempt to divert resources from the private to the public sector when the economy as a whole was expanding rapidly anyway. At any rate, through the last three quarters of 1965, whether as a result of financing the needs of trade or of cushioning the impact on capital markets of extensive fiscal operations, the money stock grew rapidly. Prices, too, began to shoot up, with about a one-quarter lag behind the money sup-ply; you can compare the figures here with the value of 1.1 percent per year from 1953 to 1961 cited in Table 7–1 found on page 153.

After the first quarter of 1966, the brakes were put on, and the rate of growth of the money stock slowed almost to zero; the velocity of money more than doubled; and, again with the one-quarter lag, the rate of inflation slowed markedly. These symptoms were in large part produced by a tight money policy, a policy which affected the intermediaries, the banks, and the customers of both types of institutions—particularly the housing market—even more than it affected the rest of the economy.

TABLE 10–4
ECONOMIC ACTIVITY IN 1965–66 IN THE UNITED STATES

| | Annual Rates of Growth | | | | |
Quarters	Real Income	Price Level	Money Stock	Velocity (Residual)	Level of Unemployment
1965, 1	8.7	0.7	2.8	6.6	4.83
2	6.9	3.2	0.2	9.9	4.73
3	6.8	1.1	3.5	4.4	4.47
4	8.4	2.2	9.7	0.9	4.20
1966, 1	5.9	3.6	6.6	2.9	3.83
2	1.8	4.2	0.4	5.6	3.83
3	4.0	3.2	0.2	7.0	3.80
4	4.5	2.8	3.6	3.7	3.67

SOURCE: *Federal Reserve Bulletin.*

In Table 10–5 I have collected some broad flow-of-funds data for the years 1964–67. The flow of funds measures the change in various financial stocks (of assets and of liabilities) for various arbitrary periods of time. Generally, in the flow-of-funds table, a distinction is made between the final users of the funds and the *intermediate* suppliers; the *ultimate* suppliers of funds, of course, are savers, primarily individuals and corporations.[11] We see, when examining Table 10–5, that the mortgage market was hard hit in 1966 and that (no doubt) the most important reason for this was a drastic drop in the funds available to MSB's and S. & L.'s, which together grew $5.8 billion less than they had in the previous year.

---

[11] The term "flow" is a misnomer here, as we defined it in Chapter 1. Frequently you will find *uses* referred to as the demand for funds and sources as the supply. This, too, is misleading, for the *net* change in any of these stocks is determined by both supply and demand.

Commercial banks also show the effects of the scramble for funds; but they more than recovered in 1967, while the MSB's and S. & L.'s were, collectively, still short of their 1964 level; and, more significantly, so were funds in the mortgage market. Since everybody seems to have lost, we cannot conclude that tight money spreads itself unevenly around the financial sector—except for life insurance companies, who also sell a product—but we

TABLE 10–5
ANNUAL FLOW OF FUNDS

	1964	1965	1966	1967
Net uses:				
Mortgages (public)	$25.6	$25.2	$17.7	$19.8
Corporate bonds	6.6	8.1	11.1	16.0
State and local securities	5.6	7.1	5.6	9.4
Foreign bonds	0.9	1.2	0.9	1.2
Other bank loans	13.6	19.8	13.0	12.9
Treasury debt (public)	2.6	−2.4	−1.9	3.4
Federal agency debt	0.6	2.9	4.8	4.0
Total	$55.5	$61.9	$51.2	$66.7
Net sources:				
Mutual savings banks	$ 4.1	$ 3.6	$ 2.5	$ 5.0
Savings and loan associations	10.9	9.3	4.6	8.9
Life insurance companies	6.4	6.7	6.7	6.4
Fire and casualty insurance	0.8	1.0	1.5	1.2
Private, noninsured pension funds	2.1	2.1	1.9	0.7
State and local retirement funds	2.7	2.9	3.2	3.8
Open-end mutual funds	0.4	0.4	1.0	−0.3
Commercial banks	21.5	27.9	17.2	36.6
Others	6.6	8.0	12.6	4.4
Total	$55.5	$61.9	$51.2	$66.7

SOURCE: Adapted from a table developed by the research department of Salomon Brothers and Hutzler, New York.

certainly see that final users are affected unevenly, depending on where they get their funds. This lesson is clear from the table, for corporations—especially—and most arms of the government seem not to have had difficulty, at least with regard to obtaining funds in the bond market.

10.6 THE SQUEEZE IN 1969

You can't have it both ways, after all. If intermediation is to frustrate monetary policy and to have the empirical effect of destablizing the demand for money, then evidence that monetary policy hits the intermediaries and that corporations are virtually unaffected[12] is evidence against the intermediary school. Indeed it leads to the opposite conclusion: help the intermediaries, rather than penalize them, if you want to *even out* the impact of monetary policy. Let us consider the 1969 credit squeeze; the data are contained in Table 10–6.

We see that the growth of the money stock was modest over the year and that the fall of free reserves indicated increasing tightness; the authorities, no doubt, were conducting a policy of tight money. During the tighest part of the period, from June through October, when the money supply grew only marginally, bank loans also grew only marginally; but over the entire period bank loans grew dramatically, increasing by $32.5 billion over the 11 months. Furthermore, the housing market and the financial intermediaries, as well as business investors, seem not to have been affected by the tight money.

What we see—as we have hypothesized in this chapter—is the influence of intermediation on the stock of credit. The link between the money stock and final credit in the system seems to have been ruptured, and even commercial banks seem to have found a way out. Things are actually made worse by including time deposits in one's definition of money, for time deposits at commercial banks actually fell by $9.1 billion in the 11 months. This is most peculiar.

We must look more closely at the sectors involved before we jump to the conclusion that intermediation was responsible for events in 1969. Let us first discuss the methods commercial banks employed to avoid the squeeze. There seem to have been three sources of funds during the period:

a)   +$8.6 billion from selling government bonds.
b)   +$0.4 billion from borrowing at the Federal Reserve.
c)   +$18 billion from an increase in cash assets.

The latter is not analyzed carefully in any published figures, but seems to stem largely from a rise in "interbank" and "other" de-

---

[12] M. I. Nadiri, "The Determinants of Trade Credit in the U.S. Total Manufacturing Sector," *Econometrica*, Vol. 37, No. 3 (July 1969).

TABLE 10-6
Money and Credit in the 1969 "Squeeze"
(\$ billion)

Month	Money Supply	Free Reserves	Bank Loans	Commercial & Finance Co. Paper, Bankers' Acceptances	Real Estate Loans by MSB	Life Insurance Co. Mortgage Loans	S. & L. Mortgage Loans	Business Investment
January	195.8	−0.480	261.1	21.8	53.6	70.2	131.4	
February	196.3	−0.596	263.1	22.9	53.8	70.4	132.1	
March	196.8	−0.701	265.0	23.7	54.0	70.5	133.0	(15.2)
April	198.1	−0.844	270.5	24.4	54.2	70.7	134.0	
May	198.3	−1.102	272.7	25.3	54.4	70.8	135.0	
June	199.0	−1.064	283.8	26.0	54.7	71.0	136.2	(17.7)
July	199.3	−1.074	283.2	28.3	54.9	71.7	137.1	
August	199.0	−0.946	280.7	29.5	55.1	71.2	138.0	
September	199.0	−0.831	284.3	29.7	55.2	71.4	138.6	(18.2)
October	199.1	−0.992	284.0	31.9	55.3	71.6	139.2	
November	199.3	−0.988	286.2	33.6	55.5	71.7	139.7	
December	199.6	−0.829	293.6	31.6	55.8	72.1	140.2	(20.1)
Change over 11 months:								
Absolute	+3.8	−0.349	+32.5	+ 9.8	+2.2	+1.9	+8.8	+ 4.9
Percent	+1.9	....	+12.4	+45.0	+4.1	+2.7	+6.7	+32.2

Source: *Federal Reserve Bulletin.*

mand deposits. What seems to have happened is that certain funds, especially Euro-dollars (dollar deposits in European banks, whether American- or foreign-owned) were tapped in the emergency. This is a type of intermediation, to be sure, but it seems to be more a technical flaw, since Euro-dollars are simply ignored in most analyses of the system. The intermediation produced by selling off government securities (but, significantly, not private securities) was helped—but not in the sense of an increase in the money stock—by the government's general support of the bond market.

Let us finish this discussion by examining the record of the MSB's and S. & L.'s to see if intermediaries intermediated. In Table

TABLE 10–7
Sources of Funds for MSB's and S. & L.'s in 1969
($ billion)

	MSB's	S. & L.'s
Deposits	+2.40	+3.96
Borrowings*	+0.08	+4.05
Net change in federal government securities held	−0.69	−1.39

* For MSB's, which did not borrow, this item represents "other liabilities."
Source: *Federal Reserve Bulletin.*

10–7, I have collected the principal sources of funds to these intermediaries. Clearly there is considerable intermediation shown in the first entry, deposits, and the third entry—the government-supported intermediation—cannot be ignored. Even so, we also cannot ignore the $4.05 billion which was lent directly to the S. & L.'s by the government. We can conclude this discussion by suggesting that on the evidence here, intermediation seems a serious factor, but that in 1969 it was only as important a factor as direct government intervention of two sorts:

a) Explicit lending, especially to the S. & L.'s.
b) Support of the government bond market.

Further, some institutional factors, notably the Euro-dollar market, also seem to be quite important.[13]

---

[13] We will continue the discussion of the Euro-dollar market in Chapter 15.

10.7 DISCUSSION QUESTIONS

1. Why did we evade the question of whether time deposits are money in Chapter 10? Is it sensible to regard them as "money at rest" rather than "money on the wing"? Does your answer depend on what the Federal Reserve does when individuals switch from time deposits to demand deposits and vice-versa.

2. A bill of exchange could be classified as money; indeed they have served as money in times past. This, in turn, suggests that not paying interest is not a fundamental part of the definition of money. Yet not paying interest is a feature of both currency and demand deposits in the United States. Can you reconcile these statements? Should we amend our definition of money in any way, to permit other forms?

3. It has been suggested that money be defined as a "means of payment" rather than as a "medium of exchange" (etc.). Explain why this implies time deposits are then not included in the definition and trade credit (credit between business firms) and credit card payments are. Would it help matters to stick to final (cash) payments in order to reconcile the two approaches? Would the means of payment quantity of money behave in the same way as the medium of exchange quantity of money?

4. An analogy was drawn between the product produced by a life insurance company and that of a bank. Explain the strengths and weaknesses of this analogy. Is the product idea itself subject to some criticism? Do intermediaries have a product then too? How do we decide what a product is, then?

5. Explain the weakness in the argument which likened the Federal Reserve, in its relation to commercial banks, to the commercial bank in its relation to financial intermediaries. Would this weakness disappear if the Federal Reserve controlled the reserve requirements of intermediaries, while letting intermediaries hold their reserves in commercial banks?

6. Can we distinguish commercial banks from intermediaries on the grounds that the former create deposits while the latter only accept them? Is there a difference in their procedures which we can exploit here? Does it matter which intermediary you are talking about?

7. MSB's and S. & L.'s are extreme intermediaries in that they borrow very short and lend very long. Compare the two types of institution in this respect. What implications does this have for their

ability to avoid a credit squeeze? Which seems better placed in this respect?

8. Discuss the reasons behind the fact in Table 10-4 that both velocity and the quantity of money fluctuated more than their sum? What, in this chapter, tends to explain this result? Is it a sign of intermediation? Does it matter that velocity was calculated as a residual?

9. If intermediaries are a cause of fluctuations in velocity, why is it that intermediaries appear to suffer in times of tight money? Are we missing some kinds of intermediation? What role might trade credit play in this picture?

10. Should one be worried that monetary policy affects the financial community unevenly? How could this possibly be avoided in ways which would not also vitiate monetary policy? Would such policy involve a good of discretion? Do we know enough about the system to suggest that such methods be employed?

10.8 FURTHER READING

Burger, Albert E. "A Historical Analysis of the Credit Crunch of 1966," Federal Reserve Bank of St. Louis, *Review* (September 1969).

Commission on Money and Credit. *Impacts of Monetary Policy.* Englewood Cliffs, N.J.: Prentice-Hall, Inc., 1962.

Dougall, Herbert E. *Capital Markets and Institutions.* Englewood Cliffs, N.J.: Prentice-Hall, Inc., 1965.

Ritter, Lawrence S. "The Flow of Funds Account: A Framework for Financial Analysis," *The Bulletin.* New York: New York University Graduate School of Business Administration, No. 52 (August 1968).

Robinson, Roland I. *Money and Capital Markets.* New York: McGraw-Hill Book Co., 1964.

Wood, John H. "Two Notes on the Uniqueness of Commercial Banks," *Journal of Finance,* Vol. 25, No. 1 (March 1970).

Chapter 11

THE TERM STRUCTURE
OF INTEREST RATES

11.1 INTRODUCTION

To this point we have avoided spelling out the formal nature of the interest rates we have worked with. Indeed, we have referred to "the" interest rate in general; and this usage is not in accordance with the facts, since each bond sold in the open market will have its own interest rate. The idea of a basic interest rate is, of course, a good one because it provides an essential simplicity to a complicated problem. The most representative bond to use in this sense would obviously be a government bond—because if any "firm" is safe, it is the government—and the usual candidate is the Treasury bill rate (90-day debt). We have another reason for keeping to government debt in this chapter: by doing so, we avoid the special complications introduced because business firms fail.

It is basic that the interest rate be thought of as the price of capital over time. The general idea, of course, is that a loan is made in exchange both for repayment conditions and for a stream of stated rental payments running from the issue date to the date of maturity. Two points, however, have not been mentioned explicitly: first, bonds can be issued for any maturity the market will take up, depending on the needs of the borrower (issuer); and, second, individuals can buy new or already issued bonds in order to improve the balance of their asset portfolios.

Obviously, we will have to establish that this single characteristic—the maturity of a bond—is important enough to warrant an entire chapter. In fact, the basic reason we are interested is that to each maturity date, running well into the future, an interest rate is attached; and that these interest rates embody the expectations of individuals about interest rates and, possibly, about general business conditions. If interest rate data can be used to forecast, we have made a clear gain; further, as we will see, these observations may be the best set of expectations quoted on any market.[1] Of course a sufficient reason for being interested in the bond market is that it is a vast market; even the bond market to which this chapter applies literally—the government bond market—is immense, as Table 11–1 suggests. By "applies literally," I should point out, I mean that the only important economic distinction among the marketable bonds summarized in Table 11–1 is the term to maturity of each category.

TABLE 11–1
The National Debt: A Summary,
December 31, 1969
($ billion)

Total gross public debt	368.2
Marketable debt	235.8
Maturing within:	
1 year	118.1
1–5 years	73.3
5–10 years	20.0
10–20 years	8.4
Over 20 years	16.0

11.2 INTEREST RATES AND YIELDS

A bond is best conceived of as a loan for a specified period of time, from the issue date (lending date) to the maturity date (repayment date), with explicit conditions for both the repayment of the loan and the "rental" payment for the borrowed money. This is a very broad definition and includes even time deposits; we should note that we also mean to include, as a special case, the perpetuities (no maturity date) issued by the British government. Most bonds in the United States are issued in units of $1,000 (we define the issue value to be the face value, F, and most are redeemed (at the redemption date) at or near the face value. The rental payments are collected over the life of the contract in the form of a coupon, C, which is stated in the original contract.

---

[1] In Chapter 13 we will discuss the accuracy of stock market predictions.

The sum of the rental payments over the life of the bond $\left(\sum_i C_i\right)$ and the final return of the sum lent (F) is greater than the original loan; this follows because the interest rate involved must be positive.[2]

11.2.1 Discounting

Let us pursue the notion of a loan between two maximizing individuals, since this reveals the mechanics of the situation most clearly.[3] If one desired to borrow $5 for a year, a maximizing lender, who had some other use for the money (and who wouldn't?) would charge him for the use of his funds. Let us suppose that the lender is in the habit of getting 5 percent per year on his funds; if so, the least he would charge is $0.25 for the year's rental, and we will assume that he does. The lender will, at the end of the year, receive the following sum, where i designates the interest rate expressed as a percentage.

$$\text{Sum received} = (1 + i) \text{ Loaned sum};\ \$5 + 0.05(\$5) = \$5.25 \tag{11-1}$$

Now, a bond is also a loan; and the price of a bond, both at issue and during its life, is derived from the following analogous equation; the equation is analogous because it is built on the same fundamental information.

$$\text{Price} \equiv P = \frac{\text{Coupon + face value}}{1 + i};\ \frac{\$0.25 + \$5}{1.05} = \$5 \tag{11-2}$$

Equation 11–2 describes the same situation as Equation 11–1, but here one sees an explicit statement of the process of the discounting of the sums to be returned in one year. Discounting is appropriate in this context, since we receive the coupon and the face value after one year; we discount by the current interest rate because that is the rate at which one can lend elsewhere. We find market bond prices quoted in the daily newspaper; we can regard the price, along with the C and F values, as an offer

---

[2] Real interest rates, in the sense of Chapter 9, can be negative, but money (nominal) interest rates cannot be, since that would imply giving money away.

[3] Maximizing, here, simply means getting the most from one's limited means.

from a borrower (or the present owner of the bond). In this
case we can apply our own discount factor, representing our alternative earnings at the same default risk, in order to see what
price we would be willing to pay for that offer. If we are willing
to pay the same price which is quoted from the borrower, we
have a deal; if he wants more, he will have to peddle his loan
papers elsewhere; if he wants less, naturally we will be happy
to pocket the difference and perhaps even buy some more. In
the latter case we earn a capital gain. In the example cited here,
if the borrower wanted $5 and we discounted by 5 percent, there
would be an even match.[4]

We get a term structure and, at the same time, get closer to
the real world when we consider loans (bonds) of more than
one period (maturity); let us return to Equation 11–1. If the loan
is to be for two years, the lender would compare the terms offered
with his own alternatives, which now could consist of 5 percent
for each year with one additional provision; since the 5 percent
is paid yearly, the interest payment for the first period can be
reinvested at 5 percent for the second year. Thus, our new version
of 11–1 is

$$\text{Sum earned} = (1 + i)(1 + i)\,\text{Loan} = (i + i)^2\,\text{Loan};$$
$$(1.05)^2\,\$5 = 1.1025(\$5) = \$5.50 \quad (11\text{–}3)$$

and our new version of the more useful Equation 11–2 is

$$\text{Price} \equiv P = \frac{C}{1+i} + \frac{C}{(1+i)^2} + \frac{F}{(1+i)^2} \quad (11\text{–}4)$$

where the last two terms represent the discounting of the second
coupon (which is received in two years) and the face value (also
received in two years), *twice*. Thus, in Equation 11–4, if the terms
are still the same as we listed, $5 plus $0.25 per year interest
(coupon), the price of the option is still $5 if the discount factor,

---

[4] Let us be clear on how we are using Equation 11–2. We, as potential
bond buyers, are faced with information on the coupon rate and the maturity
of the bond in question and with a market price (or an offer price if it is
a new bond). There will be some number i which summarizes the offer; we
will compare this number with our own alternative rate of return (r); and
if $i < r$, we will deal; in this way the market rate (r) will come to equal
the implicit rate (i) on the bond, since all inequalities will be eliminated by
market forces.

i, is 0.05. Finally, the complete generalization of Equation 11–4 is given by Equation 11–5.[5]

$$P = \frac{C}{1 + i} + \frac{C}{(1 + i)^2} + \cdots + \frac{C + F}{(1 + i)^n} \qquad (11-5)$$

Equation 11–5 is immediately useful. We find quotations on the bond market in newspapers; for a government bond this quotation might look something like the following:

6's of Jan. 1, 96–8, 82.3

We are immediately able to describe the situation, and we find the summary return on the bond (*i* in Equation 11–5) which we can compare with our alternative use for the money we might have to lend. The description just offered is for a bond with a coupon of 6 percent (usually $60), a face value (probably) of $1,000, which is due to be redeemed on January 1, 1998, but which may be called, at the option of the government, at any time after January 1, 1996. The bond was selling for 82.3 ($823) when the quotation was recorded. To find out what the bond yields—that is, to find the number *i* in Equation 11–5 which reconciles the stream of returns on the right with the price of the bond on the left—we merely consult a standard bond table. The date of the quotation was not stated (let us say April 13, 1970), and we have not noted that the bond pays the coupon in semiannual installments (most bonds do). This leaves us with

---

[5] If the bond were a perpetuity, we would write Equation 11–5 as:

$$P = \frac{C}{1 + i} + \frac{C}{(1 + i)^2} + \frac{C}{(1 + i)^3} + \cdots \text{ to infinity} \qquad (i)$$

This is not as awkward a formulation as it appears, for one can simplify the expression by using an algebraic transformation [multiply each side of (i) by $(1 + i)$ to form (ii) and subtract (ii) from (i)].

$$P(1 + i) = C + \frac{C}{1 + i} + \frac{C}{(1 + i)^2} + \cdots \text{ to infinity} \qquad (ii)$$

The result is (iii):

$$P = \frac{C}{i} \qquad (iii)$$

It is quite often this formula that economic theoreticians, for example Keynes in *The General Theory of Employment, Interest, and Money*, have in mind when they discuss "the" interest rate; but we must remind ourselves that this is a special case, not a general one, because there is no known change in the capital value as there is in Equation 11–5, if the bond is held to maturity.

an important question: What is the maturity date, 1996, 1998, or something in between? In practice one will have to be arbitrary about this, but if it is a government bond, it seems reasonable to pick the later date, January 1, 1998. With this modification, we can consult the bond table most readily and when we do, we see that the bond's yield was 7.48 percent.

This yield is market determined (or, more accurately, the price of the bond is) and is a unique number for this bond; and so in our competitive world, all similar (in this case, government) bonds of a like maturity, whatever their coupon rates,[6] will have approximately the same yield. In a perfectly competitive market, homogeneous goods will all be traded at the same price.

11.2.2 One-Period Interest Rates

The one thing which is seriously oversimplified about Equation 11–5 is that all interest rates into the future are assumed to be alike. The interest rate we have illustrated is a kind of one-year rate which is renewed (or expected to be renewed) each year at the same value. But in principle, it is more general to conceive of the rates differing for each future one-year period. Thus, let us call i_1 the rate at which money can be borrowed from the present until next year and i_{10}, for example, the rate at which money can be borrowed from the beginning of the 9th year hence to the beginning of the 10th. With these definitions in mind, Equation 11–5 can be rewritten in the much more complicated, and much more revealing, form given as Equation 11–6, with the im-

---

[6] Actually, because the coupon offers the lender the opportunity of switching his income between interest income and capital gains and because the two are not treated the same way by the tax laws, a bond with a lower coupon will tend to be favored in the market if capital gains tax rates are lower than income tax rates. The mechanics are simple enough, since if the yield were the same for a 2 percent and a 4 percent coupon of the same maturity (if a dollar got the same yield on either option), the prices would reflect the differences in the coupons. In this example, assuming the lender was considering holding the bond to maturity, the 2 percent coupon would have half as much of its coupon payments taxed at the income tax rate over the years, the difference being absorbed in the lower price which would, in either case, rise to $1,000 when the bond is redeemed. Then, if the lender's income tax rate were higher than his capital gains rate, and this is quite likely, he would prefer the bond with the lower coupon and would be willing to offer more (get less yield) for it. The market price of the 2 percent and the 4 percent bonds—indeed, all bonds in real-world markets—will reflect the average tax leverage of the participants in the market.

portant practical warning that while one can *deal* at the rates of Equation 11–6, the exact calculation of the rates is impossible, without some further assumptions.[7]

$$\text{Price} = \frac{C}{1 + i_1} + \frac{C}{(1 + i_1)(1 + i_2)}$$

$$+ \cdots \frac{C + F}{(1 + i_1)(1 + i_2) \cdots (1 + i_n)} \quad (11\text{–}6)$$

In the last paragraph, we asserted that we can deal at any of the rates i_1 to i_{10} taken singly; it will be instructive (and will help us to understand the hypotheses to follow) if we actually look at one such deal. Suppose, for example, we bought a two-year bond while simultaneously selling (or issuing) a three-year bond. The following equations (11–7) represent this arrangement.

$$\text{Buy Bond A:} \ P_2 = \frac{C}{1 + i_1} + \frac{C + F}{(1 + i_1)(1 + i_2)}$$

$$\text{Sell Bond B:} \ P_3 = \frac{C}{1 + i_1} + \frac{C}{(1 + i_1)(1 + i_2)}$$

$$+ \frac{C + F}{(1 + i_1)(1 + i_2)(1 + i_3)} \quad (11\text{–}7)$$

Since we simultaneously bought and sold for two of three years, we are insulated from changes in i_1 and i_2; what we gain on the one hand, we will lose on the other. Our net contribution to the money market is to borrow money for the third year—we will repay one year later than we pay off our three-year bond. Thus, if interest rates rise over the period, our asset (Bond A) will fall in value, while our liability (Bond B) will rise in value. If the change is in i_1 or i_2, we will not observe any change in our position; but if it is in i_3, we will have gained, since Bond A will not be affected by the change, while the price of Bond B will fall. For

---

[7] The usual way that this is done is to assume $C = 0$ and $F = 1$; then one can take the yield (from a bond table, or, often from newspaper quotations) from a 10-year bond divided by the yield from a 9-year bond and factor out the future interest rate i_{10}. This is possible because the price of Equation 11–6 is, after all, the price of Equation 11–5. Expressed generally, the rate i_{10} can be derived under the assumptions here, from the following formula,

$$\frac{(1 + Y_n)^n}{(1 + Y_{n-1})^{n-1}} = (1 + i_n)$$

where Y_n is the same as i in Equation 11–5, for an n-period bond.

the first two periods we are *covered* (hedging) against interest rate fluctuations, but for the third we are *uncovered* (taking a position) until the end of the period. We can either borrow or lend at these rates; and anyone who is, perforce, uncovered for any of the future interest rates, whether he is aware of it or not and whether he is "long" or "short," is speculating in bond prices.

11.3 ARBITRAGE, HEDGING, AND SPECULATION

We have implicitly defined a term structure, but for the sake of total clarity, let us state that either of the following series is a term structure (the exponents 1 to *n* are years to maturity):

$$\text{Of yields: } Y_1, Y_2, \ldots, Y_n \qquad (11\text{–}8)$$
$$\text{Of interest rates: } i_1, i_2, \ldots, i_n \qquad (11\text{–}9)$$

Theories of the term structure concern the determination of these structures, and in the literature as well as the real world we find rival claimants grouped under either hedging or speculative headings.

We have already illustrated these concepts, but the clearest illustration is a formal definition of the terms along with the definition of one other widely used term, *arbitrage*. To begin with the latter, we define an arbitrage operation as one in which a profit is obtained by buying a product in one market and simultaneously selling it in another at, presumably, prices which are wider apart than the sum of the transactions and (where relevant) transportation costs. We are most familiar with this technique in international finance, and we shall describe it in a practical way in Chapter 16; but we need only note that in domestic bond markets such opportunities arise only rarely, if at all, and thus we can neglect arbitrage for now. This leaves us with covered operations, in which no gains or losses aside from those planned can be obtained, versus uncovered operations.

It is tempting to describe speculation in a psychological sense, but it is not wise to do this because of the ubiquity of speculation in most Western economies. Anyone who is uncovered (unhedged) against any potential chance of loss or gain is thereby a speculator with regard to that variable. If you happen to run your automobile over the president of a large oil company, you can be relatively certain that your hedge (your automobile insurance policy) will not be sufficient to cover the damages—you are speculating, in effect, against this rather unlikely risk. In financial markets one speculates when he is not insulated against the fluctuations of the prices of his assets or liabilities—thus, widows who own only American Telephone and Telegraph common stock are, essentially, wild-eyed speculators in that they are completely uncovered against changes in the fortunes of that particular company.

One is inclined to wonder if this is not too broad a definition of speculation and, consequently, to restrict his usage of the term to a person who consciously speculates in some sense; but, on inspection, this latter definition is not that useful. The reason is that there is no way, except in certain narrow markets such as the foreign exchange market (where "amateur" speculators do not seem to dominate), to distinguish conscious speculators from the nonspeculators who are also nonhedgers. Both are in the same "position" and will respond to roughly the same stimuli, at least for any empirical test we have conceived of yet.

Hedging, in this chapter, will mean the insulation against interest rate (or bond price) fluctuations by matching the maturity of one's financial assets with the maturity of his financial liabilities. A practical example, if true, which partly anticipates the results of later sections of this chapter is that of a life insurance company, with liabilities (policies) actuarially of a very long term matched by holdings of long-term bonds and mortgages of a more or less equally long term. We have, in fact, observed something like this among insurance companies, but not to an extent sufficient to cause the yield structure to reflect this compartmentalization.

11.4 THEORIES OF THE DETERMINATION OF THE TERM STRUCTURE

One notices, as a matter of record, that yield curves (Equation 11–8) have varying shapes, among which those in Figure 11–1 represent the most likely types. While one hears of type I as the "normal" curve,[8] type IV has been quite common in recent years;

---

[8] One reason it is considered "normal" has to do with "liquidity preference," with "liquidity" referring to term to maturity (of which money has the shortest).

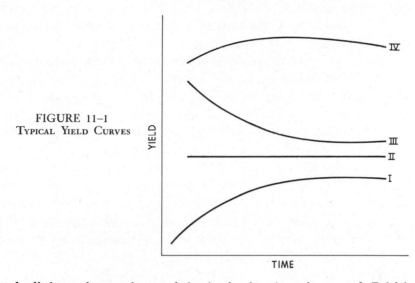

FIGURE 11–1
TYPICAL YIELD CURVES

and all have been observed in both the American and British markets since 1951. If there are no biases in the market, we might expect type II to rule, on average. In this case, everyone might be assuming that the current interest rate (i_1), whatever it is, will rule forever; this is likely if opinions are diverse or conditions unsettled. If this happens, then Equations 11–8 and 11–9 are equivalent; and we can speak of "the" interest rate as we have done up to this point in the book.

11.4.1 Speculative Behavior in Bond Markets

What is involved, then, are expectations about the future course of interest rates; and it is around the notion of firmly held and active expectations that the theories of the determination of the yield structure can be organized. The easiest, and in some ways the most plausible, explanation of each of the four curves in Figure 11–1 is that the shape is determined by the net judgment of the market as to what will happen to interest rates over the period, in comparison with the current interest rate (i_1). Thus, under the *expectations hypothesis,* curve type I represents a net effective judgment by the market that interest rates will rise; curve type III, that they will fall; curve type IV, that they will first rise and then fall; and curve type II, that they will remain constant.

But, unfortunately, it is difficult to think of ways to test such a wide-sweeping hypothesis—wide-sweeping because it can explain everything.

To take a concrete example, suppose that one expects interest rates to fall (that is, he expects bond prices to rise) over the course of the next year. If his conviction is enough to cause him to take action, he will sell off some other asset (perhaps money) and buy, say, a one-year bond. What happens in the bond market, if this occurs, is that funds are now available for one-year loans; and if our individual represents net market demand in some sense, the price of a one-year bond will be bid up, and i_1 will fall. In this way, the shape of the yield curve could be determined by speculative activity. This is the expectation hypothesis in its purest form—and the expectations tend to be self-confirming, at least in this case.

11.4.2 Hedging Behavior in Bond Markets

Hedging behavior, which is behaviorally the perfect opposite of speculation, takes two forms in bond markets. Hedging arises because of "fear" of, or, more accurately, distaste for, risk and, in this particular market, distaste for interest rate risk (or, if you prefer, bond price risk). One way in which we would look for the influence of hedging is in what is generally termed the *risk premium* which might be levied on interest rates in proportion to the length of time from maturity the bond currently is. That is, runs one explanation, the further a bond is from its maturity date, at which time all risks of changes in the level of interest rates in general will have been passed, the more likely it is that the lender might have to recall his loan (sell his asset) on unfavorable terms.[9]

In terms of our interest rate structure, Equation 11–9, what we mean to say is that each future rate (i_1 to i_n) really consists

---

[9] Put this way, it seems clear that there might easily be gamblers in bond markets, and bond yields might show some signs of this sort of activity; after all, we know that some people are willing to pay entrance fees to gambling casinos and then to undertake risks for which the average payoff is negative; a liking for risk is a known (psychological) phenomenon. In fact, Joseph Conard, whose books are recommended for further reading below, illustrates a case which he thinks might fit this description in the American bond market.

of two components; one, an expected part (i_E), and one, a *liquidity premium* part (i_L); we would then rewrite Equation 11–9 to read:

Of interest rates: $i_{1E} + i_{1L}, i_{2E} + i_{2L}, + \cdots +, i_{nE} + i_{nL}$ (11–10)

Here we run into a particularly serious problem, because it turns out that this proposition is supported by the same data as supported our expectations theory. With reference to Figure 11–1, we pointed out that the most frequently occurring yield curve was curve type I, the upsloping version; indeed, this type is the average shape for any reasonably long period. If in Equation 11–10 there are no firm expectations or if expectations average to zero, then, as a matter of arithmetic, liquidity premiums, which pile up in the yield formula, will make the average curve slope upward. But if expectations are biased toward rising rates, a bias which is reflected in realistic appraisals even at today's rates,[10] the same result, curve type I, is consistent with both the hedging and nonhedging theories; and there is no direct way out of the dilemma.

The second form of the hedging theory concerns the balance sheet evening out described in section 11.3 in our definition of hedging. This is more straightforward and implies that individual submarket rates (for example, i_{10}) will be isolated from the rest of the structure, although, perhaps, linked by the inevitable overlapping that modern financial firms obviously provide. With regard to the last point, for example, we have seen that commercial banks, whose liabilities are primarily *demand*, have assets spread all the way along the yield structure even though a large percentage are in a fairly short-term form. The implication of concentration of both assets and liabilities in the same maturity class is that such submarkets might tend to become isolated and reflect only the forces within the market, rather than development along the rest of the interest rate structure. Put this way, it is a matter of the degree of isolation of the market.

In principle, at any rate, these two general models of behavior are quite distinct; and it is fair to say that attempts to verify one or the other characteristic have dominated research in term struc-

---

[10] In the book cited at the end of this chapter, *The Five-Year Outlook for Interest Rates*, Henry C. Wallich attempts such a forecasting, using the term structure to guide him.

ture in the last 10 years. The results have not rewarded the effort; but, as the next section illustrates, the development of some practical work on economic forecasting has been a direct by-product of the formal theory.

11.5 YIELD CURVES AND ECONOMIC FORECASTING

There are two ways one might use either the structure of inter-est rates or the structure of yields in a forecasting framework. In the first place, we could attempt to verify our theories; for example, it could be argued that with substantial speculative activ-ity speculators must be right more often than they are wrong or they would tend to be eliminated by their mistakes and the field would be left to hedgers. To test this—and to reveal the existence of speculation—we might see if forecasts are accurate. In the second place, we could use the interest rates as predictions for our own purposes. That is, if interest rates are determined by speculators who are also experts on interest rate movements, we could hardly do better, unless our judgment is more expert, than to use their collective opinion, embodied in today's interest rate structure, as the best guide to the future course of interest rates.

We are going to use the British data listed in Table 11–2. We will assume away all hedging effects, since our forecasting implies the acceptance of the existence of speculative activity; this makes it clear that we are illustrating a method rather than confirming any of the theories we have proposed.

There are a lot of observations in Table 11–2 and a lot of ways we might use them. To begin with the question of verification of theory, we might ask how well the forecasts of the 10-year interest rate (let us provisionally interpret Y_{10} as a forecast) work out. In fact, as a glance at the values Y_{10} for 1955 and 1956 reveal, the interpretation of them as forecasts of Y_1 for 1965 and 1966 show guesses which are pretty wide of the mark. On the other hand, if we interpret the difference between Y_9 and Y_{10} in 1955 as a guess as to what will happen to interest rates by 1965—that is, if we interpret a positive value for $Y_{10} - Y_9$ as the market expectation that rates will rise—then we could argue that although the level was not foreseen (and it would be too much to expect that anyway), the direction of change of the level of interest rates was. It was because all 10 forecasts were for a rising rate; but this procedure is not entirely satisfactory.

If we try to arrange the curves into the broad types suggested in Figure 11–1, we will have to be arbitrary, but that cannot be helped. Let us use the following system to classify curves, based on the assumption that the difference between Y_{30} and Y_1 is a

TABLE 11–2
BRITISH GOVERNMENT YIELDS, 1955–56 AND 1965–66
(estimated by the author)

End of	Y_1	Y_2	Y_3	Y_9	Y_{10}	Y_{25}	Y_{30}	$Y_{perpetuity}$
1955 March	3.53	3.35	3.30	3.50	3.55	3.92	3.92	4.09
June	4.03	4.00	4.01	4.17	4.20	4.29	4.25	4.35
September	4.31	4.37	4.43	4.68	4.70	4.70	4.71	4.60
December	4.68	4.54	4.51	4.67	4.70	4.70	4.57	4.56
1956 March	4.90	4.94	4.98	5.13	5.14	5.01	4.90	4.84
June	4.50	4.63	4.74	5.19	5.23	5.13	4.95	4.96
September	4.93	4.83	4.84	5.22	5.27	5.30	5.12	5.06
December	4.89	4.96	5.03	5.30	5.32	5.28	5.16	5.04
1965 March	6.78	6.69	6.65	6.58	6.57	6.39	6.33	6.54
June	6.39	6.62	6.72	6.79	6.78	6.69	6.72	6.84
September	6.34	6.52	6.58	6.43	6.39	6.14	6.16	6.40
December	6.62	6.61	6.61	6.59	6.58	6.53	6.51	6.66
1966 March	6.94	6.90	6.87	6.80	6.79	6.73	6.72	6.86
June	6.72	6.86	6.93	7.02	7.02	6.94	6.92	7.07
September	6.94	6.98	7.01	7.16	7.17	7.16	7.12	7.22
December	7.02	7.05	7.02	6.77	6.73	6.72	6.81	6.85
1968 December	7.62	7.79	7.89	8.08	8.09	8.07	8.03	8.03

forecast, in the sense of indicating what direction the market expects rates to go:

$$Y_{30} > Y_1: \text{Expected rise in rates (type I)}$$
$$Y_{30} < Y_1: \text{Expected fall in rates (type III)}$$
$$Y_{30} > Y_{30} \text{ and } Y_1: \text{Expected rise, then fall (type IV)}$$
$$Y_{30} = Y_1: \text{Flat curve (type II)}$$

Table 11–3, then, presents a summary of the classification for the data of Table 11–2, with two other columns which we will use a little later. The main thing to notice, and it is important, is that there are many more negative signs in column 1 in the later period than in the earlier; that is, we have our rising curves in the early period, when interest rates are lower and might presumably be expected to rise, and our falling curves in the later period, when interest rates are at what were then considered to be historically high levels. This is the kind of thing we expect to find if speculators are at work, and it is not the sort of thing one expects from hedging behavior.

Let us try another ad hoc test on the data. Suppose we interpret the difference between Y_{30} and Y_{25} as a forecast of the change

TABLE 11–3
AN ILLUSTRATION OF PREDICTION FROM YIELD CURVES

End of		Y_{30}-Y_1	Type	Y_{30}-Y_{25}	Prediction
1955	March...........	0.39	Rising (I)	0.002	...
	June.............	0.22	Rising (I)	−0.04	Correct
	September........	0.31	Humped (IV)	−0.09	Wrong
	December........	−0.11	Humped (IV) or flat (II)	−0.13	Correct
1956	March...........	0.00	Humped (IV) or flat (II)	−0.11	Wrong
	June.............	0.45	Humped (IV)	−0.18	Wrong
	September........	0.19	Humped (IV)	−0.18	Wrong
	December........	0.27	Humped (IV)	...	Correct
1965	March...........	−0.45	Falling (III)	−0.06	...
	June.............	0.33	Humped (IV) or rising (I)	0.03	Wrong
	September........	−0.18	Humped (IV) or falling (III)	−0.02	Wrong
	December........	−0.11	Falling (III)	−0.02	Wrong
1966	March...........	−0.22	Falling (III)	−0.01	Wrong
	June.............	0.20	Humped (IV)	−0.02	Wrong
	September........	0.18	Humped (IV) or rising (I)	−0.04	Wrong
	December........	−0.21	Falling (III)	...	Correct
1968	December........	0.41	Humped (IV)	...	...

expected in the perpetuity rate of Table 11–2 from the current quarter to the next quarter. These numbers are given in column 3 of Table 11–3; thus, for example, the −0.04 in June 1955 is to be interpreted as a prediction that the perpetuity rate would fall by the end of the third quarter in 1955; it was wrong, since the perpetuity rate rose. In sum, since there were only 4 out of 14 correct predictions of the sign change, our theory has not done well at all; even so, the most we can do is reject the notion of expectations being formed in this way—that is, we cannot assert that expectations are not formed in some other way, an observation that is in line with the general evasiveness of the theory.

The second matter raised in this section concerns economic fore-casting. The behavior which makes forecasting possible is systematic speculative behavior, so that anyone who is interested in using the yield structure for purposes of predicting interest rate changes will be interested in the question of whether hedging or speculation determines the structure of interest rates. Let us take the December 1968 figure as expressing the market's collective judgment as to what is in store for British interest rates in the future. Then, if we interpret 7.62 percent as the current rate, it seems clear that the market expects rates to rise, and stay higher, for some time yet. If, in turn, we had worked this structure out because we wanted to know what to do about our own portfolio of bonds in the future and if we trusted the market's forecast, assuming we believed it to be a forecast, we might bet on a further fall in bond prices. As it turns out, if we had taken this position in December 1968, we would have made money in the next year, for interest rates did rise.

11.6 IMPLICATIONS FOR THE DEMAND FOR MONEY

In both this section and the one which follows, the importance of distinguishing between long-term and short-term rates really depends on whether or not expectations dominate along the interest rate structure. If it is expectations which dominate, then we are able to postulate that there are sufficient forces to guarantee that all interest rates move together. If all one year interest rates are equal, then we can speak of changes in "the" interest rate. If hedging dominates, then interest markets will become subdivided with respect to term to maturity, and both the demand for money and monetary policy will depend on which interest rates one is talking about.

With regard to the demand for money, the question concerns the appropriate potential substitutes for money which ought to be considered. The statement that Treasury bills are the nearest of near-monies is not correct on the basis of the superficial description of bills compared to bonds—*if* bills and bonds are perfect substitutes themselves. That is to say, the question is not a matter of definition, but a matter of what the market has determined; it is an economic question whether we use the Treasury bill rate as a determinant of the demand for money or whether we use a long term rate or, for that matter, some mixture of the two (and everything else in between). It is an economic question because it will be determined in the marketplace. In spite of this, there is a strong tendency to try to define the question away; there is, in fact, a tendency to describe the "money market" as the market in which money is exchanged for Treasury bills. As far as definitions go, as we have seen, these assets can only be near-monies in the sense of being alternative assets to wealth holders. They are incapable of performing the unique services of money—in other words, of meaningfully assisting in exchange—no matter how much the government interferes in their market.

With respect to the Keynesian speculative demand for money,[11] we have several problems. The first problem concerns a difficulty which arises whenever we use, in the demand for money, an interest rate on a close substitute to money. It is one thing to argue that Treasury bills are closer substitutes for money than anything else and that therefore their yield is the correct alternative asset "price" to employ in the demand for money, and it is quite another to assert that speculative activity occurs between bills and money. In the substitute case, a rise of the Treasury bill rate makes holding money more expensive in comparison to Treasury bills; this, in turn, would induce a simple profit-motivated move into Treasury bills. In the speculative case, a rise in the bill rate might induce speculators to bet on a fall in bill rates in the near future. This would also produce a move into Treasury bills; thus, the response is the same in either case, but the underlying market behavior is radically different. This, too, is not an easy difference to test empirically.

The second problem concerns the term structure explicitly: Which interest rate best fits the Keynesian theory, which, after all, merely postulated "an" interest rate? It turns out, although it does not settle the question for good, that if both a short-term and a long-term bond (of similar quality and carrying identical nominal features) are subject to the same change of yield, there will be greater profit in the perpetuity than in the short-term bond. Consider Table 11–4. Here we see that a dollar invested

---

[11] This was described in Chapters 3 and 9; we will return to this topic in Chapter 14.

in a perpetuity would appreciate much more than a dollar invested in a two-year bond if both bonds had the same yield, assuming that the change was instantaneous. Now, before I am accused of planting a false impression, let us note that changes in long-term bond yields generally are much smaller than changes in short-term yields. The price swings are still wider on net; but, of course, the risks are greater with a long-term bond, since one's final escape must await redemption. A pure speculator, in the Keynesian sense, using the interest rate as a proxy for the changes in bond prices which he anticipates, would probably be in longer rather than

TABLE 11–4
EFFECTS OF CHANGES IN INTEREST RATES ON LONG-TERM
AND SHORT-TERM BOND PRICES

Equation Used	Yield	Coupon	Maturity	Face Value	Price of Bond
(9–5)........	0.05	$4	2 years	$100	$ 98.14
(iii).........	0.05	4	Infinity	...	80.00
(9–5)........	0.04	4	2 years	100	100.00
(iii).........	0.04	4	Infinity	...	100.00

shorter bonds; and the perpetuity is the perfect Keynesian bond in that all of the change of yield is absorbed in a change in the price of the bond.

Let us emphasize that none of what we are saying here is a contradiction to the earlier material of this chapter. A speculator who moves out of money into bonds and moves along the yield curve looking for the greatest leverage[12] will be an important force uniting interest rates along the yield structure. That is to say,

---

[12] The leverage is obtained in two ways, one of them marketed-determined. The individual arranges with a bank or a broker to obtain a loan, using the government bonds which he buys as collateral, in order to get "long" in government bonds. The lender will, in general, ask for a minimum down payment, usually 10 percent; and if bond prices change by 10 percent (not too considerable a change in these days of fairly rapid inflation and the like), one can double his money. The problems are that bond prices may fall (more than 10 percent) and that the bank charges you more in interest payments than the bond returns to you in coupon payments. The second leverage, that determined by the market, is that produced by the fact that the yield curve changes its shape over the interest cycle; speculators will tend to iron these deviations out; and, in fact, this is one of the productive aspects of speculation in the bond market. The effect on the money market is another matter.

one reason interest rate structures begin to tip over as interest rates get very high is that speculators are operating (particularly at the long-term end) in bonds, expecting the interest rate to fall in the near future; this is a statement which is compatible with Keynesian speculation.

11.7 IMPLICATIONS FOR MONETARY POLICY

We have already pointed out that if demand curves for money are unstable—and they will be unstable if speculative activity which cannot be predicted exists—monetary policymakers will need to be aware of it. That, really, was the subject of much of our earlier work. Here we wish to ask what problems and what advantages confirmation of one or the other views of the term structure might have for the framers of our monetary policy.

Actually, in recent years, the Federal Reserve did take a stand with regard to the structure of interest rates: they argued that it was better to conduct open market operations in Treasury bills alone because that market was the only one which was broad enough to absorb the kind of change in the money stock we were likely to need if we depended on monetary policy for an effective push to the economy. One reason they did this was that they sought to effect a change in the money stock without changing interest rates and, in this case, particularly without upsetting the capital (long-term) market. This position is based on there being some separation in the markets with respect to term to maturity, for broadness or narrowness is not an issue if all rates move together because of speculative forces. We can report that explicit mention of the policy died out after a short and ambiguous trial; but, even now, one looks for open market operations primarily in Treasury bills, if one looks for them at all.

There was another wrinkle to monetary policy which was proposed in connection with the term to maturity debate, and that was called "operation twist." We observed in our discussion of monetary policy that the authorities clearly needed multiple instruments if they had multiple objectives; and, for the most part, they have been instructed to meet multiple objectives. In this particular case, the idea was that if short-term and long-term bond markets were separated by hedging influences, we could have two separate interest rate policies. The usual idea, although it is not all that feasible, was to enter the short-term market on one side, perhaps driving the short-term interest rate up to attract short-term capital flows from abroad; and to enter the long-term market on the other side, either to prevent long-term rates from following short-term rates or, more aggressively, to help the rate of growth by lowering the cost of borrowing funds for long-term investment. One could even argue that the latter might produce some fundamental structural changes by improving the real rate of growth and hence reducing the inflationary pressure of a given monetary stock. That, clearly, is basing a lot of hope on the segmentation theory.

The fact is, the policy has never been adopted, to my knowledge, and the principal reasons lie in two areas. One is that there is little hope of twisting without sizable operations, because expectations seem to tie rates together too firmly. The other arises because of the possibility that the policy will fail. Indeed, it is likely that the rise in short-term rates will draw in funds from abroad; but, at the same time, the rise in short term rates

a) Will cause a curtailment of short term investment in inventories.

b) Will cause a curtailment of consumer purchases of durable goods paid for with borrowed money.

Both could offset the stimulus to long-term investment. Thus, it is an empirical question, and the usefulness of the policy is extremely doubtful.

11.8 THE EMPIRICAL RECORD

We have already gone over a good many of the empirical possibilities in this chapter; but here we can pull things together, as well as provide some references by concentrating the discussion on the question of empirics.

David Meiselman,[13] whose work is the first really satisfying work on the empirical side of the question, has found fairly convincing evidence that expectations are an influence on American

---

[13] David Meiselman, *The Term Structure of Interest Rates* (Englewood Cliffs, N.J.: Prentice-Hall, Inc., 1962).

interest rates. One is inclined to go further than that with respect to his contribution, except that other studies have shown that a very simple model, which does not explicitly introduce human behavior at all, works as well in the same framework. Meiselman postulated that one can ask, not how the level of rates is determined, but whether or not *revisions* in future interest rates follow patterns of behavior which speculators would reasonably adopt. In particular, he asked if speculators revised their predictions in the light of their errors; he found that they did. The problem, again, was that he was not looking at speculators but at the interest rate data itself, which were *assumed* to be under the influence of speculators. His results could also have been attributed to random influences,[14] an observation which was quite damaging to his method of approach, although it did not alter the prejudices of most workers on the topic.

Tests of the predictive accuracy of the term structure of rates have mostly not provided any confirmation. Meiselman's test, just referred to, was ingenious because it avoided this whole area. It is said that all we need to establish is that interest rates respond to a reasonable type of speculative behavior rather than that expectations are accurate. But one would still think that speculators would only survive—and we know speculation exists in the money-bond market—if speculators were right more often than they were wrong; and so tests like that performed by Reuben Kessel,[15] who found that the yield curve was flat or downsloping at interest rate peaks and upsloping at interest rate troughs, seem to suggest that speculators are accurate on average. Joseph Conard[16] also found this sort of evidence.

But this is roughly where matters stand, and further tests with different data or different ways of digging out the future interest rates have not produced any additional insights into these questions. The only important gain of the rest of the work is that we have discovered that the various methods can be frustrated

---

[14] Adolph Buse, "Interest Rates, the Meiselman Model, and Random Numbers," *Journal of Political Economy*, Vol. 75, No. 1 (February 1967). We will discuss this matter fully in Chapter 13, in the context of the random behavior of stock prices.

[15] Reuben Kessel, *The Cyclical Behavior of the Term Structure of Interest Rates* (New York: National Bureau of Economic Research, 1965).

[16] Joseph Conard, *The Behavior of Interest Rates* (New York: National Bureau of Economic Research, 1966).

by using different data; but of course, this is a matter which is fairly obvious anyway.

11.9 DISCUSSION QUESTIONS

1. One reason for not conducting monetary policy in long-term bonds is that the long market is fairly thin, especially on a day-to-day basis. What would be the effect on the short-term interest rate, on expectations about interest rates, and on invesment, of a sizeable open-market purchase of long-term debt? Compare this result with that of an open-market operation in a specific security quoted on the New York Stock Exchange.

2. Life insurance companies, it is said, can find no debt long enough for them, in the American capital market. What does this imply about the shape of the yield structure, *ceteris paribus?* Does this help to explain their present asset pattern compared to, for example, the mutual savings banks?

3. We have likened a bond to a loan. Could we also link demand deposits into the structure of interest rates? How would we measure the return on demand deposits? How would we measure the term to maturity of, alternatively, demand deposits and time deposits? Where, then, does currency fit in?

4. If everyone who is uncovered is speculating, then speculation must be defined in terms of a specific risk. Explain. What risks were we describing in this chapter? Are there economic risks which can't be covered?

5. Does the thinness of certain bond markets lead to an overly high price of "cover"? What economic interpretation would you give to the word "overly" in the last sentence? Should there be some government policy to encourage the production of cover in certain markets? What role do intermediaries play in this process?

6. Why is an upsloping yield curve not conclusive evidence that the market expects rates to rise? Can we, nevertheless, use this curve to guide our predictions even if we can't justify our theory in this way? Would we, in any event, expect predictions and theory to mesh nicely in such cases? Explain.

7. Why did we construct our theory of expectations in such a way as to imply that expectations had to be acted on to be relevant? Is this analogous to our definition of the consumer choice problem in Chapter 1? Does it help make sense of our discussion of forecasting?

8. Does it seem likely that we will ever see the kind of direct evidence necessary to establish the fact that segmentation or expectations dominates the rate structure? What would you say if you knew speculators were disappearing from the market? If the governmennt changed the quantity of 10-year bonds, and the *yield* on 10-year bonds changed, would that mean the segmentation hypothesis was supported? Explain.

9. Under what theoretical circumstances could one employ a short term interest rate to represent the opportunity cost of holding money and a long term rate to represent the speculative demand? Suppose the expectations behind the speculative demand were formed on the basis of a *normal* rate of interest? How might this be measured?

10. How do speculators actually operate in the bond market? From where do they obtain their leverage? Work out a speculative deal in Treasury Bills, using actual numbers, in order to see what considerations are involved. How long can a speculator survive, with a 5 percent margin, if the interest differential is 2 percent against him?

11.10 FURTHER READING

CONARD, JOSEPH. *The Behavior of Interest Rates*, chaps. 1, 2, 6, and 7. New York: National Bureau of Economic Research, 1966.

————. *An Introduction to the Theory of Interest*, Part III. Berkeley: University of California Press, 1959.

"Federal Reserve Operations in Long-Term Securities," *Federal Reserve Bulletin*, November 1958.

KESSEL, REUBEN. *The Cyclical Behavior of the Term Structure of Interest Rates*, chaps. 1–3. New York: National Bureau of Economic Research, 1965.

MALKIEL, BURTON G. *The Term Structure of Interest Rates*. Princeton, N.J.: Princeton University Press, 1966.

MEISELMAN, DAVID. "The Policy Implications of Recent Research in Term Structure of Interest Rates," *Savings and Residential Financing, 1968 Conference Proceedings* (eds. Donald P. Jacobs and Richard T. Pratt). Chicago: United States Savings and Loan League, 1968.

PROCHNOW, HERBERT V. *The Five-Year Outlook for Interest Rates*. Chicago: Rand McNally & Co., 1968. Note especially the essay by Henry C. Wallich.

Chapter 12

AN INTRODUCTION TO THE THEORY OF PORTFOLIO CHOICE

12.1 INTRODUCTION

We have, to this point, avoided spreading too much technical apparatus around; but the useful development of portfolio analysis requires that we go some distance along the theoretical path. The whole area is without doubt the most fascinating in recent economic thinking; and the applications are so broad, ranging from monetary to personal investment problems, that one is almost bound to find something of interest to him. The general idea—which we will develop mostly by example—is to find out what governs economic decisions made in uncertain surroundings. You will immediately remark that all economic decisions except arbitrage are expected to be uncertain, and you would be correct; this, indeed, is why the "action" in economics is in uncertainty analysis. Specifically, we are going to ask what factors determine how an individual (or an institution) constructs his portfolio of assets (and of liabilities, where relevant), *including cash*. The road leads through some probabilistic and statistical concepts.

12.2 THE BASIC TOOLS OF PORTFOLIO ANALYSIS

12.2.1 Means and Variances

We begin by defining the mean of a series of n numbers in the conventional way as in Equation 12–1:

$$\text{Mean} = X = \frac{X_1 + X_2 + \ldots + X_n}{n} = \sum_{i=1}^{n} X_i \quad (12\text{–}1)$$

Consider, as an example, the three sets of yields on three common stocks,[1] American Tobacco (*AT*), American Telephone and Telegraph (*ATT*), and United States Steel (*USS*), for the period 1945 to 1954, shown in Table 12–1. While the average yields on *AT* and *ATT* are about the same, it is quite clear that the two stocks are not equivalent, for the yields fluctuate differently. A measure of the fluctuation in these figures is given by the variance; the formula appears as Equation 12–2.[2]

$$\text{Variance} = \frac{\sum_{i=1}^{n} (X_i - \bar{X})^2}{n} = \text{Var}(X) \qquad (12\text{–}2)$$

TABLE 12–1
YIELDS ON COMMON STOCK OF *AT*, *ATT*, AND *USS*,
1945–54

Date	AT	ATT	USS
1945	0.446%	0.216%	0.419%
1946	−0.088	−0.046	−0.078
1947	−0.127	−0.071	0.169
1948	−0.015	0.056	−0.035
1949	0.305	0.038	0.133
1950	−0.096	0.089	0.732
1951	0.016	0.090	0.021
1952	0.128	0.083	0.131
1953	−0.010	0.035	0.066
1954	0.154	0.176	0.908
Means	0.071%	0.067%	0.241%

SOURCE: Harry M. Markowitz, *Portfolio Selection* (New York: John Wiley & Sons, Inc., for the Cowles Foundation, 1959), p. 13.

It can alternatively be defined as the average squared deviation and is a usable measure of dispersion. For the data of Table 12–1

[1] The yield on a common stock includes the dividends paid as well as the change in the price of the stock.

[2] We may calculate an average deviation

$$\sum_{i=1}^{n} \frac{(X_i - \bar{X})}{n} = \text{Average deviation}$$

but as you can easily verify, the average deviation will be expected to sum to zero, and thus we will not be able to get an idea of the average dispersion in our series.

the three variances are:

$$V_{AT} = 0.035$$
$$V_{ATT} = 0.008$$
$$V_{USS} = 0.114$$

and both the variances and the means are illustrated in Figure 12–1. Here we see what will become very important to us when

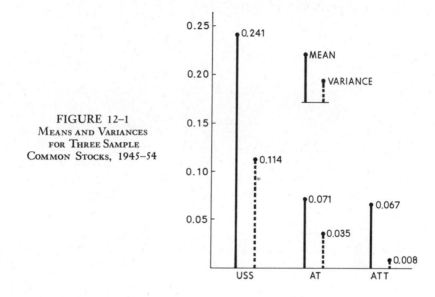

FIGURE 12–1
Means and Variances
for Three Sample
Common Stocks, 1945–54

we come to discuss economics in this chapter: a higher yield is associated with a higher variance of the yield.

12.2.2 Probabilities

When events, like future yields on common stocks, are surrounded with uncertainty, it is frequently possible to attach probabilities to the likelihood of their coming to pass. A probability is a percentage, generally, and is a positive number with an upper limit of unity, as in Equation 12–3.

$$1 > P > 0 \qquad (12\text{–}3)$$

It is obvious that probabilities can be assigned to future events when you think of picking a card from a deck of 52; indeed, if it is a "fair" deck, then you would give 1/52 (equal to a probability of 0.019) as your chance of getting the ace of spades on the first draw. Some events are certain to occur (the sun rises); and to them we would attach probabilities of 1. For example, if we picked all 52 cards, without putting any of them back, we would say that we had a 100 percent chance of getting the ace of spades. If under any circumstances we list *all* the outcomes possible, the sum of their probabilities will also be 1; this idea is expressed in equation 12–4.

$$\sum_{i=1}^{n} P_i = 1 \qquad (12\text{–}4)$$

Equations 12–3 and 12–4 constitute the formal definition of probability, as we will use it in this text.

Let us consider an example. Suppose you had the information given in Table 12–2 on the chances of winning various sums of money, let us say in a lottery. We will not worry yet about how you got the information on the probabilities, but in many situations, such as for an honest roulette wheel, there are known chances attached to each possible outcome.[3] We can construct a picture of the information in Table 12–2. In Figure 12–2 I have also drawn a curve connecting the points so as to underscore one other point about probability distributions: they are continuous.

12.2.3 Expected Values

The sort of opportunity described to this point is not economically realistic in an important sense: there is no loss involved. Even so, we can make it into an economic problem by asking how much you would pay for the gamble described there. Your answer depends on your taste (for income, as it turns out); but we could find out something about you if we faced you with a price of $235, for that is the expected value of the gamble in Table 12–2. The formula is given as Equation 12–5; the hat ($\wedge$) over the X indicates that it is a random variable or, if you wish, an uncertain outcome.

---

[3] These could also be *subjective* probabilities which you attach to the outcomes based on your knowledge of the situation. Needless to say, when we broaden the framework to the subjective, we must allow that wild guesses (so long as they sum to 1) can also be described by the model we are describing.

TABLE 12–2
A CHANCY OUTCOME

X Situation	Payoff	Probability of Winning	Expected Value
X_1...........	$100	0.025	$ 25
X_2...........	200	0.025	50
X_3...........	300	0.040	120
X_4...........	400	0.010	40
			$235

$$\text{Expected value} = E(\hat{X}) = P_1X_1 + P_2X_2 + P_3X_3 + P_4X_4$$
$$= \sum_{i=1}^{4} P_iX_i \quad (12\text{--}5)$$

The general idea behind this formulation is quite straightforward: we *weight* the value of each outcome by the chance of

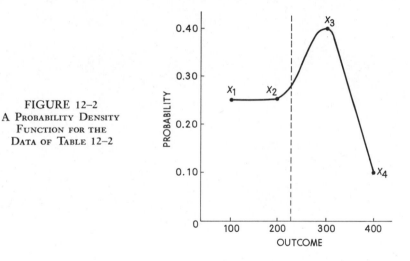

FIGURE 12–2
A PROBABILITY DENSITY
FUNCTION FOR THE
DATA OF TABLE 12–2

getting that outcome. Then, assuming everyone judges risky situations in terms of the expected value of the outcome, if I sold this situation for $240, no one would buy; but if I sold it for $230, there would be an infinite number of takers. If, in fact, the wheel were random, in the long run I would pay out $235 per spin and either go broke or break even; I couldn't make money as long as everybody judged things in this way.

It was once thought that gambling was irrational (except for the fun of it); that is, it was once thought that it was irrational to judge uncertain prospects in any way other than by their expected value. We know that gambling flourishes; even a life insurance policy is a kind of macabre bet with an insurance company—a bet you generally hope to lose in the short run. Gambling is not an irrational practice, if only because a small chance at a very big pot—a pot big enough to change one's way of life—is very hard for some to resist. Consider Table 12–3, in which the overall expected value is approximately the same as in Table 12–2. To put it another way, we might easily be willing to pay more than $235 for the gamble illustrated in Table 12–3, for the

TABLE 12–3
A Very Chancy Outcome

X Situation	Payoff	Probability of Winning	Expected Value
X_1	$ 100	0.7999	$ 79.99
X_2	200	0.0500	10.00
X_3	300	0.1500	45.00
X_4	1,000,000	0.0001	100.00
			$234.99

very small chance to become a millionaire is very tempting. In point of fact, people generally will not be indifferent between these two situations, and it all depends on what use you could make of the funds if you won them; indeed, a good deal of the psychology of the participants in the stock market is wrapped up in this example.

12.2.4 Expected Value of a Portfolio

In Table 12–1, in which we listed three stocks (*AT*, *ATT*, and *USS*), we saw the past behavior of a potential portfolio. A portfolio, generally, is any collection of securities. Thus, with one third of our funds in each of the stocks of Table 12–1, we would have one portfolio; with one fourth in each of *AT* and *ATT* and one half in *USS* we would have another. Investors will want to compare the characteristics of various portfolios rather than the characteristics of the individual stocks, except in their contribution to the portfolio. We have considered two of these characteristics in this section so far; they are

a)   Expected earnings of the portfolio as a whole.
b)   Variances of the portfolio as a whole.

Suppose, for example, that we had $1 in each of the three securities (*AT*, *ATT*, and *USS*). The expected earnings of this sum of securities is simply the sum of the individual earnings, as expressed in Equation 12–6.

$$E(\hat{S}) = E(\hat{X}_1) + E(\hat{X}_2) + E(\hat{X}_3) \qquad (12\text{–}6)$$

Thus, for the $1 in each of the securities, the expected value is

$$\$0.071 + \$0.067 + \$0.241 = \$0.379 \qquad (12\text{–}7)$$

if we use the means of past performance to guide our expectations about future earnings. In this case we really assumed that one third of our funds went into each stock; we will find it more convenient to use weighted averages (the three one-thirds are weights, summing to unity); and a reformulation of Equation 12–7 gives us Equation 12–8, the expected return of the portfolio which assigns funds equally to the three stocks and gets us away from the rather awkward dollar dimension.

$$1/3(0.071) + 1/3(0.067) + 1/3(0.241) = 0.126 \quad (12\text{–}8)$$

In the general case, Equation 12–6 would be written as Equation 12–9; you should verify this notation so that things do not begin to elude you.

$$E(\hat{S}) = W_1 E(\hat{X}_1) + \cdots + W_n E(\hat{X}_n) = \sum_{i=1}^{n} W_i E(\hat{X}_i) \quad (12\text{–}9)$$

with $\sum_{i=1}^{n} W_i = 1$.

You probably noticed that by putting all of your funds into *USS* you could earn 0.241 per $1, or $0.72 overall, which is almost double the $0.379 of Equation 12–7. Nevertheless, as we shall see, one might not choose this second portfolio, for its variance

($W_1 = 0$, $W_2 = 0$, $W_3 = 1$) is greater than that of the first portfolio ($W_1 = 1/3$, $W_2 = 1/3$, $W_3 = 1/3$). We will have to establish some criteria for dealing with the economic choice between expected variance and expected return; but for now, let us emphasize that these are expectations of future events and that they are expectations which are not firmly held. Practically nobody expects his guess about the future to be exact, and almost everybody plans for a margin of error on either side of his guess. One reason an investor might do this is that there is a chance he will need the funds during a series of unfavorable events. We use the past values of means and variances, but we know that history will not repeat itself; so we attach some doubt to our plans—and fix our portfolios accordingly.

12.2.5 The Variance of a Portfolio

The first thing to notice is that the expression for the variance, which first appeared in Equation 12–2, contains the mean, $\bar{X}$. This expression is repeated in Equation 12–10, at its two ends, while in between are two other ways of expressing the same definition.

$$\text{Var}(\hat{X}_1) = E(X_1 - \bar{X}_1)^2 = E[X_1 - E(X_1)]^2$$
$$= \sum_{i=1}^{n} \frac{(X_i - \bar{X})^2}{n} \quad (12\text{–}10)$$

We will find the two "expected value" forms handy in what follows, so it is well to note again the intuitive definition of the variance: it is the expected value of the squared deviation; it is the average squared deviation.

To get the variance of a sum, let us say of two securities, we can work with the term $E(X_1 - \bar{X}_1)^2$. If we substitute $X_1 + X_2$ and $\bar{X}_1 + \bar{X}_2$ into this term, the result is Equation 12–11.

$$\text{Var}(\hat{X}_1 + \hat{X}_2) = E[(X_1 + X_2) - (\bar{X}_1 + \bar{X}_2)]^2 = \text{Var}(\hat{S})$$
$$(12\text{–}11)$$

where $\hat{S} = \hat{X}_1 + \hat{X}_2$. Then, we can square the terms in the brackets to get

$$(X_1 + X_2)^2 + (\bar{X}_1 + \bar{X}_2)^2 - 2(X_1 + X_2)(\bar{X}_1 + \bar{X}_2)$$

or

$$X_1{}^2 + X_2{}^2 + 2X_1X_2 + \bar{X}_1{}^2 + \bar{X}_2{}^2 + 2\bar{X}_1\bar{X}_2 - 2X_1\bar{X}_1 - 2X_2\bar{X}_1 \\ - 2X_2\bar{X}_2 - 2X_1\bar{X}_2$$

Reorganizing this expression, we get:

$$(X_1{}^2 - 2X_1\bar{X}_1 + \bar{X}_1{}^2) + (X_2{}^2 - 2X_2\bar{X}_2 + \bar{X}_2{}^2 + 2(X_1X_2 \\ - X_2\bar{X}_1 - X_1\bar{X}_2 + \bar{X}_1\bar{X}_2)$$

or, finally,

$$(X_1 - \bar{X}_1)^2 + (X_2 - \bar{X}_2)^2 + 2(X_1X_2 - X_2\bar{X}_1 - X_1\bar{X}_2 - \bar{X}_1\bar{X}_2) \tag{12-12}$$

Returning to Equation 12–11, we put our new expression (12–12) for the term in brackets into 12–11 and calculate the expected values; the result is Equation 12–13:

$$\mathrm{Var}(\hat{X}_1 + \hat{X}_2) = E(X_1 - \bar{X}_1)^2 + E(X_2 - \bar{X}_2)^2 \\ + 2E(X_1X_2 - X_2\bar{X}_1 - X_1\bar{X}_2 - \bar{X}_1\bar{X}_2) \tag{12-13}$$

We will define the last term to be the covariance between $\hat{X}_1$ and $\hat{X}_2$, in which case Equation 12–11 finally appears as Equation 12–14, with the covariance appearing twice.

$$\mathrm{Var}(\hat{X}_1 + \hat{X}_2) = \mathrm{Var}(\hat{X}_1) + \mathrm{Var}(\hat{X}_2) + 2\mathrm{Cov}(\widehat{X_1X_2}) \tag{12-14}$$

There are two extensions of Equation 12–14 which we will want to consider. In the first place, a portfolio with only two securities in it is not general; the general version of 12–14 is given as Equation 12–15.

$$\mathrm{Var}(\hat{X}_1 + \hat{X}_2 + \cdots + \hat{X}_n) = \mathrm{Var}(\hat{X}_1) + \mathrm{Var}(\hat{X}_2) + \cdots \\ + \mathrm{Var}(\hat{X}_n) + 2\mathrm{Cov}(\widehat{X_1X_2}) + 2\mathrm{Cov}(\widehat{X_1X_3}) + \cdots \\ + 2\mathrm{Cov}(\widehat{X_{n-1}X_n}) \tag{12-15}$$

Thus, for a portfolio with three stocks there are three distinct covariances—and six total covariances—and the number of covariances rises very rapidly as the number of stocks considered rises. This raises the complexity of the analysis and vastly increases the expense of operating it. In the second place, we do not want to use the unweighted sum in Equation 12–14, and, for the portfolio problem, we will weight the variance of the sum by the shares of each stock held; you can prove the following expression in the same way in which we proved Equation 12–14.

$$\mathrm{Var}(W_1\hat{X}_1 + W_2\hat{X}_2) = W_1{}^2\mathrm{Var}(\hat{X}_1) + W_2{}^2\mathrm{Var}(\hat{X}_2)$$
$$+ 2W_1W_2\mathrm{Cov}(\widehat{X_1X_2}) \quad (12\text{–}16)$$

Table 12–4 gives the variances and covariances underlying the yields in Table 12–1; the variances (.035, .008, and .114) are on

TABLE 12–4
VARIANCE-COVARIANCE TABLE FOR THREE
COMMON STOCK YIELDS

	AT	*ATT*	*USS*
AT..........	0.035	0.011	0.014
ATT........	0.011	0.008	0.018
USS..........	0.014	0.018	0.114

TABLE 12–5
TWO TRIAL PORTFOLIOS COMPARED

	Portfolio 1	*Portfolio 2*
Weights (X_1, X_2, X_3)..........	$\frac{1}{3}, \frac{1}{3}, \frac{1}{3}$	0, 0, 1
Yields......................	0.158	0.301
Variances....................	0.022	0.114

the diagonal and the covariances are off-diagonal. We claimed earlier that the two portfolios we selected

Portfolio 1: $W_1 = W_2 = W_3 = 1/3$
Portfolio 2: $W_1 = 0, W_2 = 0, W_3 = 1$

had different yields and different risks (variances); the yield for the first portfolio was 0.126 and that for the second is easily seen to be 0.241. Now we have, in Table 12–4, enough information to apply Equation 12–16, but for three stocks. The results are summarized in Table 12–5.[4] We see that while Portfolio 1 yields

---

[4] The actual formula for calculating this result for the variance of Portfolio 1 is

$$\mathrm{Var}(1/3\,AT + 1/3\,ATT + 1/3\,USS) = (1/3)^2\mathrm{Var}(AT) + (1/3)^2\mathrm{Var}(ATT)$$
$$+ (1/3)^2\mathrm{Var}(USS) + 2(1/3)^2\mathrm{Cov}(AT,ATT)$$
$$+ 2(1/3)^2\mathrm{Cov}(AT,USS) + 2(1/3)^2\mathrm{Cov}(ATT,USS)$$

with the values taken from Table 12–4.

about half that of Portfolio 2, it only has a risk about one fifth of the risk of Portfolio 2; if we were investment advisors gathering information for a client, we would not be able to proceed any further until our customer told us his attitude toward risk—that is, in the range studied here, how much additional variance in his portfolio he would accept in exchange for more risk.

Then, since all his funds in *ATT* would earn him 0.083 and cost him 0.011 in risk, while all his funds in *USS* would earn 0.301 and cost 0.114, we could get him any combination between these two extreme possibilities by varying the weights. That is to say, if he gave us any one of the following pieces of information, we could select his portfolio for him:

a)   His desired yield (between 0.083 and 0.301).
b)   His desired risk (between 0.011 and 0.114).
c)   His trade-off between risk and yield.

It follows that if he does not give us this minimum information, he will have to decide what to do himself.

12.3   THE CONSEQUENCES OF CORRELATION BETWEEN SECURITIES

The covariances we have been using are somewhat awkward to deal with, so for the next point, and for much of the remaining discussion, let us talk about the *correlation* between securities. In fact, the correlation coefficient between any two securities from Equation 12–14 is simply defined as in Equation 12–17:

$$\text{Correlation coefficient} = r = \frac{\text{Cov}(\hat{X}_1\hat{X}_2)}{\sqrt{\text{Var}(\hat{X}_1)}\;\sqrt{\text{Var}(\hat{X}_2)}} \quad (12\text{–}17)$$

It is, roughly, a percentage measure of the covariation between any two variables. Table 12–6 contains the correlation coefficients for the three securities, *AT*, *ATT*, and *USS*, of our example.

Now, we have seen that the earnings on a stock and the variation on a stock are of interest to the manager of a portfolio, and we have shown that the covariation between securities is of interest because it enters into the calculation of the variance of the port-folio taken as a whole. What we have not shown explicitly is

TABLE 12–6
CORRELATION COEFFICIENTS FOR THE BASIC
EXAMPLE

	AT	ATT	USS
AT............	1.00	0.70	0.22
ATT.........	0.70	1.00	0.61
USS..........	0.22	0.61	1.00

how correlation itself enters into the picture; in fact, we will establish the following three general (and useful) propositions:

a)   Diversification may lower the average risk of a portfolio if the securities are uncorrelated.
b)   If securities are positively correlated, risk is greater than if not.
c)   A "risky" security may be "safer" than a "safe" security when either is added into a portfolio.

We will prove these points either in general or by example.

12.3.1   Diversification May Lower the Average Risk of a Portfolio

The ultimate objective of section 12.3 is to answer the question as to whether the variance and the expected earnings on a stock are adequate information to tell what effect the stock will have on a portfolio if it is added in. The answer is no, as we shall see, because the correlations between security yields also matter. We will begin with the uncorrelated case (or, if you wish, all correlations equal to zero case). In this event Equation 12–15 would look like 12–18, with all covariance terms dropped out.

$$\text{Var}(\hat{S}) = \text{Var}(\hat{r}_1 + \hat{r}_2 + \cdots + \hat{r}_n)$$
$$= \text{Var}(\hat{r}_1) + \text{Var}(\hat{r}_2) + \cdots + \text{Var}(\hat{r}_n) \quad (12\text{–}18)$$

where $\hat{S} = \hat{r}_1 + \hat{r}_2 + \cdots + \hat{r}_n$).

In order to keep things as simple as possible—and in order to look at "pure" diversification—we will assume all securities are alike; "alike" means that all yields are the same, as in Equation 12–19, and it means that all variances are the same, as in Equation 12–21 below.

$$\hat{r}_1 = \hat{r}_2 = \hat{r}_3 = \cdots = \hat{r}_n = \hat{r} \quad (12\text{–}19)$$

Then, we can calculate the average return of the portfolio by simply summing the individual returns and dividing by n, as in Equation 12–20,

$$\text{Average return} = \frac{\hat{S}}{n} \qquad (12\text{–}20)$$

and we can calculate the variance of the portfolio simply by summing all the individual variances, as in Equation 12–21.

$$\text{Var}(\hat{s}) = \text{Var}(\hat{r}_1) + \text{Var}(\hat{r}_2) + \cdots + \text{Var}(\hat{r}_n)$$

$$= \sum_{i=1}^{n} \text{Var}(\hat{r}) \quad (12\text{–}21)$$

To calculate the variance of the average return of the portfolio, we can use the information generated by our assumptions, and we can employ the propositions about the summation procedure which we explained in Chapter 2.[5] Recalling from Equation 12–16 that a constant is treated as squared when it is involved in the calculation of the variance, we can write the variance of Equation 12–20 as Equation 12–22.

$$\text{Var}(\text{Ave.Ret.}) = \text{Var}\left(\frac{\hat{S}}{n}\right) = \frac{1}{n^2}\,\text{Var}(\hat{S}) \qquad (12\text{–}22)$$

Then, using Equation 12–21 directly, for $\text{Var}(r)$ is a constant repeated n times, we can write

$$\text{Var}(\text{Ave.Ret.}) = \frac{1}{n^2}\,[n\text{Var}(\hat{r})] = \frac{1}{n}\,\text{Var}\ \hat{r} = \frac{\text{Var}\ \hat{r}}{n} \quad (12\text{–}23)$$

As n gets large—that is, as the portfolio gets more and more diversified, even if all stocks are alike—the variance of average returns (or, if you will, the risk of the portfolio) declines. We see this when we look at the last term in Equation 12–22, for as n gets very large, the variance of the average return of the portfolio clearly approaches zero. This establishes proposition (a).

12.3.2   Risk Can Be Larger with Correlation than Without

Let us continue to make the same assumptions that we used to justify proposition (a); but, of course, we must use Equation

---

[5] In particular, that $\sum\limits_{n-1}^{n} a = n \cdot a$, when a is interpreted as a constant.

12–15 instead of 12–18. Let us rewrite 12–15 in order to achieve some economy of notation:

$$\text{Var}(\hat{S}) = \sum_{i=1}^{n} \text{Var}(\hat{r}_i) + 2 \sum_{i=1}^{n} \text{Cov}(\widehat{r_i r_j}) \qquad (12\text{–}24)$$

We have employed the notation used on the first term before; but the second term, which is another form of Equation 12–15, is more complicated because it has a second subscript, which is introduced to pick up the two-way classification of covariances. This can be explained by example: pick a stock ($j = ATT$); then calculate all the covariances between that stock and all other stocks ($i = 1, \ldots, n$); repeat this for all stocks (all j), and you have all but the diagonal terms of Table 12–4, the covariance table. Then, in Table 12–4, the diagonal terms come from $\sum_{i=1}^{n} \text{Var}(\hat{r}_i)$. This procedure summarizes Equation 12–24.

Now we can rewrite our formula for the variance of the average return as in Equation 12–25:

$$\text{Var}(\text{Ave.Ret.}) = \frac{1}{n^2} V(\hat{S}) = \frac{\sum_{i=1}^{n} \text{Var}(\hat{r}_i)}{n^2} + \frac{2 \sum_{i=1}^{n} \text{Cov}(\widehat{r_i r_j})}{n^2} \qquad (12\text{–}25)$$

In this instance, as the portfolio gets very large, the first term gets very small, just as it did with Equation 12–23, but the second term does not. This result occurs primarily because there are many more terms in the numerator of the second term than there are in the first term (there are only n in the first term, one for each variance). In fact, the nth stock forms $n-1$ covariances with the remaining stocks; the $(n-1)$th forms $n-2$ with the remaining; the result is $n(n-1)$ total, and $n(n-1)/2$ distinct, covariances in the second term.[6]

The average covariance, then, is the sum of the covariances divided by the number of covariances or:

$$\text{Ave.Cov} = \frac{\sum_{i=1}^{n} \text{Cov}(\widehat{r_i r_j})}{n(n-1)} \qquad (12\text{–}26)$$

[6] The student should verify this formula.

If we put this value into the right-hand side of Equation 12–25, we get

$$\frac{n(n-1)}{n^2} \cdot \text{Ave. Covariance}$$

which simplifies to

$$\frac{n-1}{n} \cdot \text{Ave. Covariance}$$

This expression, then, will be positive no matter how large the portfolio gets, for $n - 1/n$ gets closer and closer to the value one as the portfolio grows in number (of securities). Thus, as the portfolio gets larger and larger, the variance of the whole lot

TABLE 12–7
ARBITRARY DATA FOR DEMONSTRATION OF PROPOSITION (c)

	Stock 1	Stock 2	Stock 3	Stock 4
Yield 1.................	1	0	7	0
Yield 2.................	2	2	8	3
Yield 3.................	3	7	2	3
Yield 4.................	4	8	0	4
Yield 5.................	5	−2	−2	5
Mean.................	3	3	3	3
Variance.............	2.00	15.20	15.20	2.40

declines, but approaches the average covariance instead of approaching zero. Directly, we can see that the risk of the correlated portfolio is greater than that of the uncorrelated one, and we have proved that proposition (b) is valid.[7]

12.3.3 A "Risky" Security May Be Safer than a "Safe" Security

Again, the proposition to be proved concerns the covariance between securities rather than the variance. We will use an example in this case rather than go through a fairly tedious proof. A risky security is one which has a high variance compared to the others; we will assume the data in Table 12–7, in which all securities are assumed to offer the same yield. Let us assume that

---

[7] Note that we are assuming *positive* correlation here; it is conceivable that the stocks you add would have *negative* covariances, in which case the risk would be less.

Stocks 1 and 2 are in the portfolio to begin with, and we wish to see which of the other two stocks—the risky Stock 3 or the safe Stock 4—both of which we expect to add nothing to average earnings, gives us the safest portfolio taken as a whole.

If we apply Equation 12–14 to the problem of finding the variance of the first portfolio (Stocks 1 and 2), we get

$$V(\hat{S}_1 + \hat{S}_2) = 2 + 15.20 + 2(0.60) = 18.40$$

When we add in Stock 4, we get

$$V(\hat{S}_1 + \hat{S}_2 + \hat{S}_4) = 2 + 15.20 + 2.40 + 2(0.60) + 2(2.20)$$
$$\underset{S_1 S_2}{} \quad \underset{S_1 S_4}{}$$
$$+ 2(0.80) = 26.80$$
$$\underset{S_2 S_4}{}$$

whereas, if we had added in Stock 3, we would have obtained

$$V(\hat{S}_1 + \hat{S}_2 + \hat{S}_3) = 2 + 15.20 + 15.20 + 2(0.60) - 2(5.10)$$
$$\underset{S_1 S_2}{} \quad \underset{S_1 S_4}{}$$
$$- 2(2.10) = 19.20$$
$$\underset{S_1 S_4}{}$$

So the "risky" stock is much safer than the "safe" stock; proposition (*c*) is consequently established; and, as claimed, it is the consequence of covariation dominating simple variation.

12.4 EFFICIENT PORTFOLIOS

The problem with the apparatus we have built to this point is that there seems to be no clear way to get our portfolio into shape except by trial and error; and there are a lot of stocks in the world. However, in principle one can find a much smaller *set* of possible portfolios—which we will call a set of efficient portfolios—among which the individual investor can choose, after he decides what his trade-off is between risk and yield.[8] In fact, we will define an efficient portfolio as one for which any further gain in yield is associated with an increase in risk. To put the matter another way, an efficient portfolio is one for which an

---

[8] You will recall that we are not showing exactly "how" an individual chooses between risk and earnings. That, we have said, is a matter of taste; and, in this text, we simply assume that people know their own minds and choose accordingly. Our purpose is to expose two important economic characteristics—risk versus earnings—which enter into all portfolio decisions.

investor cannot adjust his holdings (of his currently held stocks) and get more yield without at the same time getting more risk. If he can add more shares of *USS* to his portfolio, and earnings rise while the variance stays the same, then he ought to make such an addition. Indeed, the maximizer (of yield versus risk) is assumed to do just this.

Let us return to the problem of selection for three stocks which we will designate Stock 1, Stock 2, and Stock 3. Let us assume that our wealth holder has a set amount of funds; but to avoid

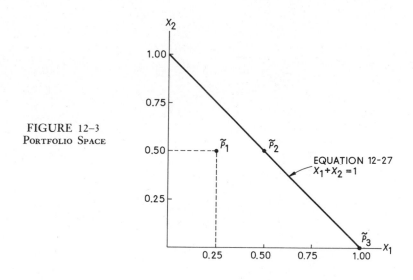

FIGURE 12–3
PORTFOLIO SPACE

the complexities of dealing in dollars, we will formulate his limits, not in dollars but in the percentage of his (given) funds. Of course, what I am suggesting is that our investor has a "budget constraint" as defined in Chapter 1, and that this budget constraint is a set of weights, where the weights are the percentages of his funds in each of the three stocks. Equation 12–27 is this budget constraint, which, we will assume, adds to unity.

$$X_1 + X_2 + X_3 = 1 \qquad (12\text{--}27)$$

We can graph this equation to gain a further perspective; in fact, in Figure 12–3 we use two dimensions (X_1 and X_2) explicitly, and Equation 12–27 is graphed as a straight-line budget constraint, in exactly the same way we have graphed earlier budget constraints. Each point in Figure 12–3 gives us the percentage of our funds held in each of the three stocks; at $\tilde{P}_1$ we have 25 percent in Stock 1, 50 percent in Stock 2, and 25 percent in Stock 3 (implicitly). At point $\tilde{P}_2$ we have split our funds equally between Stock 1 and Stock 2, and at $\tilde{P}_3$ we have all our funds in Stock 1.

We have already suggested that our expected return can be measured by Equation 12–28:

$$E = \text{Expected return} = X_1 r_1 + X_2 r_2 + X_3 r_3 \quad (12\text{–}28)$$

Thus, for $\tilde{P}_1$ of Figure 12–3 and the following arbitrary data, we have

$$r_1 = 0.10$$
$$r_2 = 0.05$$
$$r_3 = 0.07$$

and

$$E = 1/4(0.10) + 1/2(0.05) + 1/4(0.07) = 0.068$$

for example.

Let us keep things as general as possible, and eliminate X_3 (which is "invisible" anyway), in Figure 12–3 by substituting 12–27 into 12–28; the result in Equation 12–29:

$$E = X_1(r_1 - r_3) + X_2(r_2 - r_3) + r_3 \quad (12\text{–}29)$$

or, numerically (and rounded off),

$$E = 0.03(X_1) - 0.02X_2 + 0.07$$

The next step is to draw "equal earnings" lines, lines along which all portfolios return the same earnings. The idea is that the unknowns—in the choice problem—are the percentages spent on each stock; thus, if we wish our portfolio to earn 0.07, we would write Equation 12–29 as

$$E = 0.07 = 0.03X_1 - 0.02X_2 + 0.07$$

which is a straight line in the dimensions of Figure 12–3, through the origin, with a positive slope of 3/2.[9] This is illustrated as $E = 0.07$ in Figure 12–4, and one of the combinations along which a portfolio of X_1, X_2, and X_3 returns 7 percent, is seen to be

---

[9] To see this, simply write the equation as $X_2 = (-0.03/-0.02)X_1$, which is equivalent to the version in the text.

the origin (0), the point at which all our funds are in Stock 3 (and earnings are 0.07 per dollar invested). We see that $E = 0.10$ goes through $\tilde{P}_2$ and that $E = 0.05$ goes through P_3; we also see that these lines are parallel, because the slope is always 3/2, and that there are an infinite number of ways we can adjust our investor's portfolio to obtain the required earnings.

Now we are on the way to seeing the economic problem in all of this. If we decide on earnings of 0.07 (for example), then the point on the $E = 0.07$ line which has the lowest variance is

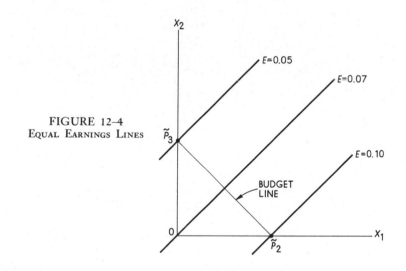

FIGURE 12–4
EQUAL EARNINGS LINES

the best point; it is also the efficient portfolio for that earnings figure, for the investor has got the least variance for his risk. Solving for the least variance is no easy matter, of course; and it does, in general, require mathematical skills beyond those required for this book. We will satisfy ourselves with a diagram illustrating the problem, and a trial-and-error solution for our mock problem.

The variance-covariance formulas—for example, Equation 12–24—are "ellipses" in two dimensions when we solve for equal variance equations.[10] One way they might appear is shown in Figure 12–5. Since the variances are ellipses, it is apparent that there

---

[10] Or, alternatively, they are "quadratic forms." A general equation for an ellipse is $X^2 + Y^2 + 2Z^2 = b$, where b is a constant. This is mathematically equivalent to Equation 12–24, with b treated as the "equal variance" mentioned in the text.

are certain points which can be eliminated right away. In particular, we can scratch out $\tilde{P}_2$ because it has the same risk as $\tilde{P}_1$, but smaller earnings—that is, $\tilde{P}_1$ and $\tilde{P}_2$ are on the same equal variance line. The center ($\tilde{C}$) does not necessarily have zero risk (it might if cash were in the portfolio), but we can see that all earnings lines above $\tilde{C}$ are inferior to some of the lines below $\tilde{C}$ because of the shape of the ellipses. In particular, for each line above $\tilde{C}$ we can find a line below which has the same earnings but lower risk.

FIGURE 12–5

SOLUTION FOR AN EFFICIENT PORTFOLIO, WITH VARIANCE
AND EARNINGS GRAPHED

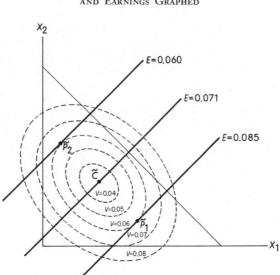

We can get all the possible "efficient" portfolios by drawing all the conceivable earnings lines below $\tilde{C}$ and moving along those lines until we come to a tangency with an equal variance line.[11] This point of tangency, as you can see, will give you the lowest risk in each case. P_1 is one such efficient point, and for each possible equal-earnings line, as drawn, there is one best (least risk) point; the locus of these points is drawn in Figure 12–6, for our arbitrary example. Thus, as you move down the efficiency locus, life gets riskier and earnings get higher; all along that line risk must be

---

[11] If you knew calculus, you would see a quick solution to the problem at this point.

traded for yield, and off that line you can always find a point on the line which is better.

The problem is now reduced to picking a point on the efficiency locus; that depends on your tastes, i.e., on your attitude toward risk, and cannot be solved by the market analyst. If, as I said before, you give him your desired risk, your desired earnings, or the trade-off between the two, he will find your portfolio from among the stocks you mutually agree to consider.[12]

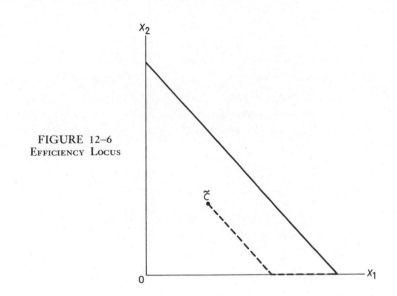

FIGURE 12–6
EFFICIENCY LOCUS

12.5 SOME COMMENTS ON APPLICATIONS IN ECONOMICS

Any economic agent which has a portfolio problem, and all wealth holding agents do, can use the methods and variations of methods of this chapter. In particular, all financial institutions—banks, as well as intermediaries—have portfolios to manage. There are three serious problems with this analysis, however.

One, already alluded to, is that the apparatus for finding the decision set (the list of efficient portfolios) is extremely expensive to operate. The principal problems here are, first, that it is expensive to obtain the information and that the solution of the problem requires solving a system of simultaneous equations—by

---

[12] As the number of stocks goes up, the cost of producing the solution goes up even more rapidly. Thus you will have to balance this cost against the gain of using the information; for institutions, machine methods might pay off, but individuals would probably not find large systems sufficiently profitable.

computer, of course—by techniques which are extremely (computer) time using. The second main problem is that we have formulated our problem in terms of only two measurable variables—earnings and risk—and thus we will obtain only two stocks in each of our efficient portfolios unless we restrict our analysis further. This can be arranged arbitrarily, for example by assuming that all stocks in the problem must be held; this assumption is more realistic for broadly defined sectors of the economy than for smaller sectors.

The last problem, and it also cannot be ducked, is that *some* statement about the investor's "risk aversion" must be made. One way this might be done is to assume some arbitrary and simple relationship between risk and earnings and then to solve for the mechanics of portfolio choice. The answers which result, some of which we will be discussing in Chapter 14, are useful, subject to the specific risk aversion assumed. This means that risk preference is generally not studied, and that there are infinitely many arbitrary relationships which could have been assumed; this is untidy but necessary, since there seems to be no "correct" model of portfolio behavior other than the one which seems to work best in a particular context. Of course, if you are working things out for yourself, the problem needn't arise, since you ought to know your own risk-earnings trade-off.

12.6 DISCUSSION QUESTIONS

1. The methods of this chapter treat upward fluctuations in stock prices in exactly the same way as they treat downward fluctuations. Is this in accordance with market practice? Why might a case be made for an unsymmetrical approach? Do margin dealings in stocks enter into the discussion?

2. Give an economic explanation of the nature of the trade-off between the mean and the variance of a portfolio of stocks. Does your explanation imply a specific attitude toward risk? What role do individual tastes play in your answer?

3. In this chapter we discussed the attachment of probabilities to future estimates of yields rather than the attachment of probability *distributions*. What would be the economic implications of adapting the second approach? Is it proper to refer to our market participants as *uncertain* about the future?

4. We did not emphasize in this chapter that one of the considerations an individual will bear in mind when he thinks about his portfolio of stocks is his expected uses of the funds in the future. Discuss some of the ways this might change our conclusions about portfolio behavior? How might this consideration make it more obviously "rational" to be a gambler?

5. Why do we use the past behavior of stock yields as the basis of our discussion of expected yields? Would you use past behavior as a guide? Would a benchmark, such as the behavior of the Dow-Jones Industrials average make the past behavior of a particular stock more relevant? Do any of your answers have any economic content?

6. Explain, perhaps in terms of some calculations you might be doing, why the apparatus of this chapter is so expensive to operate. Can you think of ways to cut things down? Does this expense help to explain why financial institutions seem to specialize in one type of risk or another? Explain, in terms of several specific types of institutions and include a discussion of other relevant factors they might consider in tailoring their portfolios so narrowly.

7. People tend to refer to stocks as risky or not risky. All stocks are risks, of course, since all companies suffer fluctuations in their earnings. Even so, why does the approach of this chapter suggest that the usage of the term *risky* in this context is not particularly well chosen? Can our usage in this chapter be given an economic interpretation?

8. Why might risk be larger with correlations than without? Can it be smaller? Give an example.

9. Why did we emphasize that individuals must actually form an opinion about risk before anyone can solve their portfolio problems? In what *specific* ways might this be done? You probably have a life-time plan (which might be a bit fuzzy at the edges); what is your implicit trade-off pattern like?

10. Why do we discuss all our economic (portfolio) problems as if we are on the efficiency locus? Is the nature of the portfolio equilibrium affected if people do not stay on the efficiency locus? Does staying on the locus have an economic cost?

12.7 FURTHER READING

MARKOWITZ, HARRY. *Portfolio Selection*, pp. 1–153. New York: John Wiley & Sons, Inc., 1959.

Chapter 13 | THE ECONOMICS OF STOCK PRICES

13.1 INTRODUCTION

No explanation of capital markets would be complete without a discussion of what we know about the determination of common stock prices, both day to day and over longer periods of time; our interest in this topic will follow two threads. In the first place we will construct a theory in which the value of the *equity* (ownership stock) of a corporation is a key economic variable. We will claim that all economic influences, both internal and external to the firm, will be reflected in changes in the value of the equity of the firm, if they affect the firm at all. Then, in Chapter 14, when we consider the application to commercial banks, we will look for the effects of monetary policy in this direction. In the second place, as with many of our peripheral topics, we are interested in the determination of stock prices themselves.

Obviously, stock prices are determined by supply and demand, but actually pinning down the determinants of these influences is frustrated on account of speculative behavior in stock markets. We will resort to several ad hoc models in our discussion—notably the "random walk" model—but at several points we will deal with more exactly specified causal models. We will tie our results into our earlier material in two ways:

a) We will explain the supply and demand for corporate debt and equity.
b) We will see what consequences the existence of an equity market has for monetary economics.

Let us begin with technical matters; we will first consider the day-to-day fluctuations of common stocks and then look briefly at the evidence for the view that in the long run, individual common stock prices will reflect the net earnings of the individual corporations. These two topics basically concern the demand for equity or, if you wish, the demand for the earnings potential of the firms. The third technical topic will consider a supply phenomenon: the factors behind the corporation's financing decision. The broad choices we will consider are to issue equity, to issue a bond, or to use retained earnings.

On a less technical level we will ask if stock prices in general can predict overall economic activity. Finally, we will examine the more popular belief that common stocks are a good hedge against inflation.

13.2 THE DETERMINATION OF STOCK PRICES

13.2.1 The Random Walk Hypothesis

There is, inevitably, a lot of myth about the determination of day-to-day stock prices; and, we must acknowledge, some of it seems verifiable. The real question, from either the amateur's or the professional economist's point of view, ultimately concerns whether or not any system of forecasting (other than prior knowledge of the future earnings of the firm) actually works. The interest of the stock trader in successful prediction is obvious, while that of the economist is somewhat less so. In fact, a wide range of economic behavior is tied up in the decision to buy or sell a common stock. The question we will begin with concerns whether or not one can use a system to outguess the market; the alternatives are to have technical competence, so as to be able to spot the arbitrage possibilities; to have insider information; or to forecast company profits, in the usual way.

It is known that the stock market is quite sensitive to what appear to be random shocks.[1] One apparent reason for this sensitivity is the thinness of the day-to-day speculative market in particu-

---

[1] When I write "stock market" from now on, I will be thinking of the New York Stock Exchange.

lar issues.[2] Thus, when a President dies or a peace rumor circulates, stock prices plunge or rise or, for that matter, gyrate rapidly, creating the illusion of fantastic profits to be made.[3] This activity draws the speculators; but the causes of the shocks are usually unpredictable and so, therefore, must be the behavior of the stock market. Once the peace rumor breaks out, it is basically too late to capitalize on the event.

One way we might find out whether systematic methods work is simply to see how much mileage we can get out of random methods of explanation.[4] It is surprisingly difficult—surprising in view of the firmness of the mythology of the stock market—to show that any particular method or any particular set of institutions can outdo the random method. The basic input to the random walk hypothesis is the idea that the principal component of tomorrow's stock price (P_{t+1}) is today's price (P_t) plus a random number (R) to deal with the peace rumor; this is expressed in Equation 13–1.

$$P_{t+1} = P_t + R \qquad (13\text{–}1)$$

When we come to predict tomorrow's price (P_{t+1}), we would take the expected value of both sides of Equation 13–1; this would give us Equation 13–2, for we expect that the mean of a series of random numbers, whose values can be as large positively as negatively, is zero.[5]

$$P_{t+1} = P_t \qquad (13\text{–}2)$$

Paul H. Cootner explains the forces thusly:

While individual buyers or sellers may act in ignorance, taken as a whole, the prices set in the marketplace thoroughly reflect the best evaluation of currently available knowledge. If any substantial group of buyers thought prices were too low, their buying would force

---

[2] The thinness results from the fact that most stockholders ignore the day-to-day fluctuations and concentrate on the current dividends and the long-run prospects of their stocks.

[3] It is actually not very easy to predict which way the market will react to a given event; although when we read about it afterward, the commentators' rationalizations often express considerable certitude as to what the prevailing attitude was.

[4] The "explanation" in this model is essentially ad hoc.

[5] Actually, it might be better to write $P_{t+1} = aP_t$ in order to account for the fact that expectations in general might be biased upward or downward. That is, stock prices could be systematically expected to rise $(a > 1)$, fall $(a < 1)$, or remain unchanged $(a = 1)$.

up the prices. The reverse would be true for sellers. Except for appreciation due to earnings retention, the conditional expectation of tomorrow's price, given today's price, is today's price.

In such a world, the only price changes that would occur are those which result from new information. Since there is no reason to expect that information to be nonrandom in its appearance, the period-to-period price changes of a stock should be random movements, statistically independent of one another.[6]

It will pay us, in coming to grips with this theorem, to think about the empirical side of the problem; what, indeed, constitutes a refutation of Equation 13–1? Actually, the best way to state our hypothesis is to note that "all" that is really claimed is that no one can forecast tomorrow's price solely on the basis of the history of price changes. In a way, this is self-evident; why should history, other than today's price—which embodies the entire influence of the past—be of any further use when it is the future for which one holds an asset? Then, it stands to reason, all who can read the newspaper and find today's price are on equal ground, at least insofar as the influence of the past is concerned.

13.2.2   Stock Prices in the Long Run

While day-to-day fluctuations in common stock prices are essentially random, it is known that individual common stock prices tend to follow the earnings of the individual corporations *in the long run.* This, indeed, comes about because speculators are operating—and operating successfully—in the stock market. As Paul H. Cootner notes,

Assuming that no investor exercises monopoly power in the market for the stock, the price at any time will be the weighted average of investor expectations, where the weights are the wealth the investor has invested or is prepared to invest in the market. If any group of investors was consistently better than average in forecasting stock prices, they would accumulate wealth and give their forecasts greater and greater weight. In the process they would bring the present price closer to the true value. Conversely, investors who were worse than average in forecasting ability would carry less and less weight. If this process worked well enough, the present price would reflect the

    [6] Paul H. Cootner, "Stock Prices: Random vs. Systematic Changes," *Industrial Management Review,* Industrial Management Review Association, Vol. 3, No. 1 (Spring 1962), p. 25.

best information about the future in the sense that the present price, plus normal profits, would be the best estimate of the future price. The existence of randomness in stock price changes does not imply that stock prices have no relationship to the real world of events, but only that investors make no systematic errors in forecasting those events.[7]

Indeed, while there is no really firm evidence in support of nonrandomness in day-to-day changes, there is evidence that successful forecasting occurs over longer periods of time. In 1965, a considerable body of data was generated by the Value-Line contest, and study of the data has revealed successful prediction. In this contest more than 18,000 contestants were asked to pick 25 stocks from a total of 350 and challenged to beat the Value-Line Investment Service over a six-month period. The first thing of note was that there was plenty of indication that the contestants did not select by a random method; some stocks were just too popular to bear out this contention. This was important to establish, for if the contestants actually picked randomly, no evidence of systematic results could be accepted.

That the contestants did not select randomly is a necessary, but not a sufficient, explanation for the observed difference. If the price changes were truly created by random behavior, the contestants could not have achieved significantly better-than-average results no matter how deliberately they made their selections. *The results can only be explained by the additional hypothesis that the price changes were not generated by a random process.*[8] [Italics added.]

Not only was the choice nonrandom, but the contestants actually generated mildly successful results for the six-month period which were extremely well-defined in the statistical sense. What guidelines the investors actually used—history or their expectations about future earnings—is not known, but it is worth noting that only 20 of the over 18,000 contestants actually beat Value Line; indeed, Value Line was well above the average, indicating, if nothing else, that experts can predict. But no technical or historical

---

[7] Paul H. Cootner, "Refinement and Empirical Testing: Introduction," in Paul H. Cootner (ed.), *The Random Character of Stock Market Prices* (Cambridge, Mass.: M.I.T. Press, © 1964), p. 80.

[8] John P. Shelton, "The Value-Line Contest: A Test of the Predictability of Stock Price Changes," *Journal of Business*, Vol. 40, No. 3 (July 1967), p. 260.

explanations tested were found to be related to individuals' or Value Line's successes; thus, the random walk hypothesis stands as essentially unrefuted, and the existence of "stabilizing" long-run forecasting stands as established, at least by this one result.

13.3 THE SUPPLY OF EQUITY AND DEBT BY PRIVATE CORPORATIONS

The discussion of this section will range from the rather parochial issues concerning the cost of capital to a variety of issues concerning the variables which influence the supply of equity and debt by corporations. We will use much of the apparatus developed in earlier chapters, but one general objective is to make clear the nature of this part of the capital market. Then, in later sections of this chapter, and in Chapter 14, we can employ our findings on the traditional monetary problems.

The "marginal efficiency of investment" approach, built in a Keynesian framework, visualizes a business firm considering an adjustment in its capital equipment as comparing the following three elements:

a)   The cost of the new equipment.
b)   The expected returns from the investment (or investments).
c)   The cost of borrowed funds or the cost of using retained earnings.

The business firm will estimate its expected net earnings (E_1, E_2, . . . , E_n) for each future period (1, 2, . . . , n) from undertaking a particular new investment. The cost (C) of the investment will then be compared with the stream of returns (R_1, . . . , R_n), with the whole project evaluated by Equation 13–3.[9]

$$C = \frac{R_1}{1 + r} + \frac{R_2}{(1 + r)^2} + \cdots + \frac{R_n + \text{Scrap value}}{(1 + r)^n} \quad (13\text{–}3)$$

This equation is a discounting formula; but in this case the rate of discount (r), which bears the alternative labels of an *internal rate of return* or the *marginal efficiency of investment* (*MEI*),

---

[9] Note that r is the "solution" to Equation 13–3, calculated after the other information has been gathered. We might refer to it as a yield, for its use is the same as the yield of Chapter 11.

is not a market variable.[10] The firm—it is said—has a series of projects; therefore, the internal rate of return can be calculated for each one. Then, with the market rate of interest reflecting the cost of borrowed funds, a profit-maximizing business firm will engage in those projects for which the internal rate of return is greater than the cost of borrowed funds, for all such projects yield expected profits.

This solution is incomplete in that no serious mention of the firm's equity is involved. The equity of a firm represents the financial interest of the owners, and, in the example just given, all funds were assumed to have been raised by bond financing on a given equity. Indeed, the analysis we just went through seems to assume that the firm will be quite indifferent toward the amount of borrowing it engages in and will operate on as thin a margin of equity as possible. This is unrealistic, and not observed in actual situations, because the interest payments on corporate debt must be made or a default will be declared. In fact, we may generalize by noting that the higher the debt-equity ratio is, the riskier life is for the stockholders of a given corporation. In practice, the amount of debt which a firm can "safely" take up depends on the variation in its earnings; if earnings fluctuate considerably, we would expect the firm to have lower debt as a percentage of its total capital.[11] We will define borrowing on a given equity as increasing the leverage of the equity; and we will ask what general principles are involved in the choice between debt and equity.[12]

Let us begin with the hypothesis that the debt-equity ratio doesn't matter to firms. This hypothesis, in its original formulation by Franco Modigliani and Merton H. Miller,[13] states that the total value of the firm depends only on its expected earnings and not on its method of financing—in particular, not on the debt-equity

---

[10] Strictly, this would be the marginal efficiency of investment if this were the marginal project.

[11] Its total capital consists of debt plus equity.

[12] And, for that matter, retained earnings.

[13] Franco Modigliani and Merton H. Miller, "The Cost of Capital, Corporation Finance, and the Theory of Investment," *American Economic Review*, Vol. 48, No. 3 (June 1958). A clearer presentation of the issues is given in Eugene M. Lerner and Willard T. Carlton, *A Theory of Financial Analysis* (New York: Harcourt, Brace, & World, Inc., 1966).

ratio. The general idea of the following proof is to show under what conditions this hypothesis will hold and then to ask if the conditions are unreal. If we accept the notion that firms should not consider the method of financing as relevant in their financing decisions, then we will be hard put to explain the relative supplies of corporate debt and equity. On the other hand, if we reject the hypothesis, perhaps because we find the assumptions too restrictive, we will probably be able to say what factors influence their decision.

We will assume that firms have no retained earnings (that is, pay out all of their net earnings), that the stock market is perfectly competitive, and that firms pay out a constant dividend for each period, forever. There will tend to be, under these conditions, a standard rate of return in each industry, in equilibrium. This rate of return, which we will call r_k, with the k an industry designation, will vary from industry to industry; but with a perfect stock market, all stock prices within the industry will adjust to the industry rate of return, so that \$1 will buy the same expected return in each firm. Consider the following two stocks:

Stock A: Dividend = \$1 per quarter
Stock B: Dividend = \$0.50 per quarter

The common stock prices for \$1 worth of stock, given an industry annual rate of return of 10 percent, will be determined from Equation 13–4,[14] where j designates the firm:

$$\text{Price} = \frac{\text{Dividend}_j}{r_k} \tag{13–4}$$

which, for the two stocks, would give share prices of

$$A: \frac{\$1 \times 4}{0.10} = \$40$$

$$B: \frac{\$0.50 \times 4}{0.10} = \$20$$

Further, as noted, \$1 will get us the same return in either firm; and if it does not, the market will eliminate the difference.

---

[14] This is the formula for a perpetuity (see Chapter 11), in case you did not recognize it; the formula applies because we are assuming that the firms pay out a constant dividend forever.

Now, suppose the firm can borrow—in a perfect market as well—and suppose that all the bonds so issued are perpetuities. In this case, all bonds, regardless of what industry they come from, will sell at the same price per dollar's worth of return. That is to say, the reason there are differences in stock yields from industry to industry is that industry earnings differ; in the case of bonds, this is not an issue, for industry-to-industry variations in corporate earnings do not affect the contracted bond yields.[15] Bonds are a homogeneous product; the bond rate of return we will designate as i, with, as noted, no industry designation. Then, Modigliani and Miller argue the following propositions:

a) The market value of any firm is independent of its capital structure (debt-equity ratio).

b) The expected yield of a share of stock depends on the leverage coefficient (debt-equity ratio).

c) The cutoff point for investment projects in any firm will be r_k and will not depend in any way on whether debt or equity is used to finance the investment.

13.3.1 The Market Value of the Firm

The first Modigliani and Miller proposition is that the market value of the company depends only on the rate of return on its assets and not on how its capital structure is arranged. If r is the rate of return on assets (A) and i is the market interest rate, then, in the absence of taxes, a company's profits will be defined by Equation 13–5, where L is the amount of debt.[16]

$$\text{Profits} = \text{Earnings} - \text{expenses} = rA - iL \qquad (13\text{–}5)$$

The essence of the first proposition is that the value (V) of the firm, defined as in Equation 13–6, for a perpetual stream of earnings is a constant which does not depend on L/E,[17] where E is

---

[15] Stock yields will also differ because of different default risk, a firm-by-firm factor which we are ignoring.

[16] We will use r instead of r_k from this point, as we will be illustrating our points within the industry.

[17] The cost of capital, taking both payments to creditors (iL) and payments to owners (rE), is defined as $C = i(L/V) + r(E/V)$. It is a rate achieved by dividing the right-hand side of $iL + rE$ by V, the market value of the firm.

the market value of equity and L is the market value of debt.

$$V = \frac{\text{Earnings}}{\text{Cost of capital}} \tag{13-6}$$

In illustration, suppose that a firm (Company A) has 100 shares of equity valued at $8 per share in the market; the market value of equity would then be $800. Suppose the firm has debt of $200 and earnings of $100; suppose the market interest rate is 0.05. The total value of the firm would be $1,000; its debt-equity ratio would be 1/4, and the rate of return on equity can then be calculated from Equation 13–5 as

$$r = \frac{\text{Profits}}{\text{Value of equity}} = \frac{\$90}{\$800} = 0.11$$

This firm has more risk than a completely unlevered firm in the same industry, obviously; therefore, its rate of return will be higher in order to compensate for the greater risk. Modigliani and Miller argue that an unlevered firm (let us say Company B), assuming that it has the same earnings of $100, will have the same market value of $1,000.

Let us accept this as an equilibrium statement and see what happens to the price of the first company's stock if it tries to increase its leverage. Since it is the reaction of stockholders which determines what happens, let us take the viewpoint of a representative stockholder, let us say one who, to begin with, holds 10 shares of Company A, the levered firm, and no shares of Company B, the unlevered one. The data so far assumed are summarized in Table 13–1. The individual stockholder will have personal leverage of 1/4, personal leverage which is equal to company leverage, since he is holding only Company A's equity. Now suppose that Company A issues $200 more of debt and retires $200 of stock, thus raising its leverage coefficient to 2/3. If this deal is profitable, as it seems to be—since the rate of return is greater than the interest rate—the value of the firm's common stock should rise; let us assert that buying up 25 percent of the outstanding stock raises the price of the common stock from $8 to $10 per share. Company A now has net earnings of $100 − 0.05 ($400) = $80; and its common stock, of which there are now 75 shares, is valued at $750.

The first thing we notice is that the Modigliani-Miller hypothesis is violated because firm A is now valued at $400 + $750 = $1,150, and Modigliani and Miller would claim that it should be valued at $1,000. The second thing is that the individual stockholder (who did not sell) in Company A now has a much higher debt-equity ratio than he originally seemed to be happy with and will want to rearrange his portfolio—in fact, he will want to sell some of his stock in Company A. The reason he will do this now can be seen clearly: the rate of return on equity is actually lower in the

TABLE 13–1
MODIGLIANI-MILLER ILLUSTRATION

	Company A	Company B
Earnings	$ 100	$ 100
Equity value	800	1,000
Debt value	200	.....
Company value	1,000	1,000
r	0.112	0.100
Cost of capital	0.100	0.100

second case than in the first—it is now 0.107—and the stockholder has a much riskier security.

If we assume the stockholder wants to keep the same trade-off between risk and yield as before (0.012 yield for 1/4 leverage) and if all stockholders are of the same mind, the equilibrium position will occur where the value of the equity is $600 for 75 shares; this means a price of $8 a share, which puts the firm back where it started and removes the advantage of leverage completely; proposition (*a*) is thus established. Let us turn to proposition (*b*).

13.3.2 The Value of a Share of Stock and the Method of Financing

Actually, in the course of proving proposition (*a*), we have established proposition (*b*) and to some extent justified proposition (*c*). Proposition (*b*) states that the yield on a share of common stock does depend on the way capital is raised. The yield on stock includes dividends plus capital gains; but, in our case, since we have assumed no retained earnings by our sample firm and since we have no capital gains, we would estimate the yield per share by dividing the net earnings of the firm by the number of shares outstanding. When we began, with $90 of earnings and 100 shares, the yield per share was $0.90; in the second case, with $80 and 75 shares, the yield per share rose to $1.07. This, indeed, is the general answer: a rise in the debt-equity ratio causes a rise in the yield per share. Now what is interesting about this is that there are some people who actually think the yield per share is an interesting number. In contrast, we have shown that nothing has changed (proposition *a*), yet the yield per share has gone up; we have shown that the yield per share is quite a misleading concept. Indeed, it is misleading because it is a nominal concept rather than a real concept; it is nominal because the number of shares is a nominal (number) concept.

We will not undertake a proof of proposition (*c*), but we ought to consider its rationale, at least. Indeed, when one is considering a new investment project under the assumptions we have adopted, the method of finance will not affect the choice of project, and the critical factor will be the rate of return which is common in the industry. Thus, we may paraphrase all three propositions by saying that the overall Modigliani-Miller hypothesis amounts to the argument that the critical element considered by the firm before it undertakes an investment project (or changes its method of acquiring finance) is what effect the project will have on the market value of the firm's common stock. If the project is expected to raise the market value, the firm will go ahead, for the market is expected to judge the additional risk as more than compensated for by the higher earnings. When put this way, the argument is eminently sensible, even if the real world does not correspond particularly well to the model world we have adopted here.

13.3.3 Some Essential Qualifications to the Argument

You are probably aware that the preceding analysis has been built on some rather special assumptions, so that its direct application to the real world would be a perilous undertaking. We are, by now, quite used to such things as "perpetual earnings" and "pure competition"; but in this case some important additional qualifications have also been slipped in. In the end, we will abandon our theorems for weaker versions, not entirely because the theorems are unsound but primarily because the *institutional* structure of our economy makes leverage profitable. To be sure, we are engaging in a kind of test of the assumptions of our model; but, you will recall, we had this in mind from the beginning of this exercise.

The most serious problems come about on account of our tax laws. These laws are so diverse and so changeable that some effects are bound to occur; even so, two simple cases destroy the direct applicability of the Modigliani-Miller model in its rigid form: the taxation of corporate earnings (double taxation) and the differential taxation of capital gains and income. Let us consider the double taxation argument more closely, since it can be illustrated directly using the data generated in the last section.

Suppose, for example, that Company A and Company B are both subject to a 50 percent corporate income tax on their net earnings. If the two firms are in equilibrium in Table 13–1, then introduction of the tax provision changes the situation, for Company A has a tax deduction in the form of interest payments of $10 which Company B does not have. Thus, the value of Company A is *understated;* and as the ratio of debt to equity grows, the value of Company A diverges from that of Company B. Since we have such a tax law, the capital structure of the firms in our economy depends on the debt-equity ratio; the Modigliani and Miller theorems still apply, but they must be qualified.

The second proposition is even more obvious, but also a little more complicated. It so happens that firms can and do finance a substantial (and variable) amount of their new investment from retained earnings. For example, consider the figures of Table 13–2 for the last half of 1968 and 1969. Here it is clear that retained earnings—a form of equity, to be sure—are by far the most important element in the generation of funds for private corporations. One reason we might reasonably be surprised at this result comes from our simple economic analysis: the implicit cost of using these funds is the same as the explicit cost of floating a bond issue; that is, the firm should charge itself the market rate of interest on its borrowings from itself.[18] The usual direct answer

---

[18] But, of course, their use does not involve extensive brokerage fees, so the saving here has some influence on the decision.

to this is that by using its own funds the firm will be able to avoid dealing for funds in a highly variable market. One of the variable elements in that market is well known: monetary policy probably affects the availability of funds to corporate users, and this unevenness they would just as soon avoid. Avoid it they did, in 1969, as the figures for new expenditures on plant and equipment in Table 13–2 suggest.

But far more important in these figures is the fact that when a firm retains its earnings rather than distributes them, the shareholders will—if the firm does not overdo the investment and reduce

TABLE 13–2
SOURCES OF CORPORATE FUNDS
(1968–3 through 1969–4; $ million)

Quarter	Corp. Pretax Earnings	Cash Dividends	Retained Earnings	Total Business Exp. on Plant & Equip.	Net Change in Corp. Bonds & Notes	Net Change, All Corp. Common & Pref. Stock
1968–3	91,500	23,600	26,500	16,790	3,402	685
1968–4	94,500	23,800	27,800	19,030	3,953	1,841
1969–1	95,500	23,800	27,900	16,040	3,676	2,433
1969–2	95,400	24,300	27,000	18,810	3,861	1,504
1969–3	92,500	24,900	24,900	19,250	3,117	1,410
1969–4	91,400	25,200	23,800	21,460	3,101	2,263

SOURCE: *Federal Reserve Bulletin.*

the profit rate—be taxed at the capital gains rate rather than at the income tax rate. Thus, for individuals with higher marginal tax rates on income[19] than on capital gains, it would pay to buy shares of a "growth stock"—i.e., a company which favored growth in the value of its common stock over increased dividends. A wide variety of such choices, even within particular industries, can be made. Again, a firm is seen to be able to affect its market value by adjusting its capital structure, so again the Modigliani-Miller hypotheses must be adjusted for this consideration.

---

[19] The marginal rates—rates on the last dollar earned—currently go to 70 percent on income; capital gains rates go to 25 percent; but the capital gains must be realized, a fact which enables some stockholders to postpone their tax payments—by means of the retained earnings dodge—until later, and earn interest on them to boot.

There are other, more specialized, qualifications which have been raised concerning the cost of capital theorems. Most of them are objections to the competitiveness and frictionless nature of the assumed world, factors which we are used to overlooking. For example, there is surely some difference between borrowing rates for big firms and for small; and there are transactions costs which make personal arbitrage expensive and which vary depending on the size of the customer's account. Further, there is the limited liability feature of owning corporate stock, so that, for example, an individual may prefer to borrow through a levered corporation rather than on his own hook.[20] We could go on like this indefinitely, but instead let us state our results somewhat more broadly than we have explained them as:

The price of the equity of a private corporation will depend on
a) the rate of return on its physical assets,
b) the debt-equity ratio of the corporation,
c) the dividend payout rate of the corporation, and
d) the cost of borrowed funds;
and it will further be constrained by
e) the availability of borrowed funds and
f) tax laws.

13.4 STOCK PRICES AND MONETARY ECONOMICS

The general points concerning common stocks and money have already been made implicitly. To spell them out a little, common stocks, like money and bonds, are a distinct sort of financial asset; and when an individual chooses among these broad categories, he will weigh return versus risk for each instrument, for we have seen that tax laws and the like make economic variables out of otherwise nominal concepts.[21] How you proceed in the further disintegration of these categories depends on the problem in hand,[22]

---

[20] The limit of liability is usually the par value of the common stock, which is often set either very low or at "no par."

[21] For stocks versus bonds it was the debt-equity ratio (in section 13.3) and for bonds of different maturities, it was the difference in coupon rates (section 11.2.1).

[22] You would need to divide bonds into long-term and short-term to deal with "operation twist" (section 11.7), with the framework of Chapters 12 and 13.

but the general framework is clear: the decision to hold money, stocks, and bonds in one's portfolio depends on the yields from these instruments versus the fluctuations in these yields, all judged from the individual's (or institution's) attitude toward risk versus earnings.

We will go into the effect all of this has on the demand for money in Chapter 14; but for now, there are two further economic questions, having to do with stocks directly, which we can take up here:

a)   Can an index of stock prices predict general activity, in which case we might want to include the index in our model of the economy?

b)   What influence does money have on stock prices?

13.4.1   The Dow-Jones Average

We have argued that common stock price changes are essentially random for short periods of time and are essentially systematic—and can be forecasted—for longer periods of time.[23] Of what use, either as a guide to the present state of the market as a whole or as an indicator of expectations, are aggregate indices such as the Dow-Jones Average (DJA) of common stock prices?

The DJA is a weighted average of the prices of 30 popular common stocks traded on the New York Stock Exchange; it is an especially crude index of prices in that it is calculated by weighting the individual stocks equally. Its principal virtue is that it is easily computed, but there are a host of problems with it as well:

a)   If two stocks fall by one point each, investors may not regard these falls as equivalent. The obvious example is the case in which one stock is selling at 1 and the other at 100; the DJA treats stocks in this naive way, by weighting them equally.

b)   The stocks may (do) have different variances and covariances, unrecognized by the index, but often recognized by individual investors; furthermore, these variances and covariances change; and these facts, too, are unrecognized.

---

[23] When I say "essentially random," I mean no more than that we have not (yet) found a good systematic explanation of their behavior.

c) Downward price movements in stocks ought not to be treated in the same way as upward movements, both because the former are not as often observed and because more people lose on downward rather than on upward movements; the DJA treats both symmetrically.

d) A stock price can change, for example because of a bad dividend, and change the DJA without "the market" in general having changed.[24]

Even so, it is very likely that the DJA is quite well correlated with the market as a whole and will be useful so long as all that

TABLE 13–3
THE DOW-JONES AVERAGE AS A LEADING INDICATOR

Date	Decline in DJA	Duration of Decline	Recession Followed
1946	23%	5 months	No
1949	16	11	Yes
1953	13	8	Yes
1957	18	6	Yes
1960	16	10	Yes
1962	27	6	No
1965	10	2	No

SOURCE: Sidney Robbins, *The Securities Markets* (Glencoe, Ill.: Free Press, 1966), p. 135

is required is very general price information. This occurs primarily because the DJA has enough different stocks (30) to be statistically representative. For particular problems of portfolio management we would want a better index; particularly important would be an index which is obviously more related to changes in the variation of stocks in the market in general. Such indices do exist, of course.

While investors may not find much help in the DJA, the government might, for the DJA is well known to be a "leading indicator" of economic activity. In fact, every downturn we have had in recent years has been signaled by a prior decline in the stock market. Table 13–3 contains one summary of recent vintage.

---

[24] We observed this phenomenon in our discussion of a price index in section 2.7.2.

The problem, though, is that the "leading indicator" leads without there being a following necessarily (in 1946, 1962, and 1965, for example). Further, not shown is the fact that the lead is quite variable in its distance from the event. About all we can say, particularly since no obvious causation exists between stock market leads and following changes in general economic activity, is that "the market" seems to "believe" something is due to happen. "The market," of course, is merely guessing.

13.4.2 Inflation and the Stock Market

When the quantity of money changes—of its own accord—the real variables in the economic system are involved in the adjustment which follows, assuming the economy is at less than full employment. Obviously, if an increase in the quantity of money has the effect of lowering interest rates and increasing corporate profits, common stock prices, in general, ought to rise. Then we should see some long-term relationship between the rate of change of the money stock and an index of stock prices; as Table 13–4 shows, we do.

Of course, the broad association in Table 13–4 is not an explanation of anything in particular, but it does indicate that when the money stock changes in an unusual manner—the kind of change associated with an abrupt change in interest rates—the stock market is likely to be affected. The problem is that easy money does not invariably lead to a stock market boom, particularly when stock market investors begin to get nervous about potential "over-expansion" and a potential plunge in stock prices. Even so, the increase in the overall "liquidity" of the economy associated with the increase in the money stock, and the increase in credit available or a decrease in its price, is bound to stimulate the stock market under ordinary conditions (possibly in 1951–52, 1955, 1959, 1963–64, and 1967–68). Further, it is likely that a slower rate of growth of the money stock will adversely affect stock prices (for example, in 1957, 1960, and 1966).

If changes in the money stock do not affect real activity, then—assuming velocity to be constant—they affect the price level. We often hear that common stocks are a good "hedge against inflation"; but, as we shall see, the quality of this hedge depends on what

TABLE 13-4

THE RELATIONSHIP BETWEEN COMMON STOCKS AND THE
MONEY STOCK IN THE UNITED STATES
(1949 through 1969)

Year	Common Stock Index: Standard & Poor Ind., 1941–43 = 100	% Change in Common Stock Index	Rate of Change of Money Stock
1949	15.00	...	...
1950	18.33	22.2	2.8
1951	20.76	13.2	4.4
1952	24.81	19.5	5.0
1953	24.84	0.1	2.6
1954	30.24	21.7	1.5
1955	42.40	40.2	3.2
1956	49.80	17.4	1.1
1957	47.63	−4.4	0.6
1958	49.36	3.6	1.2
1959	61.56	24.7	4.4
1960	59.42	−3.5	−1.3
1961	70.01	17.8	1.6
1962	65.54	−6.4	2.0
1963	73.39	12.0	3.1
1964	86.19	17.4	6.1
1965	93.48	8.4	4.7
1966	91.09	−2.6	1.9
1967	91.93	0.9	6.6
1968	98.70	7.4	7.2
1969	97.84	−0.9	1.5

SOURCE: *Federal Reserve Bulletin.*

has caused the inflation in the first place. Let us take two extreme cases:

Case 1: Inflation induced by government spending at full employment.

Case 2: Inflation induced by business spending at full employment.

Insofar as real resources stay in the private sector (Case 1), putting one's money into common stocks will be a reasonable hedge against inflation; but, if resources are drained from the private sector (Case 2), most bets will lose to some extent. Let us consider Case 2 first.

Suppose that individuals correctly expect business firms, whose prices are marked up in inflation, to have increased nominal earnings in exact proportion to the inflation. Presumably individuals will tend to switch from bonds to common stocks, because nominal returns on bonds are fixed while the nominal earnings of corporations are expected to keep exactly in line with inflation. The prices of the bonds sold will fall (and bond yields will rise) while the prices of common stocks will rise. Thus, we would expect the differences between the yields on the two instruments—calculated on an average—to be a good index of expected inflation. Furthermore, if expected inflation is closely related to actual infla-

TABLE 13–5
COMMON STOCKS AS A HEDGE AGAINST INFLATION: THE DATA
UNITED STATES, 1961–69

Year	Consumer Price Index (1)	% Change (2)	Dividend Price Ratio of Corps. (3)	Corp. Bond Yields (4)	Col. (4) Minus Col. (3) (5)	% Change in Corp. Profits (After Tax) (6)
1961	104.2	...	...	...	...	...
1962	105.4	1.15	3.37	4.62	1.25	14.7
1963	106.7	1.23	3.17	4.50	1.33	6.1
1964	108.1	1.31	3.01	4.57	1.56	16.0
1965	109.9	1.65	3.00	4.64	1.64	21.1
1966	113.1	2.91	3.40	5.34	1.94	7.3
1967	116.3	2.82	3.20	5.82	2.62	−5.2
1968	121.2	4.21	3.07	6.51	3.44	5.3
1969	127.7	5.36	3.24	7.36	4.12	1.4

SOURCE: *Federal Reserve Bulletin.*

tion, we would expect this yield difference to widen with more rapid rises in prices and to narrow when prices rise more slowly. Thus, for the period 1962–69, we see, in Table 13–5, that when inflation was slow (1961–65) the difference between bond and stock yields was equally small (and equal, for that matter) and when inflation picked up, the gap widened.

Let us turn to Case 1, the case in which additional resources disappear into the government sector. The idea here is that while business prices rise in pace with inflation, business costs rise faster (in the competition for scarce resources), so that business earnings are squeezed. In this event, common stocks would not be as good a hedge, since earnings would not keep pace with inflation, and the gap between the two yields would be less than the rate of inflation. Indeed, whenever corporate profits rise more slowly than usual, the yield gap would be likely to be less than the rate of inflation (1966–69); and whenever corporate profits rise more rapidly than usual, the converse could be true (1965). Reference to column (6) of Table 13–5 bears out that there is such a general relation.

We have seen, then, that there is a firm relation between the money stock and the stock market, and that this relation occurs in the first instance because money and stocks are alternative stores of one's financial wealth. We have also seen that under certain conditions we can estimate "expected" inflation by comparing bond yields with stock yields. Thus we certainly have demonstrated a sufficient reason for including a chapter on stock prices in a money and banking book.

13.5 DISCUSSION QUESTIONS

1. How is it possible that day-to-day fluctuations in stock prices may be random and long-period ones systematic? Is not the long run the sum of the short run? What, then, must be true about day-to-day fluctuations?

2. The "stock market analyst" usually referred to in newspapers is a shadowy figure indeed. It is noticeable, for example, that the analyst will use the same phenomenon—for example an outbreak of war in the Middle East—for opposite results. Does it follow that the analyst is talking nonsense, or is there some economic reasoning behind all this?

3. Does the thinness of the stock market have anything to do with the apparently large fluctuations in stock prices? Are the fluctuations actually very large? Look at some recent data for a typical blue chip stock—using closing prices—and work out, for various margin requirements, the profits which could have been made if your foresight had been as good as your hindsight. Comment on your results.

4. Comment on the following news item: "The market yesterday was firm, with gains outnumbering advances by two to one. The Dow-Jones industrial average was off .60 on rumors that the 747 was having engine trouble. Otherwise the market would have been higher."

5. Why is the behavior of common stock prices dominated by expectations? Which expectations serve an economic function and

which do not? How did you decide to define "an economic function" in your answer?

6. What connection is there between the "cost of capital" and the corporate supply of debt instruments? Do all debt issuing organizations go through the same procedure to arrive at their optimal strategy? Do individuals? Explain.

7. The idea that there is no intrinsic difference for the firm between debt and equity is a little hard to swallow. What was the key to that argument? Can you think of *economic* differences between the two, not caused by tax laws and the like, which we might like to mention in a more complete analysis?

8. We emphasized that the market value of a firm's equity is a key variable and, earlier, that banks are business firms. Could you work out the effect of monetary policy on the system by looking at the value of bank equity? What sorts of effects might turn up? Do expectations get in the way at all?

9. Give some additional reasons why firms use retained earnings for investment. Is monetary policy frustrated by this practice, or are there other effects, which we haven't discussed, which merely channel the pressure elsewhere? Explain carefully.

10. If common stocks are such a good hedge against inflation, why did the stock market tumble from 1965 to 1970 at exactly the same time the rate of inflation was rising? Give both a "monetary" and an "expectations" explanation and then reconcile them. You may wish to illustrate your discussion with some numbers.

13.6 FURTHER READING

Baumol, William. *The Stock Market and Economic Efficiency*, chaps. 1–3. New York: Fordham University Press, 1965.

Cootner, Paul H. (ed.). *The Random Character of Stock Market Prices*, pp. 7–16, 79–83. Cambridge, Mass.: M.I.T. Press, 1964.

Robbins, Sidney. *The Securities Market*, chaps. 2 and 3. Glencoe, Ill.: Free Press, 1966.

Robichek, Alexander A., and Myers, Stewart C. *Optimal Financing Decisions*, chaps. 1–3. Englewood Cliffs, N.J.: Prentice-Hall, Inc., 1965.

Shelton, John P. "The Value-Line Contest: A Test of the Predictability of Stock-Price Changes," *Journal of Business*, Vol. 40, No. 3 (July 1967).

Sprinkel, Beryl W. *Money and Stock Prices*. Homewood, Ill.: Richard D. Irwin, Inc., 1964.

Chapter 14

SOME IMPLICATIONS OF UNCERTAINTY ANALYSIS IN MONEY AND BANKING

14.1 INTRODUCTION

Ultimately a good deal of economics will have to be rewritten entirely in order to accommodate the findings derived from expressing events as having a probable rather than a certain likelihood of occurring. We are witnessing this development at the present; and one of the reasons we need to approach money and banking from a new angle is to appreciate the significance of, and prospects for, the new discoveries. The basis of the improvements, and it follows most directly from restating all of our monetary problems as portfolio problems, is the recognition that current economic decisions involve the future rather than the past (except as a guide); and every future event is surrounded by uncertainty. In the framework of asset choice, the future is explicitly introduced and the interest rate necessarily involved, since one holds assets for their future yields.

The general aim of this chapter is to see what use we can make of the theorems we developed in Chapters 12 and 13. The first thing we will do is recast our basic monetary problem as a portfolio problem; we will begin with the definition of money and work right through to some basic results in the demand for money. The second task is to see what happens to our understanding of the banking industry; we will be interested in bank portfolio decisions and in the official rationale of the regulation of bank interest rates, particularly the rate of zero set on demand deposits. We will see that the rationale is based on expected (destabilizing) bank portfolio behavior. Finally, we will discuss some results which have been obtained from the application of portfolio-choice methods to the study of financial intermediaries in general.

14.2 A RESTATEMENT OF THE MONETARY DEMAND PROBLEM

14.2.1 Liquidity

When we defined money in Chapter 2, we pointed out that we were making no use of the concept of liquidity; in fact, we concentrated on some functions—medium of exchange, store of value, and unit of account—and argued that currency and demand deposits are the only possessors of all three characteristics at once. If we define liquidity as "moneyness," then by the system of this book, *only* currently and demand deposits are perfectly liquid; and we have two labels for one collection of concepts. On the other hand, we can "define" money empirically as the most liquid financial asset in the system; that is, we can rank assets by their liquidity and select in one way or another a set as "money," a set as "near-money," and a set as "nonmoney." This approach— and it is used by some economists—has a number of serious problems:

a) Liquidity itself is still not easy to define.
b) The choice criterion between the three categories will have to be arbitrary and thus subject to dispute.
c) The process of definition has become empirical, which is philosophically unsound.
d) The physical thing we end up calling money will vary with the circumstances.

The general idea behind the liquidity approach is the notion that things which are perfect substitutes for each other are, economically speaking, identical; furthermore, to the extent that an item is a substitute, to that extent it is the same thing; this restates the "moneyness" position. Now since all items possess "moneyness" in the sense of being exchangeable into money, all things are partly money. If all the degrees of moneyness across the system at a moment of time could be added up, we would end up with the stock of liquidity, I suppose; but since the empirical problems are insurmountable, it seems best to shift away from this aspect of the problem toward a more positive side: What new idea is contained in the concept of liquidity?

Actually, by liquidity we generally mean the ease with which an asset can be converted into cash. This ease—and ease includes the expenses involved—depends on

a) The cost of converting the item into cash—the brokerage cost.
b) The chance that you will need to sell off the item—if it is nonmoney—before it matures.
c) The thinness of the market in which you will have to sell. (Do you know anyone who couldn't sell his house in the credit squeeze of 1969?)
d) Your typical "holding period"—the average length of time until you expect to use the funds.

This is essentially a technical explanation of liquidity; and, it seems to me, liquidity explained this way is not particularly elusive.[1] Ignoring (d), item (a) can be calculated precisely; item (b) can be estimated by the variation and covariation in your cash flows; while item (c) can be estimated by the variation and covariation in the securities market.

What I am suggesting is that what we really ought to be thinking about, when we discuss liquidity, are the characteristics of other financial assets which influence the demand for money. If the rate of return on a particular asset—let us say, a government bond—is insufficient compensation, on the margin, for the risk of holding the bond, the individual will hold money, because there is no risk of capital loss on money except for the attrition common to all financial assets due to changes in the price level.[2] The point is that one effective way to discuss the demand for money is to treat money as one item in the wealth holder's portfolio. Clearly, then, the principles of Chapter 12 would apply perfectly, and the information essential to the decision to hold money involves (1) the net return which money offers in the form of services,

---

[1] There are still problems here, however, because these aspects are not independent of each other and all directly influence the demand for each asset.

[2] Here we must distinguish between equities and bonds, for if the inflation is a "profit-inflation," then common stocks will tend to be a "refuge" for people avoiding the "tax" of the rising price level. This problem was discussed in section 13.4.2.

(2) the interest rates on all other assets, and (3) the variances and covariances of all asset yields, *including* money.

Where you begin depends on how ambitious you are; at a minimum, we will try to get genuine uncertainty about the future into our analytical framework. There are, basically, three types of models used to analyze the demand for money in the portfolio sense. There are models which study the *transactions* demand—featuring no uncertainty—in which money is held for its convenience; there are models which study the *precautionary* demand—featuring uncertainty about the time patterns of expenditures and receipts—in which money provides the service of a hedge; and there are models which study the *speculative* demand—featuring uncertainty about future yields—in which money provides the service of having no uncertainty in its return. While all of these aspects are relevant, we will concentrate on the speculative models—first in the language of Keynes, and then in the language of the portfolio models—because this is new, and interesting, material.

14.2.2 The Keynesian Speculative Demand for Money

The Keynesian version of the demand for money, which we summarized in Chapter 3, was once thought to be founded on notions of uncertainty. You will recall that we argued there that individuals formed expectations about the course of future interest rates and then took a position (speculated) in bonds or money depending on what they expected to happen to the yield on bonds. Since "speculative" behavior implies uncertain returns, it would seem that this is an uncertainty problem—but it isn't. In fact, the speculators of the Keynesian theory individually had absolute conviction (had no uncertainty) about what was going to happen to interest rates. The basic idea around which these "speculators" formed their predictions was that of a normal level of interest rates. If the market interest rate was above an individual's normal interest rate, he would expect interest rates to fall (bond prices to rise) and hold bonds. It is also important to recognize that this normal rate is an individual's view and not that of the market; there is no market normal rate (of course, there is an average normal rate) because individuals will have different opinions about what is normal. Thus, at any high interest rate, there is always someone still holding money (still believing that the normal interest is higher than that); but the higher the rate of interest, the fewer will be the number of individuals expecting (with certainty) a further rise in rates. This gives us the downsloping relation between interest rates and money holdings which we called the demand for money.

This relation, though, is based on *certainty*—it is, in a way, speculation without the enjoyment factor, for individuals face uncertain events as if they knew perfectly well what was going to happen. As Keynes notes,

> It is interesting that the stability of the system and its sensitiveness to changes in the quantity of money should be so dependent on the existence of a variety of opinions about what is uncertain. Best of all that we should know the future. But if not, then, if we are to control the activity of the system by changing the quantity of money, it is important that opinions should differ.[3]

It is important that opinions differ because it is important that the demand curve not be a horizontal straight line, but it is going too far to say that this is actually how "expectations" are formed. It seems more likely that individuals will discover—from sad experience—that their guesses are often incorrect and will grow generally cautious;[4] when individuals react as if the future they expect (on average) has some chance of not coming about, we have to deal with uncertainty.

14.2.3 A Portfolio Model of the Speculative Demand for Money

Let us assume that an individual can hold either money or a quantity of a government bond, that the interest rate on the bond is r_b, and that the yield on money is zero ($r_m = 0$).[5] We will assume the individual is interested in the relative quantities of

---

[3] John Maynard Keynes, *The General Theory of Employment, Interest, and Money* (New York: Harcourt, Brace & World, 1963), p. 172.

[4] That is, at the least, they will surround their guesses about the future with probability distributions.

[5] Note that we are implicitly assuming that there is some possibility that the individual will need his funds before the bond matures (or there is no risk). We are also assuming that there is no normal rate and that the individual pays no attention to long-time norms.

money and bonds; and it is these relative quantities which we wish to determine, at each level of interest rates. Since money has a zero yield, the individual will expect the return of his portfolio to be $r_b B$, with B defined as the percentage of funds invested in bonds, as in Equation 14–1.

$$r_b \cdot B = \text{Expected return} = \bar{X} \qquad (14\text{–}1)$$

In the analysis in Chapter 12 each of our securities had a variance and also a covariance; but because money has a zero rate of return, it is only the variance in the bond yield which matters in our estimation of the risk of the portfolio. That is, the general measure of the risk of the portfolio is

$$\text{Var}(r_b + r_m) = r_m{}^2 \text{Var}(r_m) + r_b{}^2 \text{Var}(r_b) + r_m r_b \text{Cov}(r_m, r_b)$$

but since the terms involving money are zero by virtue of our assumption of a zero yield for money, we may write the variance of the portfolio as

$$\text{Var}(r_b + r_m) = r_b{}^2 \text{Var}(r_b)$$

Then, the standard deviation (σ) of the portfolio is simply the square root of this expression, as noted in Equation 14–2.

$$\sigma(r_b + r_m) = r_b \sigma(r_b) \qquad (14\text{–}2)$$

We can solve for the trade-off between risk (14–2) and yield (14–1) by substituting 14–1 into 14–2; this process yields Equation 14–3 , in which the items we are interested in are X, the expected earnings of the portfolio and the standard deviation of the portfolio $[\sigma(r_m + r_b)]$.

$$\bar{X} = r \frac{\sigma(r_m + r_b)}{\sigma(r_b)} = \frac{r_b}{\sigma(r_b)} \sigma(r_m + r_b) \qquad (14\text{–}3)$$

If we take the standard deviation of r_b to be unrelated to the level of r_b, we can draw a family of lines, as in Figure 14–1, which describes the trade-off between risk and yield in the portfolio. Thus, the individual will be faced with an interest rate, for example r_{b1}, and will make a choice of trade-off which will imply a definite value to B (and hence to M). The actual selection of a point, say P_1, will depend on his tastes (between risk and yield); and, as before in this book, we will not be explicit about how he makes his judgment.

FIGURE 14–1
THE RISK-YIELD TRADE-OFF LINES FOR VARIOUS
INTEREST RATES

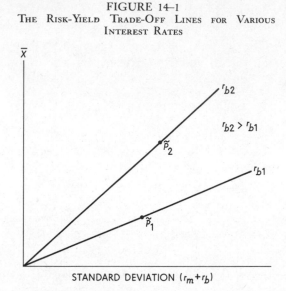

To get from this formulation to the demand for money, all we need to do is face the individual with a second interest rate. If the individual holds M_1 of money at r_{b1}, at r_{b2}—a higher rate of interest—he will hold more bonds and less money simply because he is getting a higher return without more risk. (This follows since we postulate no interdependence between the level of bond yields and the standard deviation of bond yields.) Thus, we have achieved three improvements in our basic theory; we still have a downsloping demand curve for money, but

a)   We no longer depend, as Keynes had to, on "normal" rates and "differences of opinion."

b)   We have a framework which generalizes easily and one in which money holding is just part of the general problem of asset choice.

c)   We have got closer to the real world in that in the real world there is considerable uncertainty.

14.3 COMMERCIAL BANK PORTFOLIO CHOICE

We are not going to apply our portfolio model formally to bank behavior, but we will discuss several important aspects of this behavior under three headings. These concern variations in cash flow (representing risk), variations in the yields of the items in its portfolio, and (in the context of the problem of paying interest on demand deposits) the relation between the two. Also, we will look at some of the results of portfolio studies, taking the methods used more or less for granted.

14.3.1   Variations in Cash Flows

Let us assume—as we have all along—that banks maximize their profits subject to their specific uncertainties. Earlier, when we pointed out the usefulness of arguing that banks manufacture money rather than "accept" deposits of "other people's money," we made the basic point about the suppliers of deposits. Now, however, we will examine banks as holders of an inventory of various assets in relation to their fixed liabilities; we can then argue that the bank's problem in selecting its basic portfolio is to maximize profits subject to the quantity of its cash inflows and subject to the uncertainties surrounding both cash inflow and the yields of the items in its asset portfolio.

A bank makes its profit, from the point of view we are now taking, as an intermediary rather than as a manufacturer of a product; its essential function, here, is to borrow short and lend long, deriving its earnings from performing the economic function of spreading the risk. For this service, depositors are willing to accept nothing on their deposits and to pay interest on their loans—even when the same person is involved in both transactions. The commercial bank, as we know, is not permitted to pay interest on demand deposits; thus, it has no direct means to control the cash inflow; it may vary its services, but only slowly, so the bank is more or less in the position of taking what it can get. The cash inflow to the bank will vary from period to period; consequently the bank will not be able to predict, with certainty, what amount of deposits it will have—and hence what amount of loans it can make—at a particular moment in time.[6] This uncertainty will create an inventory problem for the bank, mainly because if the bank is unable to make or renew loans, its loan customers

---

[6] We noted in section 10.6 that in 1969 commercial banks were able to switch cash funds from the Euro-dollar market to beat a cash flow problem.

will become dissatisfied and, after the pinch is over, take their business elsewhere.

We do not have much published information on the flow of deposits to and between individual banks, but for various aggregates of banks it is possible to get some idea of the magnitude of the problem. Cash flows vary over seasons, over cycles, and over a long-term trend (mainly upward), with the first two being highly irregular; consequently the "inventory" problem arises there. In Table 14–1 some figures are presented for member banks

TABLE 14–1
Private Demand Deposits: 1969

End of	Reserve City: New York	Change	Reserve City: Chicago	Change	Country Member Banks	Change	Net Change, All Three Types
1968 December.......	33.4	...	6.5	...	66.6	...	...
1969 January.........	29.3	−4.1	5.7	−0.8	60.4	−6.2	−11.1
February........	29.3	0.0	5.8	+0.1	59.4	−1.0	− 0.9
March..........	28.7	−0.6	5.8	0.0	59.7	+0.3	− 0.3
April..........	31.5	+2.8	5.9	+0.1	61.6	+1.9	+ 4.8
May............	29.6	−1.9	5.9	0.0	59.8	−1.8	− 3.7
June...........	34.4	+4.8	6.2	+0.3	63.6	+3.8	+ 8.9
July...........	29.7	−4.7	5.7	−0.5	60.6	−3.0	− 8.2
August.........	30.5	+0.8	5.6	−0.1	60.3	−0.3	+ 0.4
September......	30.3	−0.2	5.6	0.0	61.0	+0.7	+ 0.5
October........	31.6	+1.3	5.5	−0.1	61.5	+0.5	+ 1.7
November......	31.9	+0.3	5.9	+0.4	63.5	+2.0	+ 2.7
December.......	36.1	+4.2	6.8	+0.9	67.9	+4.4	+ 9.5

of the Federal Reserve System suggesting *seasonal* influences in two directions:

a) An overall seasonal, which seems strongest around
   (1) The end of the year.
   (2) The end of the fiscal year (June).
   (3) The date of income tax payments (April).
b) A slight shift of funds between classes of banks, noticeable in February, March, August, September, and October, which is otherwise obscured in the figures by the overall seasonal.

Not only is the overall seasonal factor large (running over 10 percent of the deposit base in a number of cases), but it has serious consequences for the profitability and liquidity of commercial banks, since interest rates are known to exhibit only small, if any, seasonal patterns. Further, it seems likely, in view of the dates, that the major component of the seasonal change is related to, if not caused by, fiscal activity. One way this might come about is that in stabilizing interest rates, perhaps "required" on account of sharp changes in government borrowing and perhaps on account of individual actions, the Federal Reserve necessarily must abandon the money supply. Whatever the causes, however, individual banks will have worked out their own "seasonals," in terms of both components mentioned here, and will hold inventories of cash and Treasury bills to meet the needs of their customers.

14.3.2   Bank Portfolio Management

One of the relevant variables, then, in commercial bank asset management is the variability of the commercial bank's cash liabilities. The rest, like the individual ones emphasized in Chapter 12, depend on the variability of the portfolio of the bank. In particular, since a bank can expect sizable short-run changes in its deposits, it must hold sizable short-term assets. We may begin our discussion of banks' portfolio choices by looking at the actual changes in their portfolios in 1969: Table 14–2 carries a summary.

TABLE 14–2

LOANS AND INVESTMENTS AT ALL COMMERCIAL BANKS IN 1969

($ billion)

End of	Loans	U.S. Treasury Bills and Bonds	Other Securities
1968 December	265.2	64.5	71.5
1969 January	261.1	63.2	70.5
February	263.1	59.5	70.9
March	265.0	58.5	71.4
April	270.5	58.0	72.3
May	272.7	55.4	71.8
June	283.8	54.0	72.4
July	283.2	54.7	71.3
August	280.7	54.3	70.8
September	284.3	53.2	71.2
October	284.0	54.3	70.2
November	286.2	54.8	70.5
December	293.6	54.6	70.6

These figures indicate (as emphasized in Chapter 10) that banks ran down their liquid investments (U.S. Treasury bills and bonds) as part of their general strategy of meeting the rise in the demand for loans in 1969.

We will not pursue the portfolio behavior of banks along the lines of Chapter 12,[7] but we will summarize the results of several studies which have. Again, to remind you of the problem: we assume that bankers have a certain taste relation between risk (variance) and earnings, and we then proceed to analyze the actual changes in their portfolios over a period of years. Stanley M. Besens, following a model developed by Richard C. Porter,[8] has recently published some results for state member banks of the Federal Reserve System.[9] Besens poses six hypotheses, as follow, and obtains the following results concerning them:

a) The larger the commercial bank, the larger the ratio of loans to deposits.

This proposition argues that bigger banks tend to hold a slightly "riskier" portfolio than do smaller banks; but, in fact, this behavior is the result of big banks having lower variability in their cash inflows and lower percentages of defaults on their loans. Besens finds that this hypothesis is borne out by the data.

b) The larger the proportion of a bank's deposits in demand deposits, the lower is its loan-deposit ratio.

This hypothesis follows simply because the fluctuations in demand deposits are considerably greater than the fluctuations in time deposits; and commercial banks faced with this situation would, one supposes, tend to keep more liquid than not. This, too, was confirmed in Besens' study. Consider, for example, the figures in Table 14–3, not taken from data for *individual* banks, but of some

---

[7] The reason is simply that the technical apparatus is too difficult for this book.

[8] Richard C. Porter, "A Model of Bank Portfolio Selection," *Yale Economic Essays*, in Donald D. Hester and James Tobin (eds.), *Financial Markets and Economic Activity* (New York: John Wiley & Sons, Inc., 1967); and Stanley M. Besens, "An Empirical Analysis of Commercial Bank Lending Behavior," *Yale Economic Essays*, Vol. 1, No. 2 (Fall 1961).

[9] Member banks are broken into "state" and "national" for certain purposes; the total deposits of state banks are about half of those of national banks, and the two combined have 80 percent of all deposits in the country.

TABLE 14–3

Two Determinants of the Loan-Deposit Ratio for Certain Member Banks of the Federal Reserve System, December 31, 1969

Type of Bank	Loan-Deposit Ratio	Ave. Size of Banks in Class (Total Deps.)	Demand Dep.– Total Dep. Ratio
New York	0.944	$4,258,000,000	. . .
Country member	0.643	25,000,000	. . .
National member	0.667	51,000,000	0.487
State member	0.581	59,000,000	0.463

Source: *Federal Reserve Bulletin.*

relevance nevertheless. The influence of size is strongly marked, especially by the breakdown between very large banks and fairly small ones in the first two entries; but the influence of the demand deposit ratio, which should have been higher for state member banks than for national members, is not verified. That breakdown also does not verify proposition (*a*), since state banks are somewhat larger than national banks.

Clearly, there are other factors determining the ratio of loans to deposits for commercial banks; Besens proposes four more:

c) The higher the net worth of the bank, the higher the ratio of loans to deposits; this was verified by Besens and is due, most likely, to the fact that "net worth" is really a reserve of undistributed profits available for lending. It enables the bank to hold fewer liquid assets, as such.

d) The higher the rate of return on loans, the higher is a bank's loan-deposit ratio. This statement follows directly from the argument that banks are profit maximizers. If earnings on an asset increase—but not the variability—the firm will shift its portfolio toward that asset. That, too, was verified.

e) The higher the rate of return on government securities, the lower the loan-deposit ratio. This statement is justified by the same argument as proposition (*d*) and was verified by Besens.

f) The higher the Federal Reserve rediscount rate, the lower is the loan-deposit ratio.

For the last proposition Besens got no results. The general idea is that when the Federal Reserve raises the price of borrowing from it, commercial banks will tend to increase their holding of liquid assets rather than borrow at the higher rate. This view follows the general argument behind propositions (d) and (e), but what it is not able to picture is the reluctance of commercial banks to borrow from the Federal Reserve at all (except for short-term random influences). Thus, we must conclude provisionally, member banks do not adjust their portfolios when the Federal Reserve adjusts the rediscount rate. This finding makes the usefulness of this rate somewhat doubtful, since if no portfolio changes are made, no economic effects will occur except changes in the profitability of commercial banks. No doubt, however, there will be other results from later studies modifying this finding.

14.3.3 Interest on Demand Deposits

In the extensive banking legislation of the 1930's, one of the features which was swept in was that banks be prohibited from paying interest on demand deposits; bankers themselves have sometimes seemed to favor this prohibition as keeping unfair (price) competition out of banking. The argument used then, and for that matter still used, was that banks would get involved in bidding funds away from other financial intermediaries and in so doing would have to undertake more risky (and therefore higher earning) loans and investments in order to turn a profit. The fear, clearly, was that if banks got into an overly risky portfolio, especially in times of boom, they would tend to fail in the succeeding downturn; and the failure would be socially undesirable because it would tend to undermine the entire credit structure of which banks are assumed to be the keystone.

It is possible that legislators in the 1930's actually thought that banks did engage in risky loans in the 1920's; but most of them did not, judged by almost any measure of risk. Bank failures, of which there were a great number from 1930 through 1933, were also not induced by the practice of paying interest on demand deposits, if only because the practice was not that common. As a matter of record, there was a general tendency in the legislation of the 1930's to make bank failure impossible; as things stand now, almost no amount of incompetence or dishonesty can bring down a bank, and the legislation which brought this situation about was part of the neurotic response to the disaster of the Great Depression.

A good deal of this legislation flows from a misunderstanding of the function of a commercial bank; and that function is to make money for its owners. If, in the market, risk and earnings have become perfectly balanced, as they would in a perfectly functioning competitive market, then one should not be able to obtain a higher yield without at the same time incurring more risk. This is another way of saying the individual cannot get something (more yield) for nothing (no more risk).[10] Now, this risk, *without more yield*, would be judged as contributing negatively to common stock earnings by the owners of the commercial bank. That is to say, if a bank acquires a more risky asset which has a higher yield, the common stock holders of the bank need be no better off, in general, since to them higher earnings are associated with higher risk. One consequence of this is immediate: if the stockholders feel that the higher yield is not sufficient compensation for the greater risk, they will sell the bank's stock; the value of the stock will therefore decline, in proportion. Another consequence is of more significance here: there is no good reason why higher costs would force a firm to run down its profits further. If we assume the bank had the best possible asset division to begin with, no adjustment to costs, no matter which cost item is involved, will cause it to change its position. The only exception is the case denied by the legislators: the one when further higher yielding loans are relatively riskless. All of this is another way of saying that there are risks in banking, even if there are no risks of failure.[11]

There is another problem, aside from irrelevance, in connection with the paying of interest on demand deposits and that is in connection with the value price of money in the asset (stock) dimension. If, in fact, the market price of demand deposits were

---

[10] The complete discussion of this observation, with examples, appears in Chapter 12.

[11] It is far from clear why Americans have expressed a collective (through legislation) desire that there be no risk of failure in commercial banking. Traditional economic theory, which is not entirely irrelevant, tells us that one way the market weeds out the inefficient firms is to fail them. If one interferes with the market's functioning in this way, with zero prices (interest rate of zero on demand deposits) and the like, one will probably have to pay the general economic cost of a misallocation of resources.

greater than the pegged price of zero,[12] it is quite obvious that people would hold less money and more of other interest-bearing assets than otherwise. The actual stock of money would be less than the optimum stock of money; and the actual stock of, say, time deposits would be greater than its optimum, which is to say that there would be a misallocation in the money market. One of the consequences of this misallocation is simply that there would be a revenue loss to commercial banks and a wealth (from the loss of services, including liquidity), and therefore welfare, loss to consumers in general.[13] In fact, this sort of result is what we expect whenever the government attempts to defend a disequilibrium price.

14.4 SOME COMMENTS ON WORK ON INTERMEDIARIES

We will conclude this chapter with some brief notes on some studies of other financial institutions. The general problem we are interested in concerns whether or not the existence of, changes in the extent of, or the behavior of, intermediaries poses a threat to the control of the financial community. We have argued, primarily in Chapter 10, that the effects of policy on intermediaries are more obvious than the converse, but we must beware of certain limitations of the methods used there. What, then, have the portfolio studies found out?

Actually, not very much work has been done in this area, and of particular concern is the lack of work on the short-term market, particularly for the very important (in size) savings and loan associations. There does exist some work in Britain, but the institutional differences between the United States and Britain are too great to permit of any confidence in a comparison, and I will attempt none. Nevertheless, 1 will note that the British studies do not find that (some) intermediaries act in a destabilizing way.

We do have a complete study of the portfolio decisions of a sample of life insurance companies in the United States.[14] Life

---

[12] An interest price less than zero could be levied by the bank in the form of service charges.

[13] We discussed the proofs of the points in this paragraph in Chapter 10.

[14] Leroy S. Wehrle, "Life Insurance Investment: The Experience of Four Companies," in Donald D. Hester and James Tobin (eds.), *Studies of Portfolio Behavior* (New York: John Wiley & Sons, Inc., 1967).

insurance companies undertake a rather complicated business these days, for they sell "savings" along with simple insurance; and their importance in the mortgage market, particularly for large-scale projects, certainly goes beyond the providing of funds. These companies intermediate in two senses: in the sense of spreading risk for savers and in the sense of absorbing some of the financial risk of mortality. These are two different matters, particularly since insurance per se is clearly a *product* in itself. As the manufacturers of a product, insurance companies needn't pay the same heed to variations in their cash flows: insurance is not a liability, since one can only cancel pure insurance, one cannot "withdraw" it. But as holders of savings, which generally can be withdrawn (with penalty), these companies are in somewhat the same position as commercial banks; and, in any event, both sorts of activity involve the acquisition of a portfolio to invest.

It is in the nature of the business of insurance companies that very long-term commitments can be undertaken. Insofar as they intermediate (borrow short and lend long), they are not unlike other intermediaries in function, although they can count on getting more long-term (in the sense of individuals' holding periods) savings than can savings and loan associations. Also, insofar as insurance policies are a long-term commitment and big companies are able to predict fairly closely their future cash needs, one might expect insurance companies to prefer long-term to short-term investments. Such seems to be the case.

But there is another aspect to their judgment about future risk: individual companies seem "certain" about the near future and quite "hazy" about the distant future and require a risk premium to compensate them for going long. We should note that there are two things mixed together here: *interest rate risk* and *default risk*. With respect to interest rate risk—e.g., with respect to fluctuations in bond prices—insurance companies are perfectly willing to go as long as the market can go. Indeed, the securities market doesn't manufacture a security long enough for insurance companies, which, consequently, go into very long-term mortgage commitments. One consequence is a declining "term structure of yields" on government bonds held by insurance companies. With respect to the bonds of an individual company, say General Motors, insurance companies seem to prefer short- to long-term debt, an indication that they require a risk premium to cover default risk. One consequence is a rising "term structure of yields" when differentiated on a company basis.

Insurance companies do seem to participate in the market for government securities, but it seems that they only do so on a residual basis. That is, they change their holdings of government bonds much as individuals change their time deposit balances in commercial banks, not as part of a long-term plan, but as a temporary abode of either purchasing power or savings, depending on how the winds blow. This implies that insurance companies are relatively insensitive to changes in yields on government bonds and, further, introduces a looseness into the bond market which might have further implications for monetary policy: if monetary policy is to work, wealth holders must be sensitive to changes in interest rates.

The finding that life insurance companies do not hedge against interest rate risk is also important for monetary policy because it implies (on this account) that there is no long-term compartment in which the government might operate. This finding is reinforced for life insurance companies' chief competitors, pension funds, which also seem innocent of hedging behavior.[15] If individual institutions are not hedgers, then it is likely that long- and short-term yields will be related by expectations, and that it will not be possible to push long-term rates one way and short-term rates another for very long. Thus such a policy as "operation twist" will be impossible, and the "bills only" doctrine will be irrelevant—since it wouldn't matter which end you work on if all rates go together.[16]

14.5 DISCUSSION QUESTIONS

1. Which characteristics of a market contribute most to the liquidity of the item traded in the market? Are any of these measurable? Is there any overlap between the characteristics?

2. If we phrase the question of the definitions of money as "what is money?" do we necessarily get forced into the position that the definitional problem has an empirical solution? In a recent study,

---

[15] Roger F. Murray, *Economic Aspects of Pensions: A Summary Report* (New York: National Bureau of Economic Research by Columbia University Press, 1968).

[16] The full groundwork for this discussion was laid in Chapter 11.

one author claimed, in effect, that money was that which correlated best with money gross national product. Comment, in terms of both the Keynesian and classical versions of the theory of the demand for money.

3. What is the distinction between uncertainty and risk employed in this Chapter? Is it possible to separate the precautionary and the speculative demands for money in terms of whether or not the speculators are uncertain? Is this how Keynes thought of it?

4. We said that the "normal" rate of interest was an individual rate rather than a market rate of interest. Construct an example to show why the diversity of opinions about rates leads to a downsloping demand for money. What rate does the average "normal" rate play? How might one obtain observations for this rate for the market as a whole?

5. We have utilized the fact that risk and yield will tend to offset each other to explain why the speculative demand for money slopes downward. We earlier suggested that in certain cases, when the possible pay-off was very large (but very unlikely) an individual might take the risk even though it was off the efficiency locus. Why is this so? Would this affect the derivation of the Keynesian demand curve for money? Explain.

6. These days you hear a good deal about the "cash flow" problems of corporations; indeed some firms claim they have failed due to insufficient cash flow. Is the firm's problem of cash flow analogous to the commercial bank's? What are the differences? What role might monetary policy play in the firm's dilemma?

7. Analyze, as was done in Table 14–1 for demand deposits, the "cash flow" situation for the time deposits of commercial banks. Are there noticeable seasonal components? Can you see a cyclical pattern by looking back a few years? How do the fluctuations in the two series compare?

8. One way an intermediary differs from other economic units is that the values of both assets and liabilities are portfolio problems. This is obvious for the assets, of course, but for liabilities, only the variations in the cash flow seem relevant. Reconcile this apparent dilemma in terms of the model of Chapter 4.

9. Suppose we were to permit banks to pay interest on demand deposits. Would there be an immediate economic (welfare) gain or loss as a result? How much do you think it would be? Would the effectiveness of monetary policy be hampered by this change of the environment?

10. To what extent are the following factors contributors to the very low rate of bank failure?

   a) F.D.I.C.
   b) Portfolio restrictions by various governmental agencies
   c) Mergers
   d) No interest on demand deposits
   e) Regulation Q

14.6 FURTHER READING

BENSTON, GEORGE J. "Interest on Demand Deposits and Bank Investment Behavior," *Journal of Political Economy*, Vol. 72, No. 5 (October 1964).

MURRAY, ROGER F. *Economic Aspects of Pensions: A Summary Report*, chaps. 1 and 7. New York: National Bureau of Economic Research by Columbia University Press, 1968.

TUSSING, E. DALE. "The Case for Bank Failure," *Journal of Law and Economics*, Vol. 10 (October 1967).

PART III

International Monetary Economics

Chapter 15

THE ELEMENTARY PRINCIPLES OF INTERNATIONAL FINANCE

15.1 INTRODUCTION

In this section of the book we are going to extend our simple analysis in a number of directions, but our primary task is to see what difference it makes to the analysis of Part I that there is more than one country in the world. In Part I, particularly when we came to discuss the objectives of monetary policy, we treated the international side of the problem, if at all, as a constraint on domestic policy. Now we want to do better than that: we wish to analyze the open economy, in particular the open financial economy. *Open* in this sense means that we now wish to have more than one country and to consider the individual problems as well as the collective problems which result from the fact that their citizens engage in international transactions. We will continue, however, to use the American position as the basis for our analysis.

From the first, though, we must come to grips with a serious shortcoming in our study: the theory of the subject is still somewhat sketchy at points. This has the serious consequences both that we will have to grope a little more and that our organization of the results will be both arbitrary and liable to contradiction. There is a further problem: as is often the case in recent economics, the worse the state of the area, the more diffuse and profuse is the literature one has to wade through. Apparently, the underlying cause of the relative underdevelopment of the subject is that the techniques of the Keynesian revolution, as applied to international trade, are unproductive. In Robert Mundell's words,

Good theory is good theory and there is no doubt that there was much in the *General Theory* that could be used to refresh and revise international monetary economics. But in practice the Keynesian revolution held back trade theory. Fundamental theoretical problems in macroeconomics had not been solved. The major weakness lay in the very place in which Keynes had hoped to make his major theoretical contribution, the integration of the monetary and real sectors of a closed economy. His attempt to integrate the two sectors was faulty.[1]

Now this is serious because the integration of the monetary and the real is the critical problem in international finance: in particular, we wish to know what relation there is between the flows of goods and the flows of funds between nations, and what leads to the so-called "balance of payments problem."

15.2 THE BALANCE OF PAYMENTS

15.2.1 The Balance of Payments Accounts

We will look at some data on international finance in the next section, but it is a good idea to begin here by laying out the balance sheet of an open economy; this balance sheet comes under the general heading of the balance of payments. The balance of payments is an accounting statement—of economic flows—which records the transactions between the residents of a particular country and the rest of the world. As a balance sheet, with debits and credits for a particular period of time, it must balance out. Consider the statement in Table 15–1 for the United States for the first quarter of 1969; note that debits appear with a minus sign in order to make it possible to group items in an interesting way.[2]

The "real" side of international economic activity is contained in Part I of the table,[3] which contains the so-called balance of

---

[1] Robert A. Mundell, *International Economics* (New York: Macmillan Co., 1968), p. 112.

[2] This table is hard going to the uninitiated, so the best way to proceed would be to read on and glance back at the table as the story unfolds.

[3] The word "real" has quotation marks because the entries are actually in money terms. In some respects it would be proper terminology to refer to the entries at the top of the table as having money values and at the bottom as having nominal. The text will pursue these issues.

TABLE 15–1
UNITED STATES BALANCE OF PAYMENTS, FIRST QUARTER, 1969
(figures seasonally adjusted; $ million)

	Subtotals	Totals
Part I: Balance of Trade		
Exports of goods and services............................		11,913
Merchandise..	7,469	
Military sales..	418	
Transportation..	618	
Travel...	503	
Investment income receipts............................	2,120	
Other services...	785	
Imports of goods and services............................		−11,550
Merchandise...	−7,572	
Military expenditures..................................	−1,204	
Transportation..	− 742	
Travel...	− 810	
Investment income payments............................	− 892	
Other services...	− 330	
(1) Balance on goods and services........................		363
(2) Remittances and pensions, balance....................		− 271
Part II: Financial Flows		
(3) U.S. government net grants and capital flow.............		− 793
Grants, loans, and net change in foreign currency holdings and claims...................................	−1,118	
Scheduled repayments on U.S. government bonds......	281	
Other..	44	
(4) U.S. private capital flow, net (out)....................		− 1,345
Direct investments...................................	− 928	
Foreign securities...................................	− 323	
Other long-term claims...............................	67	
Short-term claims....................................	− 161	
(5) Foreign capital flow, net, not including change in liquid assets in U.S......................................		1,633
Long-term investments................................	1,708	
Short-term investments...............................	− 76	
Other items, net.....................................	1	
(6) Balancing item (errors and unrecorded transactions)......		− 1,239
Part III: Balances		
(7) Balance A, liquidity basis............................		− 1,653
Lines (1) through (6), not seasonally adjusted...........		− 1,258
(8) Balance B, official reserve transactions basis..............		1,143
Balance A, seasonally adjusted.......................	−1,653	
Plus:		
Changes in liquid assets in the U.S. of commercial banks abroad..	−2,944	
Other private residents of foreign countries.........	− 23	
Other..	− 88	
Less:		
Changes in certain nonliquid liabilities to foreign central banks and governments......................	37	
Balance B, not seasonally adjusted....................		1,710

TABLE 15–1 *(continued)*

			Subtotals	Totals
Part IV: Transactions to Settle Balances—Not Seasonally Adjusted				
(9)	To settle balance A................................			1,258
(10)	Change in official reserves (an increase has a − sign) ..			− 48
	Gold............................	56		
	Convertible currencies...........................	− 73		
	IMF gold tranche position.......................	− 31		
(11)	Change in liquid liabilities to all foreign accounts......			1,306
(12)	Foreign central banks and governments and IMF.....	−1,707		
	Commercial banks abroad.......................	3,124		
	Other..	− 111		
(13)	To settle balance B................................			− 1,710
	Change in official reserves, item (10)................	− 48		
	Change in liquid liabilities, item (12)................	− 1,707		
	Change in certain nonliquid liabilities...............	55		

Source: *Federal Reserve Bulletin.*

trade, which was in favor of the United States during this period. But this total also contains some interesting subbalances: we see that the merchandise balance was unfavorable, as was the travel balance; and, in contrast, we see that American earnings on investment abroad far exceeded our payments to foreigners owning American securities. We also see the high foreign exchange costs of our military activity, because the military balance is also widely unfavorable. Table 15–2 summarizes the recent behavior of the real side of trade; to compare those figures with the entries in Table 15–1, you will have to convert the latter to annual rates by multiplying them by four.

TABLE 15–2
SOME EXPORT-IMPORT BALANCES IN AMERICAN TRADE, 1965–69
($ million)

	1965	1966	1967	1968	1969
Merchandise balance...........	4,772	3,926	3,860	626	1,310
Military balance..............	−2,077	−2,935	−3,138	−3,103	−3,378
Travel balance................	−1,058	−1,067	−1,549	−1,252	−1,320
Investment income balance.....	4,159	4,110	4,510	4,766	4,465

Source: *Federal Reserve Bulletin.*

There are only two large changes in the broad picture for real trade for the United States, and both of these are adverse. The deterioration of the merchandise balance is severe and somewhat alarming, for the merchandise balance no longer finances our military and travel expenditures as it did in 1965 and 1966. The point made earlier about the inevitable blending of monetary and real factors is also clearer now: the (real) merchandise deficit will have to be financed in some way (monetary); the bottom half of Table 15–1 demonstrates how. But there is another interaction to consider as well. One of the important reasons why the trade balance deteriorated, especially in 1968 and 1969, is that the rapid inflation in the United States undermined the price competitiveness of American business; some countries had slower rates of price inflation in competing products. In this case we see the possible effect of the monetary on the real, especially insofar as the inflation itself is caused by a domestic monetary expansion. The second adverse change in the figures is the approximately $1 billion annual exchange cost of the step-up in the Vietnamese war,[4] noticeable by comparing the 1966 figure with that for 1965. Of course this is only the direct exchange cost of the military activity; and insofar as the inflation itself is caused by rising government expenditures for the war, there is an indirect cost by way of the deteriorating merchandise balance.

Part II of Table 15–1 describes most of the financial side of international trade. Part I records the interest and dividends which cross borders, while Part II emphasizes the flow of money capital.[5] We study international trade because there is factor immobility between countries; but Part II of Table 15–1 is justified because one factor, capital, which needs no interpreter to be understood, moves freely between countries. In some respects, it is capital movements which justify the study of "money" trade; but, as we shall see, it is also capital flows which undermine a nation's sovereignty.

Again, an historical review of the critical figures provides the essential insight into their meaning. Table 15–3 illustrates that there is a good deal of fluctuation in the broad flows of international investment capital; the figures for foreign investment in the United

---

[4] The military balance in 1964, before the step-up, was —$2,114 million.

[5] Actually, the items here are changes in stocks, and not flows.

States show special variability. As already mentioned, these flows
are highly volatile on account of the high degree of mobility of
international capital—when returns become higher in the United
States, funds pour in. Obviously, a good deal of the balance of
payments problem for the United States involves the capital account figures summarized in Table 15–3.

TABLE 15–3
Financial Flows in the U.S. Balance of Payments, 1965–69
($ million)

	1965	1966	1967	1968	1969
U.S. government grants and capital flows..................	−3,375	−3,444	−4,224	−3,955	−3,866
U.S. private capital flows.......	−3,743	−4,310	−5,655	−5,157	−5,009
Direct investments..........	−3,418	−3,639	−3,154	−3,025	−3,060
Foreign private capital flows....	278	2,532	3,360	8,565	3,869

Source: *Federal Reserve Bulletin.*

The last empirical question we shall ask at this point concerns
the settling items from which the more popularly known "balance
of payments problem" is defined; the most interesting figures for
recent years appear as Table 15–4. The most interesting results
in the table are the trends, especially for the total financial reserves
of the United States, which have fallen slightly less than $8 billion
since 1956. As things are now arranged, a country must ultimately
settle its international debts by running down one of the reserve
items in Table 15–4; we see, in fact, that it is the United States'
gold stock, which has fallen more than $11 billion in the same
period, which has served this function in this period.[6] But one
need not pay his debts if foreign governments can be persuaded
to hold American securities or deposits in American banks in lieu
of "hard" reserves—as was not the case in the first quarter of

---

[6] The Treasury gold stock figure is the gold required to be held domestically
to back the dollar. The reason this constraint was not taken seriously in Chapter
4 is apparent from the figures in Table 15–4: the lawmakers adjust the requirements downward to correspond to the actual gold stock. One wonders,
in fact, why they bother, since if there is no effective gold constraint, nothing
"backs" the dollar and the bookkeeping entry in Table 15–4 is meaningless
(economically).

1969, as shown in line (12) of Table 15–1. One also need not pay his debts if private citizens or their agents hold more claims on the dollar than they cash in, and this also seems to have been the case in Table 15–1.

There is one final thing about Table 15–1 which should be appreciated before we begin to formalize, and that is that there are *three* official "balances" calculated there, all of which have some claim to being the official balance. That is, in the first quarter

TABLE 15–4
U.S. GOLD STOCK, HOLDINGS OF CONVERTIBLE FOREIGN CURRENCIES, AND RESERVE POSITION IN IMF, 1956–69
($ million)

End of	Total Reserve Assets	Gold Stock		Convertible Foreign Currencies	Reserve Position in IMF
		Total	Treasury		
1956.......	23,666	22,058	21,949	...	1,608
1957.......	24,832	22,857	22,781	...	1,975
1958.......	22,540	20,582	20,534	...	1,958
1959.......	21,504	19,507	19,456	...	1,997
1960.......	19,359	17,804	17,767	...	1,555
1961.......	18,753	16,947	16,889	116	1,690
1962.......	17,220	16,057	15,978	99	1,064
1963.......	16,843	15,596	15,513	212	1,035
1964.......	16,672	15,471	15,388	432	769
1965.......	15,450	13,806	13,733	781	863
1966.......	14,882	13,235	13,159	1,321	326
1967.......	14,830	12,065	11,982	2,345	420
1968.......	15,710	10,892	10,367	3,528	1,290
1969.......	16,964	11,859	10,367	2,781	2,324

SOURCE: *Federal Reserve Bulletin.*

of 1969 official reserves (from Part IV) rose by $48 million, while the traditional balance of payments (the balance on the liquidity basis) fell by $1,258 million. When one counts all the liquid items and the arranged deals between central banks, the balance on the basis of official transactions rose by $1,710 million. Thus, if we take Balance A (as defined in Table 15–1) we would be alarmed, and if we take Balance B delighted, by the performance of the foreign sectors of the American economy. We can't settle the debates of the accountants with reference to economic laws, and the extreme variability of a substantial part of the figures warns us to beware of the long run; but the obviously more inclusive measure, Balance B, does have the disadvantage, analytically, of containing some negotiated elements ("nonliquid" dealings between central banks).[7] Nevertheless, Balance B is more suggestive of the fundamental state of things and is to be generally preferred.

15.2.2 The Exchange Rate

The next step in the analysis is to separate the fundamental items in Table 15–1 from the balancing items; to do this we must understand what purpose the latter serve. This involves a description of how the international payments system works.[8]

When an individual in the United States buys a British product, he usually does so after comparing the British price with the American price (if there is something comparable made in the United States). Now there are actually three prices involved in this transaction, not two, for the American price is quoted in dollars and the British price in pounds; thus, one must also know the *rate of exchange* (the third price) between the two currencies before he knows whether or not the British price is lower. The use of the exchange rate between two countries is actually quite straightforward, although the analysis is often quite cumbersome. If, for example, the British product cost £12 delivered to the New York port and the American equivalent cost $30, then, at the current exchange rate of $2.40 per pound (or, what is exactly the same thing, 8 shillings and four pence per dollar[9]), the British price translates into $28.80 at the current exchange rate; and the best buy is, accordingly, the British product.

The exchange rate between the dollar and the pound, as things stand, is pegged, although this need not be the case. We will get to the mechanics of this situation in a moment, but for now let

---

[7] In the settling figures, explicit short-term dealings between central governments are seen to be of some importance. Below, when we come to define reserves more carefully, we will look at the historical pattern of these dealings; for the moment we find it obvious that these dealings occur depending on what happens with the rest of the international payments; and the extent to which countries will permit each other to balance off in this way obviously replaces gold as a settling item in payments.

[8] We will consider several views of how it *ought* to work in Chapter 17.

[9] Before decimalization, when these lines were written, the British pound contained 20 shillings, and each shilling contained 12 pence.

us assume that the exchange rate is a free market price determined by supply and demand. This is a relevant exercise, as you will see, even though the price does not fluctuate, because the underlying forces of supply and demand still operate even though the price cannot adjust. The American who wishes to buy the British product may either send the British dealer a check written in dollars or buy pounds at his local bank and send them in the

FIGURE 15–1
Supply and Demand for Funds: General Case

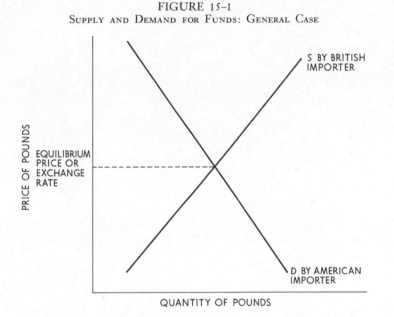

form of a cashier's check. In either event, as suggested in Figure 15–1, when we analyze the supply and demand for the British pound, in this deal, the American importer is a *demander* of pounds.[10] Similarly, a British importer is one of the ultimate suppliers of pounds (or, if you wish, demanders of dollars). All of the entries in Table 15–1 go into the supply and demand for dollars; and looking at the total represented by Balance B (unadjusted), since the overall balance was favorable, the price of dollars

---

[10] If we were analyzing the supply and demand for dollars, we would visualize the American importer as the *supplier* of the funds. It doesn't matter whether we analyze the market for dollars or the market for pounds, as they are perfect converses.

should have risen during the period, to clear the market of the surplus of $1.7 billion.

Let us construct an example, not related to Table 15–1, in order to visualize this point. Let us suppose, in Figure 15–2, that the equilibrium exchange rate in the market is $2.40 per pound. We will write this as $2.40/£1 and note that the price is expressed in dollars (per pound), so the vertical axis of the figure is denoted

FIGURE 15–2
A GOLD DRAIN FOR THE UNITED STATES

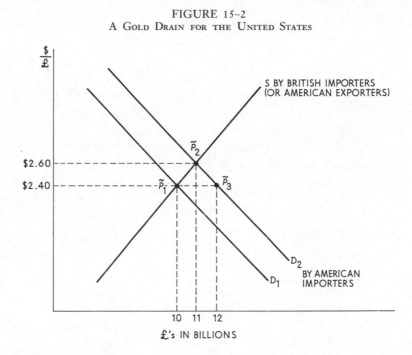

as $/£; higher points represent rises in the price of pounds and, conversely, falls in the price of dollars. At equilibrium, then, there are 10 billion pounds, thought of as a quantity, cleared in the market. Now suppose that Americans, for whatever reason, suddenly begin to spend in Britain; through the various monetary channels,[11] a rise in the demand for pounds will be felt. Let us assume the demand curve shifts to the right, to D_2.

---

[11] Usually, British commercial banks will acquire the checks (claims on the American dollar) written in dollars and will sell them on the exchange market at the current exchange rate. The American Federal Reserve and the Bank of England enter this market to keep the price stable; and in this case, the claim will end up in the New York Federal Reserve. The last steps of this process are explained in the text.

If the market price for foreign exchange (in this case the pounds desired by American importers) were allowed to fluctuate, it would rise to $2.60 as a result of the increase in demand; and at that point, there would be a clearing at 11 billion pounds. British importers, the suppliers of pounds, would offer the additional pounds because a rate of exchange of $2.60 represents a fall in the price of dollars (the new price of dollars is £1/$2.60), which means American products are effectively cheaper.

In fact, the exchange rate between the dollar and the pound is pegged by official intervention in the foreign exchange market, so the actual solution will be at $\tilde{P}_3$, as things stand. What happens is that the American government stands ready to buy or sell gold at $35 an ounce, a decision which effectively establishes the price of the American dollar in units of gold (or the price of gold in units of dollars). Other countries follow the same procedure, pegging (offering to buy and sell at the same price[12]) their currencies either to the dollar, as is the case with the British, or to gold. Gold, then, has become the ultimate "backing" of the currencies of most countries engaging in international trade. Suppose, to continue the example, that the situation of Figure 15–2 had come about in the second quarter of 1969. If there were an upward pressure on the price of the pound, the New York Federal Reserve would have to buy pounds on the open market in order to close the deals described earlier in this section. They would buy pounds either with other foreign currencies or with gold, for, of course, they could not buy them with dollars. In fact, to keep the price of the dollar stable at $2.40—or what is the same thing, keep the price of gold down to $35 an ounce—the American government would have to offer up $2 billion worth of gold.[13]

In the discussion of section 15.2.1 we referred to such dealings as *settling transactions* in the American balance of payments. Now we see how they arise: in the course of "defending" the price of gold—or, if you wish, the gold price of the American dollar—it is necessary that in lieu of the market clearing itself, settling transactions will have to be undertaken. We have, consequently,

---

[12] Actually, to avoid numerous small deals and to give the exchange rate some elbow room, the price is pegged at the center of a narrow band around the rate of $2.40 per pound.

[13] Or convertible currencies; see Table 15–4 for the stock of hard money.

defined the essence of both the fixed exchange rate system and the fluctuating system. Further, we see the essential definition of the American balance of payments problem: a persistent outward movement of ultimate reserves (as in Table 15–4 for the United States) or, if you will, a persistent tendency (stopped by gold sales) for the price of the currency to deteriorate.

15.2.3 An Analysis of the Balance of Payments

Since we would not collect many of the balance of payments figures if we did not have a system of fixed exchange rates, we will recognize that the following analysis is relevant mainly for that system. Let us note, also, the dimensional nature of Table 15–1: the figures in Part I and through Balance A in Part II are dimensionally flows, while the items beyond that are changes in stocks which, accordingly, have the same per unit time dimension.

For a particular country, at a particular time, the country's "balance," in the sense of the change in its gold reserves, can be written as in Equation 15–1.[14]

$$\text{Change in gold reserves per unit time} \equiv B_i \equiv \frac{dR_i}{dt} \quad (15–1)$$

For all (n of them) countries, this balance would be written as:

$$\sum_{i=1}^{n} B_i \equiv \sum_{i=1}^{n} \frac{dR_i}{dt} \equiv 0 \quad (15–2)$$

if the amount of gold in the system were fixed. The figures in Table 15–5 show that, indeed, this total has been declining over recent years in spite of the fact that gold production has increased somewhat. Since the volume of trade has been expanding considerably, this reveals a serious problem: we have, at the base of our system, an asset (made so by pegging its price) which is generally in diminishing supply to monetary authorities. Since there is net production of gold in the world, it is plausible to argue that the price paid by central banks is too low (it is, of course, $35 an ounce since all the currencies are tied together). A higher price

---

[14] For dt = one quarter, this would be $56 million in Table 15–1, for the first quarter of 1969; that is, there was a gold outflow of $56 million. The lower case "d" means "change in" whether referring to reserves or to time, in this section.

(e.g., $45 an ounce) would certainly make gold production more profitable and probably entice gold away from some of its other uses—those profitable between $35 and $45 an ounce. This is one answer to providing more fundamental reserves, but another lies in creating *key currencies* which central banks would be willing to hold as reserves in lieu of gold. The general idea is that anything which is acceptable as money is therefore money: that if gold and certain convertible (into gold) currencies are accepted by all, the ultimate reserves of the system could be enlarged.

TABLE 15–5
GOLD RESERVES AND PRODUCTION, 1962–69
($ million)

End of	Gold Held as Monetary Res.	United States	Rest of World	IMF	Gold Production for Year
1962.....	41,475	16,057	23,225	2,194	1,295
1963.....	42,305	15,596	24,395	2,312	1,355
1964.....	43,015	15,471	25,365	2,179	1,405
1965.....	43,230	13,806	27,285	1,869	1,440
1966.....	43,185	13,235	27,300	2,652	1,445
1967.....	41,600	12,065	26,855	2,682	1,410
1968.....	40,905	10,892	27,725	2,288	1,420
1969.....	41,015	11,859	26,725	2,310	1,420

SOURCE: *Federal Reserve Bulletin.*

Suppose only one country provided the key currency, say the United States. Its fundamental balance over a period might look like Equation 15–3:

$$B_1 = \frac{dG_1}{dt} - \frac{dL_1}{dt} \qquad (15\text{–}3)$$

where G is gold and dL_1 is its change in liabilities due to the fact that its currency is held by the rest of the world as part of their reserves. If we look at Table 15–1, we see that this equation would read

$$B_1 = -\$56 + \$73 = \$17 \qquad (15\text{–}4)$$

and that, on this account, the gold outflow of $56 million was more than offset by an increase in foreign holdings of dollars.[15]

---

[15] We should again remember that actual currency is not necessarily held, but that dollar-denoted securities (such as Treasury bills) of the United States government often are.

From the point of view of other countries, a set of equations representing their official reserves balances would look like Equations 15–5:

$$B_2 = \frac{dG_2}{dt} + \frac{dC_{12}}{dt}$$

$$B_3 = \frac{dG_3}{dt} + \frac{dC_{13}}{dt}$$

$$(15\text{–}5)$$

and so on, where dC_{12} represents the change in the amount of currency of Country 1 held by the second country, and so on.[16] Now it is apparent that when we add up international reserves, like accountants, we would get

$$\sum_{i=1}^{n} dB_i = \sum_{i=1}^{n} \frac{dG_i}{dt} + \sum_{i=1}^{n} \frac{dC_{1i}}{dt} - \frac{dL_1}{dt} \qquad (15\text{–}6)$$

and since $\sum_{i=1}^{n} (dC_i/dt) \equiv (dL_1/dt)$, that is, since the liability of the key currency country exactly equals the sum of its currency held by all other countries, aggregate reserves are not affected by such dealings, and the practice of holding key currencies simply disguises the shrinkage (due to the disappearance of gold) of the ultimate reserves of the system.

The problem with this interpretation of events centers around the word *liability*. Even if we believe that gold is the only ultimate value of the system, we still must remember that it now has this position only because its price is pegged by a consortium of central banks.[17] We might regard the promise to hold dollars given by a foreign central bank as a little short of being as "hard" as gold, but we must recognize that as long as the users continue to hold dollars, dollars are de facto reserves. Consequently, the correct conclusion to draw about Equation 15–6 is not the one drawn, but that the liability of the United States is zero (that is, $dL_1/dt = 0$).[18]

---

[16] The notation C_{12} is unfortunate but is the best we can do here. The first subscript refers to the first country, and the second refers to the other countries. There could be other key currencies than that of Country 1, in which case we would have a $C_{21}, C_{23}, C_{24}, \ldots$ for all countries holding Country 2's currency.

[17] You will recall that our domestic money stock is not effectively linked to our "monetary" gold stock.

[18] You will recall that we made a similar point about the word liability as applied to the demand deposits of commercial banks.

Let us close this particular discussion with some figures illustrating the current world reserve situation, assuming that convertible currencies are also international reserves. The figures are contained in Table 15–6; and they illustrate, as one might expect, that increasing use has been made of this source in recent years.

TABLE 15–6
THE WORLD'S RESERVES
($ million)

End of	Gold (Incl. Internatl. Organizations)	Reserve Position in IMF	Foreign Exchange	Total*
1962	41,480	3,795	20,055	65,330
1963	42,300	3,940	22,390	68,630
1964	43,010	4,155	23,850	71,015
1965	43,230	5,376	23,435	72,041
1966	43,185	6,330	24,950	74,465
1967	41,605	5,748	28,600	75,953
1968	40,730	6,488	31,325	78,543
1969	41,015	6,726	31,035	78,776

* Does not include special drawing rights (SDR's), which were activated in December 1969. The SDR scheme will be discussed in Chapter 17.

SOURCE: International Monetary Fund, *International Financial Statistics*.

15.3 THE UNITED STATES IN THE INTERNATIONAL CAPITAL MARKET

What is known in economics as the pure theory of international trade—or, alternatively, as the real theory of trade—appears as a separate study within economics because of the justifiable assumption that certain factors, especially land and labor, have little or no mobility between countries. The pure theory of trade is also distinguished because of the working assumption of the *homogeneity postulate;* this[19] amounts to the assertion that commodity demand and supply depend only on the relative prices between commodities and not on the price of money. What is peculiar about all this is that in the pure theory of trade no further explanation is ever offered about what determines the price level in each country. This, in itself, is serious; but a more damaging

---

[19] See section 9.2.4.

observation is that since capital, a critical factor of production, is mobile internationally and since capital, land, and labor are usually analyzed as substitutes for each other, the working assumption has the effect of misspecifying the problem by leaving out an adjustment mechanism which could eliminate completely the consequences of factor immobility. The point, to be specific, is that you can take the machine to the worker if the latter cannot move; and if capital is internationally mobile, the market will do just that.

Among the capital (and among the factors of production) of the world is money, which, in this day of fairly extensive convertibility, obviously has this mobility. Further than this, to take one more poke at pure trade, we cannot effectively discuss the interest rate, either real or nominal, in a moneyless world; so that whenever some but not all capital appears in a problem, along with a price (the interest rate) which only partly reflects that partial capital stock, all sorts of errors are conceivable. It is no wonder that paradoxes abound in the empirical work on pure trade.

When we wish to work with a world economy which has capital flows of significant size, as well as large trade flows, we must face the fact that things get complicated. In particular, with only two countries in the world, we have the three sets of prices mentioned in section 15.1:

a)   Domestic prices.
b)   Foreign prices.
c)   The exchange rate.

And, with capital in the problem, we also have:

d)   Domestic interest rates and stock yields.
e)   Foreign interest rates and stock yields.

Thus, the new complication—say, for American monetary and fiscal policy—concerns the influence which foreign capital has on the domestic economy.

The general argument is fairly straightforward: if a country is completely dominated by foreign capital, then it will be impossible for the country to follow an independent monetary policy. When the country tries to raise interest rates (by reducing the money supply), money will come flooding in if (money) capital is mobile. A small country in the shadow of a big one (for example, Ireland) will be one example, and a region (for example, Missouri) is another. From the point of view of monetary policy, these areas have no separate identity; furthermore, by the same standard, they are both influenced by the same phenomenon: capital flows. That is to say, if the Federal Reserve Bank of St. Louis attempts to squeeze credit in Missouri, it would be frustrated by capital flows from other parts of the country.

But in general capital is not perfectly mobile internationally; thus there is some scope for domestic monetary policy. We shall discuss various aspects of this scope in the following chapters, but before we turn to that and other more detailed tasks, I will offer some generalizations in the following paragraphs.

Because capital flows improve the worldwide allocation of resources—and thus, at least potentially, the welfare of each country—it is undesirable to restrict capital flows in the interest of the balance of payments. Further, even if you do restrict some capital flows, it will be most difficult to do so for all; therefore, the barriers will tend to be undermined anyway. In addition, there will be a distortion of the allocation of resources. Indeed, the record of recent American restrictions is poor, and the flooding in of Euro-dollars in late 1969 when domestic credit was pinched was at least partly a response to higher interest rates.

The main new point to consider, however, is the potential usefulness capital mobility has in helping the balance of payments. If the British could attract $10 billion of American short-term capital by pushing up their interest rates by 1 percent, it is likely that the British authorities might try just such an action when hard-pressed; in fact, they do. But this is a once-for-all gain—a kind of borrowing of reserves through the market—which has adverse consequences for the future in the form of (often very high) interest payments. The interest payments, of course, produce a loss of reserves for each future time period. Thus, when one is using the interest rate to draw reserves, he is borrowing against future surpluses; needless to say, the future surpluses do not necessarily appear. Higher interest rates also depress the domestic economy, another cost—stretching into the future—which ought to be calculated. We will see, by the time we are done with the topic in Chapter 18, that the system of fixed exchange rates, from which the balance of payments problem arises, is a fantastically expensive system to operate.

15.4 DISCUSSION QUESTIONS

1. Was the economy of Chapter 5, in which we introduced the idea of a balance of payments constraint, an *open economy* in the sense of this chapter? In what sense is the openness of an economy a matter of degree? Which variables would you use to measure this openness?

2. In the balance-of-payments accounts of the United States, all entries are in nominal terms. Are all items flows, then? Does it make sense to measure our reserves (or changes of reserves) in dollar terms? What happens to the size of our reserves, as we have measured them, when England devalues the pound?

3. How do you account for the significant worsening of the American merchandise balance in 1968? Dig up some figures for inflation in some of our big competitors and discuss whether or not inflation seems to be involved. Why is the investment income balance so steady?

4. The worsening of the merchandise balance of 1968, described in Question 3, was offset by a large (net) capital inflow. Were these related events? Explain. Find out whether or not the behavior of relative interest rates in the United States and abroad had anything to do with this.

5. Why do we continue to hold a Treasury Gold Stock. Does this represent "money in the bank" in any sense? Would anything happen to the price of gold if our gold stock were allowed to run down to, say, $3 billion? Are the "convertible foreign currencies" an adequate offset to the gold stock for defensive (of the exchange rate) operations?

6. It is a very good idea to go through the analysis of Section 15.2.2 carefully. The same can be said of practically all of Chapter 16. One way to do this is simply to make up a set of numbers, for a fictitious set of countries. You ought to keep in mind, as you do (and comment on, at the end), that the purpose of such systems is not to peg the price of gold but to provide some stability to world payments.

7. Suppose some other commodity than gold—say pig iron—were used in gold's role. Would the nature of the system change? Would it help matters because there is a larger quantity of pig

iron? That is, is the scarcity of gold a problem? Compare the costs of operating each system.

8. Why did we argue that the accumulated American deficit ought not to be netted out when we calculate the stock of world liquidity? Actually, what is the international equivalent of the money stock (as defined in Chapter 2)? How do we distinguish a "key" currency from any other currency?

9. If one imposes the homogeneity postulate in the study of international economies, he presumably needs some mechanism explaining how money enters the system. We did this with the money stock arbitrarily fixed by the authorities in the case of the closed economy. In the open economy, is the assumption valid any longer? How would one want to alter his discussion say in Chapters 5 and 6? Is there some analogous way of introducing money arbitrarily into the international economy? Comment.

10. If capital movements are instantaneous, in response to interest rate levels, could a country maintain its identity—in terms of fiscal and monetary policy? Explain carefully. Does this imply that it is frictions in the economic process which keep countries apart? Explain the nature of the frictions which currently operate. Is it sensible to keep the frictions alive in order to help the effectiveness of monetary policy, or is this doing things the wrong way around?

15.5 FURTHER READING

MACHLUP, FRITZ. "The Theory of Foreign Exchanges," *Readings in the Theory of International Trade*, pp. 104–58 (eds. H. S. Ellis and L. A. Metzler for the American Economic Association). Philadelphia: Blakiston Co., 1950.

MUNDELL, ROBERT A. *International Economics*, chap. 10, "The Balance of Payments." New York: Macmillan Co., 1968.

Chapter 16

THE ECONOMICS OF EXCHANGE RATES

16.1 INTRODUCTION

The facts that individuals and firms do some of their marketing in other countries and that investors consider the rate of return on foreign investment opportunities along with the domestic ones are bound to create all sorts of complications in the analysis and manipulation of the domestic economy. The complications notwithstanding, there is one price, the *exchange rate* between currencies, through which almost all of these exchanges flow. The exchange rate—to repeat our definition from Chapter 15—is the price of one country's currency in terms of another; further, it tends to be determined by supply and demand in the absence of pegging operations. Most of what we have to say in this chapter is valid for a system either of fixed or of fluctuating exchange rates; one reason this is so is that fixed exchange rates seem to mean something like temporarily fixed. Another reason is that the forces we discuss will be as valid in the determination of the quantity (given price) as of the price itself.

We will begin by carefully defining our terms and then illustrating how *spot* and *forward* exchange rates are related to each other; further, we will describe how interest rates become involved in exchange markets. Following the section on definitions, we will turn to two powerful forces—arbitrage and speculation—and their influence on exchange markets. The discussion will be broadened to include the monetary authority, in a naive way, and then we will tackle the ultimate question: Why don't we have a system of flexible exchange rates? Throughout the discussion, the focus will be on capital movements between nations.

342

16.2 THE FORMAL APPARATUS

16.2.1 The Spot Exchange Rate

We defined the spot exchange rate when we defined the exchange rate in Chapter 15, because the spot rate is the price of one currency in terms of another in terms of cash. That is, at the spot rate, one can convert his currency, sell his car, or cash in his foreign bond: it is today's rate. There is a network of spot exchange rates covering all countries participating in the international marketplace. Some of these rates fluctuate only within the narrow limits set by official pegging operations; some fluctuate from day to day; and some are simply official rates which might or might not reflect the rate on some black market in that particular country's currency. Table 16–1 illustrates a small set of these rates at a recent point in time.

TABLE 16–1
SPOT EXCHANGE RATES, JANUARY 29, 1970

Country	Spot Rate
Austria—	25.80 shillings per dollar
Belgium—	49.65 francs per dollar
Denmark—	7.4920 crowns per dollar
Holland—	3.6355 guilders per dollar
Finland—	4.17 marks per dollar
France—	5.543425 francs per dollar
Germany (F.R.)—	3.6892 marks per dollar
Greece—	30.0 drachmas per dollar
Italy—	629.50 lire per dollar
Mexico—	12.50 pesos per dollar
Norway—	7.1535 crowns per dollar
Portugal—	28.50 escudos per dollar
Spain—	69.90 pesetas per dollar
Sweden—	5.1668 crowns per dollar
Switzerland—	4.3073 francs per dollar
United Kingdom—	2.4022 dollars per pound

Insofar as the rates in Table 16–1 are pegged rates—and they all are—then deviations outside a small range around the pegs will be impossible. But even so, the *cross rates*—the rates of exchange deduced from converting first into other currencies and then into the final currency—can creep out of line. Sometimes the profits are enormous, particularly when one currency is inconvertible into gold or other currencies (as is the case with the Russian ruble); but professional traders—usually banks—who can mobilize the millions necessary to lever tiny differences into sizable absolute profits, get most of the advantage from *spot arbitrage*. Let us consider a simple example. Suppose the current exchange rates between the dollar and the pound and the franc were \$2.40 per pound and \$0.18 per franc. Now the implicit cross rate between the pound and the franc would be[1]

$$\frac{\$2.40 \text{ per } £}{\$0.18 \text{ per } F} = F13.33 \text{ per } £$$

That is, each pound fetches 13.33 francs implicitly, using the dollar rate as the base. The actual pound-franc rate might not be F13.33 but might be marginally above or below the implicit rate. Suppose that it were F13.43 and that there were no costs of transaction. Then, until the two rates were driven together (the official rate and the implicit cross rate) a New York bank could convert \$240,000 into pounds at \$2.40, getting £100,000, could convert the £100,000 into francs at the actual rate of F13.43 per pound, getting F1,343,000, and then convert the latter back into dollars at the rate of \$0.18 per franc, getting \$241,740—netting \$1,740 on the deal. Furthermore, since all of this just involved two phone calls and was effected instantaneously, a deal of 10 times the size would get profits of \$17,400. *Arbitrage*, then, serves the useful economic purpose of keeping spot exchange rates in almost perfect line.

16.2.2 The Forward Exchange Rate

Not only can one deal in currencies at the present, but there is enough interest in currency quotations in the future for there to have developed a forward market in foreign exchange. The rate of exchange in this market is known as the forward rate of exchange; regular quotations often can be found for 30-, 60-, 90-,

---

[1] The calculation should read:

$$\frac{\$2.40/£1}{\$0.18/F1} = 13.33F/£ = F13.33 \text{ per } £$$

in order to keep the units straight.

or 180-day maturities, and deals can be effected for other maturities on a custom basis. As with the spot market, the forward market arises out of the needs of trade, broadly defined. A firm may order a foreign product, for example, but not wish to pay until delivery, say 90 days after the placement of the order, and pay at a rate specified on the day the order was placed. An American importer who has agreed to buy for £20 a product offered by a British firm for delivery in 90 days has the choice of paying (1) now at the current exchange rate (hence losing interest on his money); or paying, say, 90 days later, either (2) at the current exchange rate or (3) at the spot rate ruling in 90 days. He may also (4) buy pounds now and reinvest them in pound-denominated securities until his debt is due. Consequently, he will not follow course (1) unless the cost of getting in and out of a 90-day British Treasury bill exceeds the interest gained thereby.

If the importer takes the third choice, he will have to bear the risk of foreign exchange fluctuation. That is, £20 might cost him $48 now and $52 in three months, a loss to him over choice (4) and even over choice (1). On the other hand, if he could invest his $48 at 40 percent per year—a somewhat unlikely rate in the legitimate business world—he would actually end up ahead (by 40 cents), even with the adverse change in the exchange rate. It is also true, of course, that the exchange rate need not go against him, and his own views as to what might happen will influence his decision.

If he were to adopt the second course, that of paying 90 days later at the current spot rate, he would have to enter the forward exchange market in order to find someone to bear his risk for him. He would, in fact, buy £20 for future delivery at the forward exchange rate, a rate which reflects the current spot rate and the interest costs of the operation as well as the views of speculators as to what is going to happen to the exchange rate itself over the period. The mechanics of the situation are a little complicated, but they are worth some thought. When you buy currency forward, you buy somebody's promise to provide a certain amount of money in the future. The natural provider of this money in the future is a British importer who needs the same amount, in dollars, in 90 days; he, too, will promise a delivery, of pounds in this case, and with a bank in the middle the deal can be closed with only transactions costs, and with no effect on the balance of payments, now or (in this case) later.

16.2.3 Interest Parities

In fact, under the third option of the last section, exact swaps will be rare. Instead, generally one will buy forward sterling (pounds) from his local bank which, in the first instance, will therefore take a position in pounds for 90 days. Usually, a commercial bank will cover itself in these operations; it can cover itself most effectively by buying the 90-day bills of the British Treasury; similarly, British banks seeking a cover will hold American Treasury bills. This side of the operation, the hedge against exchange risks by the commercial bank, does cause pressure on the balance of payments, for actual funds come to be transmitted (the American bank must buy pounds now to get British Treasury bills now). Of course, the deal is undone in 90 days, but that is small satisfaction if, in the meantime, the country has been forced to devalue.

Since the American commercial bank is forced to buy pounds and hold British Treasury bills, it will be limited to earning the British Treasury bill rate, say 8 percent, on its holdings. If the Treasury bill rate in the United States were 6 percent, the American bank actually would gain on the deal[2] and would be able to offer the American customer a discount on the forward contract of 2 percent per year.[3] This amounts to saying that the forward exchange rate in the market ordinarily will be expected to equal the spot exchange rate plus a term reflecting the difference between Treasury bill rates.

Formally, let us define the spot exchange rate of dollars for pounds to be $SR\$/\pounds$ which, for purposes of example, we will take to be \$2.40. The forward rate will be $FR\$/\pounds$, and we will deduce

---

[2] The American bank only gets into the deal as a result of arranging the cover for a forward deal it has made for one of its customers. A direct attempt to get the 2 percent difference involves exchange risk for the bank unless it hedges itself in the forward exchange market. When it does that, it will have to give up the 2 percent, for it will be selling pounds forward in order to get back into dollars, and that is done at a 2 percent loss.

[3] The British importer is facing a situation which is the exact opposite of this, in which he must pay a premium of 2 percent per year for his forward dollars.

what it ought to be, given an interest rate of 6 percent in the United States and of 8 percent in the United Kingdom. We have observed that if an individual takes a dollar and buys an American Treasury bill with it, he will get, in due time

$$\$1(1 + i_{US})$$

A foreigner, let us say, has a pound to invest in New York; and he will, accordingly, earn

$$(\pounds 1)SR\frac{\$}{\pounds}(1 + i_{US}) \qquad\qquad (16\text{-}1)$$

The value of the expression is measured in dollars.[4] A pound lent in this way, in a perfect capital market, should get the same as a pound lent any other way, if the risks are equivalent. One other way you can lend money is to be the other side of someone's forward exchange deal for the same period. Under the circumstances assumed, the British investor could buy dollars forward (at $FR\$/\pounds$); in the meantime, his funds will earn $\pounds 1 (1 + i_{UK})$. The commercial bank, which will cover itself by buying a U.S. Treasury bill yielding 6 percent, will quote him a rate which reflects its loss on the deal. This will be

$$FR\frac{\$}{\pounds} = (1 + i_{US} - i_{UK})SR\frac{\$}{\pounds} \qquad\qquad (16\text{--}2)$$

in dollar terms.[5]

The investor, we are assuming, has two options. That is, he can take his $\pounds 1$ and invest it at i_{UK} and buy dollars at the rate of Equation 16–2, or he can buy American Treasury bills. Both options leave him uncovered in dollars in 90 days, so in equilibrium, both options should pay the same thing. That is, the in-

---

[4] As an illustration, verify that for $\pounds 1$, at the current official exchange rate, you get a return, including the principal, in 90 days of $2.436 if the interest rate is 0.06 per year.

[5] At a spot rate of $2.40 per pound, the arithmetic would yield (recalling that 0.06 and 0.08 were annual rates):

$$(0.06 - 0.08)\frac{\$2.40}{\pounds} = -\$0.048 \text{ per pound}$$

You should note, as is not emphasized in the text, that the actual deal does not involve any money changing hands now. The formula in the text establishes a forward rate equivalent to the spot rate in dimension.

vestor can buy forward dollars for his pound, at the interest cost of

$$\left(FR\frac{\$}{£} \right) - \left(SR\frac{\$}{£} \right)$$

and he can invest his funds at the United Kingdom Treasury bill rate at

$$(1 + i_{UK})$$

or he can buy American Treasury bills at

$$(1 + i_{US})SR\frac{\$}{£}$$

Since these two options will be the same in equilibrium, a formal relation between the forward and the spot rates exists, in equilibrium. It is, clearly,[6]

$$£1\left[FR\frac{\$}{£} - SR\frac{\$}{£} \right] - £1\left[\left(1 + i_{UK}\right) SR\frac{\$}{£} \right]$$
$$= £1\left[(1 + i_{US}) SR\frac{\$}{£} \right] \quad (16\text{-}3)$$

which can be simplified to

$$\frac{FR - SR}{SR} = i_{US} - i_{UK} \quad \text{in dollar terms} \quad (16\text{-}4)$$

which is equivalent, by the symmetry of exchange rates, to

$$\frac{FR - SR}{SR} = i_{UK} - i_{US} \quad \text{in pound terms} \quad (16\text{-}5)$$

Let us, then, conclude this section of formal definitions by reinterpreting Equation 16–5. In this equation, the percentage difference between forward and spot rates, in equilibrium, is seen to be equal to the interest parities between Treasury bill rates in the two countries. For example, a recent quotation had the pound at $2.4031 with a forward discount of 5/16 cent for a three months deal. Treasury bills in New York were fetching 7.79 percent, and the Treasury bill rate in Britain was 7.53. If we apply Equa-

---

[6] Note that this equation (16–3) is an identity if Equation 16–2 always represents the actual interest charge. Whether it does or does not depends on other market forces to be described shortly. The student should verify that each option brings the investor $2.544 if the contract is taken on an annual basis.

tion 16–4 to these figures, we expect, on the basis of the interest parity, the forward rate to exceed the spot rate, as a percentage of the spot rate, by

$$0.0779 - 0.0753 = 0.0026$$

converted to the annual rates. The statement that the "forward discount was 5/16 cent" implies that the forward rate was 5/16 cent less than the spot rate (of $2.4031), or $0.0032. This times four and divided by $2.4031 gives a left-hand side of -0.0053 which, you can easily see, is of the wrong sign. That is, the interest parity did not hold; and this generally is the case, because the types of deals we described only partly complete the picture of the market.

16.2.4 Arbitrage and Speculation: The Mechanics

We have already described one arbitrage, that involved in ironing out the discrepancies in cross spot rates, and we should point out that there is an exact equivalent in ironing out the discrepancies in cross forward rates. But because speculators enter the forward exchange market, as described in the last section, other opportunities arise for arbitrage. The speculator is defined as someone who expects the exchange rate to change; he deals in market trends rather than in real values. He will speculate against the dollar in the spot market by holding his assets in pounds. This one-way deal creates adverse pressure on the balance of payments, of course; and this, by itself, tends to make speculation a one-way street. But there are monetary consequences which tend to cancel out some of this effect.

In the first place, his purchase of foreign securities tends to drive down foreign interest rates and, presumably, drive up domestic ones. Assuming that interest rates were perfectly balanced in the first place, a discount appears on the dollar, much as we had in our example. Insofar as this is all that happens, the operation stops here, on the surface. But funds are available to the banking system in the United Kingdom, backed, if you will, by a U.S. gold drain. If a British banking firm, let us say, were to acquire a dollar deposit which it consequently wished to convert into pounds at the Bank of England, the banking system would acquire more reserves and, consequently, more high-powered money. And *if the Bank of England did not sterilize the increase in reserves* by a reversing open market operation, the domestic money supply would expand, interest rates would drop, and domestic prices would tend to rise.[7] The drop in the interest rate would further widen the forward discount on the dollar, and the rise in the foreign price level would tend to improve the U.S. balance of trade and hence the balance of payments. But since the lags are so complicated and the parameters of the process are unknown, it is best not to pursue this situation any further.

There is scope here, by the way, for the Federal Reserve to channel the initial adverse effects of this operation on the balance of payments into the forward exchange market. In particular, if the Federal Reserve (or the Bank of England) bought pounds forward for 90 days (say from British banks), a deal which, in effect, involves only a promise to deliver the pounds when the American speculator wishes to return to dollars, British commercial banks would tend to cover immediately by buying American Treasury bills, a transaction which would tend to reverse the gold drain and, incidentally, restore the interest parity. Other destabilizing effects on the balance of payments can be contained in this way. But the essence of the operation is a kind of counter-speculation which tends to remove the teeth from one of the really disturbing features of speculation in exchange rates. That is, speculation uncountered tends to produce evidence, in the form of a reserve drain, that the currency is weakening and that the speculation is justified. This self-reinforcement, whether deliberate or not, presents the real possibility that speculation might be destabilizing,[8] bringing down currencies.

One reason the forward rate and the spot rate could depart from parity is simply that a large number of firms and individuals are going uncovered simply because they expect no change in exchange rates. This is formally speculation, of course, but we must recall that arranging forward cover is an expensive nuisance. Even so, many firms have been badly hit in the currency devalua-

---

[7] This is one of the factors behind Germany's concern, in recent years, about its "imported inflation." Leland B. Yeager, *International Monetary Relations* (New York: Harper & Row, 1966), chap. 23.

[8] The argument as to whether or not this has been the case is discussed in section 16.3.1.

tions and revaluations of recent years.[9] Another form of speculation, often of the accidental sort, involves the timing of payments
and receipts. The individual, for example, might "speculate"
against the dollar by settling his French wine debts more rapidly
than his American wine debts (his wine dealers may not go along
with this); this is the *leads-and-lags* method of speculation, which
can be quite sizable over short periods of time and is as complicated
as the techniques of foreign exchange.

Arbitrageurs will enter the forward market in a way other than
by smoothing out cross forward rates. In particular, there might
be an interest-arbitrage incentive when forward rates get substantially out of line with interest parities. This arbitrage, of course,
requires cover—at the market rate—and due to high transactions
costs (partly because this deal involves operations in both the forward market and the Treasury bill market), it is said that a fairly
wide difference between interest parities and forward rates is necessary to motivate it. This permits some flexibility in the relationship between the forward and spot rates; similarly, there are a
variety of short rates and risk factors in the market, and limits
to the funds arbitrageurs have at their disposal further limits their
ability to operate to reduce the difference.[10]

16.3   PURCHASING POWER PARITY: A NAIVE MODEL OF MONETARY INTERACTION

We have already suggested that relative price *levels* between
countries have something to do with the flow of trade and, consequently, with the balance of payments. The general idea is clear
enough, although when we try to formulate it precisely, the whole
thing becomes somewhat of a nightmare. That is, if there is a
fall in the price of a British product, other things being equal,
there should be a tendency for the British to sell more and the
Americans less, assuming both deal in the product in question.
Then, to connect up the ends, the fall in the individual British
price should be associated with a fall in the British price level,

---

[9] A revaluation is a (rare) upward movement of an exchange rate. The
Germans revalued in 1961 and in 1969.

[10] Recall that arbitrage involving the evening out of cross rates does not require
funds.

and all should be associated with an improvement in the British balance of payments. But the pit is yawning before us.

Let us push a little further before we see if an example helps us. In the classical theory of international payments, applied to two countries, assuming the conditions of the quantity theory of money apply in both countries, a country which experiences a rise in its price level[11] will experience a gold outflow, which will tend to reduce the monetary base and reverse the change in the price level. The general assumption underlying the mechanisms seems to be the idea that there is an *automatic gold standard*—a country experiencing a gold inflow will permit its money supply to expand and its price level will follow suit. Then one can conclude "that the equilibrium rate of exchange between two currencies is such as gives equality in their purchasing power."[12] Indeed, in one version, this is exactly how it is stated:

$$ER = \frac{\bar{P}_A}{\bar{P}_B} \qquad (16\text{--}6)$$

where A and B identify the countries, and $\bar{P}$ is the price level.

Recently, some assumptions have come to be included in the analysis, as direct empirical tests of Equation 16–6 have not been entirely successful. Two of the most important of these assumptions are

a) There are no lags in the adjustment process.
b) All goods are traded internationally.[13]

Assumptions, you will recall, need not be valid; and these certainly are not. The second, for example, requires that services be traded internationally, and this is a bit hard to accept. Of course, once we recognize that all prices need not be used in the theory, we can merely reformulate things in terms of those goods which are actually traded when we seek to test the theory.

---

[11] It is never clear how this comes about in the first place. We will begin at the beginning, in what follows, and will discover that it is not easy to get the classical result.

[12] W. M. Scammell, *International Monetary Policy* (New York: St. Martin's Press, 1962), p. 58.

[13] Among the others are (often) the assumption of the homogeneity postulate on real demands and the absence of friction. The first was described in Chapter 9.

Since it is difficult to generate observations about flexibility in the modern system of fixed exchange rates, we will not take up the actual verification of the theory. We should note, however, that most modern adherents of the purchasing-power parity doctrine would abandon the rather rigid formulation implied in Equation 16–6 to something like the following empirically oriented version:

> While the absolute interpretation of the purchasing-power parity doctrine appears unsatisfactory, it is a different question whether changes in the relative purchasing power of national currencies can provide an indication of the required degree of adjustment in exchange rates.[14]

Now we seem to be asking the general question, What contribution to the determination of the exchange rate between two countries does a comparison of the two price levels make? Let us attempt an example.

Assume there are just two countries (A and B) in the world and that there are three goods: X_1, X_2, and money. Let us also assume that there is a domestic gold stock in each country, linked arbitrarily to the quantity of money (for example, that in Country A, one ounce of gold can be converted into \$7). The velocity of money will be assumed to be constant in each country, and each country has flexible prices, competition, and full employment. That is a strict classical world. Both of these countries are closed, to begin with; and we ask, What happens when they start trading—that is, when we consider them in an open system?

The price levels in the two countries are given by Equation 16–7.

$$\bar{P}_a = W_{1a}P_{1a} + W_{2a}P_{2a} \qquad W_{1a} + W_{2a} = 1$$
$$\bar{P}_b = W_{1b}P_{1b} + W_{2b}P_{2b} \qquad W_{1b} + W_{2b} = 1 \qquad (16\text{–}7)$$

If the system is as described, changes in the price level can come about only on account of:

a)   Changes in the quantity of gold in each country.
b)   Changes in the relative weights, $W_{1a,b}$, $W_{2a,b}$.

---

[14] Bela Balassa, "Purchasing Power Parity Doctrine," *Journal of Political Economy*, Vol. 72, No. 6 (December 1964), p. 590.

Now, when we open the system to trade, we must consider the adjustment mechanism. Since we are interested in the determination of the exchange rate, we will assume that it is variable; thus, equilibrium between the two countries can be thought of as occurring due to the flow of gold. If, when we start trade, an ounce of gold can buy more X in Country A than in Country B, gold will tend to flow toward Country A. Country A will experience an increase in its money stock and, with commodities going out and the money stock expanding, in its price level. Country B will be experiencing the reverse.

The exchange rate between the two countries will thus settle down to an equilibrium where gold has the same purchasing power everywhere. Now, suppose the quantity of gold produced in Country A rises: the money stock will expand and so will the domestic price level; similarly, the price level in Country B will expand, *for world prices must be the same everywhere*. If we (continue to) assume that the goods X_1 and X_2 are produced equally efficiently in the two countries, there is no reason for the exchange rate to alter between the two countries unless the relative weights W_1 and W_2 change in the two countries. They will change unless we also assume that all individuals are both alike and have the same incomes.

Actually, the exchange rate is fictitious in this world—there is only one price level which matters, and that is the price level which gives us the purchasing power of gold. The purchasing power of money is automatically "determined" by the statements that all the weights, velocity, and the banking multiplier, are constant in each country. Thus, the statement that the exchange rate reflects the relative price levels is an empty one—capital (gold) mobility has really eliminated all but the accounting distinctions between nations. In other words, there is a meaningful price level in the analysis, but it is the purchasing power of gold, not of money. Indeed, in any system with perfect capital mobility, this is going to be the outcome.

If we wish to get something out of the classical analysis of the mechanism, we must allow the weights for the price level to change or the data (e.g., velocity) to change. But arbitrary changes in the weights must be induced by the types of changes we usually rule out in the classical world: changes in tastes, changes in relative productivity, and changes in the distribution of income. No matter which of these we alter, we will not be able to predict price level changes easily.

The only sensible thing to do, at this point, is to abandon this classical world in favor of one with conditions closer to our own. Without interest rates in the model—without a variable velocity—we cannot really deal with the capital flows our economic system has. That is, we permit gold to flow in the classical world, but deny that it is a capital item by ruling out interest rates. The admission that capital moves from country to country is a serious one for organized international trade theory.

16.4 FIXED VERSUS FLUCTUATING EXCHANGE RATES

Perhaps the most vexed question in international monetary economics is whether or not to have the price of foreign exchange fluctuate so that the market will clear itself. Indeed, in defining the problem, I have stated the best argument in favor of a fluctuating rate: the market would clear itself, so that the complicated and patently unstable clearing systems of our day would be unnecessary. The discussion recently has been broadened into the analysis of *optimum currency areas*, a catch-phrase which highlights the essence of a fixed exchange system: currencies convertible automatically into gold are convertible automatically into each other. That is, a currency area consists of a set of countries whose exchange rates are tied together so that, in effect, they have one currency; the optimum currency area is a reference to trying to solve the problem of deciding which countries belong in the best area from the world point of view.

16.4.1 The Traditional Debate

Let us begin with the traditional debate. The main advantages to a freely fluctuating exchange rate have already been described in passing:

a)   The resources—such as gold and brain power—which go into the present system will be free to seek other employment; this is a substantial gain.

b) The instruments which the authorities use to stabilize the exchange markets will be free for other uses.

c) The system will clear itself and will tend to be more stable than the capricious system we now have.

Point (*a*) is clearly true, but (*b*) and (*c*) are hotly debated. Let us begin with (*c*), where the debate is hottest.

The general idea behind the "clearing itself" position—associated with Milton Freidman[15]—is that if the change in the exchange rate is believed by speculators to be temporary, individuals will adjust their future holdings (perhaps through the forward market) so that an offsetting influence due to the covering action of banks will act to reverse the original fluctuation in the exchange rate.[16] Of course, the critical point here concerns whether or not speculators actually adopt this stabilizing attitude. If not—if, for example, speculators anticipate a fundamental change in the exchange rate—their actions will drive the rate toward the new, anticipated level. Indeed, under any system, any rate the speculators pick will be achieved if they are strong enough. Further, if speculators simply throw out the past in their calculations, small cycles in exchange rates will tend to be enlarged, with some positive probability of a real disaster. Roy Harrod, as the following quotation suggests, fears such a disaster.

This, of course, assumes that there is complete confidence in the maintenance of the fixed rate. But with flexible rates, a downward movement of 1 percent has no such significance. No one knows whether in future the rate will move further down or have a reverse movement. At any point of time the betting may well be 50–50.[17]

---

[15] Milton Friedman, "The Case for Flexible Exchange Rates," in Milton Friedman (ed.), *Essays in Positive Economics* (Chicago: University of Chicago Press, 1953).

[16] If, for example, the spot exchange rate (£/$) rose and you expected it to fall in 90 days, you might buy pounds forward (remember that the current price forward, in the absence of interest parities and other irregularities, is simply the current spot rate plus transactions costs). The American commercial bank, which has agreed to sell you pounds in 90 days, will tend to cover its risk by holding a British Treasury bill. But in currently demanding pounds to effect this transaction, they will tend to reverse the original movement: the supply of dollars will expand when the price of dollars rises.

[17] Roy Harrod, *Reforming the World's Money* (New York: St. Martin's Press, 1965), p. 46.

Under these conditions any jolt in the structure can generate wider swings in the rate, and wider swings will increase the costs of foreign trade by adding a risk factor to all deals. More seriously, the risks of investment in foreign countries (deals which are not so easily covered in the forward market) will be increased, with the result that there will be less investment.

Actually, the argument of the last paragraph is empirical at its root. We are asking, in fact, whether in moving to a system of fluctuating exchange rates speculative activity (which could destabilize markets) will increase uncertainty in foreign exchange markets. There have been a number of serious attempts to state the conditions under which speculators will destabilize (and some to test the proposition empirically). One such, again associated with Friedman, is the idea that if speculators destabilize, they must lose money. That is, if speculators buy when rates are low and sell when they are high, they will make money and will stabilize the market in the sense of pushing up low rates and pushing down high rates. In the converse case—when speculators destabilize—they will lose money. Thus, if speculation is destabilizing, speculators will disappear.

The preceding argument leans pretty heavily on the idea that there is a normal exchange rate, and it ignores a lot of technical possibilities having to do with the way exchange markets work. Even worse, it neglects the redistribution of funds among speculators which we are used to in the domestic stock markets. As with roulette, on which the expected payoff is negative, some speculators will gain, so fresh money will always be around so long as there is sufficient activity in the market. Speculators could ride rates up and down, losing funds on net, but some speculators could do quite nicely. An even more fundamental objection—more in the framework proposed by Friedman—is that if speculators buy when rates are rising (but low) and sell when they are falling (but high), they will tend to profit and to make the rises and falls steeper.

I will not attempt to predict what might happen in practice, but there are several ways a flexible system may be defended, even if fluctuations are sizable. For one, the forward market could be expected to broaden its scope under flexible exchange rates, providing (at a cost) cover against short-run fluctuations, however the fluctuations are generated. Another is that countries can simply defend the exchange rate by dealing in foreign exchange themselves, much as they do under the present system. In this case, it is speculators versus the authorities, and it seems at least likely that the authorities will be stronger, and will grow stronger over time.

Point (*b*) above concerned the freeing of at least one instrument of policy by cutting loose the exchange rate. It is just as well to note that some writers, when they use the word flexible, do not mean perfectly flexible, but only flexible within a fairly wide range. Of course any degree of flexibility less than complete implies holding official reserves to support the limits, whatever they are; so the system would be basically the same as our present one, differing only in degree. Thus, the use of instruments would broadly be the same. This use, applied generally to outflows of reserves, arises because any outflow will be matched by some kind of internal policy—either supression of one or more sectors to affect the "real trade" flows or a rise in the price of credit to affect short-term capital flows. Further, a long standing "deficit" will invite even deeper structural changes, and the use of other instruments.[18]

16.4.2 Optimum Currency Areas: A Modern Perspective on the Debate

To get back to the theory of optimum currency areas, the question can now be posed more exactly: Should the entire world (as it almost is) be one currency area (i.e., bound together by fixed exchange rates); should each country be a currency area in itself, as Friedman's proposal seems to imply; or is there some other system, such as the present set of customs unions, which

---

[18] The British balance of payments has been generally soft since the 1920's. In recent years a stiff domestic incomes policy, partly aimed at increasing the competitiveness of British industry, has been applied. In earlier periods, the policy of "stop-go" was followed (it is not entirely replaced by the incomes policy): that is, in periods of crisis, firm controls were laid on, often in a "package" affecting many sectors at once, and when the tide turned (and the economy had ground to a halt), the measures were let off. Short-term interest rates, subsidies, limits on bank lending, minimum down payments on consumer durables, and tax rates were among the devices included in the package.

would be more economic?[19] The question is not an academic one, if only because it is under some slight consideration in the world; we have also had several periods of limited flexibility recently, notably Canada's from 1950 to 1962 and again in 1970, and West Germany's in late 1969.

Of course a currency area with only one national currency implies a financial structure with a single central bank; further, given the sentimental attachment people (are thought to) have toward their national units, such schemes seem far in the future.[20] Thus, in any currency area, we have to deal with sets of fixed rates which are maintained cooperatively rather than necessarily; a certain amount of instability, therefore, is to be expected. But there is a more fundamental difference as well, for with a poorly designed currency area, regional shifts in spending patterns will have undesirable effects. For example, consider two countries, A and B, which have a shift of demand from Country B to Country A. Assuming separate currencies, then, if Country A raises interest rates to restrain the price rise—thus sterilizing the effect—B will suffer deflation and unemployment. This, indeed, might describe German policy since World War II. If A and B have the same currency and a central bank with the responsibility of eliminating unemployment, if any region suffers unemployment due to a shift in spending, the central bank will increase the money supply. This imparts an inflationary bias to poorly drawn currency areas; further, you will recognize the process of the validation of a structural force common to the cost-push theories of inflation.[21]

Thus we find a trade-off established between unemployment and the rate of inflation in the world which can be lessened by constructing currency areas so that such internationally induced

---

[19] There are overlapping free trade areas, customs unions, and formal agreements in the world. The first, for example the European Free Trade Association (EFTA, which includes Britain in its membership) has a common internal tariff structure and individual external tariffs. The Common Market, at present, is a customs union—i.e., has a common internal and external tariff structure. It will be a common market, as the term is defined for analytical purposes, when there is free mobility of factors between the countries. "Kennedy rounds" and the General Agreement on Tariffs and Trade (GATT) are examples of the last-named.

[20] This is one of the objectives of the European Common Market. Indeed, when final factor mobility is achieved, the adoption of a common currency will be attended without difficulty. These discussions are going on.

[21] This process is discussed in Chapters 6 and 7.

effects are held to a minimum. Flexible exchange rates might solve the problem between Country A and Country B; but if there are disparities within Country A as well, then the attempt to reach an internally caused problem due to regional shifts of demand in A, along with a balance of payments problem with B, requires more than one instrument. The one instrument, you will recall, is monetary policy with either fixed exchange rates or fluctuating exchange rates. The answer, of course, lies in treating the unemployment in one of the regions of A with some other device, such as a form of fiscal policy.

It is quite obvious that either the possession of other effective instruments to deal with conflict between objectives or *sufficient factor mobility* (in which case the unemployment problem solves itself) will eliminate the problem. For example, if all factors are used in all productive purposes, then if any factor is perfectly mobile, permanent unemployment is inconceivable in any event; and the optimal currency area is the world. If no factors have perfect mobility, then it is an empirical question as to how the boundaries are to be drawn, assuming no other instruments are available. To return to the practical example of the Common Market, since one of the principle objectives of that organization is to achieve at least perfect capital, and substantial labor, mobility, a common currency (or, if you will, ultimately stable internal exchange rates) will follow other reforms without incident.

16.4.3 Canada's Fluctuating Exchange Rate[22]

When one important country goes onto a flexible exchange rate while all other major countries do not, we do not really have a sufficiently flexible system to judge flexibility empirically. This is because intrinsically, only one price—in this case the Canadian offer for gold—has been freed. Even so, largely as a chapter in political economy, the Canadian experience is revealing. Let us begin with the actual events.

From October 1950 until June 1961, the Canadian exchange rate was freed. The rate began at a discount to the dollar, but

---

[22] As this section draws heavily on Chapter 24 in Yeager, *op. cit.*, it seems best to point this out now. The conclusions are presented in a different language, however, and the whole discussion is brought up to date.

by 1952 was at a substantial premium to the dollar. The chief cause of this premium seems to have been a fairly massive inflow of capital which continued into 1956. The capital inflow, of course, would have strengthened the Canadian balance of payments if Canada had been on a fixed rate; and it had the consequence of contributing strongly to the driving up of the exchange rate, which reached its peak in August 1956. Interest payments, which reversed the flow of payments and accelerated inflation,[23] led to a reversal of the move upward; and the Canadian dollar "slipped" steadily from 1956, dipping sharply to a discount again in the last six months of the period.

During this time, month-to-month and average fluctuations in the rate were fairly modest, reaching excessive rates (still less than 6 percent on an annual basis) only at the beginning and the end of the period. Some of this orderliness was due to official Canadian intervention in the foreign exchange market—particularly in 1950 and 1960—but the average intervention (judged simply by the size of dealings) seems to have been less than half that of the period before the rate was cut loose. While we cannot interpret the Canadian experience directly as a lesson in freely flexible rates, the relative absence of strong speculation—except at crisis periods such as 1950, 1957, and after 1960—is worth something as an empirical refutation of destabilizing speculation. The speculative activity which did exist could have arisen because it was well-known that the authorities were in the market; and, from 1956, it might have been suspected by speculators—validly in 1960—that the authorities might return to a fixed rate at a rate lower than the market rate of the late 1950's. The authorities might pick a lower rate because it would be easier to defend.

Why, then, did Canada go off the free rate?[24] One of the issues was political and concerned the increasing dominance—because of capital flows—of Canadian business by American investors. Actually, control of the exchange rate was not fundamentally involved here, because Canada and the United States are a single currency area because of capital flows. One could put controls

---

[23] See section 16.4 on purchasing power parity.

[24] In 1970, they returned to a free rate after a prolonged period of surplus. Perhaps, therefore, it is fair to say that the interval from 1961 to 1970 was the aberration.

on capital under any system of exchange rates, so we must judge the attack on the flexible system as partly confused and partly emotional. To put the economic point more strongly—nationalism aside, if there are strong capital flows between nations, it doesn't matter what exchange system is adopted between them, for the capital flows will simply undermine the nominal independence of the monetary authorities supposedly emanating from flexible rates.[25] Indeed before, after, and during the period of flexible exchange rates, the Canadian and U.S. price levels moved together, suggesting that they were a common currency area with a common price level.

16.5 DISCUSSION QUESTIONS

1. Does it make much sense to talk about the exchange rate as a price determined by supply and demand when the prices actually determined are those of product prices in the first instance? Is the problem raised here similar to that first raised in Chapter 15 over whether a supply of dollars is automatically a demand for pounds (in a two-country world)? Explain.

2. It was suggested that some countries set official exchange rates which are away out of line with what the market would set. What are the consequences (assuming a rate set well above the market rate) of such actions? For example, what happens to the balance of payments accounts which are, presumably, figured at one set of rates but (depending on the ability of traders) reflect transactions conducted at another? Are capital accounts especially likely to be in error? Explain.

3. Recently, the European Common Market proposed that in the course of working toward a common monetary system, they were going to keep cross exchange rates much closer together. How would this be effected? Is there any difference between what they would do here and an alternative policy of each country narrowing the gap around its price vis-à-vis the dollar? Explain carefully, in terms of optimum currency area theory.

4. Give reasons, in addition to those cited in the text, why forward rates might get out of line with spot rates. Is there any *necessary* relation? Would it make sense to interfere in the forward market

---

[25] This makes the results of the two systems the same.

directly in order to assist in evening out fluctuations in the spot rate?

5. Work out an example, on an arbitrary set of recent quotations using three countries and both spot and forward rates, of the mechanics of Section 16.2. Comment on your findings in terms of the explanations in this chapter; be sure that you attempt to reconcile all the peculiarities in the results, as these must have some underlying economic explanation (with the word *economic* being defined quite broadly).

6. Why, do you suppose, do many business firms let themselves go uncovered in their foreign exchange dealings. Would it make sense as a government policy to build up the forward market so that such dealings would be cheaper? Why is it so expensive, then, and what can be done about it?

7. The speculator in interest rates seems to serve an economic function, while the speculator in foreign exchange markets might not. Is this a reasonable statement? What role does government intervention in the two markets play in defining this difference? What would you say if the country discussed had been Brazil?

8. Why is the purchasing power parity theory an obvious extension of classical thinking into the international sphere? Are more assumptions needed to get things going, or are those of Chapter 10 sufficient? Comment on whether or not these assumptions are in the classical spirit and whether or not they alter the nature of the monetary analysis.

9. How did we manage to link the problem of fixed versus fluctuating rates with the question of optimum currency areas? If the United Kingdom were included in the Common Market—after the Common Market had achieved a common currency—would the system be more or less likely to stay together? Explain, and illustrate your generalizations with recent data, where possible.

10. Canada has gone off its fixed exchange rate again. Has the Canadian economy changed in some way since 1961? Illustrate. Are there considerable political overtones to your discussion? Are the Canadians more or less autonomous (and in what sense?) under the new system?

16.6 FURTHER READING

FRIEDMAN, MILTON. "The Case for Flexible Exchange Rates," *Essays in Positive Economics* (ed. Milton Friedman). Chicago: University of Chicago Press, 1953.

HARROD, ROY. *Reforming the World's Money*, chap. 2. New York: St. Martin's Press, 1965.

HOLMES, ALAN R., and SCHOTT, FRANCIS H. *The New York Foreign Exchange Market*. Federal Reserve Bank of New York, 1965.

KENEN, PETER B. "The Theory of Optimum Currency Areas: An Eclectic View," *Monetary Problems of the International Economy* (eds. Robert A. Mundell and Alexander K. Swoboda). Chicago: University of Chicago Press, 1969.

MUNDELL, ROBERT A. "A Theory of Optimum Currency Areas," *International Economics* (ed. Robert A. Mundell). New York: Macmillan Co., 1968.

SCAMMELL, W. M. *International Monetary Policy*, chaps. 2 and 3. New York: St. Martin's Press, 1962.

YEAGER, LELAND B. *International Monetary Relations*, chaps. 5, 6, 10, 11, and 24. New York: Harper & Row, 1966.

Chapter 17

REFORM OF THE INTERNATIONAL PAYMENTS MECHANISM: A DEBATE

17.1 INTRODUCTION

The literature on reform of the payments system is diffuse and studded with inconsistencies. Since there has never been—apart from the classical "automatic mechanism"—a viable theory to employ, the literature has been subject to no clear constraints on its growth. I am not going to offer a theory here, but I am going to run through the proposals that have been served up to see which are palatable from the point of view we have built up in this text. In the end we will be able to show some signs of progress, but we will be far from establishing a consensus.

The principle task of this chapter is to expose the nature and weaknesses of the clearing system we have and to offer a critique of its effectiveness. The present system is built on the ideal of multinational cooperation and at its center has the International Monetary Fund, a kind of super bank, whose purpose is to police the system rather than to control the stock of (international) high-powered money. We will begin with the IMF, including a brief discussion of its origination; but the thrust of this chapter will be toward the debate over the reform of the present system. We will spend some space, at the end, on the recently enacted *special drawing rights* scheme.

17.2 THE DEVELOPMENT OF THE INTERNATIONAL MONETARY FUND

The general idea underlying most of the payments plans put forward since the 1930's has been to build a self-correcting mechanism similar to that attributed to domestic economies with a central bank. The idea is to have final payments made in a medium which countries cannot directly create; the hope is that there will then be a natural discipline to the system insofar as the quantity of the medium itself does not readily respond to pressure. Gold, which is most often thought to serve best in this role, is a commodity, unfortunately, and in diminishing supply. Thus, systems relying on gold alone are faced with an annoying scarcity; the result has been a series of efforts to come up with either an alternative (commodity) or a supplement (whether commodity or not). The technique actually employed has been to support the price of gold. Since the 1930's, the price of gold has been $35 an ounce simply because that is the buy-and-sell price of the Americans.[1] But on top of gold, because of the failure of new production to match the new demand by central banks, we have seen a variety of ad hoc arrangements between countries. These are, categorically:

a) Bilateral currency swaps in one form or another (monetary incest).

b) Agreed (usually bilaterally) indebtedness between countries (key currencies).

c) Multicountry (usually with IMF approval) arrangements to hold one another's debts (the sterling area).

d) International credits (IMF quotas or special drawing rights).

These arrangements have arisen out of the wreckage of the gold standard.

When a country pegs itself into the fixed rate system, it pledges itself to fight adverse balance of payments situations with its reserves—gold plus convertible (into gold or dollars) currencies. When it runs out of reserves, a country must either borrow or undertake some sort of structural reform. It does not follow, unfortunately, that all countries forced to undertake structural re-

---

[1] Since one can always buy and sell at $35 per ounce, the only times prices outside that range occur are when speculators expect the United States to devalue (or revalue, to refer to lowering the price of gold). There has always been a certain amount of black-market operation in gold, and recently a two-tier system of gold dealings has operated, with speculators and private dealers permitted to have their say in their own market. In fact, the price of gold in this market has gone over $40 an ounce, although it is generally only a little above $35.

forms actually had structural problems, and recognition of this possibility led directly to the International Monetary Fund, an international organization empowered to lend to a deficit country after a suitable review of its problems. The IMF arose out of the discussions begun during World War II, and its final charter reflects two quite different views of what was needed, the British and the American.

Let us begin with the consensus. It was generally agreed that

a)   Exchange rate changes ought to be rare.
b)   The IMF ought to have the power to inspect trouble spots.
c)   The IMF ought to provide an efficient clearing mechanism for international payments.

However, when it came to actually making over the mechanism itself, and in particular to defining the lending power of the IMF, the dispute became intense.[2]

The British put forward a proposal engineered largely by John Maynard Keynes. The Keynes plan called for an international currency—called Bancor—which was to be valued in gold but to be untied to any particular central bank. The world central bank, then, would clear payments and compare deficits and surpluses with the quotas—which we could call deposits—assigned to each nation. Countries would still have gold and convertible currency balances, but could channel short-run problems to the IMF. The latter, in turn, would always be "solvent," since one country's deficit is another's surplus: the IMF would lend to deficit countries from the surplus of other countries. This did not deal with structural problems; to handle these, the Keynes version of the IMF would have the power to force deficit countries to

a)   Devalue.
b)   Put controls on outward capital transactions.
c)   Pay up.
d)   Leave the IMF.

Surplus countries were not to be treated so harshly in the Keynes plan, and this generated a bias which has continued to this day. To be sure, there was a very timid suggestion that persistent credit

---

[2] We shall see, in the course of our discussion of the special drawing rights scheme (vintage 1967), that the dispute goes on to this day.

surpluses at the IMF might be canceled if the country in question could not justify itself, but this was a long way from policing chronic surpluses. We shall return to this bias from time to time, because it is one important contributor to the present instability of the payments system.

The American plan, known as the White plan (for Harry Dexter White), was much less visionary and opted for a simple quota system and for no international currency or super central bank, either in substance or in form. The American plan was the one which was adopted eventually; after being modified, it had much in common with the Keynes plan, especially in terms of the assigning and policing of quotas. Where it did differ (aside from the notion of an international money) was in being much more firmly against exchange rate changes; suggesting, in fact, that only a "fundamental disequilibrium" be treated by an exchange rate change, and then only after agreement by four fifths of the members. On the question of surplus countries, the White plan was even less restrictive than the Keynes plan; thus, in the negotiations only a "scarce currency clause" was added onto the White plan. This provision permitted the IMF to declare a persistent creditor country's currency "scarce" and to allow countries to discriminate against it. However, because of the persistent belief, still not eradicated, that deficit countries—and not surplus countries—are to blame when things go wrong, this clause has never been invoked beyond the advisory stage.[3]

Offhand, it does not seem likely that the losers in any economic game, particularly one in which monopoly elements are present, are responsible for more than their share of the blame for their losses. Over and over again, for example, the West German government—which has run "embarrassing" surpluses since the middle 1950's—has claimed that it has no responsibility for other countries' deficits. Its position, roughly, is that its surpluses have been thrust upon Germany by the foolish policies of other countries, notably Britain. It is obvious that both parties have a responsibility in the gold exchange standard, for a surplus somewhere implies

---

[3] We shall see more fully, in Chapter 18, that in the "international disequilibrium" system we live in, no such position is valid; this is true even under the gold standard or the gold exchange standard, as we have experienced them.

a deficit somewhere else. Indeed, a surplus country must permit the domestic price level to rise and change interest rates so as to encourage a capital outflow; it is not obvious that the Germans have done this, and we do know they have tried to restrain what they call imported inflation. Japan, another country with a surplus, uses subsidies to frustrate the system.

TABLE 17–1

IMF POSITIONS OF SELECTED COUNTRIES, NOVEMBER 30, 1969

($ million)

Countries	Gold Subscription	Currency Subscription	Quota	Actual Fund of Currency Holdings	Fund Reserve Position*
United States.......	1,290	3,870	5,160	3,196	1,964
United Kingdom.....	610	1,830	2,440	4,507	−2,067
France............	246	739	985	1,484	− 499
Germany..........	300	900	1,200	898	852
Italy..............	156	469	625	330	780
Canada............	185	555	740	361	444
Japan.............	181	544	725	274	524
Areas:					
Latin America.......	484	1,480	1,964	1,875	352
Middle East........	168	502	690	687	− 17
Other Asia........	296	1,451	2,312	2,280	− 533
Other Africa.......	173	638	988	921	− 110
Total**.......	4,942	15,568	21,272	22,468	...

* Minus sign indicates use of fund credit.

** The figures in the table are meant to be suggestive only and, because unimportant items are left out, the figures cannot be reconciled completely, either by columns or by rows.

SOURCE: International Monetary Fund, *International Financial Statistics*.

The IMF itself grew out of meetings held at Bretton Woods, New Hampshire in 1944. While many of the disagreements aired during the early years of World War II had been ironed out by that time, the question of the size of quotas had not; in fact, the formula, the size of the quotas, and the method of administering them had to be worked out. The system adopted set rather low limits to these quotas, and several revisions have been made subsequently; the American figure, originally set at $2,750 million had risen to $5,160 million by the end of 1969. The IMF positions as of the end of November 1969 of a sample of countries is set out in Table 17–1. In this table the *quota* is defined as a sum of gold and currency "deposits," and *borrowings*—for example, for the United Kingdom and France—consist basically of fund holdings of currency in excess of the subscribed amount. This, it seems to me, adequately illustrates the mechanics of IMF operations.

There are several other "contributions" made by the Americans which have become embodied into the IMF's articles. One of these concerns the voting procedures. The Americans wanted—and got—a system of voting weights proportional to the size of the quota subscribed. This has given America veto power over most structural matters—for which an 80 to 85 percent vote is necessary—and it is one reason why many people feel the system is American rather than international. Other blocs of countries, particularly the Common Market, could also have veto power, but generally none of the potential blocs vote in common. Perhaps the objection to the American monopoly is overrated, but it is just as well to point out that several other American attitudes have become embodied in the IMF both in spirit and in practice, including:

a) Hostility to fluctuating or even changing exchange rates.
b) A preference for free trade in general.

Many countries would object to these either as principles or as sound economic policies.

17.3 PLANS FOR REFORM: A MUDDLE

17.3.1 Overall Exchange Rate Change Plans

The variety of proposals about exchange rates is fairly large. At one end is the school of thought—the "hard money" school—which believes that gold is the fundamental value in any economic system and, somewhat illogically, that exchange rates should never be changed. Certainly that system would be an exciting one, for it would never be in equilibrium; indeed, we are actually trying to operate a version of this system today. At the other end we have the school of 100 percent flexibility. The latter has the disadvantage (as we saw in Chapter 16) that wild swings in rates (if they occurred) would upset the system and possibly reduce the volume of trade and investment. The fluctuating system has the advantage that freeing the price of gold leaves the managers of the economy with an instrument to use elsewhere; for when they peg the price of gold, they use up an instrument—changes in the quantity of reserves—to achieve their objective. Therefore, assuming that balance of payments problems don't arise because of policy mistakes elsewhere, the issue depends on the trade-offs between (alleged) international instability and the effectiveness of the freed instrument in its other uses.[4]

Usually, however, the discussion over exchange rates concerns the frequency and nature of revisions in these rates. The most widely held view in this general area is probably the *wider band* notion of flexible exchange rates. The argument generally given is that the limits of the present set of pegs (1 percent on each side of parity) are too close together, with the result that stabilization dealings are often required for very short-run influences. Indeed, we end up offsetting seasonal factors and are kept "busy" offsetting the innumerable, and often trivial, "random" shocks which hit the payments system. Of course it isn't really clear how wide the band ought to be, and obviously some theory will have to be developed about this. With a wider band system there is still some chance that a nation will "run out" of assets, and thus some form of international reserve—gold, no doubt—will be needed in a large quantity. One thing we can say is that it seems likely—but not certain, by any means—that if we widened the bands in our present system, we would, for the moment, need fewer reserves.[5]

Another, more complicated, proposal of this sort is known as the *crawling peg*. The general idea is to permit a persistent pressure on the currency, or even on the price of gold, to be met with a series of gradual adjustments. It would be most difficult to figure out where to set a rate by looking at the results of our "managed disequilibrium" system; but in view of the general feeling that

---

[4] In Chapter 18 we will point out that more than one instrument is actually used by many countries in adhering to their assigned parities. This fact changes the weight of the above argument in favor of fluctuating rates.

[5] The actual suggestions made are usually for 2 to 3 percent on each side (the smaller band) or 4 to 5 percent (the broader band). The latter would permit a range of fluctuation, up to 10 percent, a range wide enough for most of our few experiences with flexible rates.

a good deal of systematic devaluation is needed in the world, one suspects that the pegs in this system would tend to crawl upwards—in dollars per ounce of gold—at least in the early days of the system. A lot of economists favor such a proposal, but it has to be worked out carefully, for if the crawl is too rapid, speculators will be able to profit. The way to keep speculators off balance is to keep the crawl down to an annual rate of 2 to 3 percent. This would tend to keep the gain below the interest cost of financing the speculation—and in any event, too low to be interesting—and would be a workable system, in general.

There are other such plans, of course. There is a plan which would combine the crawling peg with the wider band; this is known as the *movable band*. There is a proposal that all countries simply have the right—often argued to be implicit in the Bretton Woods agreement—to change their parities up to 2 per cent per year without consultation with the IMF. The general argument behind all of these schemes is that increased flexibility would put the system back on its feet: that trying to keep rates within a 2 percent range is impossible, given the volatility of trade and capital flows in our world.

17.3.2 Unilateral Adjustments

The IMF permits changes in exchange rates when a "fundamental disequilibrium" can be established, but the countries which have devalued in recent years have ignored this criterion as well as the IMF. I do not see how the word "fundamental" is going to be defined; and since all countries are generally in at least visible disequilibrium—a surplus being just as undesirable as a deficit—it is possible that what is in fundamental disequilibrium is the system itself. One proposal, more as a matter of fact than as anyone's thought-out plan, is to conduct once-for-all devaluations on a unilateral basis whenever parity becomes "indefensible." But there is a curious thing about hit-and-run devaluations: they might not work, and usually too little is known in advance about their chances of success for prediction to be anything but hazardous.

When a country devalues its currency, whether or not it gains (and the rest of the world loses) mainly depends on the slopes of the supply and demand schedules for foreign exchange. The overall effects of a devaluation are extremely complicated, but one question which could be asked concerns the effect on the trade balance of the devaluing country, in money terms. Let us take the British as our example; then, the actual effect, in the simplest possible framework, is the result of four influences:

a)   The response of British consumers to the rise in foreign prices.
b)   The response of British business firms to the rise in foreign prices.
c)   The response of foreign consumers to the fall in British prices.
d)   The response of foreign business firms to the fall in British prices.

It is traditional, but not necessary, to ignore (*b*) and (*d*), so we will; the analysis, then, generally continues in terms of the elasticities of demand measured for (*a*) and (*c*).[6]

The elasticity of demand is defined as the percentage change in some quantity (here, spending on goods) induced by a 1 percent change in the price of the quantity (here, the price of the currency). Let us define E_F as the elasticity of demand of foreign consumers for British products:

$$E_F = \frac{\%\ \Delta \text{ in foreign demand for British goods}}{\%\ \Delta \text{ in prices of British goods}}$$

and E_D as the elasticity of the demand of British consumers for foreign products:

$$E_D = \frac{\%\ \Delta \text{ in British demand for foreign goods}}{\%\ \Delta \text{ in prices of foreign goods}}$$

The change in the exchange rate between the pound and all other currencies changes both prices, and both elasticities can be and have been measured; further, the effect on the balance of payments—the net change of total spending in terms of foreign currencies—can be evaluated from these two measures.

Let us assume the data for Case 1 illustrated in Table 17–2. We wish to know, in this case, whether devaluation brings net

---

[6] We will neglect the income effects of the price changes, and we will ignore changes in costs (for example, due to the rise in the costs of imported materials); thus, the analysis here is not general, although it points things in the right direction.

claims on British currency or on foreign currencies—that is, what we want to know is the net effect of devaluation. The value of 0.5 for E_D indicates that British purchasers, who think in terms of pounds, will cut spending by 5 percent in pounds if foreign prices (the exchange rate) rise by 10 percent. This is a net gain to the British balance of payments; let us do a calculation so that the point here is perfectly clear. Assume that the devaluation is 10 percent—that is, that the percentage of change in dollars to pounds is 10 percent, from, say, $2.40 to $2.16 per pound. Assum-

TABLE 17–2
Two Cases Illustrating "Stabilizing" and "Destabilizing" Devaluation

| Elasticities* | Case 1 | Case 2 | Net Effect Illustrated | |
			Case 1	Case 2
E_D	0.5	0.5	$2400/$2052	$2400/$2052
E_F	0.3	0.8	$2400/$2008	$2400/$2117
			Net Gain or Loss to British Balance of Payments	
$E_D + E_F - 1$	+0.2	−0.3	−$44	−$65

* These demand elasticities ought to be negative, but it is traditional to treat them as positive.

ing that £1,000 was spent at the original exchange rate, total claims on the pound of $2400 would result; in turn, the elasticity of 0.5 implies that spending by British citizens on American products would fall, in dollar terms, by no more than 5 percent (to include both the cut in pound spending and the fall in the exchange rate). The calculations are as follow:

$$\text{Original exchange rate: } \frac{\$2.40}{£1} \cdot £1000 = \$2400$$

$$\text{Devalued exchange rate: } \frac{\$2.16}{£1} \cdot £950 = \$2052$$

That is, fewer pounds are spent on American products at a lower exchange rate, so that the net use of dollars (in terms of gold, ultimately) has fallen by $348; this is beneficial to the British balance of payments.

The other side of the coin is American spending on British products. Along a demand curve, the relation between total spending and elasticity is as follows:

a)   Elasticity = 1: A fall in price produces *no change* in spending.
b)   Elasticity > 1: A fall in price produces a *rise* in total spending.
c)   Elasticity < 1: A fall in price produces a *fall* in total spending.

In our example we have case (*c*) for E_F, for both 0.8 and 0.3 are less than unity. Let us consider the first case: assume that Americans spent £1,000 ($2400) on British products in the first instance, so that the original British balance of payments was balanced. The 10 percent fall in the exchange rate produces only a 3 percent increase in the quantity demanded of British products in dollar terms (for Americans think in dollars). That is, originally Americans provided $2400 to get £1000, but in the second instance they spent 7 percent less (in dollar terms); in fact they spent $2008, as the following calculation makes clear:

$$\frac{\$2.16}{£1} \cdot £930 = \$2008$$

Thus, the devaluation has actually put the British into deficit, since they spent $2052 in the new situation but only acquired $2008 by foreign trade.

If we assume the elasticities in Case 2, the only calculation which needs to be changed is the last one. This time there is only a 2 percent fall in American spending on British products; the calculation reads as follows:

$$\frac{\$2.16}{£1} \cdot £980 = \$2117$$

and the British acquire net claims on the dollar of $2117. The devaluation was successful, and the balance of trade—and the balance of payments—rose by $65. The condition $E_D + E_F - 1$ represents the so-called stability condition, assuming that there is no supply in the analysis.[7] Whether or not a devaluation will "work"

___

[7] If, in fact, we include supply, the result would generally be $E_D + E_F < 1$. See Leland B. Yeager, *International Monetary Relations* (New York: Harper & Row, 1966), chap. 8, for a full discussion of the general case. His general case, as well as ours here, neglects income and cost effects.

under the restrictive assumptions necessary to generate this expression depends on the sign of it. The dichotomy is, simply,

$E_D + E_F - 1 > 0$, Stability: Devaluation works.
$E_D + E_F - 1 < 0$, Instability: Devaluation makes things worse.

Before one devalues, these days, there are political factors which have to be considered. For example, American agreement has seemed to be a necessary prerequisite for a British devaluation; and, compared to other countries, an American devaluation is an

TABLE 17–3
SOME ESTIMATES OF PRICE ELASTICITIES IN FOREIGN TRADE,
1951–66

Country	E_D	E_F	$E_D + E_F$
United States	0.54	1.51	2.05
United Kingdom	−0.22	0.44	0.22
Japan	0.72	0.80	1.52
West Germany	0.24	−1.70	−1.46
Italy	0.13	0.03	0.16
France	−0.17	2.27	2.10
Sweden	0.79	−0.67	0.12
Australia	−0.83	0.17	−0.66
Switzerland	0.84	0.58	1.42
Denmark	1.66	0.56	2.22
Norway	0.78	−0.20	0.58

SOURCE: H. Houthakker and M. Magee, "Income and Price Elasticities in World Trade," *Review of Economics and Statistics*, Vol. 50, No. 2, (May 1969), p. 113.

impossibility, partly on political grounds, for all other countries are likely to follow them: such is the fate of a key currency. One set of recent figures for elasticities is contained in Table 17–3. It is far from a sensible set, but based on the simple analysis of this section, the result of three recent exchange rate changes can be evaluated. The data suggest—using our stability criterion—that a United Kingdom devaluation would be unsuccessful and that a French devaluation would be successful. More interesting is the figure for West Germany: if −1.46 is correct in any sense, then the two attempts to reduce Germany's surplus by revaluation (an upward movement of the exchange rate) would actually increase its surplus. This seems peculiar, but the point should be emphasized: the consequences of either a revaluation or a devaluation are not obvious. It is naive to think that the German revaluation would necessarily reduce the country's surplus, and no qualifications on the analysis will destroy the possibility of instability completely.[8]

The consequences for a system of managed but unilateral exchange rate changes are immediate. Adjustments in exchange rates can be made, at least with some theoretical justification; but the data are so poor, as things now stand, and the likelihood of mistakes is so high (6 of the 11 countries in Table 17–3 had $E_D + E_F < 1$), especially if simple rules of thumb are followed, that arbitrary exchange rate changes to overcome local problems is unlikely to work except on an inefficient trial and error basis.

17.4   REFORMING THE ROLE OF THE UNITED STATES

17.4.1   The Price of Gold

The first thing one could do in the present situation is to create international reserves by raising the price of gold. The present price of gold (in terms of currencies, of course) is, for all practical purposes, $35 per ounce. The general idea of a rise in the price of gold is that the world's gold stocks would then buy more currency—that is, be worth more currency—and if domestic price levels did not respond, or responded only slowly, there would be, effectively, more reserves in the system. Of course, people who held currency reserves would not be benefited.

The objections to the plan, the basic rationale of which is simply bringing the price of gold into line with the rest of the world's inflated prices, are primarily emotional or moral. Some would find it offensive that the hoarders of gold would benefit; others would object to the gains going to the big gold producers—Russia and South Africa—on moral grounds. Even more politically, one school of thought feels that gold is a device by which the materialist imperialist powers subjugate other nations; while a widely different view is simply that it is naive to think that stabilizing the price of gold will stabilize the payments system

---

[8] It is worth reflecting on the results of the recent British and French devaluations and the German revaluation, for the predictions of Table 17–3 seem to have been borne out, at least thinking casually.

better than the market could. The political philosophies behind these two views, as usually expressed at any rate, couldn't be further apart, but the policy recommendation is the same. One other objection, perhaps the real one in all of this, is that the price of gold has become confused with the price of the dollar; defending the dollar price of gold has become a matter of national pride to Americans, who, after all, have reserved the right to make the decision. As Roy Harrod notes:

> The prestige point is a false one, because the real humiliation—but that is too strong a word—occurred when the dollar lost value in terms of goods, in consequence of the war-time and post-war inflations. Nothing can be done now to alter this. . . . A rise in the dollar price of gold would merely be an official recognition of what has long since been a fact, the reduced value of the dollar.[9]

The main argument in favor of raising the price of gold has already been given: world reserves will thereby be increased by a stroke of the pen. It is not a very good idea to repeat the performance time after time—although the fear of speculators, which is the main reason for stating that qualification, may be a neurotic one. But there are other methods for increasing the total of world reserves, not involving exchange rates; these methods are, unfortunately, somewhat less direct. We have discussed the IMF; and, clearly, the only important reasons for not expanding its role are either the belief that the world is too liquid or reasons which are political, moral, or emotional.

17.4.2 The American Deficit

With regard to the American deficit, the literature is almost as diffuse as it is on the price of gold. William McChesney Martin, who argues that the "price of gold is not the problem," assumes that the continuing American deficits are an undesirable way of providing reserves, an assumption which enables him to dismiss all forms of "key currency" reserves without further analysis. His position is typical of a good deal—but far from all—of the official thinking on the topic. Even so, the language employed is typically heavily metaphoric and is built on an analogy with the private

---

[9] Roy Harrod, *Reforming the World's Money* (New York: St. Martin's Press, 1965), p. 63.

banking system, an analogy which cannot be sustained. Witness Martin's summary of the issues:

A continuing U.S. deficit of substantial size is neither desirable nor tolerable. Such a deficit saps the international liquidity position of the nation, by continually building up liquid liabilities abroad or continually reducing U.S. reserves, or both. A steady worsening of our liquidity position—*even while our net worth is improving*—cannot be sustained indefinitely. As a reserve currency, the dollar is widely held around the world. It is natural that holders of dollars look to our gold and other reserves, expecting us to maintain a *reasonable* relationship between our liquid reserves and our short-term liabilities, *just as depositors look to the funds held in reserve by their banks.*[10] [Italics added.]

It is alarming to discover that a man who had such influence in guiding the system actually seems to think that a commercial bank's reserves are used to fight currency drains and states an analogy which requires (at the least) that "the international liquidity" (whatever that means!) he refers to be a medium of exchange.[11] But the biggest problem, as discussed in Chapter 15, is his use of the scare word "liability" in this context, which implies that some day we must pay up ("cannot be sustained indefinitely"). The fact is, unless you assume it away, that there is no necessary limit to the American (or other key currency) deficit, nor is there any obvious reason for other countries to want the system to end. Certainly, the system as presently conceived is a simple one; and central bankers can sit down and, by agreeing to extend each other "credit," provide reserves; this, in turn, will give them more elbowroom to follow conflicting policies domestically and internationally. Since the deficit creates a reserve by agreement, and not by virtue of lowering transactions costs directly, the only limit to the system is the limit to agreement. There are two views to be considered—the rest of the world (the "creditors") and the American (the "debtors")—and from both points of view the key currency system is viable.

We can also ask whether or not America's creditors have any interest in collecting their debts. It is likely, to begin with, that

---

[10] William McChesney Martin (then chairman of the board of governors of the Federal Reserve System), "The Price of Gold Is Not the Problem," *Federal Reserve Bulletin*, February 1968.

[11] Most "liquid" nongold reserves are actually held in the form of short-term government securities, not currency.

the American deficit has arisen on account of an increase in the demand for some form of acceptable reserves. From this point of view, the deficit is analogous to the demand deposits of commercial banks; and the world is, on net, better off for having its reserves, whatever the form. No one would suggest that banks (as a whole) ought to pay up, for if they did, our financial system would collapse. By analogy, so long as the dollar is the basis of the system, that basis must be protected, but not at all costs, until a viable alternative can be achieved. We observe an unprecedented rise in foreign trade, under the "dollar exchange standard"; and, although it is presumptuous to argue that the dollar basis is necessary to this development, it is equally presumptuous to overlook its contribution, particularly when other solutions are politically difficult.

On the other hand, one ought to be reminded that an American deficit means that Americans buy more abroad than foreigners buy in the United States, so that transfers of real goods from abroad to the United States continually offset the runup of American "liabilities." This confers what is known as a *seigniorage* gain to the United States, a gain which has an exact equivalent in the form of the profit of a commercial bank. One way we can argue this point is to call the United States, in this role, a financial intermediary, in that it borrows short (the deficit on a liquidity basis) and lends long (in the form of a capital flow to the rest of the world). Needless to say, the carving up of the seigniorage gain of providing international reserves—between, say, the United States and South Africa—is a messy political problem, on which opinions are likely to differ widely. Even so, there is no system of creating reserves which does not have a seigniorage problem; but, at least from the American point of view, the profit from the American monopoly is so handy that I cannot see why Mr. Martin suggests that Americans drop it. In addition, this kind of reserve is created at essentially no resource cost; and it is, therefore, to be much preferred to gold reserves, *insofar as it is equally acceptable to central bankers*. What private citizens think doesn't matter anyway, since individuals are not allowed to trade in gold.[12]

---

[12] The last part of this sentence describes the critical feature of the gold exchange standard, which we now use, in comparison with the gold standard (in which such trades of gold are permissible).

17.5 THE CENTRALIZED RESERVES PLANS

You will have observed that most of the proposals for reform of the system so far discussed involve increasing total reserves in one way or another.[13] One ought to have some idea of how much is needed, I suppose, but it is the fashion in most of the literature just to *assume* that an increase is needed—because it is thought, for example, that the system has been under increasing strain in recent years. The observation usually follows a notice that world trade has expanded more rapidly than liquid reserves, a fact which is of no particular significance, since it is fluctuations in reserves which matter. Nor is it easy to establish which balance of payments crises are undesirable—and could be prevented if we had more reserves—and which are desirable from some point of view—such as punishing the chronic deficit countries. In the final analysis you might decide to have no crises, in which case you might as well have fluctuating exchange rates for all the stability you will have achieved. But let us assume that the object is to get more reserves somehow, that fluctuating exchange rates are undesirable, and that the key currency notion requires more confidence in one another's national integrity than modern nations can stomach.

17.5.1 Super Central Banks

One key requirement of most of the proposals to this point is that national autonomy—the right to deal yourself in and out of the system—should not be surrendered; but when one drops this condition and begins to think of the possibility of having a super central bank, even more stupid than the ones we have,

---

[13] We haven't established, and it would be most difficult to do so, as we shall see in Chapter 18, that an increase is needed. But since the literature doesn't, we won't either. Some feel that world reserves are actually too high and adduce as evidence that there is a worldwide inflation—that is, that prices are rising everywhere—and the purchasing power of gold has fallen. There is no particular reason to worry about the value of gold; but it is not easy to link up a series of domestic inflations with "reserves" when, in fact, the links have been cut by sterilizing gold inflows. Under an automatic gold standard, when no nonmonetary noise exists, this could be the case; but otherwise—in our world—things are not so obvious. We will not find the answer as easily as that.

all sorts of possibilities emerge. There are three main threads to all the schemes to centralize reserves. The first proposal, which first appeared in the Keynes plan as outlined above, calls for borrowing facilities and a clearing mechanism using an international money (Bancor) which is backed by 100 percent quotas (reserves). This is daring stuff for central bankers; even so, Robert Triffin has suggested that a super IMF have not only the power to open lines of credit but also the power to create reserves by "credit" and "green-market" operations; he suggests one quota "dollar" for five Bancor "dollars." Let us consider this seductive approach more closely.

The first thing to notice is that the super IMF will exercise influence—centralized influence—over domestic economies. Some people will not be able to read any further, and many will count it as a disadvantage; but for the rest, let us note, this is partly a false issue, since outside constraint is a feature of our present system anyway. Americans will not have noticed this, since the present system actually does not constrain them much; but recent British economic history is dominated by balance of payments crises which may have been caused by an inadequate international payments system. This is outside influence, and it is more undesirable in the event that the British deficit is caused by someone else's successful attempt to generate a surplus.

Triffin's main reason for recommending the surrender of sovereignty is revealed in the following statement.

And third—to my mind the most urgent consideration at the moment—what is the proper composition of reserves? How can we live with several different types of reserve assets which countries can shift from one to another at any moment of time?[14]

That is, Triffin denies, and there certainly are instances to support his view, that sovereign nations can be trusted to keep politics out of their handling of their reserves. Basically, then, Triffin is concerned with the American deficit, and it is the confidence issue which he raises. Consider, for example, what France, holding dollar liabilities, might do to the total of reserves if she politically opposed the United States' "paying" the exchange cost of the Vietnamese War by running a deficit. This is murky stuff, to be sure, but

---

[14] Robert Triffin, "The Triffin Approach," in Randall Hinshaw (ed.), *The Price of Gold* (Baltimore: Johns Hopkins Press, 1967), p. 48.

we are bound to answer that France will not be able to collar all the world's gold in the process; and there is no limit to the dollar liabilities other countries could accept in their place.[15] The big loser in such an operation is more likely to be France—and perhaps it even happened that way, particularly if the United States discriminated against French products in order to straighten out the balance. Further, the destruction of reserves would only be dollar for dollar, in contrast to the currency panics we considered earlier, so it is not very alarming either. Under a Triffin one to five plan, by the way, with some national autonomy, things could be much worse.

17.5.2   Special Drawing Rights

In September 1967, the member countries of the IMF agreed to permit a new type of automatic reserve, the special drawing right (SDR), to exist. The SDR represents something "new," at least technically, in the international payments mechanism because of its resemblance to the original proposals of the Keynes plan. In particular, SDR's have the general properties of being

a)   Unchallengable by participating countries.
b)   Not contingent on any structural reforms in the deficit country.

Thus—and the second point is especially relevant—they will be used as a matter of right and will be a permanent addition to international reserves. SDR's, accordingly, are a kind of international money, useful insofar as they are acceptable in exchange by governments. SDR's are not a real liability of any government, since no firm provision for the "repayment" of the "loan" is made; of course, referring to such stand-by arrangements as "credit" is not very precise anyway, since credit in the ordinary sense is not involved.

Actually, the use of the word credit is not authorized in this context, even if it is appropriate; nor is there any reference to reserves or to borrowing. The term special drawing rights, in fact,

---

[15] If an organized anticapitalist group wished to destroy the American banking system by withdrawing its funds from commercial banks in order to generate banking multiplier effects, the Federal Reserve in the course of its almost automatic stabilizing would render the protest invisible.

was a concession to those countries—notably France—which were firmly opposed to an international money. While we have such a money now—for the SDR is a new form of money—it is not called money, nor is it referred to by any of the acceptable synonyms for money. Such is politics.

There is also some confusion surrounding the intention and scope of the plan (which has been adopted). This has arisen primarily because SDR's are only in very limited use and may not soon be significant in volume—after all, it does depend partly on the extent to which they are needed.[16] The mechanics of the system have something to do with the slow implementation, in particular the voting and quota system, which is the same as for the IMF itself. Both the United States (as of 1968) with 22 percent of the voting strength, and the Common Market (without Britain) with 17 percent, can veto any proposal to implement the plan. In particular, an 85 percent vote is necessary to pass on any proposal to put the plan into effect; and changes in the sizes of the quotas are also subject to United States veto. Thus, the mechanism is set up and operative, but widespread use of the system probably awaits either the end of European surpluses in general or the unwillingness of the rest of the world to increase their holdings of dollar-denominated securities; as we have seen, this situation has not yet come to pass.[17]

Once SDR's come into large-scale use, they would not be subject to control; one consequence has been lively interest in the magnitude of the funds. There is no limit to the amount which can be "accepted" by central banks, but several factors cause this to be an interesting debate. For one thing, since the SDR's are proportionate to the IMF quotas, the United States stands to be assigned 22 percent of any rights granted.[18] Thus, in some ways it is logical for the United States to view the scheme as a standby in case the present system, with the dollar as the key currency,

---

[16] At the present writing, the only major user has been the United Kingdom, and its use (SDR 100 million) makes a fairly trivial contribution to its overall balance of payments.

[17] One should also mention that the United States might decide to end its role as the key currency nation.

[18] There is a minor monetary point here: the SDR certificates, like the gold certificates provided by the U.S. Treasury, end up as assets of the Federal Reserve System. That is to say, like gold, SDR's "back" the dollar.

comes under strain. Other countries also agree; particularly the French, who at one time argued that we cannot have the SDR's until the American deficit is ended. This implies, since the payments system is based on dollar liabilities, that SDR's will be generally acceptable only if the present system collapses.

17.6 DISCUSSION QUESTIONS

1. Throughout the discussion of Chapters 15 through 18, the straw man has been a system of fluctuating exchange rates. Draw up a list of asserted advantages and disadvantages for such a system, based on reading other sources as well as this text, compare them in quantitative terms, and decide whether or not it wins.

2. Does it make sense to equate the stability of the payments system with the rigidity of the price of gold? In what senses is this case the perfect analogue of the stability of the interest rate argument in Chapter 6? In what ways does it differ?

3. What are the dangers inherent in a system built entirely of bilateral currency swaps of the type known as monetary incest? Would "perfect incest" produce a payments system functioning like a freely fluctuating exchange rate system?

4. The rhetoric of international finance suggests that deficit countries are to blame, but the analysis does not. Is it possible that it is easier to cure a deficit than to cure a surplus (gifts aside)? Is this because of rigidities in the system? Do your answers to these questions have political overtones? Spell them out.

5. The fact that both the White and the Keynes plans recommended that exchange rate changes ought to be rare suggests that consensus need not produce sense. What other widely accepted "principles" of the payments system can be attacked along the same lines? Why, then, do we get a stronger political aroma from this area than from any other we have studied in this course?

6. The uneven voting procedures of the IMF have not produced as much dissent as one might have expected. Why is this so, do you suppose? Is there a tacit agreement that the banker of the system—the USA—should have veto power? Even so, underdeveloped countries have been critical—what is their argument?

7. Construct a numerical example of a crawling peg system for the dollar. What did you assume about interest rates? Does the effectiveness of this procedure depend on foreign countries in any way? Explain.

8. There has been a lot of flap about the meaning of the term *fundamental* in fundamental disequilibrium. Define this term in several ways and test your definitions against the common usages. Is it possible to have a fundamental disequilibrium in a world economy which has unrestricted capital movements? What role do institutional constraints seem to play in the popular definitions of the word *fundamental?*

9. The lesson of section 17.3.2. is that one never can know whether a devaluation will work until after the fact, if at all. From a policy point of view this makes unilateral devaluations a "random walk." Comment on these views.

10. Roy Harrod noted that the real humiliation for the dollar came when the dollar lost value in terms of goods. Is he talking about the dollar internationally or nationally? What is the relation between his definitions of the prestige issue and the usual definition? Is there an implicit use of the purchasing power parity doctrine lurking in the background or is that, too, unspecified?

17.7 FURTHER READING

GRUBEL, HERBERT G. "The Distribution of Seigniorage from International Liquidity Creation," *Monetary Problems of the International Economy* (eds. Robert A. Mundell and Alexander K. Swoboda). Chicago: University of Chicago Press, 1969.

HARROD, ROY. *Reforming the World's Money,* chaps. 3 and 5. New York: St. Martin's Press, 1965.

HINSHAW, RANDALL. *The Price of Gold,* essays by Lord Robbins, Jacques Rueff, and Robert Triffin. Baltimore: Johns Hopkins Press, 1967.

MACHLUP, FRITZ. *Plans for Reform of the International Monetary System.* Princeton, N.J.: Princeton University Press, 1964.

———. *Remaking the International Monetary System.* Baltimore: Johns Hopkins Press (for the Committee for Economic Development), 1968.

MARTIN, WILLIAM MCCHESNEY. "The Price of Gold Is Not the Problem," *Federal Reserve Bulletin,* February 1968.

YEAGER, LELAND B. *International Monetary Relations,* chap. 8. New York: Harper & Row, 1966.

Chapter 18

THE ECONOMICS OF INTERNATIONAL FINANCE

18.1 INTRODUCTION

In the last three chapters we have emphasized that under the present conditions, capital flows must be included in any analysis of international trade—and, for that matter, in any analysis of the domestic economy. The most basic task remaining is to make some effort to see how the system actually works: to see what variables determine the supply and demand for reserves.

We will concentrate on two aspects of the economics of international finance in this chapter. One concerns the supply and demand for reserves by monetary authorities, with the emphasis on the adequacy of these reserves for their (assumed) purpose. The second concerns the scope left to monetary policy, in an open economy, in the context of limited capital mobility. In this connection we will also comment on the Euro-dollar market, whose recent astronomical growth rate has produced new headaches for the monetary authorities.

18.2 THE SUPPLY AND DEMAND FOR LIQUID RESERVES

18.2.1 Some Crude Solutions

The first question concerns the adequacy of international reserves for the task assigned to them. How you tackle this question depends partly on what role you think reserves ought to play, but we will begin by remaining neutral on that issue and looking at some other viewpoints. We have quoted and referred to the general idea that the world's reserves "ought" to grow in proportion to the expansion of world trade. That is, assuming that the total was about right in, say, 1958, we could ask whether or not the system has generated reserves in proportion to the expansion of world trade since then. The figures are contained in Table 18–1, and they indicate that the proportion of reserves "financing" exports fell from 62.5 percent in 1958 to 41.1 percent in 1967, 10 years later.

TABLE 18–1
WORLD RESERVES AND EXPORTS, 1958–67
($ million)

Date	Total Reserves	World Exports	U.S. Reserves	U.K. Reserves
1958	57,555	91,970	22,540	3,105
1959	57,405	97,180	21,504	2,801
1960	60,285	107,880	19,359	3,719
1961	62,360	112,580	18,753	3,318
1962	62,905	118,320	17,220	3,308
1963	66,275	129,020	16,843	3,147
1964	68,505	144,500	16,672	2,316
1965	70,250	156,490	15,450	3,004
1966	71,980	171,390	14,882	3,100
1967	73,600	178,700	14,830	2,695

SOURCES: World exports data from United Nations, *United Nations Statistical Yearbook.* Other data from International Monetary Fund, *International Financial Statistics.*

The examination of such ratios implies there is some connection between the level of total reserves and world trade: that reserves finance trade in some sense.[1] We can refer to this idea as the "crude quantity theory of reserves," for such it is; and, like the crude quantity theory of money itself, its verification cannot be ascertained merely from an examination of the figures. One reason this is so is that a lot of other influences are at work on the balance of payments; but a more fundamental reason is that reserves are used by central banks to support the exchange rate, and not by individuals as such. More particularly, a rise in the flow of world exports could be associated with a rise in pegging operations or with a fall. It all depends on whether the system itself tends to push outside the limits imposed on it by the fixed exchange rate

---

[1] In another sense all that we observe in Table 18–1, if we argue that the level of reserves is demand-determined, is a rise in velocity.

system; whether it does push outside is not directly related to the level of world trade. To put the case another way, it is not the level of high-powered money which is related to the transactions demand for cash, but the level of "currency plus demand deposits"; international reserves, *in a special sense,* are a kind of high-powered money.

A more promising approach is that which relates the need for reserves to the fluctuations in world trade, rather than to the level of trade as such. If we look at some recent figures which suggest that more developed countries suffer a smaller percentage of fluctuation in their exports than do underdeveloped, then we might argue that the world actually needs fewer reserves as a percentage of exports: that the general growth of world trade brings greater stability to the payments system. But this case is simply the crude Keynesian theory of reserves, to give it an arbitrary name parallel to that attached to the "levels of exports" argument. The idea is that if trade fluctuations increase in absolute amounts, countries will have to hold larger reserves against contingencies—exactly like individuals holding precautionary balances of money. But, once again, we must note that only countries and not individuals are interested in the reserves. It is probably true that individuals hold larger balances as uncertainty increases; but it is not fluctuations in trade, in exports, or in capital movements, but fluctuations in the balance of payments itself—taken as a whole—which countries are interested in. Again, this has nothing to do with world trade as such; and if exports fluctuate all over the place but the exchange rate does not tend to go through the limits imposed on it (because imports fluctuate as well), no further reserves are required by the system. To put it another way, the "balance of payments problem" is the problem of balancing payments—in accounting terms—and that is not easily related to private economic decisions.

18.2.2 The Demand for Liquid Reserves

We must assume that the demanders of official reserves—gold, IMF quotas, dollars, and SDR's—are all the countries in the world except the United States. The suppliers, then—the bankers of the international system—are the IMF, the United States, and the (net) gold-producing countries. The cost of producing reserves varies with the type of reserve produced, with the following summary describing the principal nominal features of each unit.

a)   *Gold* is expensive to produce; and, at today's prices, many mines are unprofitable. Gold is often regarded as the "hard" money behind the system; and some nations, for example France, have held a larger proportion of their reserves in the form of gold for this reason.

b)   The *IMF quotas* are based on gold and currency subscriptions and, since they are backed 1:1, are almost as "hard" as gold. Their use has increased steadily over the years, but is still minor compared to dollars or gold. They are almost costlessly produced.

c)   The *dollar*, as the paper "liability" of the United States, is basically costless to produce (but not to administer); but there is considerable doubt about the stability of the dollar system on account of:

   (1)   The fear that the United States will suddenly decide to reduce its liabilities—irrationally—thus tumbling the the system down.

   (2)   The fear that other countries will permit a run on the dollar, or that one will occur in its own right.

d)   The *SDR*, a new form of IMF credit, has a fractional backing, but is not yet widely used.

These differences notwithstanding, we will turn to the discussion of the demand for reserves as if all forms were alike.

If the argument is that it is the monetary authority of a country which desires the reserves, then as good a starting place as any is the argument that the authorities will judge their needs on the basis of the past behavior of their official reserves. This behavior—following the discussion of Chapter 12 on portfolio decisions—consists of

a)   The variance of past changes.
b)   The mean of past changes.
c)   The duration of past changes.

That is, insofar as a country tends to have had large past changes in reserves, with a long and uncertain duration, the country will wish to hold a larger balance than otherwise. In one such study, the actual reserves of a set of 14 countries were compared to the desired reserves. The results are presented as Table 18–2. Actual reserves are compared with what are assumed to be desired reserves; the desired reserves are calculated by looking at the past behavior of reserves and constructing a prediction of what the authorities would want, assuming they used this method to judge

TABLE 18–2

THE DEMAND FOR INTERNATIONAL RESERVES: VARIATION METHOD
(all entries in $ million; 1962)

Country	Actual Reserves	Desired Reserves	Excess Reserves
Austria................	1,081	1,042	39
Belgium................	1,753	1,406	347
Canada................	2,547	2,270	277
Denmark...............	261	982	−721
Finland...............	317	765	−448
Germany..............	6,964	7,287	−323
Italy.................	3,644	2,145	1,499
Japan.................	2,022	1,411	611
Netherlands...........	1,946	1,824	122
New Zealand..........	171	946	−775
Norway...............	304	818	−514
Sweden...............	801	976	−175
Switzerland...........	2,872	2,266	606
United Kingdom........	3,311	3,856	−545
Totals...........	27,994	27,994	0 = World Excess Reserves

SOURCE: Peter B. Kenen and Elinor B. Yudin, "The Demand for International Reserves," *Review of Economics and Statistics*, Vol. 46 No. 3 (August 1965), p. 249.

their needs. Thus we see that the United Kingdom, for example, would have liked to hold $545 million more of foreign reserves than it had; and, similarly, Italy had more than it "needed." A redistribution system such as the IMF could solve individual problems by arranging to have Italy "lend" (in effect) to the United Kingdom.[2]

---

[2] Because of the way the desired reserves were calculated (from past actual reserves), and because the figures are cross-sectional at a moment in time, the excess reserves sum to zero. Thus we cannot make any observations about the adequacy of reserves; we need a supply function, as the text goes on to point out.

The virture of this method of approach is that it renders it unnecessary to link fluctuations in trade with fluctuations in the balance of payments: the "demand" is generated by using only balance of payments figures. We are, consequently, avoiding confusing the demand for foreign money by individuals with the demand for foreign reserves by central banks. Even so, the approach leaves out a number of critical aspects. One of these is that reserves can be created by unilateral agreement, depending on what country you are talking about. Reserves can also be created by general agreement, such as the SDR scheme; this, too, is not picked up by looking at the past behavior of reserves. Reserves may also be created by a number of direct means, and it is these methods which cause the most confusion about how to study the adequacy of our present system.

18.2.3 Optimal International Reserves

One way a country can create foreign exchange reserves— reserves of dollars, for example—is simply for, say, Britain to buy American Treasury bills with its own currency. The American government will acquire pounds which it *can* use to buy British Treasury bills; the British will have dollars (in the form of Treasury bills); the consequence is that both countries will be more liquid than they were, in the sense that each holds more foreign exchange. This deal can be worked in currency as well, and it is a good deal simpler that way; the United States may simply buy pounds with dollars, which the Bank of England stores as its reserves—this device has been referred to as "monetary incest" because it makes a mockery of any system of counting reserves.

When we talk about individual countries rather than the system as a whole, however, it clearly does not make sense to argue that demand creates supply, for individual countries can get more or less than their share of the pot depending primarily on what domestic policies they follow. The imposition of domestic constraints—by fiscal and monetary policies—imposes costs on the government in the form of rising unemployment (or a loss of income) and in the form of a reduction of investment (or a fall of the growth rate). These costs of obtaining reserves through domestic deflation—to lower the demand for foreign goods and to lower the price level—must be included if we are to appraise the adequacy of reserves. Thus, in one such study,[3] the results of which are reported in Table 18–3, the level of world reserves is almost twice that which the world needs (*Optimal Reserves*) when both demand and supply are taken account of.

TABLE 18–3
OPTIMAL INTERNATIONAL RESERVES, 1963
($ million)

Country	Actual Reserves	Optimal Reserves	Excess Reserves
Austria.................	1,229	442	787
Belgium................	1,940	869	1,071
Canada.................	2,603	866	1,737
Denmark...............	470	251	219
Finland................	347	257	90
Germany...............	7,650	3,773	3,877
Italy...................	3,283	1,893	1,390
Japan..................	2,058	1,770	288
Netherlands............	2,101	933	1,168
New Zealand...........	143	290	−147
Norway................	354	104	250
Sweden................	758	379	379
Switzerland............	3,078	616	2,462
United Kingdom........	3,147	3,810	−663
Totals...............	29,161	16,253	12,908

SOURCE: H. R. Heller, "Optimal International Reserves," *Economic Journal*, Vol. 126, No. 302 (June 1966), p. 307.

We cannot really quarrel with these figures—which imply excess world liquidity and, probably, a worldwide inflation—but we can point out that the cost side might be seriously overstated for most countries because of the presence of two cost items—a measure of deflation and the interest rate. What I am suggesting is that only one measure (perhaps unemployment) is appropriate, because domestic monetary authorities actually pay little attention

---

[3] Heller, in the study to be referred to in the table, actually has a measure of domestic deflation and an interest rate; but the latter is justified as measuring the opportunity cost of holding idle reserves rather than as proxying the damage to the rate of growth of the economy. The reason this is objectionable is that central banks generally do not (or should not) pay any attention to interest rates, at least on their own (profit-and-loss) account.

to the growth rate. There is, in fact, direct evidence that unemployment can be linked to the balance of payments. The results of three such studies are presented in Table 18–4.

These numbers say, for example for 1955–68, that the British deem a billion dollars of reserves worth almost 1 percent unemployment; this also means that if they are offered a billion dollars less of reserves, they will need almost 1 percent less unemployment to keep them happy. The German valuations for the entire period are about the same and are a little hard to understand, for Germany was obviously less needy in that it ran a persistent surplus. The

TABLE 18–4
TRADE-OFFS BETWEEN UNEMPLOYMENT AND $1 BILLION
OF LIQUID RESERVES FOR THE UNITED KINGDOM AND GERMANY

Country	Trade-Off*
United Kingdom: 1951–64, total	1.07%
1951–64, crisis periods	1.79
1955–68, total	0.86
Germany: 1953–68	0.70
1961–68	1.84

* $1 billion of foregin reserves was worth this percentage of unemployment.
SOURCES: United Kingdom: Douglas Fisher, "The Objectives of British Monetary Policy, 1951–1964," *Journal of Finance*, Vol. 23, No. 5 (December 1968); and "The Instruments of Monetary Policy and the Generalized Trade-Off Function for Britain, 1955–1968," *Manchester School*, Vol. 38, No. 3, September 1970.
Germany: Douglas Fisher and Hugo M. Kaufmann, "An Examination of the Techniques of German Monetary Policy: 1953–1968" (unpublished paper).

secret lies in the last figure, for the subperiod 1961–68. Germany's reserves rose during that period so she probably lowered interest rates and enjoyed a domestic expansion; in this case she was a good neighbor and profited by it.[4] The general meaning of these figures seems to be that both the Germans and the British are willing to pay roughly the same amount, in terms of unemployment, in both normal and crisis periods.

What is desired, then, would be an analysis of the problem of what reserves a country would want to hold in comparison with what it has, along with the costs which a central bank has to pay for failure. It is of no use to treat central banks as individuals, and there is no point in totaling up "liabilities" as if central banks had to pay up; it is also not relevant to think of reserves

---

[4] There was a revaluation in early 1961 which may have been destabilizing, as defined in section 17.3.2.

as money or, even, as liquidity. So much of this system is arti-
ficial—or, if you prefer, institutional—that formal economic analysis requires rather sharply new approaches to wring out any results.
Even so, we do seem to have made progress; but we have left
one important question to the very end: What freedom does a
country have to pursue domestic policies when it has surrendered
itself to the fixed exchange system? We have seen that some governments have been forced to choose between unemployment and
gold bricks and have opted for gold bricks when they did not
have "enough." Is there a way around this problem? Would more
instruments or a system of clearing without gold bricks work better in the sense of increasing a government's ability to manipulate
its domestic economy? Further, what damage to these systems
does the increasing mobility of capital cause?

18.3 MONETARY AND FISCAL POLICY IN AN OPEN ECONOMY

If the picture of the world clearing system is described accurately by the tables in the last section, then adherence to a fixed
exchange system *in which there is some tendency for exchange
rates to fluctuate* outside the bands around the pegged rate presents
each domestic economy with the problem of meeting the costs
of imbalance. We can argue that in many cases some change in
an exchange rate might restore equilibrium within the system; but
if that is impossible, some other change is required—especially
a change in an instrument which will affect the domestic economy.
Indeed, one point we need to appreciate right from the beginning
is that any country wishing to participate in the present gold exchange standard must employ an instrument of policy on that
task. The reason—a very simple one indeed—is that the system
requires that each country keep its exchange rate near parity by
operating in the exchange market. When each operates in a market,
it uses up an instrument to influence a policy objective—the exchange rate.

The way this is done, you will recall, is by a country dealing
in gold and convertible currencies at the central bank level. Insofar
as gold and convertible currencies can be created at will by each
country, no further obvious action is required; but if a country

in deficit is forced to supply gold and convertible currencies by affecting the dealings of private individuals—for example, by generating a recession—it will have to employ still another instrument in the task. Let us risk an analogy with the American Federal Reserve system. Insofar as the Federal Reserve has a large stock of Treasury bills, it can conduct selling open market operations and reduce the money supply. But when its portfolio is exhausted and the objective is not yet achieved, it must reach for another instrument—perhaps changing the level of reserve requirements—in order to continue to follow its instructions. To complete the analogy, we note that a central bank which is in danger of running out of its stock of international reserves is forced—even more compellingly, it seems—to apply another instrument to the task of stabilizing the exchange rate.

The most logical choice of a standby instrument—at least, logical when you realize that it is a central bank which is conducting both operations—is some other monetary weapon. Either control of interest rates or control of the money supply might do the job; the choice would depend on whether the authorities think the impact effect of a rise in interest rates—by attracting short-term capital funds—would be greater than the impact effect of open market operations. The reason is that the latter is thought to work more, if at all, on the level of prices (compared to foreign prices) and is, consequently, much slower and, partly as a consequence of its slowness, more uneven in its impact. Ultimately, the two will amount to about the same thing, for the authorities cannot control both the quantity and the price of anything in the long run.[5]

Suppose, then, that a country is experiencing an inflow of reserves: that the balance of trade, for example, is persistently favorable. So far as we have specified things, if the authorities inflate the domestic economy and push down on interest rates, things will tend to get better. But there is another aspect to the interaction between countries which may confuse the issue: the monetary base of the system will be growing as well, because individuals—

---

[5] The qualification "about" is meant to warn you of two things: one, that the long run is an abstraction and, two, that the way you approach an equilibrium will have something to do with the nature of the equilibrium, if only because institutional changes will occur in the process.

and hence commercial banks—are acquiring reserves. That is, when you acquire a claim on a foreign currency and deposit it in your commercial bank, expecting to get dollars, and the Federal Reserve (as it has to) covers the transaction, the commercial bank will have gained reserves. Further than this, inflation of the domestic economy will be fairly general and not just in the export industries essential to the workings of purchasing power parity. This inflation will generally be deemed undesirable; and, in fact, one way surplus countries have dealt with the problem of imported inflation is to sterilize the impact effect of the surplus on the money supply and to use the interest rate weapon on the surplus.[6] We have used up one instrument, open market operations, to fight inflation; and another, interest rate policy, to fight the surplus. Recalling that gold and currency reserves are dealing with the payments mechanism, we see that we have used up three short-run instruments to achieve one short-run objective: a stable payments mechanism. But we do not have enough instruments to hold the system together in the long run when capital flows go to work; and, more seriously, the short-run stability we have actually achieved is not all that impressive.

18.3.1 Matching Instruments and Objectives

When we have more than one instrument and more than one objective, we raise the question of the matching of instruments and objectives. Two questions have been asked in the literature: Which instrument, a monetary or a fiscal one, is more appropriate for maintaining external balance? And, does it matter to the answer which system we use—that with fixed exchange rates or that with fluctuating exchange rates? The first thing to appreciate is that all instruments can be shown to affect all objectives but in differing degrees. As Robert A. Mundell has put it,

It will be found in most cases that each instrument influences all target variables, although the *relative* impact of a given set of instruments on a certain pattern of targets, if they are independent, will nevertheless be different. A useful guide that can be used in this connection is the *principle of effective market classification*, according to

[6] Leland B. Yeager, *International Monetary Relations*, chap. 23, "The German Struggle Against Imported Inflation" (New York: Harper & Row, Inc., 1966).

which an instrument should be matched with the target on which it exerts the greatest relative influence.[7]

Actually, this "principle" is much more empirical than the preceding quotation seems to imply, but we will get to that problem after we consider the Mundell theorems.

Let us assume, with Mundell, that there are two goals, viz:

a)   Price stability.
b)   Balance of payments equilibrium.

We do not include unemployment as a domestic goal, for if we do, we will need another instrument; this is important, for much of the uniqueness we achieve depends on things being uncomplicated. We cannot have prices inflexible, for if we do (that is, if we have both exchange rates and prices between countries fixed) the balance of payments equilibrium will be unattainable. The next thing we must do is describe the basic problem facing the hypothetical country—that is, describe the environment under which it is operating. There are four possibilities, as follows, with an example in each case from recent history.

Case 1:   Inflation with a balance of payments surplus (Germany since 1955).
Case 2:   Inflation with a balance of payments deficit (Britain since the end of World War II).
Case 3:   Depression with a balance of payments surplus (United States in the 1930's).
Case 4:   Depression with a balance of payments deficit (Britain in the 1930's).

Obviously, your responses depend on where you are in this "real-world" setting. For example, if you are suffering Case 2, then a rise in interest rates will operate on both the inflation (to reduce it) and the balance of payments deficit. Even so, you would only by the wildest of accidents find the interest rate alone adequate to deal with the degree of attainment you desire. The consequence is that you need another instrument: let us assume it is changes in the budget surplus induced by changes in income tax rates.

---

[7] Robert A. Mundell, *International Economics* (New York: Macmillan Co., 1968), p. 203.

The Mundell theorem, then, is that under fixed exchange rates

. . . monetary policy ought to be aimed at external objectives and fiscal policy at internal objectives, and that failure to follow this prescription can make the disequilibrium situation worse than before the policy changes were introduced.[8]

We will assume the conditions of the last paragraph; and we will assume that the initial impulse comes from a worsening of the balance of trade. Let us graph the two tools we have and compare internal with external equilibrium. In Figure 18–1 the foreign balance schedule is illustrated; assuming that both instruments do

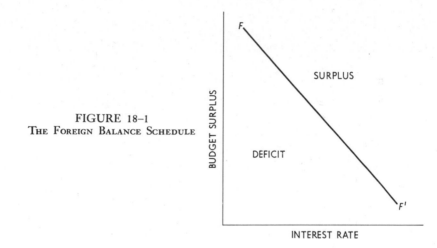

FIGURE 18–1
THE FOREIGN BALANCE SCHEDULE

affect the balance of payments, the general idea behind Figure 18–1 is that a fall in the interest rate worsens the balance of payments, because of the capital outflow, and requires an offsetting rise in the budget surplus to reduce domestic demand—especially that for foreign products—and restore order. The curve *FF'* has no clear meaning in itself, you should note, but is a boundary between surplus and deficit; a country would try to get on the boundary by varying the policy instruments at its disposal.

Internal balance can be described in a similar way; the result is Figure 18–2. This schedule, which represents equilibrium between the production of goods and total spending on goods, slopes downward as well. The reason can be seen by noting that a rise

---
[8] *Ibid.*, p. 233.

in the interest rate will tend to decrease domestic expenditures and induce depression unless it is offset by an increase in government spending (that is, a decrease in the budget surplus). It is also important to notice another Mundell assumption, which is that exports are constant in the model, so that the balance of trade is the same at every point on *XX'*. The reason this is so is that *XX'* is a full-employment line, so that we are assuming that total spending on domestic goods is constant, just as it is on exports. If imports were larger at $\tilde{P}$ than at $\tilde{E}$, domestic spending abroad

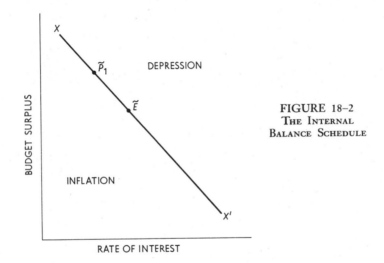

FIGURE 18–2
THE INTERNAL
BALANCE SCHEDULE

would be that much greater than foreign spending at home, and employment would not be full.

When we combine these figures, we find that, as drawn in Figure 18–3, they have only one point in common: $\tilde{E}$, for equilibrium.[9] At this point we are in balance of payments equilibrium, being on *FF'*, in addition to having full employment without inflation along the *XX'* line. Let us consider a simple case: suppose that we are at point $\tilde{P}_1$, at which we have the problem of inflation along with a balance of payments surplus, the situation faced by Germany since 1955. Suppose the German authorities attempted to apply the income tax policy to solve the external problem;

---

[9] With capital mobility, *FF'* must be steeper than *XX'*; see *ibid.*, p. 236, for a complete discussion. This discussion is also resumed later in the text.

this would push them to $\tilde{P}_2$, at which point the foreign trade part of the problem would be solved (we are on *FF'*), but the domestic inflation would be worse. Then suppose the German authorities tried a rise in interest rates to deal with the domestic inflation: they might end up at $\tilde{P}_3$ for their trouble, and $\tilde{P}_3$ is clearly worse than $\tilde{P}_1$. The theorem holds for the case illustrated; in contrast, applying monetary policy to the external problem and fiscal policy

FIGURE 18–3
Overall Equilibrium

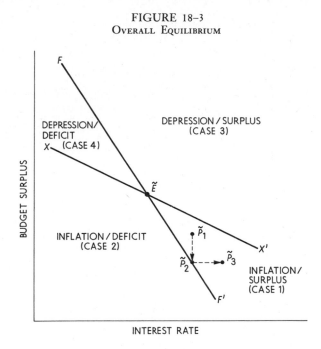

to the internal problem would lead us to $\hat{E}$, the equilibrium point of the system.

What is crucial to this argument, of course, is that the slope of *FF'* be steeper than that of *XX'*. We said that any capital mobility at all would give us this result, but we did not say why. The first thing to appreciate is that with no capital mobility the rate of interest will not affect the balance of payments, so that the *FF'* line will coincide with the *XX'* line. To see the more usual case with some—but not, as we shall see, perfect—capital mobility, consider the situation depicted in Figure 18–4. Assume that the interest rate falls to $\tilde{P}_1$, taking the system off the equilibrium point, $\check{E}$. In that quadrant we have inflation with a persistent deficit, the British problem. Now suppose we push to $\tilde{P}_2$ with our domestic tax policy. This restores full employment domestically, and spending at $\tilde{P}_2$ is the same as at E. We pointed out that the assumptions of full employment and constant exports imply that imports are the same at $\tilde{P}_2$ as at $\check{E}$; thus the balance of trade is the same at all points on XX'. It then follows that

FIGURE 18–4
THE EFFECT OF SHORT-RUN CAPITAL MOBILITY ON
THE MUNDELL THEOREM

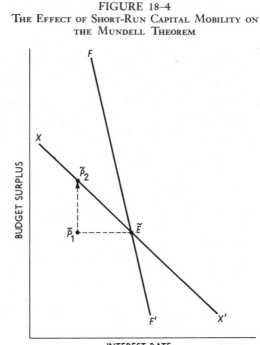

our balance of payments deficit, compared to $\check{E}$, must be due to adverse capital movements at the low interest rate; and, it follows immediately, FF' lies to the right of XX'—that is, overall equilibrium requires a rise in interest rates.

There are a number of important qualifications to this result which, in the last analysis, must remain as an interesting possibility. One thing we might ask concerns what happens to the situation in a system of flexible exchange rates: the answer is that the theorem is reversed, so long as we hold to comparable conditions.[10]

---

[10] *Ibid.*, chap. 17.

There are also a number of other qualifications which grow out of several attempts to see how things work out in the real world: for example, the attempt to make policy recommendations for specific countries at different times. One of these concerns interactions between the instruments; if fiscal policy has monetary implications (e.g., affects the interest rate), then there is a range in which monetary policy works better on domestic than on foreign imbalance. There are similar qualifications if there are interactions between the objectives; again the system becomes more sensitive to changes in the basic situation. In one extreme case, that in which there is *perfect* capital mobility, monetary policy will be ineffective in any event.

The most serious shortcoming of all concerns the effect interest payments have on the results. We pointed out, in section 15.3, that attracting capital in the short run—by using high short-term interest rates—creates a long-run balance of payments problem because the interest payments run in the opposite direction. It turns out, on the basis of simple calculations, that even for fairly short periods of time, the Mundell theorems are reversed. This comes about because domestic deflation by means of tax rate changes need not have strong interest rate effects and so, on this account, has an advantage over tight money. Thus the very capital movements which establish the Mundell theorem in the short run provide its undoing in the long run.

18.3.2   The Euro-Dollar Market

Capital, then, is critical because the (long-run) effectiveness of all our monetary instruments depends on there being, at most, limited international capital mobility. Recently, in the Euro-dollar market, we have seen an illustration of how corrosive capital movements are, and there is no better way to close this book than to show how easily things can become undone.

Euro-dollars are dollar-denominated deposits in European banks, whether the banks be branches of American banks or banks which are foreign to the United States.[11] What has happened in recent years is that corporations (and individuals) operating in Europe have tended to acquire dollars and, instead of processing them

---

[11] There is also an active Euro-pound market.

in the usual way, have deposited them in special dollar accounts in Europe. The reason corporations have done this is a simple one: these accounts, which are generally only for large denominations, earn higher interest rates than the alternatives, which, in Table 18–5, are judged to be United States Treasury bills.[12]

The unusually high rate of 19.63 for Euro-pounds in August 1969 probably reflected the fear of a French devaluation at that time. One way for French commercial banks to escape a devaluation, particularly over weekends, is to borrow Euro-pounds or, for that matter, Euro-dollars. The Euro-pound market is a

TABLE 18–5
Euro-Currencies Rates in 1969
(percent per year)

End of	Euro-Dollar Rate London	Euro-Pound Rate, Paris	U.S. Treasury Bill Rate
February	8.50	10.88	6.32
April	8.56	13.81	6.05
June	10.56	14.06	6.23
August	11.31	19.63	7.37
October	10.00	11.50	7.19
December	10.06	10.25	8.30

Source: Bank of England, *Quarterly Bulletin.*

fairly thin one, which probably accounts for the excessively high rates observed.

It is not easy to get a grip on the size of the Euro-currency market because the official statistic gatherers have only recently gotten on to the consequences of this extremely mobile form of capital. In September 1969, the two most important holders of Euro-dollars had $48.2 billion between them, $23.2 billion in U.S. banks abroad and $25 billion in U.K. banks; and this is not the entire market, by any means. Further, both of these totals have grown rapidly in recent years; for example, the U.K. figure for 1967 (average) was $9.6 billion.

The importance of the Euro-dollar market for monetary policy depends on the country considered. In the United Kingdom, the

---

[12] Actually, the U.S. Treasury bill rate is only a proxy, since most deals on both sides of the Euro-dollar market are very short term.

lending of dollars which are not directly controlled by the authorities represents a potential (actual in 1969) threat to efforts to control domestic credit expansion. The threat to the United States comes from the ability of U.S. banks to repatriate these funds. Indeed, in 1969, this seems to have happened on a large scale. You will recall, from section 10.6, that American commercial banks were able to call on an item entitled "other deposits" in order to maintain their lending. The principal component of the $18 billion so obtained—possibly as much as $10 billion—was Euro-dollars. Thus it is that capital flows, granting that this is a special case, undermine domestic monetary policy.

18.4 DISCUSSION QUESTIONS

1. We noted that world reserves have not expanded as rapidly as world trade. Does this imply that the demand for reserves has been frustrated? Construct an equation of exchange to fit this situation. What do you need to complete the system? What economic interpretation can you give to your "velocity" term?

2. Central governments could be treated as managers of portfolios of various assets and liabilities. If we did so, what would we use as rates of return? Explain carefully.

3. Should one add up the total of gold, dollars held abroad, and IMF quotas? Is the system a fractional reserve system supported by dollars, a fractional reserve system supported by gold, neither, or both?

4. Why do we worry about the duration of past changes in reserves as well as the variance? Was this element ever introduced explicitly into our theory of the demand for money? Explain. Are the duration and the variation related in any way? Would your answer differ if you assumed that speculators dominate in the market?

5. In the discussion of optimal international reserves, two different supply relations for reserves were suggested: one featuring interest rates (representing opportunity cost) and one representing domestic monetary policy. Are these merely two versions of the same thing or are there important differences? Be careful in your answer because it should be possible to merge these two views under *some* assumptions.

6. Why do we pick on unemployment as the proxy for the cost of having a fixed exchange rate system? Is one of the implications that

a system of fluctuating exchange rates would reduce unemployment on a worldwide basis? Explain carefully, since an affirmative answer is potentially political dynamite.

7. Compare the United States with the United Kingdom in terms of the number of instruments actually employed in defending the currency. Are some of the differences due to institutional factors? Were you tempted to use the term *fundamental disequilibrium* at any point in your discussion?

8. If there is perfect capital mobility between nations, what happens to the Mundell thesis? How did you define capital mobility? Has the mobility of capital increased or decreased in recent years? What evidence did you look at in making your decision?

9. Go through the argument as to why the Mundell theorem cannot be proved (in its simple form) when we break down GNP into its components. It is noticeable, nevertheless, that countries do apply the theorem, in the sense of its recommendation of "effective market classification"? Consider the United States, Germany, and the United Kingdom in your answer.

10. We end up, then, with the latest wrinkle in monetary economics: the Euro-dollar. What is the relevance of this market? What happens to forward cross rates in the Euro-dollar market? What is happening in this market at present?

18.5 FURTHER READING

MUNDELL, ROBERT A. *International Economics*, chap. 14, pp. 201–207, chaps. 15, 16 and 17. New York: Macmillan Co., 1968.

INDEX

A

Accelerator effect, 161
Accord, the United States, 122
Aggregation
  and demand for money, 67–68
  problem defined, 25–27
  relation to problem of definition, 30–31
Andersen, Leonall C., 146
Arbitrage
  defined, 241
  in international trade
    forward, 349, 351
    spot, 342–44
Assumptions
  continuity, 16
  principles of, 12
Availability of funds, 226–31, 293
Axioms
  general nature of, 11
  specific in microeconomic theory, 15–16

B

Balance of payments; *see also* Capital flows; Exchange rates; *and* Reserves, international
  accounts, 324–30
  American deficit on, 378–80
  analysis of, 334–37
  as an objective of monetary policy, 106–8, 397–403
  problem
    defined, 328–30, 333–34, 388–89
    and speculation, 349–51
    of surplus countries, 367–68
    and reserves, 388–89
    settling items, 328–30, 333–34
Balance sheet
  of Balance of Payments, 324–30
  see also under each type of financial institution
Bancor, 367, 382
Bank of England, 121, 132, 350, 392
Banking Act of 1933, 184
Banking holidays, 179–81

Banks, banking; *see also* Reserves, bank and financial intermediaries, 219, 222–31, 314–16
  as financial intermediaries, 309–10
  in international trade, 344–51
  and portfolio analysis, 277–78
  portfolio behavior of, 302, 308–14
  and real balance effect, 208
  and term structure of interest rates, 245
  uniqueness of, 222–26
  in United States
    balance sheet, 88
    business of, 91–95
    competition in, 96–98, 314–16
    costs in, 93–95
    failures, 179–84, 314–16
    history of, 170–91
    investments of, 88, 311–16
    loan-deposit ratio, 312–14
    loans, 230, 311–16
    revenues of, 92–93
    size, 96–98, 312–14
Barger, Harold, 178
Barter economy, 31–33, 35, 161–64
Baumol, William, 301
Benston, George J., 320
Besens, Stanley M., 312
Bill of exchange, 218
Bills only policy, 252, 318
Bonds
  characteristics of
    coupon, 57–58, 235–41
    face value, 57, 235–41
    maturity of, 57–58, 234–41, 244, 249–53
    yield of, 57–58, 235–55
  speculation in, 243–55
  types of; *see also* Perpetual bonds *and* Treasury bills
    corporate, 285–94
    government, 234–39, 304, 313, 318
Bretton Woods, 369, 372
Britain, 106–8, 132, 235, 243, 246–49, 316, 330–34, 345–52, 368–70, 373–77, 391–92, 394, 404–5
Broad money; *see* Money
Bronfenbrenner, Martin S., 29

409

*This book has been set in 11 point and 10 point
Janson, leaded 2 points. Part and chapter numbers and titles are in 16 point Helvetica. The
size of the type page is 26 by 43 2/3 picas.*